8

Scott Foresman

Teacher's Edition

ESL

Accelerating English Language Learning

Authors

Anna Uhl Chamot

Jim Cummins

Carolyn Kessler

J. Michael O'Malley

Lily Wong Fillmore

Consultant

George González

Longman

ACKNOWLEDGMENTS

Illustrations Unless otherwise acknowledged, all illustrations are the property of Scott, Foresman and Company. Page abbreviations are as follows: (T) top, (B) bottom, (L) left, (R) right, (C) center.

Deborah Wolfe/Skip Baker **43, 46**(B)–**47**(R); Shawn Banner **12**(T), **26–37, 180**(C)–**181**(B,R); Clare Jett/Jennifer Bolton **128, 214**; Melissa Turk/Ka Botzis **83**(T); Edward Burton **90, 101, 194–195**(B); Deborah Wolfe/Anthony Cericola **87**(TR); Ebet Dudley **16**(TL), **19**(R), **20**(TL); American Artists/Lane Dupont **13**(L), **38**; Allan Eitzen **126–127, 199**(T), **228**; Cornell & McCarthy/Doris Ettlinger **154–155**(BC); Bill Farnsworth **164–171**; Howard S. Friedman **120**(B); Laurie Harden **76**; American Artists/Doug Henry **114**; Richard Salzman/Denis Hilton-Campbell **14, 48–49, 157**; Dilys Evans/Laura Kelly **10**(T), **138–139**; Mattleson Associates/Karen Kluglein **8–9, 22**(B)–**23**(T); Bob Lange **24**(L), **68**(T), **118–119, 125**(T), **130–131, 189**; Gayle Levee **50–57**; Carol Chislovsky/David Lund **216–217, 224–225**; Carol Chislovsky/Peg Magovern **183**; Mapping Specialists **70–71, 80, 86**(T), **156**(B), **159**(T), **185**(T), **188**(R); Carol Chislovsky/Paul Mirocha **190**; Square Moon/Elizbeth Morales **17**(T), **21, 25**(TR); Deborah Wolfe/Andy Myer **152**; Deborah Wolfe/Saul Rosenbaum **94**(T), **100**(T); Carla Simmons **163**; Holly Hahn/Steve Snodgrass **206–213**; Richard Salzman/Wayne Anthony Still **156**(T); Carol Chrislovsky/Cathy Trachok **160**(T), **174**(R)–**177**(B), **200–201**; Christina Tugeau/Meryl Treatner **4**(L)–**5**(R), **12**(R); Elaine Wadsworth **10–11, 75**; Elizabeth Wolf **58, 63**(B), **72**(T), **73**(T), **74, 172.**

Literature 26–37: From LITTLE BROTHER OF THE WILDERNESS by Meridel Le Sueur. Copyright © 1947 by Meridel LeSueur. Reprinted by permission of Alfred A. Knopf, Inc. **50–57:** "Why the Monsoon Comes Each Year" reprinted by permission of G. P. Putnam's Sons from FAIRY TALES FROM VIET NAM, retold by Dorothy Lewis Robertson. Copyright © 1968 by Dorothy Lewis Robertson. **102–113:** From THUNDER AT GETTYSBURG, text copyright © 1975 by Patricia Lee Gauch, illustrations copyright © 1975 by Stephen Gammell. Reprinted by permission of G. P. Putnam's Sons. **140–147:** From THE SOLAR SYSTEM by Maura Gouck. Copyright © 1993 by the Child's World, Inc. Reprinted by permission. **164–171:** From SARAH, PLAIN AND TALL by Patricia MacLachlan. Copyright © 1985 by Patricia MacLachlan. Reprinted by permission of HarperCollins. **184–187:** Reprinted with the permission of Atheneum Books for Young Readers, an imprint of Simon & Schuster from GREAT LIVES: HUMAN RIGHTS by William Jay Jacobs. Copyright © 1990 by William Jay Jacobs. **206–213:** From LETTERS FROM RIFKA by Karen Hesse. Copyright © 1992 by Karen Hesse. Reprinted by permission of Henry Holt and Co., Inc.

Poems and Songs 14: "Turn! Turn! Turn! (To Everything There Is a Season)" words from the Book of Ecclesiastes, adaption and music by Pete Seeger. TRO © Copyright 1962 (Renewed) Melody Trails, Inc., New York, NY. Used by permission. **58:** "Lotsa Winds" from CRACKERS AND CRUMBS by Sonja Dunn. Copyright © 1990 by Sonja Dunn and Lou Pamenter. Reprinted with permission of Pembroke Publishers Limited. **75:** "Raindrop" from THERE'S MOTION EVERYWHERE by John Travers Moore. Copyright © 1970 by John Travers Moore. Reprinted by permission. **76:** "Good Day Sunshine" by John Lennon and Paul McCartney. Copyright © 1966 by Northern Songs Ltd. Copyright renewed. All rights controlled and administered by EMI Blackwood Music Inc. under license from SONY/ATV Songs LLC. All rights reserved. International copyright secured. Used by permission. **126–127:** "Here Comes the Sun" by George Harrison. Copyright © 1969 by Harrisongs Ltd. International Copyright Secured. All rights reserved. **128:** "Brazilian Moon Tale" by Jane Yolen reprinted by permission by Philomel Books from WHAT RHYMES WITH MOON? text copyright © 1993 by Jane Yolen, illustrations copyright © 1993 by Ruth Tietjen Councell. **190:** "Brother, Can You Spare a Dime?" by E. Y. Harburg and Jay Gorney. Copyright © 1932 (Renewed) Warner Bros. Inc. Rights for extended renewal term in U.S. controlled by Glocca Morra Music and Gorney Music Publishers. Canadian rights controlled by Warner Bros. Inc. All rights reserved. Used by permission of Warner Bros. Publications US Inc., Miami, FL 33014. **228:** "Hang Out the Flags" from CRICKETY CRICKET! THE BEST LOVED POEMS OF JAMES S. TIPPETT. Copyright 1933, renewed © 1973 by Martha K. Tippett. Used by permission of HarperCollins Publishers.

Photography Unless otherwise acknowledged, all photographs are the property of Scott, Foresman and Company. Page abbreviations are as follows: (t) top, (c) center, (b) bottom, (r) right.

v(t) Erich Lessing/Art Resource, (br) TSADO/NASA/Tom Stack & Associates; **2**(t), **3**(tl, tr, b) Superstock, Inc.; **8** Courtesy U.S.D.A.; **12** UPI/Corbis-Bettmann; **13**(c) Focus on Sports, Inc.; (t) REUTERS/Jean Paul Pelissier/Archive Photos; **16, 17**(b) Superstock, Inc.; (t) Jim Strawser/Grant Heilman Photography; **18** Larry LeFever/Grant Heilman Photography; **19** Runk/Schoenberger/Grant Heilman Photography; **20, 22, 23, 25**(t, b), **39**(t, b), **40–41, 40**(t) Superstock, Inc.; (bl) NSSL/NOAA; **41**(b) Grant Heilman/Grant Heilman Photography; **41**(t) Holt Confer/Grant Heilman Photography; (c) Arthur C. Smith III/Grant Heilman Photography; **42**(c, r) Superstock, Inc.; (l) NASA; **46–47** Superstock, Inc.; **59**(b) NSSL/NOAA; (r) Grant Heilman/Grant Heilman Photography; **60**(b) Superstock, Inc.; **60–61**(background) NASA; **61**(b) © CNES 1988; **65**(b) NASA; **66**(t) James Deeton/Tony Stone Images; (c, b), **70**(t), **71**(b), **72** Superstock, Inc.; **77** NASA; **78–79**(background), **78**(inset) North Wind Picture Archives; **79**(t, br-insets) Granger Collection, New York; (bl-inset) Collection of Mr. William S. Powell; **80**(c) Brown Brothers; **81, 82**(b) North Wind Picture Archives; **82**(t) Brown Brothers; **83**(b) Southern Historical Collection CB#3926, Wilson Library, The University of North Carolina at Chapel Hill; (t) Library of Congress; **84**(cl) North Wind Picture Archives; **84**(t, b, cr), **85**(t, bl, br) Granger Collection, New York; (c) North Wind Picture Archives; **86–87, 88** Granger Collection, New York; **89**(t, b) Sophia Smith Collection, Smith College; **91** Library of Congress; **92** Granger Collection, New York; **93**(t) Library of Congress; **93**(b), **94–95** Granger Collection, New York; **95**(t) Library of Congress; **96**(b) Superstock, Inc.; (t) Granger Collection, New York; **97**(b) Jack Novak/Photri, Inc.; (t) Granger Collection, New York; **98**(r) U.S. Signal Corps Photo, National Archives, Brady Collection; (l) Granger Collection, New York; **99**(b) Library of Congress; (t) Brown Brothers; **115**(b) Library of Congress; (t, c) Granger Collection, New York; **116**(b) Steven Hunt/Image Bank; (t) TSADO/NASA/Tom Stack & Associates; **117**(b) NASA/JPL/TSADO/Tom Stack & Associates; (t) Superstock, Inc.; (c) NASA/Airworks/Tom Stack & Associates; **118–119**(background) Bill & Sally Fletcher/Tom Stack & Associates; **120–121** Superstock, Inc.; **120**(t) NASA/Tom Stack & Associates; **123** Bill & Sally Fletcher/Tom Stack & Associates; **124**(t) Egyptian National Museum, Cairo/Superstock, Inc., (bl) Erich Lessing/Art Resource, (br) Pollak/Art Resource; **125**(b) Erich Lessing/Art Resource; **129**(b) TSADO/NASA/Tom Stack & Associates; Bill & Sally Fletcher/Tom Stack & Associates; **130–131** Photri; **130**(t, b), **131**(t) NASA; (c) NASA/JPL/TSADO/Tom Stack & Associates; **132** JPL/TSADO/Tom Stack & Associates; **133**(b) USGS/TSADO/Tom Stack & Associates; (c) NASA; (t) NASA/TSADO/Tom Stack & Associates; **134**(b) NASA/ESA/Tom Stack & Associates; (c) Photri; (t) Superstock, Inc.; **135**(t, b) JPL/NASA; **136**(b) Corbis-Bettmann; (tr) NASA; (tl) Photri; **137**(br) NASA; (bl) JPL/Tom Stack & Associates; (tr) Photri (tl) NASA; **140** JPL/TSADO/Tom Stack & Associates; **141**(inset) Superstock, Inc.; (background) Mike O'Brine/Tom Stack & Associates; **142** Photri; **143** JPL/TSADO/Tom Stack & Associates; **144** NASA/JPL/Tom Stack & Associates; **145**(l) Superstock, Inc.; (r) NASA; (background) Mike O'Brine/Tom Stack & Associates; **146** Photri; **147** NASA/Airworks/Tom Stack & Associates; **148** NASA; **149**(r) Corbis-Bettmann; (l) NASA; **150**(b) JPL/Superstock, Inc.; (t) Corbis-Bettmann; **151**(b) JPL/Photri; (t) Corbis-Bettmann; **153**(t, b) NASA; (background) Bill & Sally Fletcher/Tom Stack & Associates; **154** Granger Collection, New York; **155**(b) Stock Montage, Inc.; (c) Superstock, Inc.; **158**(t, b) Granger Collection, New York; **159**(b) Gary Irving/Tony Stone Images; **159**(t), **160, 161, 162**(b) Granger Collection, New York; **162**(t) James P. Rowan/Tony Stone Images; **173, 174–175**(c), **174**(b) Granger Collection, New York; (t) Superstock, Inc.; **175**(tr, b), **176**(b) Granger Collection, New York; (t) North Wind Picture Archives; **177**(b) Granger Collection, New York; (t) Corbis-Bettmann Archive; **178**(b) Stock Montage, Inc.; (t, c) Corbis-Bettmann; **179**(b) Superstock, Inc.; **179**(tl, tr), **180**(t, b) Granger Collection, New York; **181** Stock Montage, Inc.; **184** Culver Pictures Inc.; **185, 186**(t) Granger Collection, New York; (b) National Archives; **187**(b) Superstock, Inc.; (t) Library of Congress; (c) Carnegie Hero Fund Commmission; **188, 189** Granger Collection, New York; **190** UPI/Corbis-Bettmann; **191**(b) Granger Collection, New York; (tl, tr) Superstock, Inc.; **192–193** Mark Richards/PhotoEdit; **192**(bl) Bob Daemmrich; (br) F. Lee Corkran/Sygma; **192**(t) Corbis-Bettmann Archive; **193**(t) Superstock, Inc.; (b) Sophia Smith Collection; (c) David R. Frazier; **195** John Neubaugh/PhotoEdit; **196–197**(b) 1995 Dennis Brack/Black Star; **196**(t) UPI/Corbis-Bettmann; **198**(t) Willie L. Hill Jr./Stock Boston; (b) Billy E. Barnes/PhotoEdit; **199** Ben Van Hook/Black Star; **202**(t, b) Superstock, Inc.; **203**(b) Koni Nordmann/Focus/Matrix International, Inc.; (t) Corbis-Bettmann Archive; **204**(b) 1988 Andrew Popper/Popperfoto; **204–205**(t) Jacob Riis Collection, Museum of the City of New York; **205**(b) © 1988 Andrew Popper/Popperfoto; **217**(b) UPI/Corbis-Bettmann; **218** U.S. Capitol Historical Society/National Geographic Photographer George F. Mobley; **219** Paul Conklin/PhotoEdit; **220**(t) Superstock, Inc.; (b) Paul Conklin/PhotoEdit; **221** 95 Dennis Brack/Black Star; **222** Superstock, Inc.; **223** Sygma; **226** © 1995 Tribune Media Services, Inc. All rights Reserved.; **227**(b) Superstock, Inc.

ISBN 0-13-027502-6

Pearson Education
10 Bank Street, White Plains, New York 10606

2345678910 BAM 05040302010

CONTENTS

AUTHORS

ANNA UHL CHAMOT is an associate professor in the area of ESL teacher preparation at George Washington University. Previously Associate Director of the Georgetown University/Center for Applied Linguistics National Foreign Language Resource Center, she also managed two Title VII Special Alternative Instructional Projects in the Arlington, Virginia, Public Schools. She has co-authored two books with J. Michael O'Malley, *Learning Strategies in Second Language Acquisition* and *The CALLA Handbook: How to Implement the Cognitive Academic Language Learning Approach.* Other publications include content-ESL books in history and mathematics, a textbook series based on the CALLA model, *Building Bridges: Content and Learning Strategies for ESL* and *The Learning Strategies Handbook.* Dr. Chamot holds a Ph.D. in ESL and applied linguistics from the University of Texas at Austin and a Master's degree in foreign language education from Teachers College, Columbia University.

JIM CUMMINS is a professor in the Modern Language Centre and Department of Curriculum, Teaching and Learning of the University of Toronto. His research focuses on the challenges educators face in adjusting to classrooms where cultural and linguistic diversity is the norm. Among the books he has published related to ESL and bilingual education are: *Bilingualism and Special Education: Issues in Assessment and Pedagogy; Bilingualism in Education: Aspects of Theory, Research and Practice* (with Merrill Swain); *Minority Education: From Shame to Struggle* (with Tove Skutnabb-Kangas); *Brave New Schools: Challenging Cultural Illiteracy Through Global Learning Networks* (with Dennis Sayers); *Negotiating Identities: Education for Empowerment in a Diverse Society;* his most recent book is *Language, Power and Pedagogy: Bilingual Children in the Crossfire* published by Multilingual Matters in 2000. Dr. Cummins received his Ph.D. from the University of Alberta, Canada. In May 1997, he received an Honorary Doctorate in Humane Letters from the Bank Street College of Education in New York City.

CAROLYN KESSLER is professor emerita (ESL and Applied Linguistics) at the University of Texas at San Antonio. She has extensive experience in teacher education for meeting the needs of linguistically and culturally diverse populations. Among recent books and monographs authored or co-authored are: *Cooperative Language Learning: A Teacher's Resource Book; Literacy con Cariño: A Story of Migrant Children's Success; Making Connections: An Integrated Approach to ESL* (a secondary program); *Parade* (a K–6 EFL program); and *Teaching Science to English Learners, Grades 4–8.* Her research interests include the integration of content area learning with second language and literacy development, adult and family literacy and language learning, and second language acquisition for both children and adults. Dr. Kessler received her Ph.D. in linguistics from Georgetown University.

J. MICHAEL O'MALLEY was Supervisor of Assessment and Evaluation in Prince William County Public Schools in Virginia, where he established a performance assessment program in grades K–12. He was previously Senior Researcher in the National Foreign Language Resource Center at Georgetown University and for six years was Director of the Evaluation Assistance Center at Georgetown University. Dr. O'Malley was co-developer with Anna Uhl Chamot of the Cognitive Academic Language Learning Approach (CALLA). CALLA was introduced by O'Malley and Chamot in 1986 and was the subject of both their 1994 work *The CALLA Handbook* and their earlier work on the research and theory underlying the approach. J. Michael O'Malley was a true leader in the field of learning strategies, assessment, and ESL instruction. He helped shape the future of ESL and contributed greatly to the way ESL instruction is given and monitored. He touched the lives of all who knew him and worked with him. Dr. O'Malley died in 1998.

LILY WONG FILLMORE is a professor in the Graduate School of Education at the University of California, Berkeley. Her specializations are in the areas of second language learning and teaching, the education of language minority students, and socialization for learning across cultures. Over the past 30 years, she has conducted numerous studies of children learning English as a second language in classroom settings. These studies have examined the sources of variation in the learning of English by children from kindergarten through the middle school; classrooms as social settings for language learning; how setting variables and instructional practices influence second language learning; cultural influences on language learning; and primary language shift and loss in immigrant and Native American children. She is project director and principal investigator for the Family, Community, and the University Partnership, which prepares professionals to work in educational institutions in American Indian communities in the Southwest. Dr. Wong Fillmore received her Ph.D. in linguistics from Stanford University.

GEORGE GONZÁLEZ is a retired professor in the School of Education in the field of bilingual education and ESL at the University of Texas Pan-American. He is highly regarded for his work as a consultant in school districts throughout the Southwest. The author of many ESL instructional materials, Dr. González has also worked as a consultant for the Education Service Center—Region XX in San Antonio.

CRITIC READERS

Sandra H. Bible
Elementary ESL Teacher
Shawnee Mission School District
Shawnee Mission, Kansas

Anaida Colón-Muñiz, Ed.D.
Director of English Language Development and Bilingual Education
Santa Ana Unified School District
Santa Ana, California

Debbie Corkey-Corber
Educational Consultant
Williamsburg, Virginia

Barbara Crandall
Carol Baranyi
Illean Zamlut
ESOL Teachers
Lake Park Elementary School
Palm Beach County, Florida

Lily Pham Dam
Instructional Specialist
Dallas Independent School District
Dallas, Texas

María Delgado
Edison Middle School
Milwaukee Public Schools
Milwaukee, Wisconsin

Dr. M. Viramontes de Marín
Chair, Education/Liberal Arts Departments
The National Hispanic University
San Jose, California

Virginia Hansen
ESOL Resource Teacher
Palm Beach County, Florida

Timothy Hart
Supervisor of English as a Second Language
Wake County
Raleigh, North Carolina

Lilian I. Jezik
Bilingual Resource Teacher
Corona-Norco Unified School District
Norco, California

Helen L. Lin
Chairman, Education Program
Multicultural Arts Council of Orange County, California
Formerly ESL Lab Director
Kansas City, Kansas, Schools

Justine McDonough
Trish Lirio
Sheree DiDonato
Jupiter Elementary School
West Palm Beach, Florida

Teresa Montaño
United Teachers Los Angeles
Los Angeles, California

Loriana M. Novoa, Ed.D.
Research and Evaluation Consultants
Miami, Florida

Beatrice Palls
ESOL and Foreign Language Supervisor
Pasco County, Florida

Rosa María Peña
Austin Independent School District
Austin, Texas

Alice Quarles
Assistant Principal
Fairlawn Elementary School
Dade County, Florida

Thuy Pham-Remmele
ESL/Bilingual K–12 Specialist
Madison Metropolitan School District
Madison, Wisconsin

Jacqueline J. Servi Margis
ESL and Foreign Language Curriculum Specialist
Milwaukee Public Schools
Milwaukee, Wisconsin

Carmen Sorondo
Supervisor, ESOL, K–12
Hillsborough County, Florida

Lydia M. Trujillo
Hot Topics Consultants
Pueblo, Colorado

Susan C. VanLeuven
Poudre R-1 School District
Fort Collins, Colorado

Rosaura Villaseñor, M.A.
Educator
Norwalk, California

Cheryl Wilkinson
J.O. Davis Elementary School
Irving Independent School District
Irving, Texas

Phyllis I. Ziegler
ESL/Bilingual Consultant
New York, New York

The Philosophy of *ScottForesman ESL*

ScottForesman ESL accelerates English language learning through the use and application of the following principles.

Thematic Units

In theme- or topic-based lessons, curriculum content is presented thematically to provide the basis for language learning. Topic-related language and concepts are recycled over a period of time, ensuring their conceptualization and making students increasingly able to communicate their ideas on the topic. Each level of *ScottForesman ESL* contains six thematic units; each unit contains two related chapters. In each unit students are exposed to a rich array of language and activities based on the major topic. As students work through each unit, the variety of text types, formats, and activities enables them to master both the language and the concepts.

Balanced Skills

In each chapter of *ScottForesman ESL,* students develop all of the four language skills—listening, speaking, reading, and writing. This balanced approach ensures communicative proficiency. Authentic texts, both fiction and nonfiction, give ample reading practice. "Talk About It" and "Write About It" sections in each chapter offer practice in listening, speaking, and writing. The "Writer's Workshop" in Books 2–8 leads students through the writing process. These sections, along with the abundant optional activities, give students the time and opportunity to achieve communicative competence.

Phonics

Within the context of the stories and content text in Scott Foresman ESL, students develop phonics concepts through a four-step process: *Identify, Hear, See and Say,* and *Write.* It is by listening and responding to the voice of the teacher that students learn the variations of the English sound system, develop phonological awareness, practice pronunciation, and build background in the language. *Newcomer Phonics* and *Word By Word Phonics Picture Dictionary* offer step by step, in-depth phonics instruction.

UNIT 3 • CONFLICT
The Civil War
Tell what you know.
What is war?
These pictures are from the 1860s, during the U.S. Civil War. What things do the pictures tell about the war?
Talk About It
What wars do you know about? What countries did the fighting? Why did they fight?
78
79

The Cognitive Academic Language Learning Approach (CALLA)

ScottForesman ESL follows the principles of CALLA: it teaches grade-level topics from the major curriculum areas; it develops academic language skills; and it provides explicit instruction in learning strategies for both content and language acquisition.

Learning Strategies

Learning strategies are actions or thoughts that students can apply to challenging tasks. *ScottForesman ESL* integrates learning strategies instruction into each part of the learning process by providing guidelines for teaching the strategies and for helping students develop an awareness of their own learning processes.

Cooperative Learning

Throughout *ScottForesman ESL,* cooperative learning activities give students opportunities to work in groups to share what they know and to learn new information and skills. For a cooperative group to be successful, there should be a common, agreed upon goal and assigned individual roles for achieving that goal. In fact, cooperative learning activities are characterized by three components: (1) Positive interdependence—members rely on each other to achieve the end product; (2) Individual accountability—each member is responsible for information that is used to achieve the group's goal; (3) Face-to-face interaction—members work and talk together. In addition, cooperative learning may entail (4) Group processing—the group reviews what they did in terms of the group process or group mechanics; and (5) Development of social skills—members use group maintenance skills to keep the process going and task skills to perform what is required.

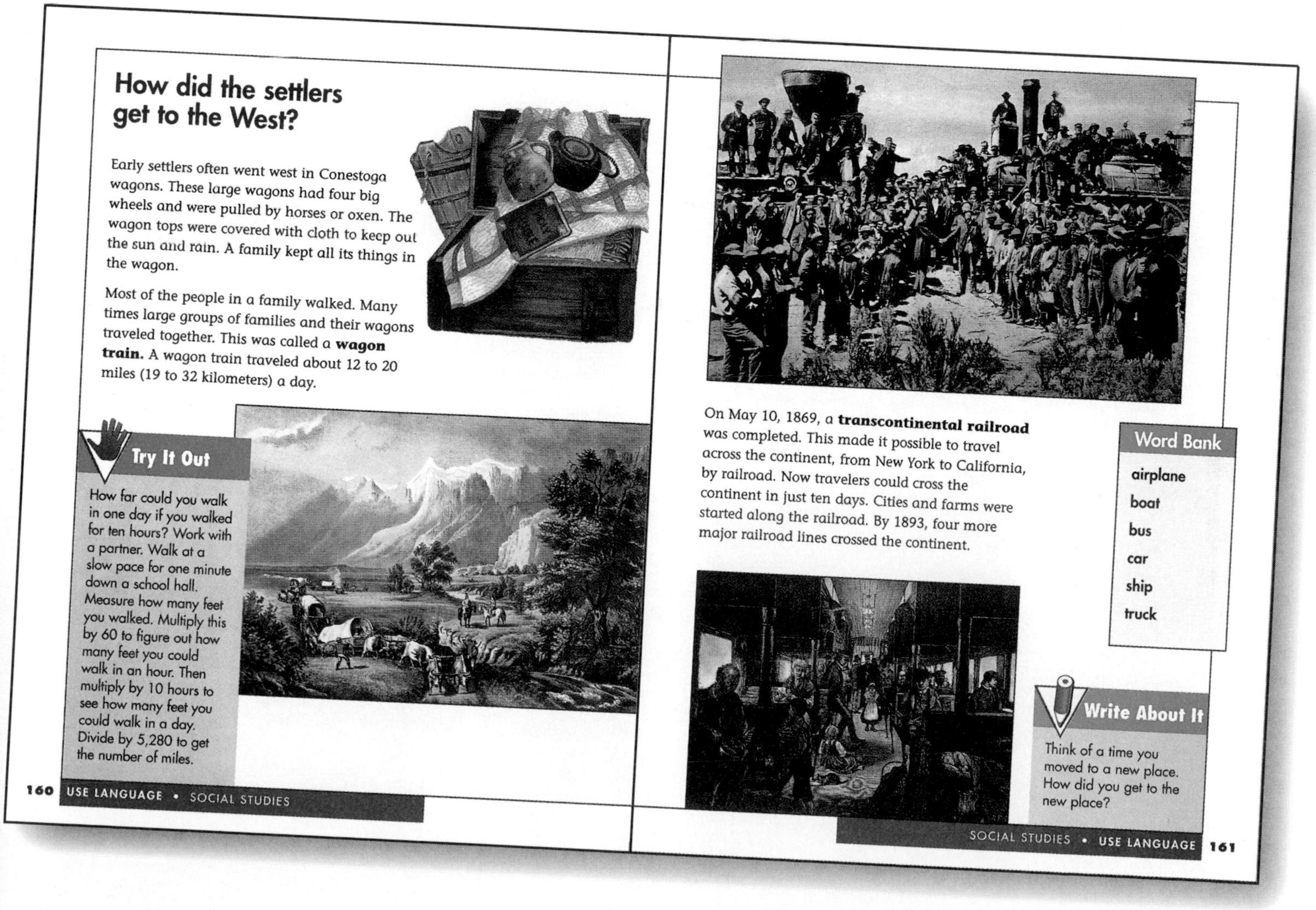

How did the settlers get to the West?

Early settlers often went west in Conestoga wagons. These large wagons had four big wheels and were pulled by horses or oxen. The wagon tops were covered with cloth to keep out the sun and rain. A family kept all its things in the wagon.

Most of the people in a family walked. Many times large groups of families and their wagons traveled together. This was called a **wagon train.** A wagon train traveled about 12 to 20 miles (19 to 32 kilometers) a day.

Try It Out

How far could you walk in one day if you walked for ten hours? Work with a partner. Walk at a slow pace for one minute down a school hall. Measure how many feet you walked. Multiply this by 60 to figure out how many feet you could walk in an hour. Then multiply by 10 hours to see how many feet you could walk in a day. Divide by 5,280 to get the number of miles.

160 USE LANGUAGE • SOCIAL STUDIES

On May 10, 1869, a **transcontinental railroad** was completed. This made it possible to travel across the continent, from New York to California, by railroad. Now travelers could cross the continent in just ten days. Cities and farms were started along the railroad. By 1893, four more major railroad lines crossed the continent.

Word Bank

airplane
boat
bus
car
ship
truck

Write About It

Think of a time you moved to a new place. How did you get to the new place?

SOCIAL STUDIES • USE LANGUAGE 161

Integrated Curriculum

Each chapter in *ScottForesman ESL* develops language, concepts, and strategies related to a particular area of the curriculum. As students gain control over new material, it is vital that they understand how to transfer this knowledge and understanding to other areas of the curriculum and to "real life." In the "Connect" section of every chapter, students apply what they have learned to a new curriculum area and to the reading of authentic literature. Throughout the program, students learn how language and ideas cross the curriculum and how they can be applied in their content area classes.

Home/ School Connections

ScottForesman ESL fosters a "community building" approach to education so teachers and parents can work together collaboratively as co-educators of children. In this approach, families are key participants in the academic success of children learning English, so learning communities develop in which the culture of hope, possibility, and promise can flourish.

Multicultural Understanding

Americans are a multicultural people. *ScottForesman ESL* recognizes the need to respect and preserve each group's culture, while at the same time acknowledging the interdependence of these cultures, the unity of our nation, and respect for others. Throughout the program, the variety of activities take into consideration students' different learning styles and backgrounds. And by presenting topics that are interesting and relevant to students, the program helps them understand their different backgrounds and facilitates communication among them, their families, and the rest of society.

CHAPTER 11

Citizenship

All Are Equal

A **citizen** is a person who is a member of a nation. A person can be a citizen by being born in a place. A person can also become a citizen by choosing to live in a place. About 250 million people live in the United States. More than 225 million of these people are citizens. Most of these people were born in the United States. They are citizens for that reason.

Many other citizens chose the United States as their home. They began life in some other country, and they came to the United States as immigrants. After living here for five years, they can become citizens.

Many immigrants become citizens because, in the United States, all people are equal before the law. This means that all people must be treated the same. This **equality** before the law is an important reason that many immigrants want to become citizens.

Write About It

Why did your family immigrate to the United States? Why did other people you know immigrate?

194 LEARN LANGUAGE • SOCIAL STUDIES

SOCIAL STUDIES • LEARN LANGUAGE 195

Authentic Literature

Authentic children's literature such as that which appears in *ScottForesman ESL* is perhaps the most reliable and consistent source of academic English input children can have. By using such texts, teachers can help children develop the vocabulary, structures, and background knowledge they need to comprehend the intellectually challenging language of the classroom.

Authentic Assessment

Assessment is authentic when it enables students to communicate successfully their strengths and educational needs and when the results can be used to improve instruction based on accurate knowledge of students' progress. Authentic assessment activities in *ScottForesman ESL* include teacher observation, self assessment, peer assessment, performance assessment, and portfolio assessment. Traditional language and listening assessments are also included, as are standardized test instruction and practice.

Self-Esteem

Children thrive in an atmosphere in which their language, culture, and values are acknowledged and respected and in which they can succeed. *ScottForesman ESL* encourages students to affirm their heritages and to celebrate them in the classroom. Activities are suggested throughout in which students demonstrate and explain aspects of their own and their families' lives and cultures. Optional activities provide opportunities for all students—from beginners through advanced—to be successful by demonstrating their accomplishments both individually and in cooperative groups.

Why the Monsoon Comes Each Year

Retold by Dorothy Lewis Robertson

The Princess Mi Nuong was sad. She sat quietly with downcast eyes while a handmaiden combed her glossy, black hair and idly smoothed a fold in the silk of her gown. When the last jade pin was fastened in her hair and the handmaiden held up a mirror, she pushed it away without even glancing in it. She already knew what the mirror would show her: a tiny new wrinkle between her eyes. It was this new wrinkle that made her sad. She was growing old and she was husbandless.

Language Tip
Vocabulary
A monsoon is a seasonal wind that brings heavy rains to South Asia every year. This folk tale is from Vietnam, a country in Southeast Asia.

50 CONNECT LANGUAGE • SCIENCE/LITERATURE

It wasn't that she was ugly or lame or bad tempered. She had had many suitors. Some were handsome and many had come from foreign lands, but not one had gained the consent of her father, the Emperor. Like many fathers with only one child, he believed that no one was good enough for his charming daughter. For her he wanted someone rich and distinguished and, above all, powerful. Years had passed since the last suitor had proposed and been declined, and it looked as though the Princess would remain single forever.

Language Tip
Vocabulary
A suitor is someone who wants to marry someone. Mi Nuong needed her father's consent to be married. She needed her father to say yes.

SCIENCE/LITERATURE • CONNECT LANGUAGE 51

COMPONENTS

Student Book

The 240-page, hard-cover *Student Book* contains six curriculum-based, thematic units of two chapters each. Each unit contains a full-length piece of authentic literature plus poems, songs, and other shorter literature pieces. Book 1 contains a Children's Reference Section. Books 2–8 contain a Writer's Workshop, which leads students through the writing process.

Teacher's Edition

The spiral-bound *Teacher's Edition* contains reproduced student pages with complete instructions for presenting each page along with Options for Reaching All Students. Each unit features a planning guide, a list of resources, suggestions for a unit project, *Activity Book* and test answers, and wrap-up activities.

ACTIVITY BOOK

Language Development Activity Book with Standardized Test Practice

The *Activity Book* contains a variety of language practice along with instructions for and practice in taking standardized tests.

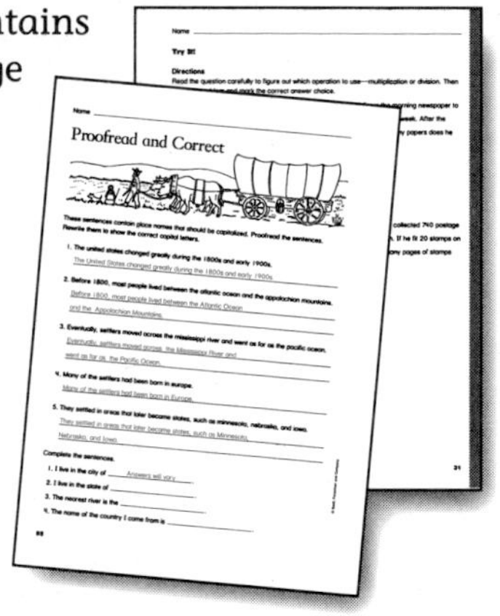

LET'S TALK CARD

Let's Talk!

Ninety-six cards provide conversation starters at three levels: Beginning, Intermediate, and Advanced.

BLACKLINE MASTER

Teacher's Resource Book

The reproducible pages in the *Teacher's Resource Book* contain scoring rubrics, checklists, and rating scales; graphic organizers; letters to families in Cambodian, Cantonese, English, Spanish, Haitian Creole, and Vietnamese; and language and listening assessments for each chapter of the program.

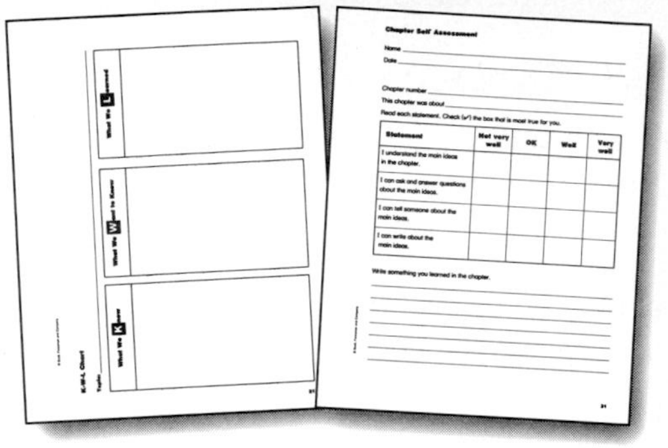

Newcomer Books

A (Grades 1–2),
B (Grades 3–5),
C (Grades 6–8)

These books, which contain age-appropriate lessons in survival English, were designed to ease new students into English and the American school system.

Newcomer Teacher Suggestion Book

One book per grade, which focuses on social and academic language development, provides teachers with lesson-by-lesson *Student Book* support for newcomers.

HomeLink Penguin Readers

Six classic stories per grade that students can read on their own.

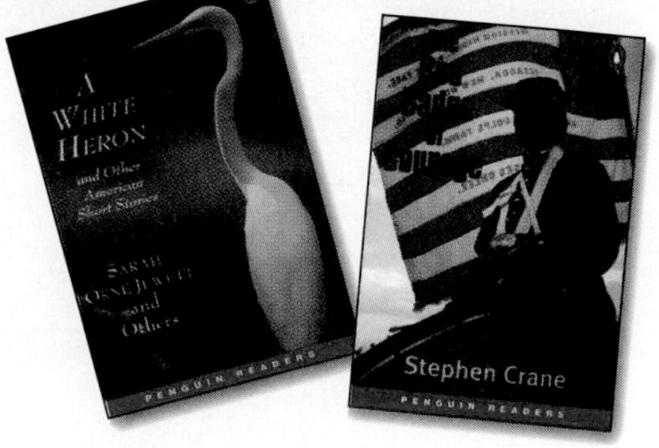

GREEN TAPE

Audio Tapes

Eight audio tapes per level contain all the stories, songs, poems, and rhymes for that book plus a listening assessment for every chapter.

PICTURE CARDS

Picture Cards

Seventy-two full-color, labeled cards with 144 pictures can be used to introduce and reinforce vocabulary in a variety of games and exercises.

Storytelling Anthologies

One collection per grade of multicultural literature selections enhances students' listening skills and provides lessons and activities to ensure comprehension.

Phonics

Program of literacy activities for newcomers to develop phonemic awareness and sound-symbol correspondence for English sounds and letters. Includes student workbook, picture cards, audio program, and teacher's guide.

DISK

Writer's Notebook

Writer's Notebook Software helps students explore their knowledge, thinking, and creativity by combining personal journal writing with computer technology. Writing prompts are included for each chapter and each major literature selection.

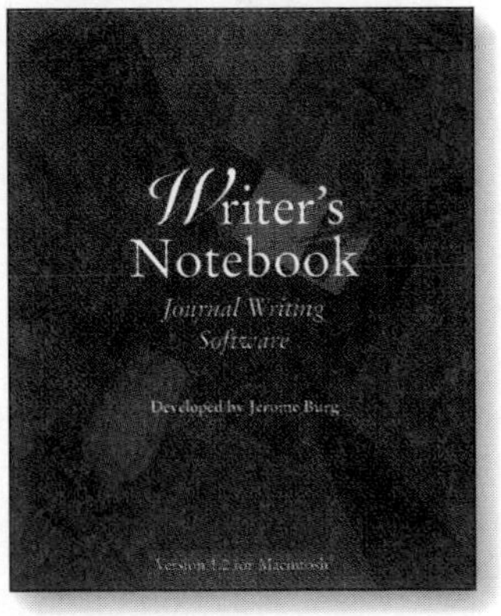

For more activities and ideas, visit the ScottForesman ESL website at: www.longman-elt.com/sfesl

ORGANIZATION

The Teacher's Edition

Each level of *ScottForesman ESL* contains six thematic units; each unit contains two related chapters. Each unit of the *Teacher's Edition* contains these features.

Planning Guide

The Planning Guide lists the objectives and the vocabulary focus for each chapter. A chart for each chapter shows the content focus, language awareness objectives, and learning strategies for each lesson in the *Student Book*.

Resources

A list of Resources for each chapter includes Support Materials, Phonics Reference and Support Materials, Storytelling Anthology, Let's Talk Cards, Assessment Materials, Support for Newcomers, HomeLink Readers, and a bibliography of books for extended reading and of related technology products.

Resources

Chapter 2

Support Materials

PICTURE CARDS: Numbers 2, 8, 14, 17, 18, 21, 27, 33, 36, 38, 42, 52, 57, 67, 70

ACTIVITY BOOK: Pages 12–21

RED TAPE: Side 1: *The Story of Johnny Appleseed*, pages T26–T37

DISK: Writer's Notebook

Phonics

PHONICS: *Newcomer Phonics*, pages 20–21

Assessment Materials

BLACKLINE MASTER: Language Assessment, Blackline Master 42; Listening Assessment, Blackline Master 43

WHITE TAPE: Side 1: Listening Assessment, page T39

Listen carefully to each description. Then write the number of the description next to the part of the picture it describes.

1. The pistil is found inside a flower. It makes and holds egg cells. It is where pollination takes place.

2. Petals are the outside parts of flowers. They come in many different sizes and colors. Most flowers have several petals.

3. Stamens are found inside the petals of a flower. They are long and thin and make pollen.

Support for Newcomer

Newcomer Teacher Suggestion Book, Chapter 2, pages 10–11

For Extended Reading

From Flower to Fruit by Anne O. Dowden, Ticknor & Fields, 1994. Text and drawings explain how flowers mature into seed-bearing fruit. **Level: Advanced**

How Leaves Change by Sylvia A. Johnson, Lerner Publications, 1986. Discover how leaves go from green to brilliant oranges, reds, and yellows as part of their natural life cycle. **Level: Average**

How Seeds Travel by Cynthia Overbeck, Lerner Publications, 1982. Find out how seeds travel by wind, water, and animals, and how they reproduce. **Level: Average**

Incredible Plants by Lesley Dow, Time-Life Books, 1997. This colorful overview of the plant world identifies the parts of a plant, flowering and food plants, medicine from plants, and much more. **Level: Beginning**

Looking at Plants by David Suzuki, John Wiley & Sons, 1992. Learn about the characteristics, parts, growth, and care of plants in this well-written book. **Level: Average**

The Plant-and Grow Project Book by Ulla Dietl, Sterling Publishing Co., 1993. Students learn how to grow their own plants and learn how they mature. **Level: Advanced**

Related Technology

The Way Plants Grow, Queue, Inc., 1996. Students learn about the growth cycle of plants.

T1d

CHAPTER 2

Life Cycles of Plants

Objectives

Name the parts of a plant.
Name the four main parts of a flower.
Describe the life cycle of a plant.
Tell how plants and animals are interdependent.
Identify the parts of plants that people can eat.

Vocabulary Focus

Parts of plants, such as *flower, leaf, root, stem.*
Parts of flowers, such as *pistil, stamen, sepal.*
Stages of a plant's life cycle, such as *seed, pollen, grain, flower.*
Parts of plants people eat, such as *seeds, stems, roots.*

Lesson	Content Focus	Language Awareness Objectives	Learning Strategies
Preview pp. 16–17 Tell what you know.			
Present pp. 18–19 Parts of a Flower	Science	**Language Function** Words That Describe	Use pictures for meaning.
Practice pp. 20–21 Life Cycle of a Flowering Plant	Science	**Phonics** Initial Consonant *p*, Consonant Blends *pl* and *pr*	Follow a sequence.
Practice pp. 22–23 Eating Plants	Science	**Grammar** Count and Noncount Nouns	
Connect pp. 24–25 Numbers in Plants	Science/Math	**Vocabulary** Position Words	
Connect pp. 26–37 *The Story of Johnny Appleseed*	Science/ Literature	**Spelling** Capitalization of Place Names **Language Function** Expressing Intention with *Going to* or *Will* **Grammar** Past Tense	Make inferences. Recognize cause and effect. Visualize story details.
Connect p. 38 Recipe for Waldorf Salad	Science/ Reading	**Spelling** Punctuation	
Assess p. 39 Tell what you learned.			

T1b

Unit Project

This optional project is designed to be completed over the two chapters of the unit. Typically, this is a hands-on, cooperative project that results in a product students can share with friends and family. Letters to invite family participation in each project are provided in Cambodian, Cantonese, English, Spanish, Haitian Creole, and Vietnamese. At the end of the project, family and friends are invited to school to share the results.

Activity Book Answers

The *Activity Book* pages for every chapter of the book are reproduced in mini format with the answers in place. Answers to the practice standardized tests can be found on the *Assess* page of each chapter.

Page-by-Page Teaching Suggestions

Student Book pages are reproduced in the *Teacher's Edition* with complete instructions for presenting each page, for developing language awareness, and for modeling learning strategies. *Options for Reaching All Students* suggest activities for beginning and advanced students and mixed-ability groups, as well as ideas for peer or cross-age tutoring, cooperative learning, and home connections.

Wrap-Up

Following the page-by-page teaching, the Unit Wrap-Up contains suggestions for individual, small group, and class activities based on the unit theme. Suggestions are given for discussing what the students have learned in the unit and for sharing the unit project with family and friends. Signs of Success, a unit checklist, provides a quick way to assess students' progress.

Themes and Topics

The themes and topics for Book 8 of *ScottForesman ESL* are the following:

Unit 1:	**Change—Cycles of Life**
Chapter 1:	Growing Up
Chapter 2:	Life Cycles of Plants
Unit 2:	**Challenges—Weather**
Chapter 3:	Changing Weather
Chapter 4:	Predicting the Weather
Unit 3:	**Conflict—The Civil War**
Chapter 5:	The United States Before the Civil War
Chapter 6:	War Between North and South
Unit 4:	**Relationships—The Solar System**
Chapter 7:	The Sun
Chapter 8:	The Planets
Unit 5:	**Journeys—A Growing Nation**
Chapter 9:	Settling the West
Chapter 10:	Industry Changed the Nation
Unit 6:	**Justice—Citzenship and Government**
Chapter 11:	Citizenship
Chapter 12:	Government

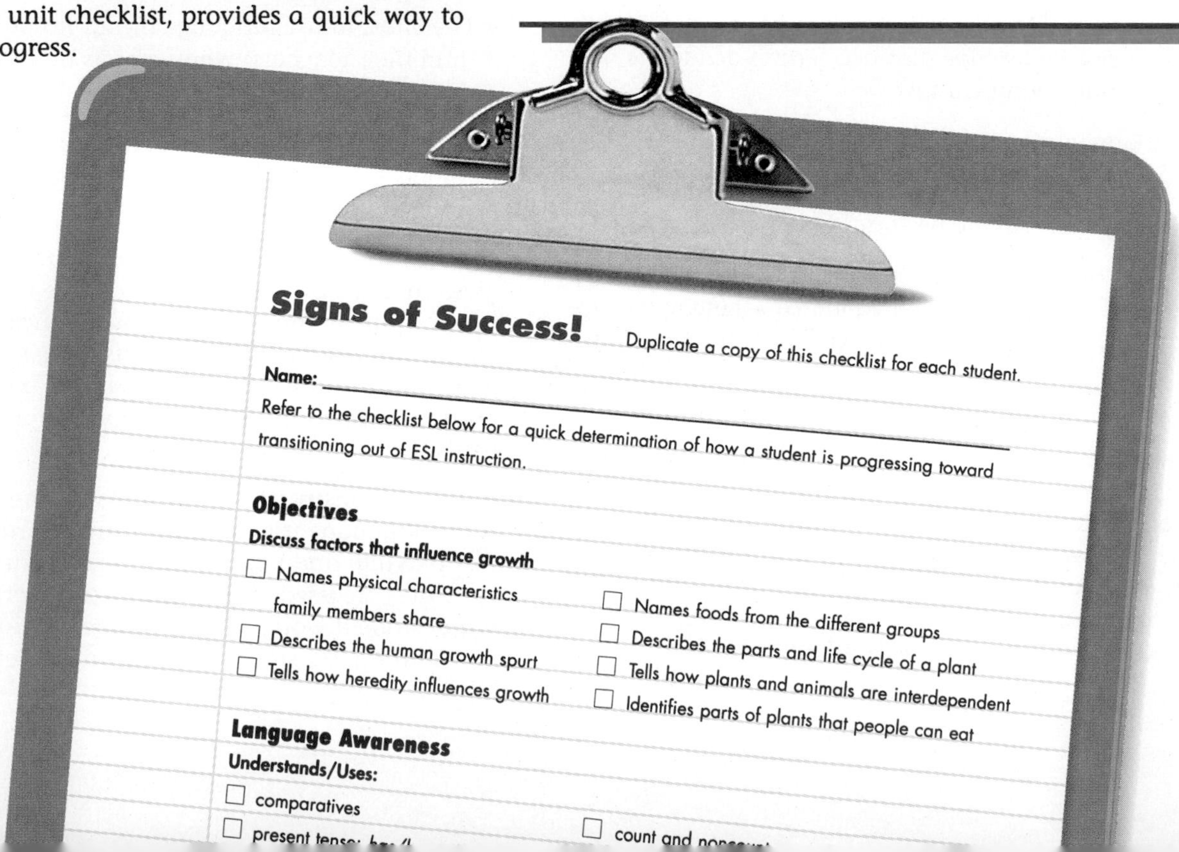
Signs of Success! Duplicate a copy of this checklist for each student.

Name: ____________________

Refer to the checklist below for a quick determination of how a student is progressing toward transitioning out of ESL instruction.

Objectives

Discuss factors that influence growth

- ☐ Names physical characteristics family members share
- ☐ Describes the human growth spurt
- ☐ Tells how heredity influences growth
- ☐ Names foods from the different groups
- ☐ Describes the parts and life cycle of a plant
- ☐ Tells how plants and animals are interdependent
- ☐ Identifies parts of plants that people can eat

Language Awareness

Understands/Uses:

- ☐ comparatives
- ☐ present tense
- ☐ count and

The Lesson Plan

JIM CUMMINS

The five step instructional sequence of each chapter in *ScottForesman ESL* provides the means for teachers to implement effective instructional strategies in ways that affirm ESL students' developing sense of self.

Preview

There is general agreement among cognitive psychologists that we learn by integrating new input into our existing cognitive structures, or schemata. Our prior knowledge and experience provide the foundation for interpreting new information.

In a classroom of English language learners from diverse backgrounds, prior knowledge about a particular topic may vary widely. Simple transmission of the information or skill may fail to connect with the prior knowledge and experience of some students. Other students may have relevant information in their first language but not realize that there is any connection with what they are learning in English.

Every chapter in *ScottForesman ESL* begins with a *Preview* section, designed to activate students' prior knowledge through pictures and brainstorming as a whole class or in small groups or pairs. Finding out what students know about a particular topic allows the teacher to supply relevant concepts or vocabulary that some or all of the students may be lacking but which will be important for understanding the chapter. Building this context permits students to understand more complex language and to pursue more cognitively demanding activities.

In addition to making the learning process more efficient, activating prior knowledge also accelerates academic progress in other significant ways:

- It stimulates students to use the target language.
- It permits teachers to get to know their students as individuals with unique personal histories.
- It creates a classroom in which students' cultural knowledge is expressed, shared, and validated—thereby motivating students to participate more actively in the learning process.

Present

Input in English can be presented orally or through written text. In either case, comprehension can be facilitated through the use of photographs, illustrations, maps, graphs, diagrams, and other graphic organizers such as Venn diagrams, semantic webs, and time lines. This kind of scaffolding enables ESL students to participate effectively in instruction even when their knowledge of the language is still quite limited.

The *Present* section of every chapter in *ScottForesman ESL* introduces language and concepts through a wide variety of scaffolding devices and learning strategies. This linguistic and contextual support gives students access to the language of text, a language very different from the language of interpersonal conversation. In the language of text, the vocabulary usually consists of words that are less frequent than those in everyday conversation; grammatical constructions are more complex because meanings must be made more explicit; and meaning is not supported by the immediacy of context and interpersonal cues (e.g., gestures, intonation). A wide variety of learning strategies is presented to help students become independent interpreters of this language. (See pp. xxi–xxii.)

Academic success depends on students gaining access to and comprehending the language of books and school discourse. *ScottForesman ESL* provides the support students need as they learn school English as a source of comprehensible input.

Practice

Active language use in both oral and written modalities is important for both cognitive and linguistic growth. At a cognitive level, writing about or discussion of complex issues with the teacher and peers encourages students to reflect critically and refine their ideas.

Linguistic growth is stimulated by active language use in at least three ways.

- Students must try to figure out sophisticated aspects of the target language to express what they want to communicate.
- The effort to use language brings home to students (and their teachers) what aspects of language they need assistance with.
- Teachers are given the opportunity to provide corrective feedback to build language awareness and help students see how the language works.

The *Practice* section of every chapter in *ScottForesman ESL* gives students the active language use they need to develop both cognitive and linguistic competencies. Students are also encouraged to express *themselves*; in other words, to explore their own feelings, ideas, and experiences in a supportive context and thereby become more aware of their goals, values, and aspirations.

Among the instructional strategies that encourage this active language use are cooperative learning, drama and role playing, and peer or cross-age tutoring. All of these strategies are used to promote creative writing and publishing of student work, which are of central importance in accelerating ESL students' academic growth.

Connect

An integrated curriculum crosses subject areas and connects various curriculum components into a meaningful whole. This leads students to a deeper understanding of both the concepts they are learning and the language used to describe those concepts.

The *Connect* section of every chapter in *ScottForesman ESL* gives students practice in applying the language and strategies they are learning to a new area of the curriculum. It also provides the opportunity for students to apply their expanding understanding of language and concepts to the reading of authentic literature. (See pp. xviii–xx.)

Assess

Instruction and assessment are closely linked. Assessment involves monitoring of students' content learning and oral and written language use in order to provide appropriate guidance and feedback to the students.

The *Assess* section of every chapter in *ScottForesman ESL* provides a wide variety of assessment tools. In the Student Book, "Tell What You Learned" checks understanding of content and provides self-assessment. In the *Teacher's Edition,* "Options for Assessment" provides ideas for language and writing assessment. The Audio tapes and *Teacher's Resource Book* contain a listening assessment for every chapter; the *Teacher's Resource Book* contains additional language assessment; and the *Activity Book* contains instructions and practice for standardized tests.

In addition, the *Teachers Resource Book* contains a wide variety of rubrics, rating sheets, checklists, and forms for teacher, peer, and self assessment. (See pp. xxiii–xxv.)

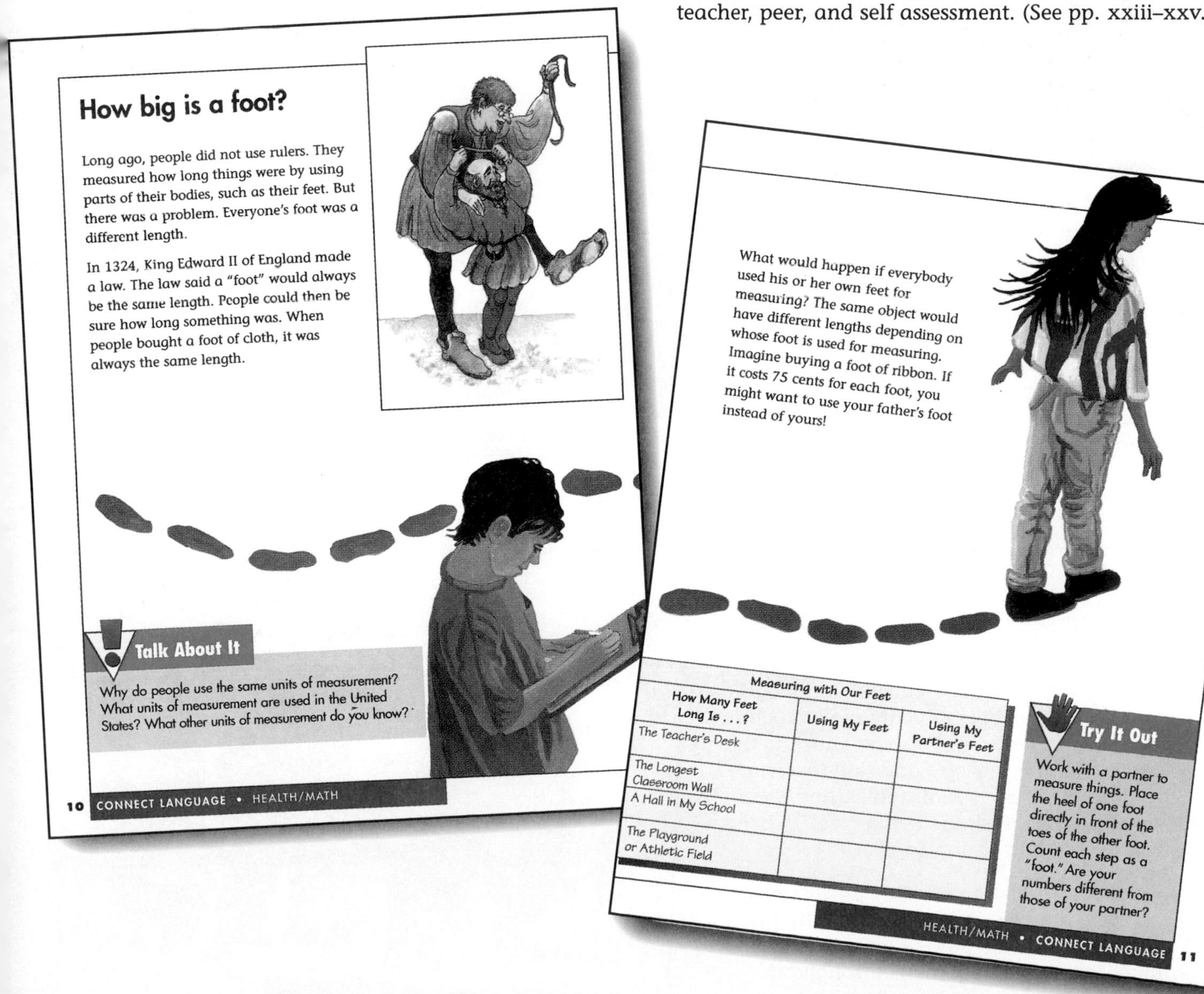

How big is a foot?

Long ago, people did not use rulers. They measured how long things were by using parts of their bodies, such as their feet. But there was a problem. Everyone's foot was a different length.

In 1324, King Edward II of England made a law. The law said a "foot" would always be the same length. People could then be sure how long something was. When people bought a foot of cloth, it was always the same length.

Talk About It

Why do people use the same units of measurement? What units of measurement are used in the United States? What other units of measurement do you know?

10 CONNECT LANGUAGE • HEALTH/MATH

What would happen if everybody used his or her own feet for measuring? The same object would have different lengths depending on whose foot is used for measuring. Imagine buying a foot of ribbon. If it costs 75 cents for each foot, you might want to use your father's foot instead of yours!

Measuring with Our Feet

How Many Feet Long Is . . . ?	Using My Feet	Using My Partner's Feet
The Teacher's Desk		
The Longest Classroom Wall		
A Hall in My School		
The Playground or Athletic Field		

Try It Out

Work with a partner to measure things. Place the heel of one foot directly in front of the toes of the other foot. Count each step as a "foot." Are your numbers different from those of your partner?

HEALTH/MATH • CONNECT LANGUAGE 11

Cognitive Academic Language in ESL Instruction

ANNA UHL CHAMOT & J. MICHAEL O'MALLEY

The Cognitive Academic Language Learning Approach (CALLA) is an instructional model for meeting the academic needs of ESL students in American schools. It is designed to assist ESL students to succeed by providing beginning or transitional instruction in either standard ESL programs or bilingual programs.

The CALLA model includes three components and instructional objectives in its curricular and instructional design:

- topics from the major school subjects,
- the development of academic language skills,
- explicit instruction in learning strategies for both content and language acquisition.

Content subjects are the primary focus of instruction in CALLA. Content, rather than language, drives the curriculum. Language modalities (e.g., listening, speaking, reading, writing) are developed for content-area activities as they are needed, rather than being taught sequentially. Academic language skills can be developed as the need for them emerges from the content. Language skills will be most meaningful when students perceive that they are needed in order to accomplish a communicative or academic task.

There are at least four reasons for incorporating curricular content into the ESL class.

- Students develop important knowledge in all subject areas. Throughout *ScottForesman ESL,* students learn grade level concepts and processes in science, social studies, mathematics, and other academic areas, thus providing a foundation for their content-area classes.
- Students learn the language functions and skills needed for success in content areas. Every lesson of the *Teacher's Edition* of *ScottForesman ESL* suggests language awareness activities designed to strengthen students' abilities to practice these functions and skills.
- Many students exhibit greater motivation when learning content than when they are learning language only. Students in *ScottForesman ESL* are motivated not only by the topics presented but also by knowing that they are developing the concepts and skills associated with science, mathematics, social studies, and literature. They perceive that they are doing "real" schoolwork instead of merely learning English.
- Students learn the strategies necessary for success in curriculum areas. These learning strategies are the mental processes and behaviors students use to access their learning. Extensive suggestions throughout *ScottForesman ESL* provide guidelines for learning strategy instruction. *Academic language* is the language that is used by teachers and students for the purpose of acquiring new knowledge and skills. This kind of language differs in many ways from social language, the language that is used for interaction in social settings. Academic language is more difficult and takes longer to learn than social language. It may be less interactive than social language and may provide fewer context clues, such as gestures, to assist comprehension. Academic language has very specific purposes, including imparting new information, describing abstract ideas, and developing conceptual understanding. These purposes are cognitively demanding, thus increasing the comprehension difficulties students experience.

Academic language consists primarily of the functions needed for authentic academic content. These functions include explaining, informing, justifying, comparing, describing, proving, debating, persuading, and evaluating. To accomplish these functions requires the use of both lower-order and higher-order thinking skills. *ScottForesman ESL* enables students to practice the functions and thinking skills needed to engage in specific content activities. Discrete language elements such as vocabulary, grammatical structures, spelling, and pronunciation are integrated into this practice.

Facts About Immigration

Some decades have been times of great immigration. Other decades have not. Study the chart and answer the questions.

Immigration to the United States, 1900 to 1990	
Decade	**Number of People**
1900s	8,795,386
1910s	5,735,811
1920s	4,107,209
1930s	528,431
1940s	1,035,039
1950s	2,515,479
1960s	3,321,677
1970s	4,493,314
1980s	7,338,062

200 CONNECT LANGUAGE • SOCIAL STUDIES/MATH

There are at least five reasons for focusing on academic language skills in the ESL classroom.

- For ESL students, the ability to use academic language effectively is a key to success in grade-level classrooms.
- Academic language is not usually learned outside of the classroom setting.
- Grade-level teachers may assume that all of their students already know appropriate academic language, when, in fact, ESL students in their classes have often acquired only social language skills.
- Academic language provides students with practice in using English as a medium of thought.
- Students may need assistance in using learning strategies with academic language, just as they do with content knowledge and skills.

ScottForesman ESL responds to each of these reasons. In its content-based lessons, both teachers and students use academic language to communicate, analyze, and explain. It provides the exposure students need to develop academic language functions and thinking skills. It prepares students for transition into grade-level classrooms. Throughout the program, guidelines are given for:

- modeling academic language appropriate to content topic;
- providing practice in listening to information and answering higher level questions;
- creating opportunities for using academic language through cooperative activities;
- having students describe, explain, justify, evaluate, and express understanding of and feelings about topics and processes;
- having students read and write in every major curriculum area.

Learning Strategies, the third key element in CALLA instruction, are important for language learning and for learning academic content. Learning strategies are the mental processes and overt behaviors students use to assist their learning. Strategies are taught explicitly in CALLA to help students develop metacognitive awareness of their own learning and to become self-directed learners. Knowing how and when to use learning strategies is especially important for ESL students who are learning both a new language and challenging academic content.

In *ScottForesman ESL,* learning strategies are taught in every lesson. Students are prompted to use various learning strategies for language and content activities. The *Teacher's Edition* contains suggestions for introducing, modeling, practicing, extending, and assessing learning strategies. (See pp. xxi–xxii.)

ScottForesman ESL incorporates the major principles from CALLA, which are based on cognitive research and learning theory. The CALLA model has been successful in accelerating ESL students' academic achievements in school districts nationwide.

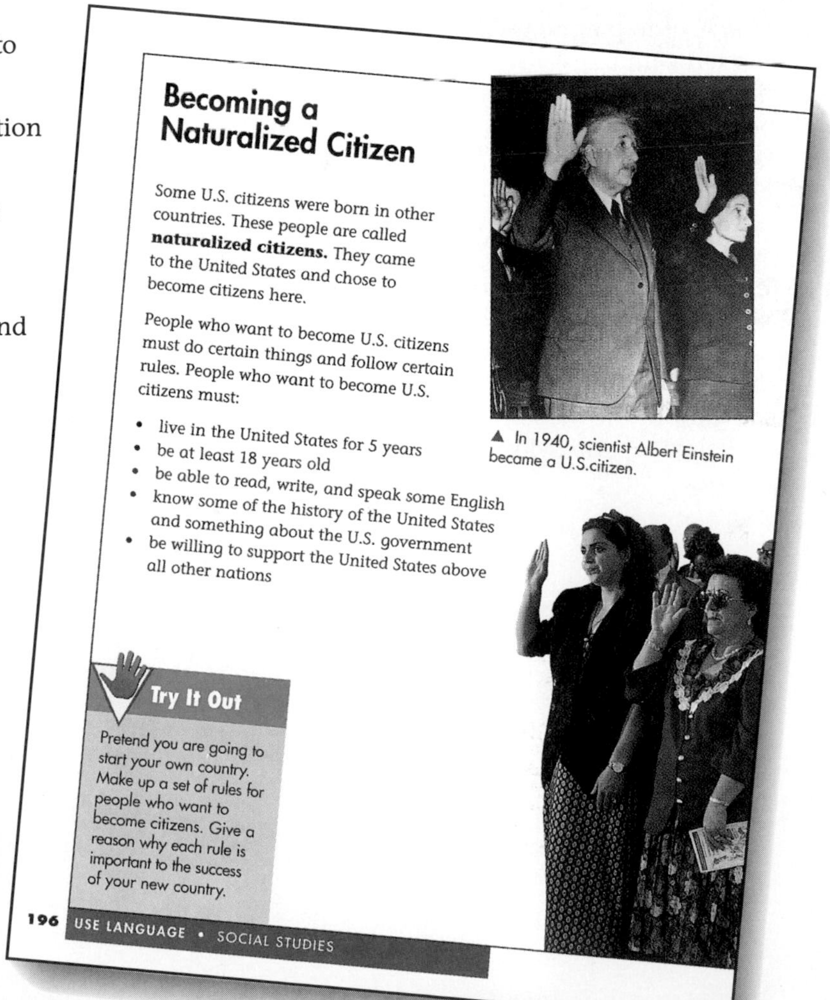

Becoming a Naturalized Citizen

Some U.S. citizens were born in other countries. These people are called **naturalized citizens.** They came to the United States and chose to become citizens here.

People who want to become U.S. citizens must do certain things and follow certain rules. People who want to become U.S. citizens must:

- live in the United States for 5 years
- be at least 18 years old
- be able to read, write, and speak some English
- know some of the history of the United States and something about the U.S. government
- be willing to support the United States above all other nations

▲ In 1940, scientist Albert Einstein became a U.S.citizen.

Try It Out

Pretend you are going to start your own country. Make up a set of rules for people who want to become citizens. Give a reason why each rule is important to the success of your new country.

196 USE LANGUAGE • SOCIAL STUDIES

Authentic Literature in ESL Instruction

LILY WONG FILLMORE

How do children acquire those aspects of language knowledge and proficiency that figure in intellectually demanding communication? Few children, whether native speakers of English or learners of English, are fully proficient in this type of language when they first enter school. Children who have had books read to them at home, or who have learned to read in their primary languages, will have some familiarity with the language of written texts. But all will need to develop it further to handle the language demands of school. For most, authentic children's literature such as that appearing in *ScottForesman ESL* is a major source of input for academic language, whether in the native or a second language.

Let us look at a piece of literature, "The Night of the Stars" by Douglas Gutierrez. The story tells of a man who did not like the night because there was no light. He goes to the mountaintop from which he thinks night comes and tries to get it to stop obscuring the light of day. But the man is told that nothing can be done, because the light is hidden behind the night. The man thinks about this, and eventually comes up with a solution:

> "Once more he went to the mountain. The night was like an immense awning, covering all things. When at last he reached the highest point on the mountain, the man stood on his tiptoes, and with his finger poked a hole in the black sky. A pinprick of light flickered through the hole. The man who did not like the night was delighted. He poked holes all over the sky. Here, there, everywhere, and all over the sky little points of light appeared. Amazed now at what he could do, the man made a fist and punched it through the darkness. A large hole opened up, and a huge round light, almost like a grapefruit, shone through. All the escaping light cast a brilliant glow at the base of the mountain and lit up everything below . . . the fields, the street, the houses. Everything."

Now one might wonder how a piece of literature such as this one, offering a mythic account of how the stars and the moon came to be, might figure in the interpretation of language such as that found in a science text. Isn't an account like this one contradictory to the science materials that the students are reading? The answer is this: texts like this delightful piece of literature give children access to the language itself. The language of stories gives access to vocabulary, structures, phrasings, and discourse processes that children, whether they are native speakers of English or learners of English, must eventually learn. Let us look at what the readers of "The Night of the Stars" will find as input in this passage:

Vocabulary: Among the words the readers will encounter are nouns such as *mountain, awning, point, tiptoes, pinprick, light,* and *glow*; verbs such as *reach, flicker, shine, poke,* and *amaze*; adjectives such as *brilliant, immense, huge, round,* and *highest*; and adverbials such as *everywhere* and *below*. Notice that this vocabulary is specific and precise—it tells the reader where the man went and what he did and more. It tells the reader about the event in language that evokes images and feelings and qualities.

According to some experts, vocabulary size and breadth are crucial determinants of reading and overall academic performance. School-age children acquire much of the new vocabulary they learn by reading books. Children reading a text such as the one we are looking at may or may not learn all the words that they do not already know. Whether they do or do not understand every word is not usually critical to the understanding of the story. But having read it, they will have encountered the words used in it. This gives them a passing acquaintance with the ones that are new to them, and of how they are used in this particular text. The next time they encounter these words, they will have some usage information available in memory that may just help them figure out what they mean. The point is, it takes a great deal of reading to learn the words that are crucial to the understanding of texts with real meaning payloads.

Structure: Our story has a relatively simple past narrative—all of the events take place in past time. Most of the verbs are in the simple past tense. But the time relations among the parts of this story are not all that simple. The first two sentences might appear to be a simple sequence of events: The man went to the mountain. Once there, he checks out the night-time sky, and likens it to an immense awning. It is somewhat more complex than that, however.

"Once more" indicates that the man has gone to the mountain before, and "he went to the mountain" describes what he was doing in this event, but not necessarily the completion of the activity. The next sentence—"the night was like an immense awning, etc.," is a description of what the man perceived or thought while he was on his way to the mountain, rather than what he saw once he arrived. How do readers know that? Because in the next sentence, the temporal clause, "when at last he reached the highest point on the mountain" tells them that only then was the journey completed. This then suggests that the second sentence describes the man's observations before the completion of the journey. Does this make any difference to the readers? It probably doesn't—at least in terms of their understanding and enjoyment of the story. However, when readers figure out or are helped to see how the events described in this story relate, they pick up a bit more information about how English works with respect to temporal relations.

Background knowledge: Just as readers must apply their linguistic knowledge to the interpretation of the texts they read, so too must they make use of their knowledge of the world and their prior experiences in reading. No text contains every bit of information needed to understand it fully. Writers generally assume a level of prior language knowledge and cultural and real world experience when they write. If they believe that the intended readers are unlikely to be familiar with certain words or concepts, they will define or discuss them. Otherwise, they simply presuppose that the readers will be able to apply their knowledge of language and of how it works to the reading and interpretation of the text, and that they will draw on their knowledge of the world and on their experiences to fill in the gaps in the text. The ideal reader then is one who has the cultural background, experience, and linguistic knowledge to do just what the writer hopes the readers of the text will be able to do when they read it.

That fact presents a special problem to educators who are concerned with finding or preparing appropriate instructional materials and texts for children from diverse cultural and linguistic backgrounds. How can these children deal with texts that are as complex as those used for mainstream students? How can they possibly comprehend materials that presuppose cultural background, knowledge, and experiences that they don't already have? Shouldn't they be given materials that are culturally familiar, that deal with the world as they know and have experienced it?

I will argue that the education of children irrespective of their background would be greatly diminished if educators were to choose materials for them that were in any way narrowed or lowered in level because of putative deficiencies in the children's backgrounds. Such decisions must take into account the role authentic and challenging materials play in building children's background knowledge and in supporting language development. Authentic literature gives English learners access to the vocabulary, grammar, and discourse conventions of the language they are learning. Children also gain the very kind of background knowledge that they need to have to deal with materials they read in school from the literature and textbooks they have already read. This argument might seem rather circular, at first glance. How do children get the background they need in the first place? And what kind of useful background could they possibly get from a story like "The Night of the Stars"?

Consider the cognitive skills it takes to make sense of such scientific ideas as supernovas or the time it takes light to travel from a star to earth. How does anyone understand concepts like these without actually having experienced them? How do scientists and theorists come up with ideas like brown dwarfs and black holes? I will argue that this kind of thinking begins with the development of the imagination. One way to develop the imagination is by reading and thinking about stories like "The Night of the Stars." The ability to conceptualize possible worlds is not entirely unrelated to the ability to create and consider impossible ones, of the sort involved in that story. There may be nothing in our story that leads directly to knowledge that will enable a reader to understand a newspaper story about the discovery of a new black hole. Yet, the reader who, as a child, was able to imagine someone standing on top of a mountain, poking holes in the night-time sky thereby creating stars will no doubt find it easier to understand than one without such early experiences.

Authentic texts such as those in *ScottForesman ESL* are perhaps the most reliable and consistent source of academic English input children can have. However, texts do not by themselves reveal how the language in them works, nor do they provide many clues as to what the words that appear in them mean or how they are used. Such materials work as input when teachers do the following:

- provide the support learners need to make sense of the text
- call attention to the way language is used in the text
- discuss with learners the meaning and interpretation of sentences and phrases within the text
- point out that words in one text may have been encountered or used in other places
- help learners discover the grammatical cues that indicate relationships such as cause and effect, antecedent and consequence, comparison and contrast, and so on

In short, teachers help written texts become usable input—not only by helping children make sense of the text, but by focusing their attention on how language is used in the materials they read. Done consistently enough, the learners themselves will soon come to notice the way language is used in the materials they read. When they can do that, everything they read will be input for learning.

Presenting Stories in ESL Instruction

GEORGE A GONZÁLEZ

Reading authentic literature presents special challenges to ESL students. Some students may understand details, but not see the big picture. Others may grasp the gist of a story, but not have the language to explain their understanding.

Sentences

Choosing and presenting the important sentences of a story can convey the most significant and salient ideas of the selection and represent critical story elements. These sentences can form a story map that includes related story elements, such as characters, events, problems, feelings and opinions, setting, time, and conclusion. The important sentences can also convey knowledge and information such as linguistic patterns.

Words

Children who cannot understand and use a wide repertoire of words in their oral language often encounter problems with reading comprehension. For these children, idioms and words that represent new concepts or new labels can be especially challenging. Throughout *ScottForesman ESL* are suggestions for words and terms to be presented to these students.

The following six methods for oral teaching of new vocabulary in context help make words meaningful, relevant, and enjoyable.

Personalization

Relate the word to a situation familiar to children.

example: bad mood

The baby is in a bad mood; he is not happy; he has been crying all day.

Demonstration

Demonstrate the action implied by the word, stating what you are doing as you do it.

example: kneel

I will kneel on the floor; I am kneeling on the floor; I have knelt on the floor.

Dramatization

Act out a situation illustrating the meaning of several words.

example: shake, fall, shuffled, collapsed, couch

Exemplification

Recite several examples of sentences in which a particular word or expression could be used.

example: unpleasant

The weather today is unpleasant. It is unpleasant to be scolded. The odor near the garbage cans was unpleasant.

Illustration

Guide children to draw pictures or to manipulate picture cards that depict the objects or concepts.

Definition

Define words or terms through description followed by a repetition of the word.

example: decision

I have decided to go to Nashville to visit friends.
It is my decision.

Sounds

Children who cannot perceive, discriminate, or produce the sounds of English may experience difficulties with word attack skills and spelling. Throughout *ScottForesman ESL*, the "Language Awareness" sections contain lessons on pronunciation and sound/letter relationships that are exemplified in the text. As students become acquainted with the sounds in context, they will develop a sensitivity to and an awareness of the English sound system and at the same time improve their comprehension.

The *ScottForesman ESL* Audio Tapes afford the opportunity for children to listen to the sounds of English within the context of authentic literature—over and over again.

Gestures and Body Language

Children who cannot express in English their ideas about a story will often be able to show their understanding by pantomiming elements of the plot or the emotions of the characters. Help them by pointing out the body language and facial expressions of characters in the illustrations. Demonstrate with students the way people in different cultures use gestures and other paralinguistic language. Compare, for example, the ways people wave hello or good-by, the distance people stand from one another when conversing, and the ways people show deference or respect.

Activities throughout *ScottForesman ESL* suggest ideas for helping students use pantomime, gestures, and body language to help convey what they want to get across in English.

Learning Strategies in ESL Instruction

ANNA UHL CHAMOT

Learning strategies are actions or thoughts that students can apply *on their own* to a challenging task. Learning strategies can be applied to language-related tasks, such as listening to or reading a text, speaking, or writing, or to tasks related to subject matter content, such as information and processes in science, mathematics, social studies, literature, art, and music.

ScottForesman ESL integrates learning strategies throughout and provides guidelines for teaching the strategies and helping students develop an awareness of their own learning processes. The intent of the learning strategies instructional component of *ScottForesman ESL* is to help all students develop their ability to learn independently.

ScottForesman ESL teaches students how to apply a number of useful learning strategies for school subjects. Students are encouraged to make use of their own background knowledge through discussions and brainstorming activities. They are taught to make a plan for carrying out an activity, for monitoring themselves as they work, and for evaluating their own achievements. Other learning strategies taught in *ScottForesman ESL* include predicting, making inferences, classifying, summarizing, note-taking, using picture clues, cooperating with classmates, and asking questions for clarification. Each chapter of *ScottForesman ESL* presents learning strategies that assist in preparing for a task (INTO strategies), for working on a task (THROUGH strategies), and for evaluating and extending a task (BEYOND strategies).

ScottForesman ESL integrates learning strategies instruction into each part of the learning process. The *Teacher's Edition* provides specific suggestions for presenting learning strategies throughout the *ScottForesman ESL* instructional sequence.

Preview

The purpose of this step in learning strategies instruction is to help students become more aware of their own learning processes, thus developing their metacognition, or understanding of their own thinking. The teacher begins by helping students identify their prior knowledge about strategies already familiar to them. The types of strategies students are already using can be quite diverse, especially in the case of students whose previous schooling has been in other countries. Most students are quite interested in finding out about their classmates' varying approaches to learning, and teachers can capitalize on this natural interest in suggesting new learning strategies to try.

Ways to identify students' prior knowledge about learning strategies include class or small group discussions in which students compare their individual approaches to working on a particular task, such as reading a story or following directions for a science experiment. More formal ways to identify existing learning strategies are through student interviews, questionnaires, or personal journals.

Present

In presenting a learning strategy, teachers need to be explicit and direct in their explanation, as this helps students develop awareness of strategic thinking. One of the most effective ways to present a strategy is through teacher modeling, in which teachers think aloud about their own use of the strategy. *ScottForesman ESL* provides examples of think-aloud scripts *(Model a Strategy)* that teachers can use or adapt to demonstrate different strategies.

In addition to modeling the strategy, teachers should also name it, tell students how it will help them learn, and explain when to use it. Naming a strategy makes it more concrete for students and helps focus class discussions about strategy use. Posters of learning strategies associated with easily remembered icons are helpful in reminding students about the names and uses of the strategies they are learning.

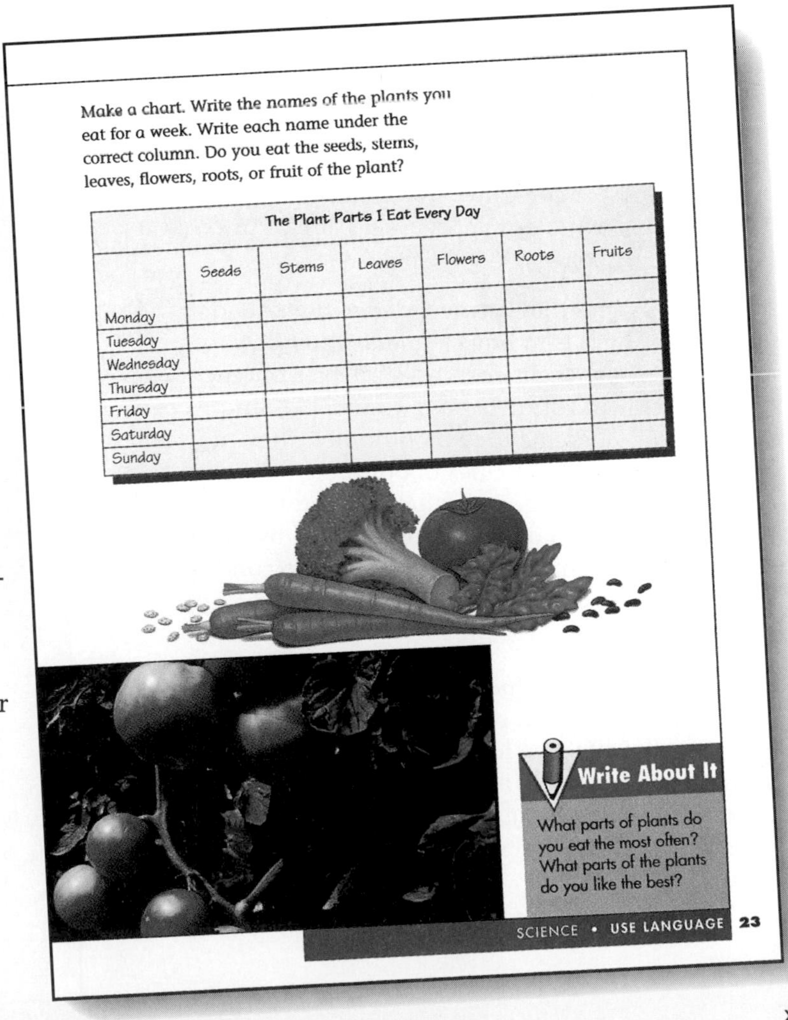
Make a chart. Write the names of the plants you eat for a week. Write each name under the correct column. Do you eat the seeds, stems, leaves, flowers, roots, or fruit of the plant?

The Plant Parts I Eat Every Day

	Seeds	Stems	Leaves	Flowers	Roots	Fruits
Monday						
Tuesday						
Wednesday						
Thursday						
Friday						
Saturday						
Sunday						

Write About It

What parts of plants do you eat the most often? What parts of the plants do you like the best?

SCIENCE • USE LANGUAGE 23

Students also need to understand that the purpose of learning strategies is to provide them with tools that they can use to help themselves in learning. Finally, teachers need to be sure that students understand that knowing *when* to use a strategy is as important as knowing *which* strategy to use.

Practice

As with any type of process or procedure, students need ample practice opportunities in applying learning strategies to their language development and subject matter learning. Learning strategies can be practiced with any task or activity that presents a challenge or a problem to be solved—very easy tasks can be accomplished successfully without consciously using learning strategies!

The rich variety of activities in *ScottForesman ESL* provides extensive opportunities for practicing the learning strategies presented. For example, stories, poems, and informational articles provide opportunities for using different kinds of reading strategies. Projects, reports, experiments, and other hands-on activities can be enhanced with planning, monitoring, and self-assessment strategies. Group discussions and cooperative learning activities are excellent vehicles for developing strategic competence in cooperation and questioning for clarification.

Connect

When students extend a strategy to a new context or connect two or more strategies in a unique approach to a problem, they are well on their way to becoming independent and self-regulated learners. Teachers can assist this process by asking students to brainstorm new ways to use a strategy or combine strategies and by suggesting that they try a strategy in another class or in a setting outside of school.

Another activity that connects learning strategies to students' own lives is to have students interview family members about their learning strategies or teach a favorite learning strategy to a younger sibling. When upper grade students read biographies, they may find it interesting to look for clues about the types of learning strategies that a famous person may have used. Finally, students can learn about strategies used by athletes, artists, dancers, musicians, actors, writers, and other contributors to students' life experiences.

Assess

Students need to evaluate how well different strategies are working for them so that they can build their own repertoire of effective learning strategies. Debriefing discussions after practicing one or more strategies can help students think through their use of strategies and pinpoint moments when a strategy really worked—or did not work—for them.

More formal ways for students to evaluate their own strategy use is through checklists, learning logs, or journals in which they describe their use of different learning strategies. Some teachers have also found that having students compare their performances on similar tasks with and without using a learning strategy is an effective strategy evaluation activity. The most important contribution that teachers can make in student self-evaluation of strategies is to provide many opportunities for students to reflect on, discuss, and write about their insights into their own learning processes.

Learning strategies are fun to teach and fun to learn. Students enjoy talking about their thinking, and teachers gain deeper insights by listening to their students' thoughts. Students who have already developed effective learning strategies should be encouraged to share them with classmates and to continue using them even as they are acquiring additional strategies. Eventually, students will take the responsibility for choosing their own personal repertoire of learning strategies and making their own decisions about when and how to apply the strategies.

The approach to learning strategies instruction in *ScottForesman ESL* helps students deal with challenging tasks, gain an appreciation of their own learning process, and develop both their language skills and their knowledge and understanding of content area subjects.

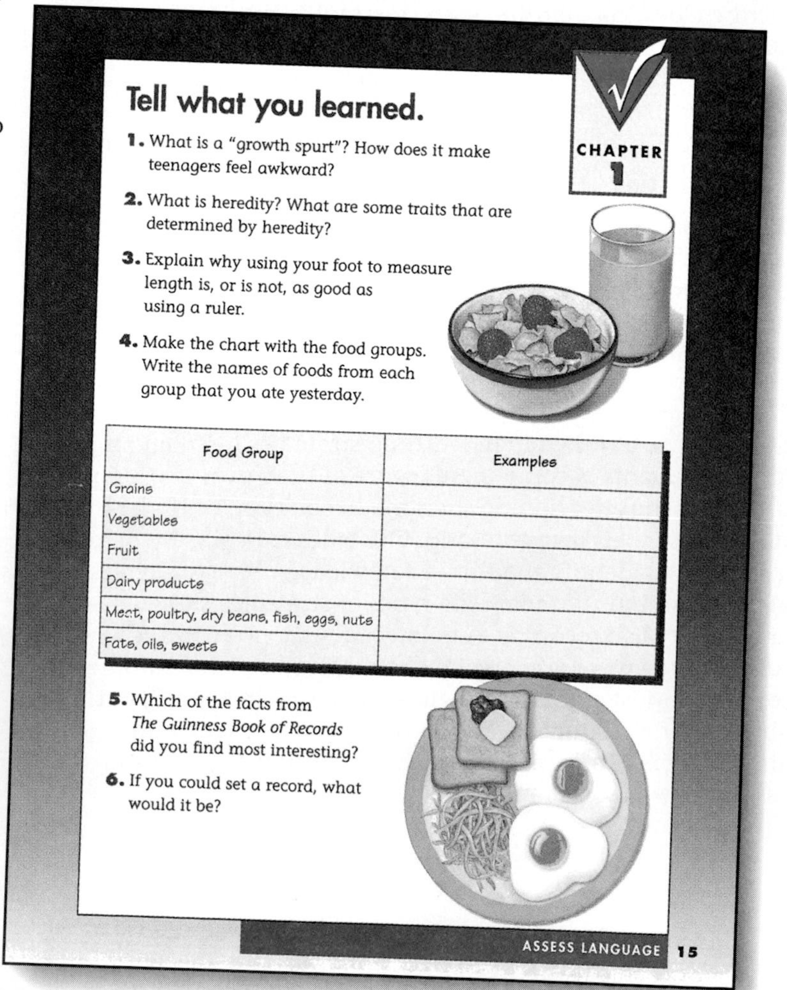

Tell what you learned.

CHAPTER 1

1. What is a "growth spurt"? How does it make teenagers feel awkward?
2. What is heredity? What are some traits that are determined by heredity?
3. Explain why using your foot to measure length is, or is not, as good as using a ruler.
4. Make the chart with the food groups. Write the names of foods from each group that you ate yesterday.

Food Group	Examples
Grains	
Vegetables	
Fruit	
Dairy products	
Meat, poultry, dry beans, fish, eggs, nuts	
Fats, oils, sweets	

5. Which of the facts from *The Guinness Book of Records* did you find most interesting?
6. If you could set a record, what would it be?

ASSESS LANGUAGE 15

Authentic Assessment in ESL Instruction

J. MICHAEL O'MALLEY

Assessment is authentic when it enables students to communicate successfully their strengths and educational needs, and when the results can be used to improve instruction based on accurate knowledge of student progress. Such assessment mirrors good classroom instruction, and it gives students ongoing feedback that enables them to reflect on their accomplishments, identify future learning needs, and develop goals and strategies for attaining them. As a result, this type of assessment empowers students to become self-directed learners and empowers teachers to use assessment information for instructional improvement.

The authentic assessment activities in *ScottForesman ESL* are integrated with and complement instruction. Because the assessment is part of instruction, it should not require significant additional time to prepare and conduct. Students do not need to stop learning for authentic assessment to occur.

The approach to assessment taken in *ScottForesman ESL* addresses four major issues: *who* conducts the assessment, *when* assessment occurs, *what* is assessed, and *how* assessment is accomplished. Each of these is important to ensure that assessment is authentic:

- Who—Assessment is conducted by students, teachers, and parents working in partnership to improve instruction and learning.
- When—Assessment is ongoing and enables both teachers and students to maintain a continuous record of student progress.
- What—The processes and strategies involved in learning as well as the products of learning are assessed.
- How—The assessment is designed to assist students with all levels of proficiency in English to communicate what they know and can do.

Three critical components of authentic assessment in *ScottForesman ESL* are the use of *scoring rubrics, benchmark standards,* and *informed judgment.*

Scoring rubrics are holistic scoring scales that identify what students know and can do at different levels of performance on classroom tasks. Typically, there may be four or five levels of proficiency or achievement defined on a scoring rubric.

Benchmark standards identify clearly for students and teachers the expected levels of performance based on specific tasks. That is, you might determine that all students should be performing at level 4 or 5, the highest levels of performance, on oral proficiency. With rubrics and benchmarks, students understand the nature of the performance expected as they progress through each level of proficiency and achievement toward mastery.

Informed judgment is based on scoring rubrics and benchmark standards. The judgment may be expressed by the teacher, the student, peers, or parents. This aspect of authentic assessment assures that responsibility for educational judgments about students is assumed by those in the classroom and others most closely associated with the child.

The assessment procedures in *ScottForesman ESL* assess students' knowledge through all four language skills—listening, speaking, reading, and writing. And because *ScottForesman ESL* integrates language development with literature and other academic content—including math, science, and social studies—the assessment provides information on the knowledge and procedural skills students use in all subjects.

Assessment activities in *ScottForesman ESL* are contained in the *Student Book,* the *Teacher's Edition,* the *Activity Book,* and the *Teacher's Resource Book. ScottForesman ESL* also provides sample forms, checklists, rubrics, and other guidelines to be used or adapted for assessment. (For additional forms, checklists, and rubrics, see *Authentic Assessment for English Language Learners: Practical Applications for Classroom Teachers* by J.M. O'Malley & L. Valdez Pierce, Addison-Wesley, 1996.)

A key element in authentic assessment is the use of multiple assessments, providing students with varied opportunities to demonstrate their learning and accomplishments. *ScottForesman ESL* includes all of the following: *teacher observation, self-assessment, peer assessment, performance assessment,* and *portfolio assessment.*

Teacher Observation

Teachers often make daily classroom observations to check on a student's progress or to plan for instruction. *ScottForesman ESL* provides suggestions on how to conduct observations through sample checklists, rating scales, and forms on which to note student behaviors that are directly relevant to the lesson.

Checklists identify specific behaviors to be observed and provide a form on which to indicate that the behavior occurred or how frequently it occurred. Examples of behaviors that might appear on a checklist are: scanning to find information while reading, using various cues for word meaning in context, making an outline or graphic organizer to plan an essay, or explaining successfully a problem-solving approach to a peer. A checklist of unit objectives appears at the end of each unit of *ScottForesman ESL.*

Rating scales are similar to checklists but provide an opportunity to indicate the degree to which a particular behavior occurred. For example, you can use a 3-point scale to indicate the level of control the student exhibited over specific aspects of writing, such as sentence formation—consistent control, reasonable control, or little or no control. A rating scale might also enable you to indicate if the student behavior occurred independently or with peer or adult support. Several examples of rating scales appear in the *ScottForesman ESL Teacher's Resource Book.*

Anecdotal records are notes describing behaviors that provide a rich indication of student progress when reviewed over the course of a school year. You can describe a specific behavior along with the learning materials, setting, student grouping, and time and place the behavior occurred. An example of a form for an anecdotal record appears in the *ScottForesman ESL Teacher's Resource Book.*

ScottForesman ESL provides varied procedures to observe student learning and performance as learning is taking place. You can identify individual students to observe in advance and plan the occasion when you will conduct the observation. In this way, you can manage the observations efficiently.

Self-Assessment

The importance of self-assessment cannot be overstated. Self-assessment is the key to student empowerment because it gives students an opportunity to reflect on their own progress toward instructional objectives, to determine the learning strategies that are effective for them, and to develop plans for their future learning. With self-assessment, students are active participants in deciding what and how much to learn and in setting the criteria by which their learning is evaluated.

To encourage self-assessment, you should share scoring rubrics with students and elicit their input on improving the rubrics. You can also share *anchor papers,* i.e., samples of student work that represent each point on the scoring rubric. After students review the anchor papers, they can then rate their own work or the work of their peers. Additional ways to encourage self-assessment include *K-W-L Charts, Reading Logs, Journals,* and *Self Ratings.*

K-W-L Charts are charts students complete using three columns to reflect what they *Know* about a topic before an instructional activity, what they *Want* to know from the lesson, and what they *Learned* from the lesson after its completion. The rows on the chart can reflect specific topics covered. For example, a lesson on Plants We Eat might cover Parts of the Plant, Types of Plants, and How Plants Grow. Suggestions for K-W-L Charts appear throughout *ScottForesman ESL.*

Reading Logs are records students keep of the reading they have completed. These might be categorized by genre and include the title, author, topics, and date on which the reading was completed, as well as the student's personal response to the reading and important concepts or information to remember. A Reading Log form appears in the *ScottForesman ESL Teacher's Resource Book.*

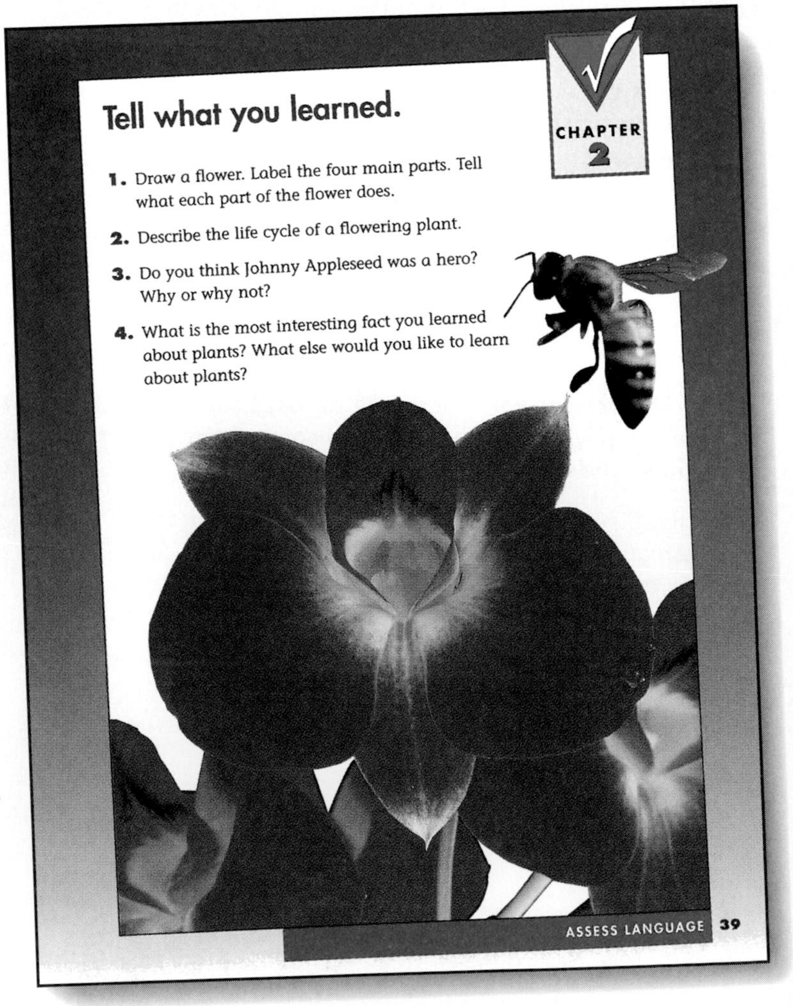
CHAPTER 2
Tell what you learned.
1. Draw a flower. Label the four main parts. Tell what each part of the flower does.
2. Describe the life cycle of a flowering plant.
3. Do you think Johnny Appleseed was a hero? Why or why not?
4. What is the most interesting fact you learned about plants? What else would you like to learn about plants?
ASSESS LANGUAGE 39

Journals are students' narrative diaries of what they have learned in each subject area. The journal may be kept daily and might mention the topics, what was difficult, what was easy, what strategies helped in learning, and what the student wants to know next.

Self-Ratings are the students' use of a scoring rubric to rate their own performance. For example, the use of a rubric for writing might include composing, style, sentence formation, word usage, and mechanics (spelling, capitalization, and punctuation).

ScottForesman ESL provides opportunity for self-assessment at the end of each chapter in the *Student Book* (page 31 in the *Teacher's Resource Book*). In addition, the *Teacher's Resource Book* contains a variety of forms and logs that students can use to monitor their own progress (pages 8–12).

Peer Assessment

In addition to rating their own products and learning processes, students can rate the work of their peers as readers, writers, and learners. Students can rate the oral and written work of their peers, identifying areas that can be improved as well as areas that are presented effectively. These ratings can be based on scoring rubrics that students develop themselves or on rubrics provided by teachers. Students may need both guidance and assurance that peer feedback will be stated positively. One of the main advantages of self and peer assessment is that students internalize the standards for learning more readily than they would from teacher assessment alone. Another advantage concerns time management for teachers, who need only spot-check student performance rather than spend time rating every single product from each student. See page 16 in the *ScottForesman ESL Teacher's Resource Book* for a sample peer assessment form.

Performance Assessment

This type of assessment includes exhibitions of student-constructed work such as written products, science demonstrations, oral presentations, retellings, pair interactions, discussions, drawings, and graphic organizers. Some student products can be exhibited in the classroom, presented and described by the student or by groups that worked together, or documented by video or audio recorder. The student work can be evaluated by the teacher, by the student, and by peers using a scoring rubric that reflects different levels of performance. Rubrics used in performance assessment typically integrate language and content in a holistic scoring procedure that may also reflect the processes used in solving problems or in reaching conclusions.

Portfolio Assessment

A portfolio is a collection of student work that shows growth over time. The portfolio may contain written products, worksheets, self-assessments, or audio tapes. It is useful to document learning, to identify student strengths and needs, to help in making instructional decisions, and to provide evidence of student progress in student and parent conferences. The keys to a successful portfolio are student involvement and self-assessment. Students should play a major role in deciding what goes into the portfolio and how the work is evaluated, so they can feel ownership over their learning.

There are at least three different types of portfolios: a *collections portfolio,* containing virtually everything the student has produced; a *showcase portfolio,* focusing on the student's best work; and an *assessment portfolio,* illustrating growth with respect to specific instructional objectives. *ScottForesman ESL* encourages the use of assessment portfolios, which are efficient for assisting students and teachers in planning for future learning activities. For all portfolios, we suggest using a *portfolio cover sheet* that identifies specific portfolio entries, the date of each entry, and the type of each entry (e. g., written product, tape, peer assessment, checklist). A variety of forms and checklists are provided in the *Teacher's Resource Book* for teacher, self, and peer portfolio assessment (pages 14–18).

The multiple forms of assessment included in *ScottForesman ESL* provide students with varied opportunities to communicate what they know and can do, what learning processes work effectively for them, and what progress they have made over time. Such opportunities put students in a better position to manage their learning and to become self-directed learners.

To take advantage of assessment information, you need to review periodically the student portfolios, your own anecdotal records and ratings, and other evidence of student progress in light of goals established for instruction. The scoring rubrics and benchmark standards are essential parts of authentic assessment that give you indications of how successful students have been in learning and what worked and did not work in your own instruction. Use this information in planning your instructional activities, in student conferences, and in communicating with parents. You can also use it to assist in placement decisions, to communicate with other teachers, to report to administrators, and to anticipate the results of end-of-year testing. By using the assessment information in *ScottForesman ESL* effectively, you can help to ensure that all your students enjoy maximum learning success!

Home/ School Connections in ESL Instruction

CAROLYN KESSLER

Parents are children's first teachers; the home is the first learning community. Here children acquire their first language and develop a world view shaped by the community of which they are a part. Their experiences as they grow in this community provide a wealth of knowledge about what they believe, value, do in daily encounters, and what they perceive about how the world around them works. As children whose home language is other than English enter the schooling process, they not only meet new teachers and a different community, but often a new world view. Connecting home and school in light of this linguistic and cultural diversity is a challenge for both parents and teachers.

ScottForesman ESL provides the means for teachers and parents to work together collaboratively as co-educators of their children. Educating children so that they can succeed academically in an English-speaking environment is the goal of this collaboration.

Home-school partnerships as developed in *ScottForesman ESL* integrate life at home with that of the school in a "community-building" approach. In this approach, collaborative work between children and parents at home finds an audience at school. The teacher's role is to draw on the funds of knowledge that children have from their home and life experiences and to connect what happens inside the classroom to what happens outside. Under these conditions learning English takes on real meaning.

This community-building approach encourages students to develop their own voices as they interact with others, including family and community members. The home-school connection draws extensively on resources from the home. Among them are the support and encouragement parents give for their children's educational undertakings, frequent parent-child conversations, the exchange of ideas and information about concrete situations or problems children experience, and taking action to solve problems.

Because of the power of family stories in transmitting cultural values and attitudes that can contribute to school success, *ScottForesman ESL* encourages the telling of family stories. In this participatory approach, teachers learn about the community with which their students are identified and work towards building communities of learners in their classrooms where cultural and linguistic differences brought from home are understood and valued.

In the *ScottForesman ESL* community-building approach, the many dimensions of a student's life, including culture and the social context of the home and community, are viewed as rich resources for learning. Teachers value, use, and build on children's prior knowledge through tapping into the funds of knowledge that learners bring to school.

Children from diverse backgrounds have a wealth of cultural capital— experiences, knowledge, attitudes, beliefs, aspirations, and skills that are passed from one generation to another. Activities designed to incorporate children's cultural capital in the classroom validate the home culture. Approaches and strategies, however, that recognize and build on culturally different ways of learning and seeing the world rely on teachers making efforts to know about and understand the socio-cultural contexts of their students' lives. When efforts are made, teachers are in a much stronger position to join parents as full partners in their children's schooling.

ScottForesman ESL provides many opportunities for the development of this partnership. Each unit of the program suggests a unit project to be carried out by the students as a class. Letters to family members inviting their participation in the project are provided in six different languages (Cambodian, Cantonese, English, Spanish, Haitian Creole, and Vietnamese). At the completion of each project families are invited to visit the classroom to see what the children have accomplished.

In addition, *ScottForesman ESL* provides suggestions throughout each chapter for ways to build community. These suggestions include:

- children reading aloud at home to parents in either the home language or English;
- children carrying out research with family members on their family's social history through interviews of parents, grandparents, and other family members;
- parents and children collaborating on writing projects, such as publishing books about their family history, making time lines of family history, making a map of family migrations, keeping portfolios of their work together;
- families telling stories that transmit family beliefs, cultural values, attitudes, aspirations, self-images;
- children telling their stories at school, sometimes in their first language with explanations given in English by the children or a bilingual staff member or volunteer;
- teachers inviting parents to school to read a book in their home language or provide a presentation drawing on some particular area of interest or expertise.

Families are key participants in the academic success of children learning English. When families join in a partnership with the school, learning communities can develop in which the culture of hope, possibility, and promise can flourish.

BIBLIOGRAPHY

Anderson, R.C., & P. Freebody. "Vocabulary Knowledge" in J. T. Guthrie, ed. *Comprehension and Teaching: Research Reviews.* International Reading Association, 1981.

Auerbach, Elsa. *Making Meaning, Making Change.* Prentice Hall, 1992.

Bartlett, F. *Remembering: A Study in Experimental and Social Psychology.* Cambridge University Press, 1995.

Berg, E. C. "Preparing ESL Students for Peer Response." *TESOL Journal,* 8 (2), 1999.

Celce-Murcia, M., D. Brinton, & J. Goodwin. *Teaching Pronunciation.* Cambridge University Press, 1996.

Chamot, A.U., & J.M. O'Malley. *The CALLA Handbook: Implementing the Cognitive Academic Language Learning Approach.* Addison-Wesley, 1994.

Clemmons, J., et al. *Portfolios in the Classroom: A Teachers Sourcebook.* Scholastic Professional Books, 1993.

Cummins, Jim. *Negotiating Identities: Education for Empowerment in a Diverse Society.* California Association for Bilingual Education, 1996.

Cummins, Jim, & Dennis Sayers. *Brave New Schools: Challenging Cultural Illiteracy Through Global Learning Networks.* St. Martin's Press, 1995.

Cummins, Jim. "Linguistic Interdependence and the Educational Development of Bilingual Children." *Review of Educational Research,* 49 (2), 1979.

Enright, D. Scott, & Mary Lou McCloskey. *Integrating English: Developing English Language and Literacy in the Multilingual Classroom.* Addison-Wesley, 1988.

Fathman, A.K., M.E. Quinn, & C. Kessler. *Teaching Science to English Learners, Grades 4-8.* National Clearinghouse for Bilingual Education, 1992.

Freeman, Yvonne, & David Freeman. *Between Worlds: Access to Second Language Acquisition.* Heinemann, 1994.

Genesee, Fred, ed. *Educating Second Language Children: The Whole Child, the Whole Curriculum, the Whole Community.* Cambridge University Press, 1994.

Glazer, S.M., & C.S. Brown. *Portfolios and Beyond: Collaborative Assessment in Reading and Writing.* Christopher-Gordon, 1993.

Gonzalez, V., et al. *Assessment and Instruction of Culturally and Linguistically Diverse Students with or At-Risk of Learning Problems.* Allyn & Bacon, 1997.

Hayes, C.W., R. Bahruth, & C. Kessler. *Literacy con cariño: A Story of Migrant Children's Success.* Heinemann, 1991.

Hudelson, Sarah. *Write On: Children Writing in ESL.* Prentice Hall Regents, 1989.

Kessler, Carolyn, ed. *Cooperative Language Learning: A Teacher's Resource Book.* Prentice Hall Regents, 1992.

Larsen-Freeman, Diane, & Michael H. Long. *An Introduction to Second Language Acquisition Research.* Longman, 1991.

Lightbown, Patsy, & Nina Spada. *How Languages Are Learned.* Oxford University Press, 1993.

McCaleb, Sudia P. *Building Communities of Learners: A Collaboration Among Teachers, Students, Families, and Community.* St. Martin's Press, 1994.

Miller, G. "How School Children Learn Words" in F. Marshall, ed. *Proceedings of the Third Eastern States Conference on Linguistics.* The Ohio State University, 1986.

Ogle, D. "K-W-L Group Instruction Strategy" in A.S. Palincsar, et al., eds. *Teaching Reading as Thinking.* Association for Supervision and Curriculum Development, 1986.

O'Malley, J.M., & A.U. Chamot. *Learning Strategies in Second Language Acquisition.* Cambridge University Press, 1990.

O'Malley, J.M., & L. Valdez Pierce. *Authentic Assessment for English Language Learners: Practical Approaches for Teachers.* Addison-Wesley, 1996.

Pressley, M., & V. Woloshyn. *Cognitive Strategy Instruction That Really Improves Children's Academic Performance,* 2nd ed. Brookline Books, 1995.

Reid, J.M., ed. *Learning Styles in the ESL/EFL Classroom.* Heinle & Heinle, 1995.

Richard-Amato, Patricia A., & Marguerite Ann Snow, eds. *The Multicultural Classroom: Readings for Content-Area Teachers.* Longman, 1992.

Rigg, Pat, & Virginia G. Allen, eds. *When They Don't All Speak English: Integrating the ESL Student into the Regular Classroom.* National Council of Teachers of English, 1989.

Rong, X.L., & J. Preissle. *Educating Immigrant Students: What We Need to Know to Meet the Challenges.* Corwin Press, Inc., 1998.

Rumelhart, D.E. "Schemata: The Building Blocks of Cognition" in Spiro, R.J., B.C. Bruce, & W.F. Brewer, eds. *Theoretical Issues in Reading Comprehension: Perspectives from Cognitive Psychology, Linguistics, Artificial Intelligence, and Education.* Erlbaum, 1980.

Scarcella, Robin. *Teaching Language Minority Students in the Multicultural Classroom.* Prentice Hall Regents, 1990.

Short, D.J. "Assessing Integrated Language and Content Instruction." *TESOL Quarterly,* 27 (4), 1993.

Snow, M.A., & D. Brinton. *The Content-Based Classroom: Perspectives on Integrating Language and Content.* Longman, 1997.

Spangenberg-Urbschat, Karen, & Robert Pritchard, eds. *Kids Come in All Languages: Reading Instruction for ESL Students.* International Reading Association, 1994.

Sternberg, R.J., & J.S. Powell. "Comprehending Verbal Comprehension." *American Psychologist,* 38 (8), 1983.

Warschauer, Mark. *E-Mail for English Teachers: Bringing the Internet and Computer Learning Networks into the Language Classroom.* TESOL, 1995.

Professional Associations

National Association for Bilingual Education, 1220 L Street NW, Suite 605, Washington, DC 20005

National Center for Research on Cultural Diversity and Second Language Learning, Center for Applied Linguistics, 4646 40th Street NW, Washington, DC 20016-1859

Teachers of English to Speakers of Other Languages, Inc.
700 S. Washington St., Suite 200, Alexandria, VA 22314-4287

Newcomer Book C was designed for students in grades 6, 7, and 8 who are new to the English language. All of the activities represent real-life situations centered around school themes that are age- and grade-level appropriate.

Each lesson is divided into four types of activities. The *Preview/Present* section allows students to activate prior knowledge of words, concepts, and language.

Present/Practice and *Practice* give students the opportunity to practice the new language. Use the *Assess* section to check understanding and to review or reteach any material students may have found difficult. Then help students mark the boxes in the "I can" section to assess their progress.

Lesson 1 *My Class* (pages 1–4, 41)

Tell what you know. Name the items. Have students talk about the picture and act out the conversation in groups.

Say the numbers. Help pairs practice counting.

Write the numbers. Say the numbers. Model the activity. Then have pairs complete it.

How many? Count the items in the picture. Have students count the chairs *(five)*, and then count the other items in the picture. Continue, having pairs count classroom objects.

Count the items in your classroom. List the names of classroom objects on the board. Have students count how many of each item is in the classroom. Have partners make their own lists.

Ask a friend. What do you have? Have students choose classroom objects and act out the conversation with partners.

Play the matching game. Have pairs cut out the cards on page 41, place them facedown, and mix them. Each student chooses two cards. When the numbers match, they keep the cards if they can say "I have (four) (books) and (four) (chairs)." The student with the most cards at the end wins.

Circle the number. What is in the classroom? Circle the words. How many do you have? Write the word. Model the Assess activities, and then have students work independently.

Lesson 2 *About Me* (pages 5–8, 43)

Tell what you know. Name the items. Have students practice naming the vocabulary with partners.

Say the alphabet. Present the alphabet by using alphabet flash cards. If students need additional help, use the Blackline Masters on pages xxx and xxxi in the Teacher's Edition.

Say the numbers. Help students read and say the number words. Have them practice counting from 11 to 21.

What numbers? Write and say. Have students practice counting to 26.

Draw a line. Help students read the words and decide where they go on the form. Have partners complete the activity.

Ask a friend. Write. Fill out a student form on the board. Then have students fill out the forms with partners.

Write the secret word. Read the number code with students. Write an example on the board, and help students write the secret word. Have partners complete the code.

Make an address book. Show students a completed address book from page 43. Have them work in small groups.

Circle the word. Write the letters. Write about you. Model the Assess activities, and then have students work independently.

Lesson 3 *On Time* (pages 9–12, 45)

Tell what you know. What time is it? Say the times. Use a clock to model the times. Have pairs practice saying them.

Say the colors. Have students identify objects by name and color, and then practice saying the color words with partners.

Say the shapes. Have partners identify classroom objects by name, shape, and color.

Write and say the times. Help students say the times on the clocks. Have partners complete the activity.

Circle the word. Have partners complete the activity.

Draw and color. Make a pattern. Help students complete a pattern on the board. Then have pairs complete the activity.

Measure the shapes. Write the numbers. Have students cut out the ruler on page 45 and do the activity with partners.

Play the matching game. Have students cut out the cards on page 45, mix them up, and place them facedown. Partners take turns choosing two cards. If they match, he or she must say the time correct in order to keep the cards.

Write the times. Circle the word. Write about yourself. Draw the times. Model the Assess activities, and then have students work independently.

Lesson 4 *My Week* (pages 13–16, 47)

Tell what you know. Say the days of the week. Use a calendar to present the days of the week.

Say the months. Have students practice saying the months. Talk about important dates or holidays they know.

It's Wednesday. Put the pictures in order. Help students put the pictures in chronological order with partners.

Circle the word. Help students decide which word is missing. Have students complete the activity with partners.

Write. Use the words in the box. Have pairs talk about the pictures, read the words, and then complete the activity.

Make your schedule. Have students cut out and complete the schedules on page 47. Have partners compare their schedules.

What's today? Circle the word. Circle the word. Write your schedule for Wednesday. Model the Assess activities, and then have students work independently.

Lesson 5 *My School* (pages 17–20, 49)

Tell what you know. Walk students through school and point out the places like those in the pictures.

Say the times. Use a toy clock to practice the times.

Who are they? Say. Help students identify the people. If possible, introduce actual school personnel.

Circle the word. Have partners complete the activity.

Write the word. Help students compare the pictures to the picture on page 17. Have pairs do the activity.

Who are the people in your school? Write names of school personnel on the board and read them aloud. Then have partners complete the activity.

Write about your classes. Help students read the column titles and complete one item orally before having them complete the rest of the activity.

Play the game. Have students cut out the game board and cards on page 49. Students take turns choosing a card and identifying the items or completing the command. If correct, they move the number of spaces shown on the card. The first student to reach "finish" wins.

Draw a line. Circle the word. Write about you. Model the Assess activities, and then have students work independently.

Lesson 6 *Getting Ready* (pages 21–24, 51)

Tell what you know. Name the items. Have students talk about the picture and then use the vocabulary to say what they are wearing.

Say the weather. Use pantomime to present the weather.

Draw a line from the weather to the clothes. Circle the word. Model the activities, and then have students work in pairs.

Read the descriptions with a partner. Practice with a partner. Model the activities, and then have pairs complete them.

Draw and write your own description. Have students use the top of the page as a model, and then read their work in pairs.

Play the matching game. Have students cut apart the cards on page 51. Model how to play the matching game. The student who can make the most matches wins.

Draw the clothes. Write the weather. Model the Assess activities, and then have students work independently.

Lesson 7 *Working at School* (pages 25–28, 53)

Tell what you know. Name the activities. Use pantomime to introduce the vocabulary.

Name the activities. Use pantomime to present the vocabulary.

Draw the pictures. Say the words. Practice with a partner. Have students do the first activity independently. Then have pairs role-play the conversation, changing the response each time.

Draw lines from the people to the items. Use realia to introduce the items. Model the activity before students complete it.

Act it out. Have a partner guess. Have pairs cut out the cards on page 53. They can then take turns acting out and guessing the activities.

Read the story. Have individuals read the sentences aloud.

Circle the word. Write the words. Model the Assess activities, and then have students work independently.

Lesson 8 *Lunchtime* (pages 29–32, 55)

Tell what you know. Name the food. Model the conversation with a volunteer. Use realia to introduce the vocabulary.

Say the words. Use realia to present the vocabulary. Have students practice the words with a partner.

Draw pictures. Write the words. Ask your friends. Take a survey. Have individuals do the first activity. Then model asking about and recording a friend's favorite food.

Read the story. Draw a picture. Write the words. Ask volunteers to read the sentences. Then have students do the second activity, using the story as a model.

Make a meal. Show students a completed meal from page 55 before they do the activity independently. Invite them to share their work with a partner.

Draw the food. Write the words. Write. Use the words in the box. Model the Assess activities, and then have students work independently.

Lesson 9 *After School* (pages 33–36, 57)

Tell what you know. Name the activities. Model the conversations. Use pantomime to introduce the vocabulary.

Practice with a friend. Ask your friends. Take a survey. Model the conversation, and then have pairs practice. Have students ask friends about a favorite activity and write their responses.

Draw pictures. Write the words. Have students share their drawings and sentences in small groups.

Read the sentences. Circle the sentence. Review the pronouns he and she before students do the activities.

Make a book. Show a completed book from page 57 before students do the activity.

Draw pictures. Write the words. Model the Assess activities, and then have students work independently.

Lesson 10 *My Neighborhood* (pages 37–40, 59)

Tell what you know. Name the places. Invite students to talk about or pantomime what happens in each place.

Name the activities. Use pantomime to introduce the vocabulary.

Practice with a friend. Have pairs act out the conversation.

Circle the word. Ask a volunteer to read each possible response. Model the activity before students do it.

Name the directions. Look at the map. Write the directions. Use TPR to have students turn in each direction.

Make a map. Show a completed map from page 59 before students do the activity.

Write the directions. Circle the sentence. Model the Assess activities, and then have students work independently.

Name: ______________________

A A

a a

B B

b b

C C

c c

D D

d d

E E

e e

F F

f f

G G

g g

H H

h h

I I

i i

J J

j j

K K

k k

L L

l l

M M

m m

Name: ______________________________

N N

n n

O O

o o

P P

p p

Q Q

q q

R R

r r

S S

s s

T T

t t

U U

u u

V V

v v

W W

w w

X X

x x

Y Y

y y

Z Z

z z

Planning Guide

CHAPTER 1

Growing Up

Objectives

Name physical characteristics family members share.

Describe the growth of boys and girls between ages 9 and 15.

Tell how heredity influences growth.

Name foods from the different food groups.

Vocabulary Focus

Similar features found in family members, such as *eye color, height, weight.*
Elements of family characteristics, such as *traits, heredity, genes.*
Good foods that promote growth, such as *fish, potatoes, strawberries, rice.*
Words used to measure human traits, such as *feet, pounds.*

Lesson	Content Focus	Language Awareness Objectives	Learning Strategies
Preview pp. 2–3 Tell what you know.			
Present pp. 4–5 How We Grow	Health	**Grammar** Comparatives	
Practice pp. 6–7 Heredity and Growth	Health	**Grammar** Present Tense: *Has/Have, Is/Are*	Understand key words.
Practice pp. 8–9 Food and Growth	Health	**Grammar** Plural Forms	Use a chart.
Connect pp. 10–11 How big is a foot?	Health/Math	**Grammar** Possessive Adjectives	Understand directions.
Connect pp. 12–13 Fun Facts	Health/Reading	**Grammar** Superlatives	
Connect p. 14 "Turn! Turn! Turn!"	Health/Literature	**Vocabulary** Opposites	
Assess p. 15 Tell what you learned.			

CHAPTER 2

Life Cycles of Plants

Objectives

Name the parts of a plant.

Name the four main parts of a flower.

Describe the life cycle of a plant.

Tell how plants and animals are interdependent.

Identify the parts of plants that people can eat.

Vocabulary Focus

Parts of plants, such as *flower, leaf, root, stem.*

Parts of flowers, such as *pistil, stamen, sepal.*

Stages of a plant's life cycle, such as *seed, pollen, grain, flower.*

Parts of plants people eat, such as *seeds, stems, roots.*

Lesson	Content Focus	Language Awareness Objectives	Learning Strategies
Preview pp. 16–17 Tell what you know.			
Present pp. 18–19 Parts of a Flower	Science	**Language Function** Words That Describe	Use pictures for meaning.
Practice pp. 20–21 Life Cycle of a Flowering Plant	Science	**Phonics** Initial Consonant *p*, Consonant Blends *pl* and *pr*	Follow a sequence.
Practice pp. 22–23 Eating Plants	Science	**Grammar** Count and Noncount Nouns	
Connect pp. 24–25 Numbers in Plants	Science/Math	**Vocabulary** Position Words	
Connect pp. 26–37 *The Story of Johnny Appleseed*	Science/ Literature	**Spelling** Capitalization of Place Names **Language Function** Expressing Intention with *Going to* or *Will* **Grammar** Past Tense	Make inferences. Recognize cause and effect. Visualize story details.
Connect p. 38 Recipe for Waldorf Salad	Science/ Reading	**Spelling** Punctuation	
Assess p. 39 Tell what you learned.			

Resources

Chapter 1

Support Materials

PICTURE CARDS
Numbers 2, 4, 8, 11, 14, 15, 19, 25, 26, 27, 28, 33, 34, 36, 37, 38, 42, 44, 48, 49, 51, 52, 54, 55, 56, 57, 59, 60, 66, 67, 70, 72

ACTIVITY BOOK
Pages 2–11

RED TAPE
Side 2: "Turn! Turn! Turn!" page T14

DISK
Writer's Notebook

LET'S TALK CARD
96 cards to start conversations.

STORYTELLING
Storytelling Anthology: *Worlds Together*

Phonics

PHONICS
Newcomer Phonics, pages 49, 56

Assessment Materials

BLACKLINE MASTER
Language Assessment, Blackline Master 40

Listening Assessment, Blackline Master 41

WHITE TAPE
Side 1: Listening Assessment, page T15

Listen carefully as an expert explains the Food Pyramid. Circle the names of foods she mentions.

Young people need to eat the right foods to stay healthy and grow well.

At the bottom of the Food Pyramid are grains. Grains include common foods such as bread. Young people need to eat more foods from the grain group than from any other group.

At the next level of the pyramid are fruits and vegetables. Young people should eat several servings of both fruits and vegetables every day. Fruits such as apples and oranges are easy to get and good to eat. Carrots are one good vegetable to eat as a snack.

See that you eat the right number of servings from the bottom of the pyramid each day.

Support for Newcomers

Newcomer Book C, Survival language for absolute beginners. For overview, see pages xxviii–xxix.

Newcomer Teacher Suggestion Book, Chapter 1, pages 8–9

HomeLink Penguin Readers

White Fang

For Extended Reading

Amazing Schemes Within Your Genes by Dr. Fran Balkwill, First Avenue Editions, 1994. Students learn how genes function, adapt, and mutate to form the special person each human is. **Level: Beginning**

How the Y Makes the Guy by Norbert Landa and Patrick A. Baeuerle, Barron's Educational Series, 1998. Find out how genes combine to make a boy or a girl and how genes determine a person's characteristics. **Level: Average**

Human Body by Steve Parker, DK Publishing, 1999. This comprehensive overview of the human body including captioned color photographs. **Level: Advanced**

Ingenious Genes by Norbert Landa and Patrick A. Baeuerle, Barron's Educational Series, 1998. This book about genetic engineering explains how scientists copy and change genes within living cells. **Level: Average**

Nutrition: What's in the Food We Eat by Dorothy Hinshaw Patent, Holiday House, 1992. Why do people need protein, fiber, and sugar? Students find out how the food they eat affects their day-to-day lives in this informative book. **Level: Average**

Related Technology

Exploring Genetics and Heredity, Queue Inc., 1994. Checks for understanding and keeps a record of completion for each student.

Resources

Chapter 2

Support Materials

PICTURE CARDS

Numbers 2, 8, 14, 17, 18, 21, 27, 33, 36, 38, 42, 52, 57, 67, 70

ACTIVITY BOOK

Pages 12–21

RED TAPE

Side 1: *The Story of Johnny Appleseed,* pages T26–T37

DISK

Writer's Notebook

Phonics

PHONICS

Newcomer Phonics, pages 20–21

Assessment Materials

BLACKLINE MASTER

Language Assessment, Blackline Master 42

Listening Assessment, Blackline Master 43

WHITE TAPE

Side 1: Listening Assessment, page T39

Listen carefully to each description. Then write the number of the description next to the part of the picture it describes.

1. The pistil is found inside a flower. It makes and holds egg cells. It is where pollination takes place.

2. Petals are the outside parts of flowers. They come in many different sizes and colors. Most flowers have several petals.

3. Stamens are found inside the petals of a flower. They are long and thin and make pollen.

Support for Newcomer

Newcomer Teacher Suggestion Book, Chapter 2, pages 10–11

For Extended Reading

From Flower to Fruit by Anne O. Dowden, Ticknor & Fields, 1994. Text and drawings explain how flowers mature into seed-bearing fruit. **Level: Advanced**

How Leaves Change by Sylvia A. Johnson, Lerner Publications, 1986. Discover how leaves go from green to brilliant oranges, reds, and yellows as part of their natural life cycle. **Level: Average**

How Seeds Travel by Cynthia Overbeck, Lerner Publications, 1982. Find out how seeds travel by wind, water, and animals, and how they reproduce. **Level: Average**

Incredible Plants by Lesley Dow, Time-Life Books, 1997. This colorful overview of the plant world identifies the parts of a plant, flowering and food plants, medicine from plants, and much more. **Level: Beginning**

Looking at Plants by David Suzuki, John Wiley & Sons, 1992. Learn about the characteristics, parts, growth, and care of plants in this well-written book. **Level: Average**

The Plant-and Grow Project Book by Ulla Dietl, Sterling Publishing Co., 1993. Students learn how to grow their own plants and learn how they mature. **Level: Advanced**

Related Technology

The Way Plants Grow, Queue, Inc., 1996. Students learn about the growth cycle of plants.

Project

Garden of Change

This optional project can be completed over the next two chapters. In this project, students will be making two displays: family "trees" and a display of drawings or models of plants from their home countries. See the Unit Wrap-Up, page T39a, for more ideas on sharing the project with family members.

What You'll Need

Collect the following kinds of items:

- resource materials with visuals about plant life
- construction or other colored paper, cardboard
- coat hangers
- mixed media materials, which might include green yarn, tape, glue, a roll of paper, cellophane, poster paints, felt-tipped markers

Strategies You'll Use

- Understand chronology
- Understand cause and effect
- Use a model
- Brainstorm

Beginning the Project

Explain that you will be creating displays relating to families and plants. Tell students they will be making family trees and drawing plants that grow in their home countries.

Home Involvement

Send the Letter to the Family, Blackline Masters 34–39, to families to explain that students will be creating "family trees." Encourage families to discuss their relatives from present and past generations. The letter also asks families to discuss plants that grow in their home countries.

Creating the Garden of Change

Have students review the cycles of growth for plants and humans in their Student Books. Then tell students they are going to create visual representations of their families.

First, have students collect materials to make a family tree. Have them make a "leaf" for each family member. It could include a picture and basic information, such as age, job or school, and hobbies. Students can tie the leaves to a coat hanger. For students who come from non-traditional families, explain that their family trees can contain anyone they think of as family, including adoptive and biological parents, foster parents, step-families, and so on.

Discuss with students the fact that their family trees show people as they are now. Talk about change over time by discussing the fact that grandparents were once children and so on.

Then, have students make drawings or models of plants from the cardboard and construction paper. Encourage students to research the plants that grow in their home countries and to label their plants.

Daily Discussion

As the unit progresses, brainstorm ways to decorate your classroom in keeping with the theme "Garden of Change."

Take a few minutes each day for one or two students to present their own "Family Tree."

Encourage students to share family photographs during their presentations.

Suggest that students describe their impressions of their relatives' lives in their home countries and the changes that moving to the United States may have meant for their families.

Once this part is finished, have students present the plant models they have made.

Arrange to hang the family trees in one area of the classroom and to display the drawings or models of plants.

See page T39a for ideas about sharing the garden with families and friends when the module is completed.

Growing Plants

As a complement to the project, students could be encouraged to set up an area in the classroom or in the neighborhood to plant a garden. (Some communities offer the possibility for people to set up gardens on public land.) Have students decide on what plants to grow. Encourage students who are experienced in growing things to organize the project. Also encourage students to plant as wide a variety of plants as will grow in your area. If the class includes visually impaired students, try to grow plants that have strong fragrances and interesting textures.

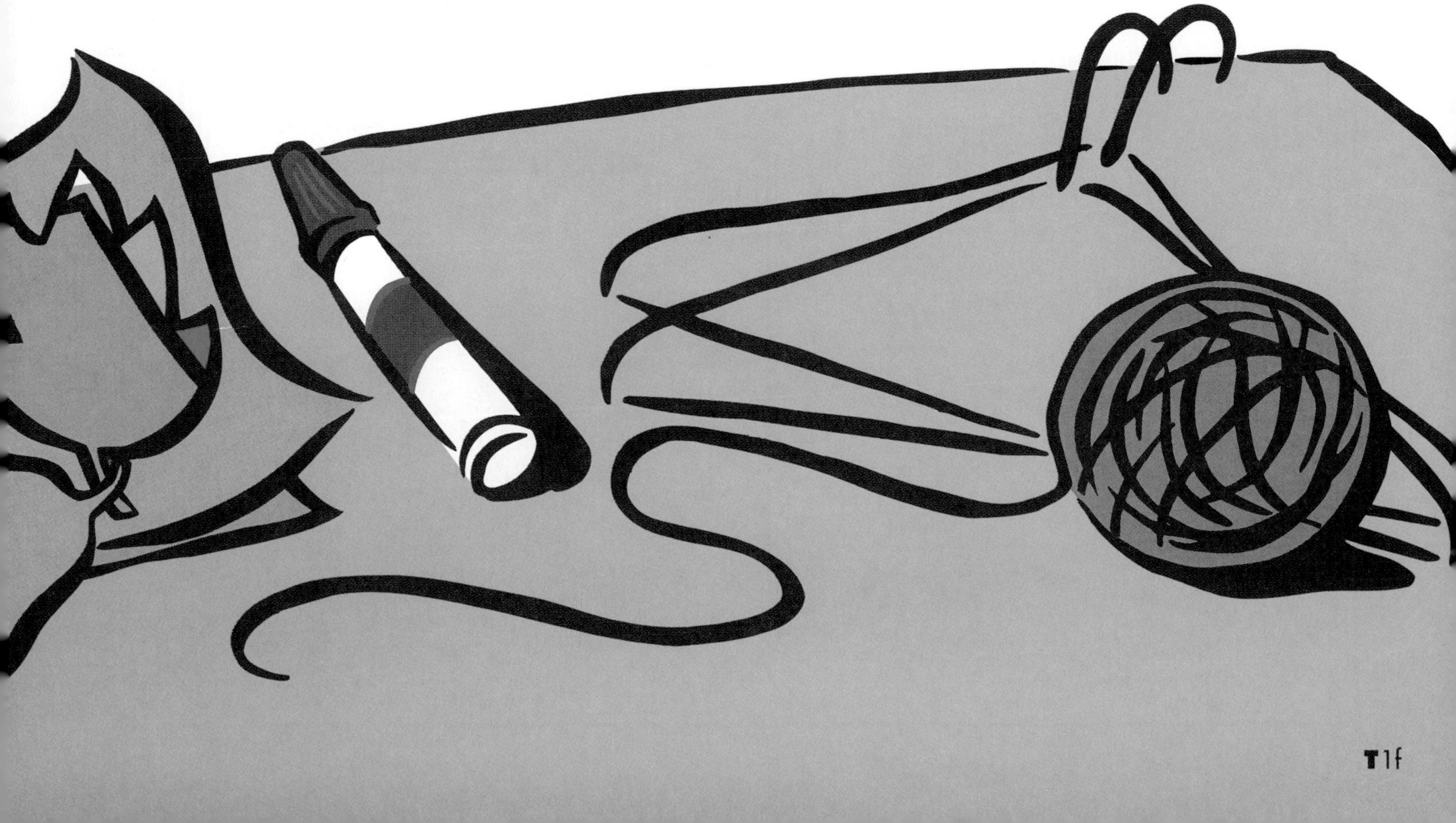

Activity Book

Chapter 1

Name ______________________

Comparisons

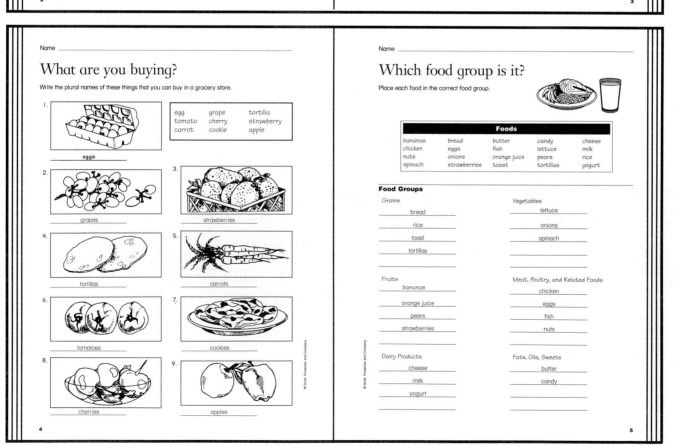

Maria
Age 13
5 feet tall

Selena
Age 16
5 feet, 6 inches tall

Antonio
Age 10
4 feet tall

Maria and her brother and sister are always comparing themselves. Study the information under the pictures. Then complete the comparisons.

Age

1. Maria is younger than Selena.
2. Maria is older than Antonio.
3. Antonio is younger than Maria.
4. Antonio is younger than Selena.

Size

5. Selena is taller than Maria.
6. Antonio is shorter than Selena.
7. Selena is taller than Antonio.
8. Maria is shorter than Selena and taller than Antonio.

Now compare yourself to two friends or family members.

Age

I am ______________________

I am ______________________

Size

____

____

Name ______________________

What are your traits?

Complete the paragraphs with the words from the box. You may use each word more than once.

has	have	is	are

You have certain traits. Your height, your hair color, and your eye color are all traits. Another trait is the age at which you get your growth spurt.

You and your parents probably have many of the same traits. For example, if your parents have dark hair, you probably have dark hair. And if your parents are short, you probably are short. If your father has blue eyes, you may have blue eyes, too. If your mother is thin, you may be thin too.

Your traits are determined by your genes. Genes are passed from parent to child. Half your genes are from your mother and half are from your father. This mixture determines your traits. The passing of genes from parents to children is called heredity.

Name ______________________

What are you buying?

Write the plural names of these things that you can buy in a grocery store.

egg	grape	tortilla
tomato	cherry	strawberry
carrot	cookie	apple

1. 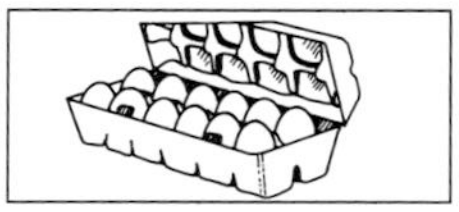
eggs

2. 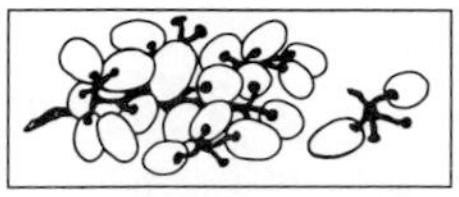
grapes

3. 
strawberries

4. 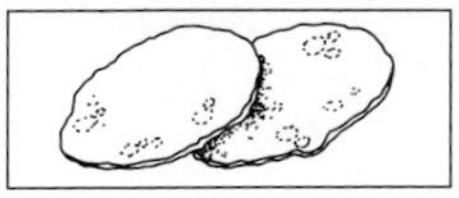
tortillas

5. 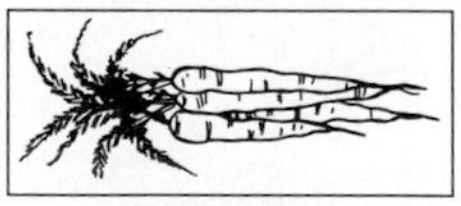
carrots

6. 
tomatoes

7. 
cookies

8. 
cherries

9. 
apples

Name ______________________

Which food group is it?

Place each food in the correct food group.

Foods				
bananas	bread	butter	candy	cheese
chicken	eggs	fish	lettuce	milk
nuts	onions	orange juice	pears	rice
spinach	strawberries	toast	tortillas	yogurt

Food Groups

Grains
- bread
- rice
- toast
- tortillas

Vegetables
- lettuce
- onions
- spinach

Fruits
- bananas
- orange juice
- pears
- strawberries

Meat, Poultry, and Related Foods
- chicken
- eggs
- fish
- nuts

Dairy Products
- cheese
- milk
- yogurt

Fats, Oils, Sweets
- butter
- candy

Name ______________________________

My Favorite Foods

List your ten favorite foods. Then write each one in the correct part of the food pyramid.

1. Answers will vary.
2. ______________
3. ______________
4. ______________
5. ______________
6. ______________
7. ______________
8. ______________
9. ______________
10. ______________

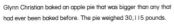

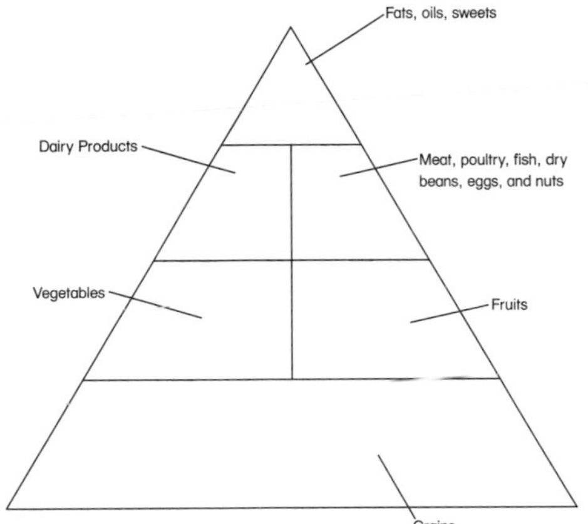

Name ______________________________

Measuring with Our Feet

Work with a partner to measure things. Place the heel of one foot directly in front of the toes of the other foot. Count each step as a "foot." Write your answers in the chart. Are your numbers different from those of your partner?

Measuring with Our Feet		
How Many Feet Long Is . . .?	Using My Feet	Using My Partner's Feet
The Teacher's Desk	Answers will vary.	
The Longest Classroom Wall		
A Hall in My School		
The Playground or Athletic Field		

Name ______________________________

World Records

Write a headline for each story. Be sure to use the superlative in each headline. Watch out! Where are most of these foods on the food pyramid?

1. The Largest Pie

Glynn Christian baked an apple pie that was bigger than any that had ever been baked before. The pie weighed 30,115 pounds.

2. The Oldest Cake

A museum in Switzerland has a cake that is older than any other cake in the world. It was found in a tomb in Egypt and was baked over 4,000 years ago.

3. The Longest Banana Split

Some people in Pennsylvania created a banana split that was longer than any other. It was 4.55 miles long.

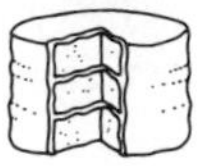

4. The Tallest Cake

Beth Cornell and her helpers built a cake that was taller than any other. It was 101 feet, 2 1/2 inches tall and had 100 layers.

5. The Largest Cookie

The people of Ripon, Wisconsin, baked a cookie that was larger than any other. It contained 600 pounds of sugar and almost 4 million chocolate chips.

6. The Longest Burrito

Some people in California built a burrito that was longer than any other. It was over 2,000 feet long and contained 738.5 pounds of tortillas.

Name ______________________________

Opposites

Draw lines to connect each word in the first column with its opposite in the second column.

Words	Opposites
1. big	slow
2. young	night
3. bottom	sell
4. laugh	short
5. day	end
6. in front of	small
7. begin	top
8. fast	cry
9. tall	old
10. buy	in back of

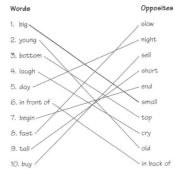

Complete the sentences. Use words in the opposites list.

1. The foods you should eat are on the __bottom__ of the pyramid. The foods you should eat very little of are on the __top__ of the pyramid.

2. Girls __begin__ their growth spurt at the ages of 9 to 12. Boys __begin__ their growth spurt at the ages of 11 to 15.

Activity Book

Chapter 2

Name ______________________

The Parts of a Plant

Label the parts of the flower. Use the words in the box.

petal	leaf	stamen
pistil	stem	

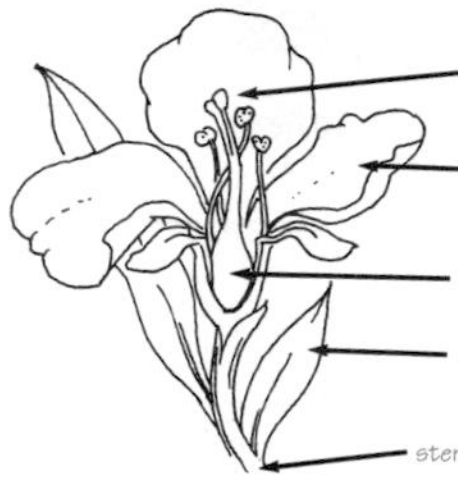

Write sentences that describe the flowers. Choose from the words in the box or use words of your own.

curved	large	straight	wide
small	narrow	pointed	

1. Answers will vary.

2. ______________________

Name ______________________

Animals, Insects, and Plants

Finish the words. Use *p*, *pl*, or *pr*.

Animals and insects pl ay an important role in the life of pl ants. Bees and other insects help pl ants p ollinate. They carry p ollen from the stamens of a pl ant to the p istils. The wind may also carry p ollen from one pl ant to another.

After p ollination, the flower dries up and falls off. Now the pl ant pr oduces seeds. The seeds might fall to the ground. The wind or animals might carry them to another pl ace. The seeds then grow into new pl ants. The new pl ants pr oduce flowers. And the cycle of the pl ant repeats itself.

Create an imaginary flower. Draw a picture of it and describe it.

____

Name ______________________

The Plants I Eat

Think of the plant parts you eat during one week. Write the name of each plant part in the correct column of the chart.

The Plant Parts I Eat Every Day

	Seeds	Stems	Leaves	Flowers	Roots	Fruits
Monday						
Tuesday						
Wednesday						
Thursday						
Friday						
Saturday						
Sunday						

Answer the questions.

1. Which category of plant part do you eat most often? Answers will vary.
2. Which category of plant part do you eat least often? ______________________
3. What is your favorite plant part? ______________________

Name ______________________

What did Mike buy?

Mike just returned from the grocery store. The things he bought are on the table. What did he buy?

Mike bought these things:

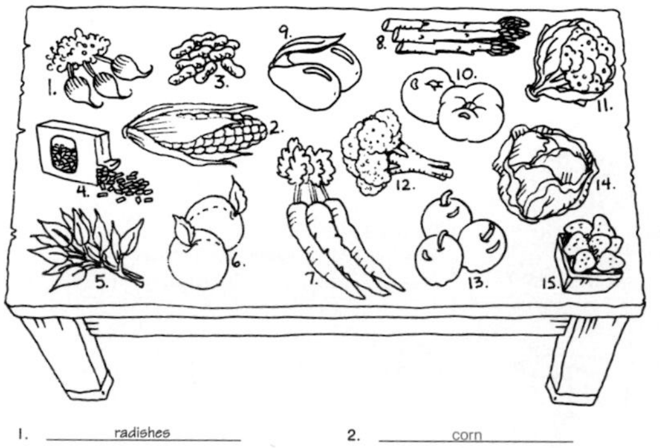

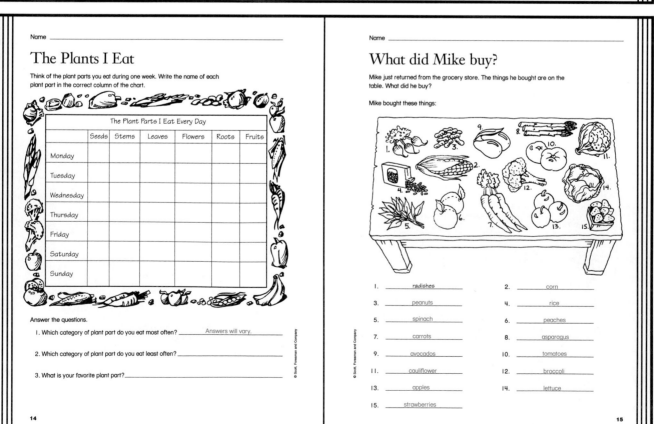

1. radishes
2. corn
3. peanuts
4. rice
5. spinach
6. peaches
7. carrots
8. asparagus
9. avocados
10. tomatoes
11. cauliflower
12. broccoli
13. apples
14. lettuce
15. strawberries

Name ______________________

Where is the bee?

Tell where the bee is in each picture. Choose from the words in the box. Use each word only once.

above	below	inside
at the bottom of	in front of	on top of

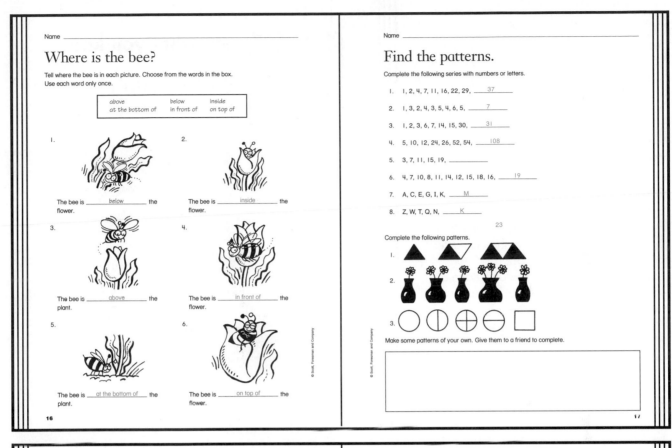

1.

The bee is ___below___ the flower.

2.

The bee is ___inside___ the flower.

3.

The bee is ___above___ the plant.

4.

The bee is ___in front of___ the flower.

5.

The bee is ___at the bottom of___ the plant.

6.

The bee is ___on top of___ the flower.

Name ______________________

Find the patterns.

Complete the following series with numbers or letters.

1. 1, 2, 4, 7, 11, 16, 22, 29, ___37___
2. 1, 3, 2, 4, 3, 5, 4, 6, 5, ___7___
3. 1, 2, 3, 6, 7, 14, 15, 30, ___31___
4. 5, 10, 12, 24, 26, 52, 54, ___108___
5. 3, 7, 11, 15, 19, ______
6. 4, 7, 10, 8, 11, 14, 12, 15, 18, 16, ___19___
7. A, C, E, G, I, K, ___M___
8. Z, W, T, Q, N, ___K___

23

Complete the following patterns.

1.

2.

3.

Make some patterns of your own. Give them to a friend to complete.

Name ______________________

Why?

Form sentences by drawing lines to connect one choice from column 1 with one choice from column 2. Each sentence should tell why something happened in "The Story of Johnny Appleseed." Use each choice only once.

1. It was lonely making America
2. Apple trees are beautiful
3. Jonathan Chapman never threw an apple core away
4. The child in Pennsylvania was crying
5. The child stopped crying
6. Jonathan decided to pick the seeds out of the apple mash
7. The men laughed at Jonathan and called him Johnny Appleseed
8. Johnny Appleseed was a friend to birds, beasts, and humans

because he wanted to plant apple trees across the West.

because he never carried a gun and left wonderful apple trees wherever he went.

because they thought his plan was silly.

because he loved apple trees.

because they have blossoms in the spring and apples in the fall.

because it was such a big country.

because Jonathan promised to plant apple trees where the child was going.

because he didn't want to leave the apple trees.

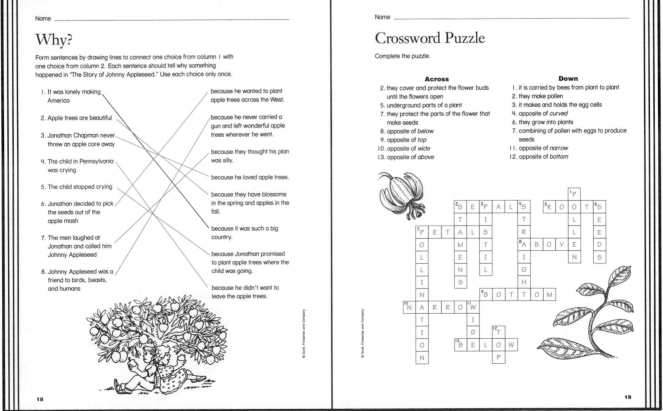

Name ______________________

Crossword Puzzle

Complete the puzzle.

Across

2. they cover and protect the flower buds until the flowers open
5. underground parts of a plant
7. they protect the parts of the flower that make seeds
8. opposite of *below*
9. opposite of *top*
10. opposite of *wide*
13. opposite of *above*

Down

1. it is carried by bees from plant to plant
2. they make pollen
3. it makes and holds the egg cells
4. opposite of *curved*
6. they grow into plants
7. combining of pollen with eggs to produce seeds
11. opposite of *narrow*
12. opposite of *bottom*

UNIT 1

Preview

Activate Prior Knowledge

Brainstorm Vocabulary

Describe yourself to the students, using words that apply to the categories in the Word Bank and accompanying your words with explanatory gestures, such as pointing to your eyes. Say, for example, *I have brown eyes. That's my eye color. I am tall. That's my height.* Ask students to describe themselves. Write each characteristic on the board. Have them compare characteristics that may change over the years with those that do not.

Create a five-column chart. Label each column with one of the terms from the Word Bank. Have students classify the characteristics on the board into the appropriate columns. Make sure that students have at least one characteristic in each column, and encourage them to add other characteristics. If some students have difficulty coming up with describing words, provide them with several choices and help them choose one or more characteristics that apply to them. Be sensitive to self-esteem issues adolescents often have about physical appearances.

Develop Language and Concepts

Present Pages 2 and 3

Have students examine the photographs. Help them use the words in the Word Bank and those they brainstormed earlier to describe the people in the pictures. Then have them describe people in their own family. Read and discuss the Tell What You Know and Talk About It questions.

Cycles of Life

Word Bank

- body shape
- eye color
- hair color
- height
- weight

Tell what you know.

How are the people in a family alike?

How do people change over the years?

Options for Reaching All Students

Beginning

Writing: Describe Yourself

Have students use words from the class chart to write short descriptions of themselves. Prompt them with cloze sentences such as *I have _____ eyes. I have _____ hair.*

Advanced

Writing: Interview Friends and Family

Have students interview a family member or friend about ways he or she has changed over the years. Start by brainstorming different interview questions students can ask. Then have students write brief biographical sketches focusing on the changes. Encourage students to illustrate their written text with photos or drawings.

Cooperative Language Experience

Field Trip

Lead students on a walk outdoors. Help them identify nonliving things in nature that show signs of change—cloud shapes, rock shapes, cracked sidewalks, rusted metal objects, a dry stream bed, or eroded soil. As a whole group, have students write and illustrate a story about their observations.

Talk About It

Do you have brothers or sisters? In what ways do you look alike?

THEME/KEY CONCEPTS

Change is a part of all life. Both humans and plants have life cycles characterized by growth and change.

Chapter 1

- Between the ages of 9 and 15 years, boys and girls experience a growth spurt.
- Heredity influences growth.
- The Food Pyramid shows the amounts and kinds of foods to eat to ensure proper growth.

Chapter 2

- Flowers play an important role in the life cycle of most plants.
- Plants are an important source of food for animals and people.

Home Connection

Share Family Pictures

Ask students to bring in family photographs. Have them examine and describe the similarities and differences between their family members. Then ask students to name ways in which they themselves resemble other family members. Be sensitive to the fact that some students may not be biologically related to all or any of the people with whom they live. These students may simply describe the physical characteristics of family members, rather than naming resemblances.

QuickCheck

Parts of the Body

Make sure that students can name the basic parts of the body. Advanced learners can draw and label a self-portrait. Beginning learners can point to body parts on their bodies as you name them.

Present

Activate Prior Knowledge

Use Pictures

Show students pictures of children of various ages. Have students guess the children's ages. Ask if they think each child is younger or older than they are. Have students put the pictured children in order from youngest to oldest.

Ask students how their size and interests have changed since they were five years old. Ask what they liked to do then and if it is different from what they like to do now.

Develop Language and Concepts

Present Pages 4 and 5

Read the text with students, making sure they understand such expressions and terms as *growth spurt* and *awkward.*

Measure a student's height to demonstrate feet and inches, meters and centimeters.

Then talk about issues such as these:

- When we stop growing, why are some of us shorter or taller than others?

Help students discuss the questions in Talk About It.

FYI Bone Growth

Physicians can use X-rays to tell if a child will continue to grow. A layer of cartilage at the ends of long bones indicates that growth is continuing. If the cartilage has changed to bone, growth has ceased.

CHAPTER 1

Growing Up

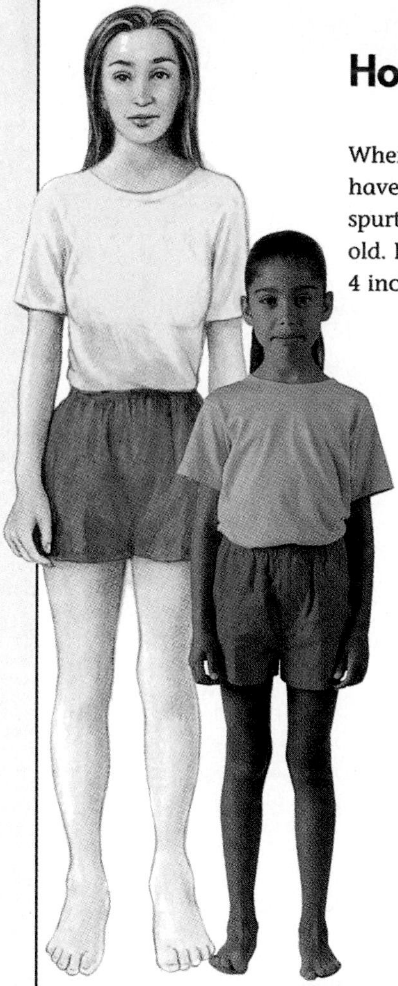

How We Grow

When girls are between 9 and 13 years old, they have a growth spurt. Boys have their growth spurt when they are between 11 and 15 years old. For example, a 14-year-old boy might grow 4 inches (10 centimeters) in one year.

Growth Spurt in Girls
The growth spurt usually begins earlier in girls than in boys.
Girls gain the most weight about the age of 12 or 13.
Girls reach their adult height about the age of 18.

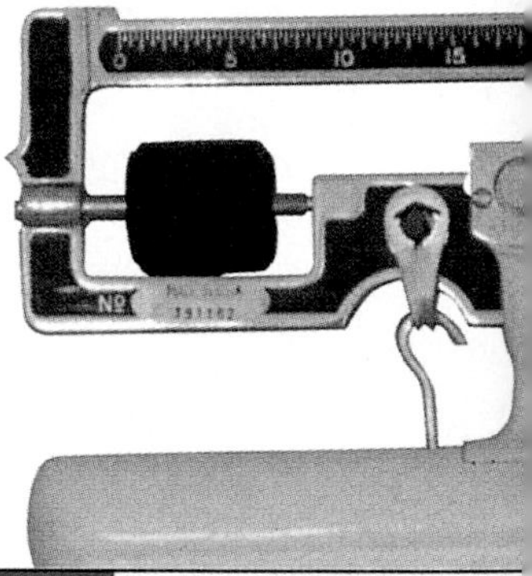

Options for Reaching All Students

Beginning

Art: Footstep Mural

Give students a roll of butcher paper. Ask students, one at a time, to stand on the paper while partners trace an outline of their feet. Have students write a label for each set of footprints, such as *Annamaria Vasquez, at 13 years, 6 months, after she arrived from Paraguay.*

Advanced

Science: Growth Time Line

Have students work in small groups. Ask them to use the charts and information from the text to make a time line showing ages of growth spurts, ages when most weight is gained, and ages at which adult height is reached. Students may want to create separate time lines for boys and girls. They can then post them one above the other easier visual comparisons.

Mixed Ability

Math: Measure Height

Give pairs a tape measure. Have them measure each other's height in inches. Have one student stand against a wall covered with a strip of paper while the other places a mark on the paper and measures the mark's distance from the floor. Use a soft tape measure to measure the body length of any students in wheelchairs. Add these heights to the paper strip.

At these ages, young people's bodies suddenly grow more quickly. Their feet and hands get bigger. Their arms and legs get longer. But other parts of their bodies do not grow as fast.

The different rates of growth cause some problems. Many young people feel awkward when they move. But soon the other parts of their bodies grow too. The young people begin to lose their awkwardness.

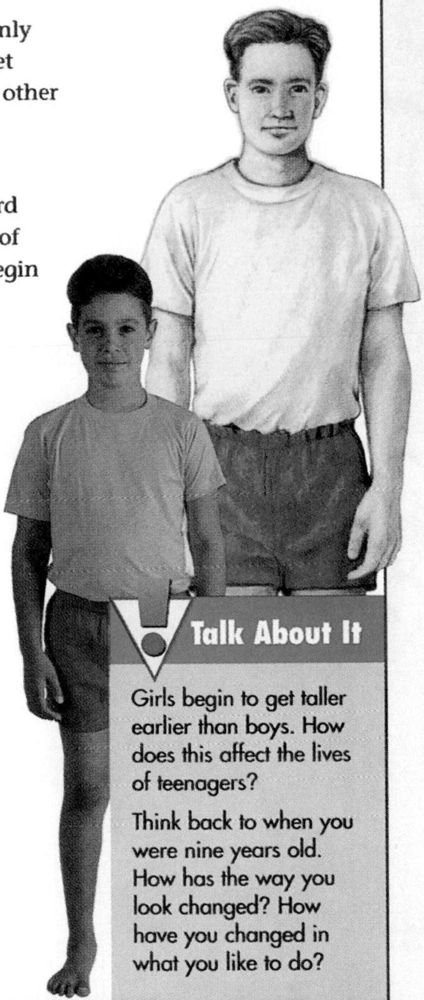

Growth Spurt in Boys
The growth spurt usually begins later in boys than in girls.
Boys gain the most weight about the age of 14 or 15.
Boys reach their adult height about the age of 20.

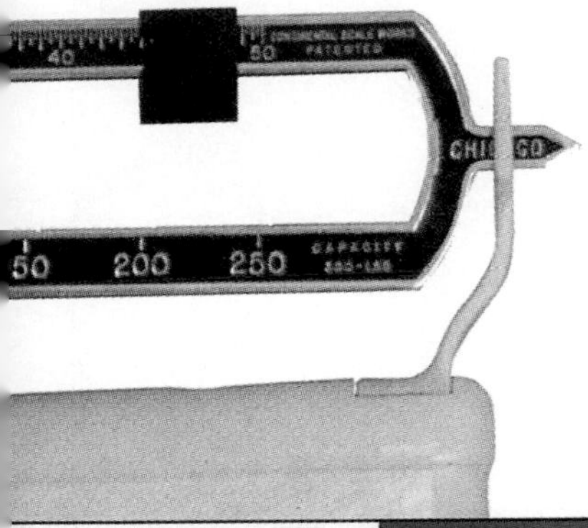

Talk About It

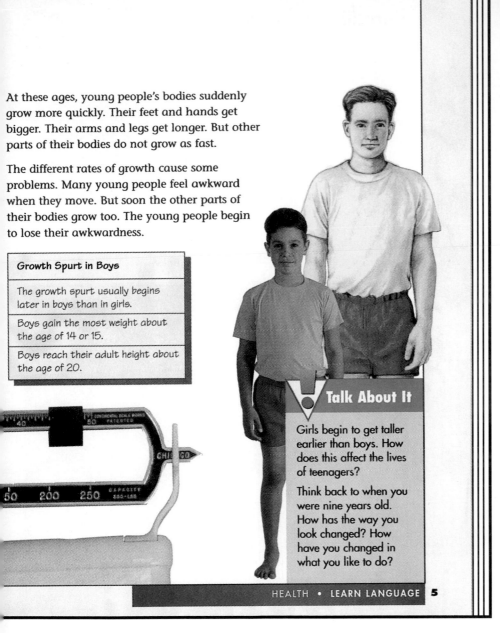

Girls begin to get taller earlier than boys. How does this affect the lives of teenagers?

Think back to when you were nine years old. How has the way you look changed? How have you changed in what you like to do?

Language Awareness

Grammar
Comparatives

ACTIVITY BOOK

Point out that some words in the text and charts compare two things or actions. Write the following sentence on the board:

Their arms and legs get <u>longer</u>.

Explain that comparative words often end in *-er*. Ask students to find other examples in the text *(bigger, earlier)*. Compare your size to that of a range of students, using both *bigger* and *smaller* and *shorter* and *taller*. Then have students compare length and sizes of various classroom objects. Use Activity Book page 2.

Assess

Use the questions in Talk About It for assessment. Students should be able to

- explain what the growth spurt is and say about when it occurs

LOOK **AHEAD**

In the next section, students will learn how heredity affects growth and other characteristics.

Peer or Cross-Age Tutoring

Language: Summarize

Have students work in pairs of mixed ability to summarize the text on pages 4 and 5 in their own words. Give them the option of summarizing orally or in writing.

QuickCheck

Numbers

Make sure that students can say the numbers 1 through 20 in English. Students who do not yet speak English can point to the numbers 1–20 as a partner says the numbers aloud.

Practice

Activate Prior Knowledge

Review Vocabulary

Have students look back at the photos on pages 2 and 3. Review words such as *parents, children, tall, short,* and so on. Ask students why they think members of a family may look alike.

Develop Language and Concepts

Present Pages 6 and 7

Read the text with students. Discuss the definitions of *traits, heredity,* and *genes.* Use the diagram of Veronica's family tree to help students see how traits, heredity, and genes are related. Ask students what traits they think they inherited from their mother, father, grandmothers, and grandfathers. Be sensitive to adopted children and others who may be uncomfortable with this activity.

Model a Strategy

Understand Key Words

Model how using key words can improve understanding when reading:

When I see a word in boldface type, I know that word is important. Such words are usually explained in the text. For example, on page 6, the word traits appears in boldface in the first sentence, and it is defined in the next sentence.

Words in boldface are key words. They give important clues about the subject. I know its important to try to learn all the words in boldface.

Heredity and Growth

You have certain **traits.** Traits include your height, hair color, and eye color. They also include the ages at which your growth spurt begins and ends. You get your traits from your parents. The passing of traits from parents to children is called **heredity.**

Traits are passed from parents to children in **genes.** Genes make you look like your parents. You get half your genes from your mother and half from your father. This mixture of genes determines your traits. For example, if your parents are tall, you probably will be tall. Your parents will pass on to you their trait for tallness.

Options for Reaching All Students

Beginning

Language: Identify Family Members

PICTURE CARDS

Give students a list of family words, such as *mother, father, son, daughter, parents, grandparents, cousin, aunt,* and *uncle.* Also give them pictures such as Picture Card 28 (family) and ask students to speculate about the relationships of the people.

Advanced

Writing: Compare Two Family Members

Have students write a short comparison of two family members. They may compare members of their own family or another family. Have them start by making a Venn diagram of similarities and differences.

Mixed Ability

Art: Create a Family Tree

Have students draw their own family trees. The drawings can resemble the illustration on page 7, show trees with family members pictured on the branches, or simply show a collage of people students consider as their family. Some students may wish to depict a family from literature or a popular TV show.

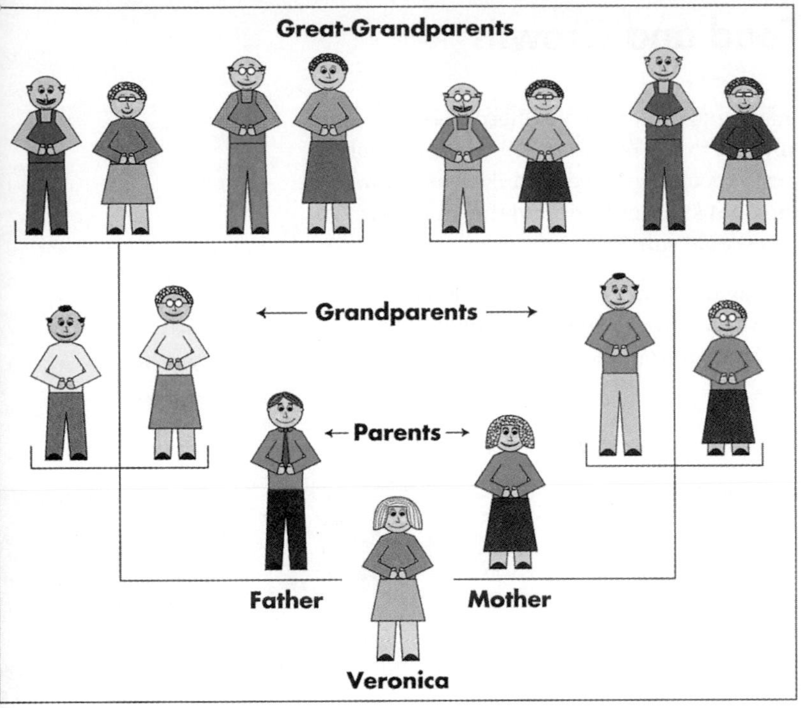

Look at the family tree. Notice how some of Veronica's parents, grandparents, and great-grandparents were tall. They passed on the trait for tallness to her.

Talk About It

How are genes and growth related?

What traits do you share with your family?

Language Awareness

Grammar

Present Tense: *Has/Have, Is/Are*

ACTIVITY BOOK Present forms of *to have* and *to be* in the context of descriptions. Start by describing yourself. *(I am short. I have blue eyes.)* Encourage students to describe themselves. Use members of the class to extend practice to *you* (singular), *he/she, we, you* (plural), and *they. (Ivana is tall. Antonio has brown hair.)* Present all forms of the verbs in the present tense. Use Activity Book page 3.

Assess ✓

Use the questions in Talk About It for assessment. Students should be able to

- make a connection between traits, such as the timing of a growth spurt, and genes inherited from parents
- use Word Bank terms from page 2 to describe traits shared by family members

LOOK **AHEAD**

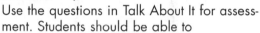

In the next section, students will learn how their food choices play a part in their growth.

Peer or Cross-Age Tutoring

Language: Summarize

Have students work in pairs of mixed ability. Ask students to tell each other two things they have learned from the text. Encourage more proficient students to help others form statements about the text.

QuickCheck

Family Relationships

Make sure that students can name family relationship words. Use Veronica's family tree as a way to prompt use of the words, but also practice terms that describe extended or non-traditional families.

Practice

Activate Prior Knowledge

Brainstorm Vocabulary

PICTURE CARDS

Use the Picture Cards of foods, such as 2 (apple), 4 (bananas), 8 (bread), 11 (butter), and so on. Have students identify each food by naming or pointing to it. Then have them name foods they ate yesterday. List the foods on the board.

Develop Language and Concepts

Present Pages 8 and 9

ACTIVITY BOOK

Read the text and the Food Pyramid with students. Use realia or pictures to present the Word Bank words. Help students place each food from the Word Bank in the appropriate section of the Food Pyramid. Then help them categorize the foods they brainstormed earlier.

Have pairs of students of mixed ability work on the Write About It activity. Discuss the lists with the entire class.

Discuss the pictures on page 9. Then have pairs of students work on the Try It Out activity. Use Activity Book pages 5 and 6.

Model a Strategy

Use a Chart

Model using a chart:

When I see a chart, I know it will often highlight key information, so I study it carefully. For example, the Food Pyramid on page 8 contains important facts about healthful eating.

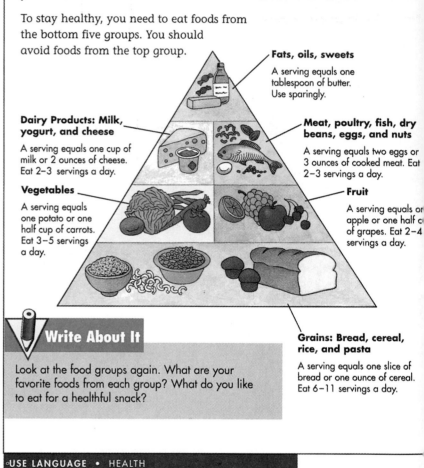

Food and Growth

In order to grow well, you need to eat the right kinds of foods. You also need to eat the right amounts of them. The Food Pyramid shows the right kinds of foods and the amounts you should eat.

To stay healthy, you need to eat foods from the bottom five groups. You should avoid foods from the top group.

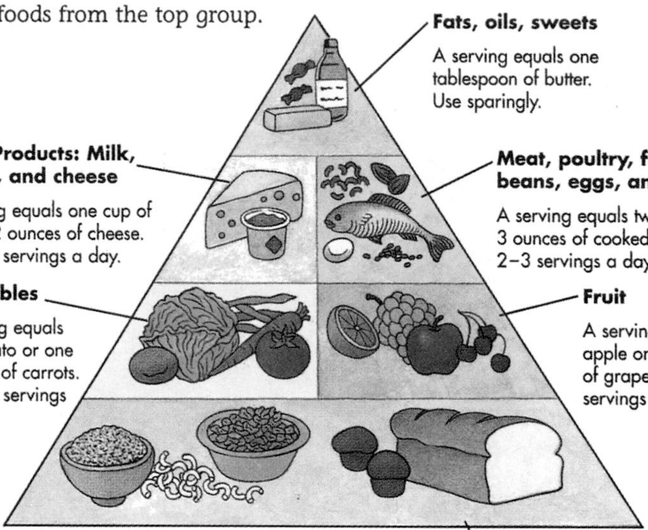

Fats, oils, sweets
A serving equals one tablespoon of butter. Use sparingly.

Dairy Products: Milk, yogurt, and cheese
A serving equals one cup of milk or 2 ounces of cheese. Eat 2–3 servings a day.

Meat, poultry, fish, dry beans, eggs, and nuts
A serving equals two eggs or 3 ounces of cooked meat. Eat 2–3 servings a day.

Vegetables
A serving equals one potato or one half cup of carrots. Eat 3–5 servings a day.

Fruit
A serving equals or apple or one half c of grapes. Eat 2–4 servings a day.

Grains: Bread, cereal, rice, and pasta
A serving equals one slice of bread or one ounce of cereal. Eat 6–11 servings a day.

Write About It

Look at the food groups again. What are your favorite foods from each group? What do you like to eat for a healthful snack?

Options for Reaching All Students

Beginning

Health: Picture Pyramid

Have small groups create their own picture pyramid of the food groups. Have each group copy the outline of the Food Pyramid and its sections on pasteboard. Students can then fill each section with magazine pictures or drawings of foods belonging to that group. Some students may benefit from placing realia (boxes and cans of food, fruits) on the pyramid.

Advanced

Language: School Lunch Menu

Have groups use the information in the Food Pyramid to create a school lunch menu for a week. Encourage them to include a variety of foods, including favorite foods from the home countries, in their menus. Suggest groups create an organizer that will help them identify and track the type of foods and number of servings to show that their menus are nutritious.

Mixed Ability

Math: Measurements

Bring in a set of measuring cups, measuring spoons, a small food scale, and foods from each of the six groups. Help students understand the meaning of *ounce, cup, teaspoon,* and *tablespoon.* Ask students to estimate a serving size for each food. You can also use nutrition labels that indicate serving sizes. Then have students work in groups to measure single servings of the foods.

Word Bank

eggs
fish
orange juice
potatoes
rice
strawberries
toast
tortillas

Try It Out

Look at the different breakfasts. What food groups do they include? Talk with a partner, and decide what you would choose for a healthful breakfast. Then decide on healthful meals for lunch and supper.

Language Awareness

Grammar
Plural Forms

ACTIVITY BOOK

Explain that most nouns are made plural by adding *-s*. Illustrate by listing words in the text such as *oranges, eggs,* and *grapes* on the board. Have students identify the singular forms of those words.

Then explain that not all plurals are formed simply by adding *-s*. Write the examples *cherries, potatoes,* and *tomatoes* on the board. Have students identify the singular forms of those nouns. Then help them discover how the plurals were formed. Ask students to find other plural nouns in the text on pages 8 and 9. Use Activity Book page 4.

Assess ✓

Students should be able to

- name the food groups in the Food Pyramid and give examples of each
- identify food choices that promote healthy growth

LOOK**AHEAD**

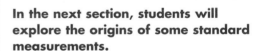

In the next section, students will explore the origins of some standard measurements.

Cooperative Language Experience

Field Trip

Arrange a tour of a local supermarket. If possible, invite an expert, such as a dietitian or the school nurse, to explain how to make wise choices when shopping for food. Encourage students to read and compare food labels. As a class, write a language experience story about the trip. Invite students to dictate words or sentences for you to write.

Home Connection

Create an Eating Chart

Ask students to make a chart of everything they eat for three days. The chart should contain one row for each food group and one column for each day. Have them write the foods and amounts on the chart. (Beginning learners may use pictures to record what they ate.) When the chart is complete, have students assess the healthfulness of their eating patterns.

Writer's Workshop

Write About Favorite Meals

Refer students to the Writer's Workshop on pages 230 to 236 of the Student Book. Ask students to describe their favorite special family meal, including what the occasion is and what is served. Encourage students to use vivid adjectives to describe the meal.

Connect

Activate Prior Knowledge

Brainstorm Vocabulary

Bring in various tools for measuring, such as rulers (one in inches and one in centimeters) and a tape measure. Have students measure items in the classroom in both standard English and metric systems.

Develop Language and Concepts

Present Pages 10 and 11

ACTIVITY BOOK

Read the text with students. Focus on the importance of using standardized units of measure. Encourage students to think of situations in which accurate measurements are important, such as cooking, sports, home building, and medicine. Discuss the questions in Talk About It. Then have pairs of students work on the Try It Out activity. Students can use Activity Book page 7. Students with motor difficulties might measure classroom objectives with their hands instead of their feet.

Model a Strategy

Understand Directions

Model the importance of understanding directions before starting an activity:

Before I start an activity, I make sure I understand what I need to do and how to do it. For example, before I fill in the chart on page 11, I will make sure that I know exactly how to use my feet to measure objects. That way, I won't make mistakes and I won't need to do the same work over.

How big is a foot?

Long ago, people did not use rulers. They measured how long things were by using parts of their bodies, such as their feet. But there was a problem. Everyone's foot was a different length.

In 1324, King Edward II of England made a law. The law said a "foot" would always be the same length. People could then be sure how long something was. When people bought a foot of cloth, it was always the same length.

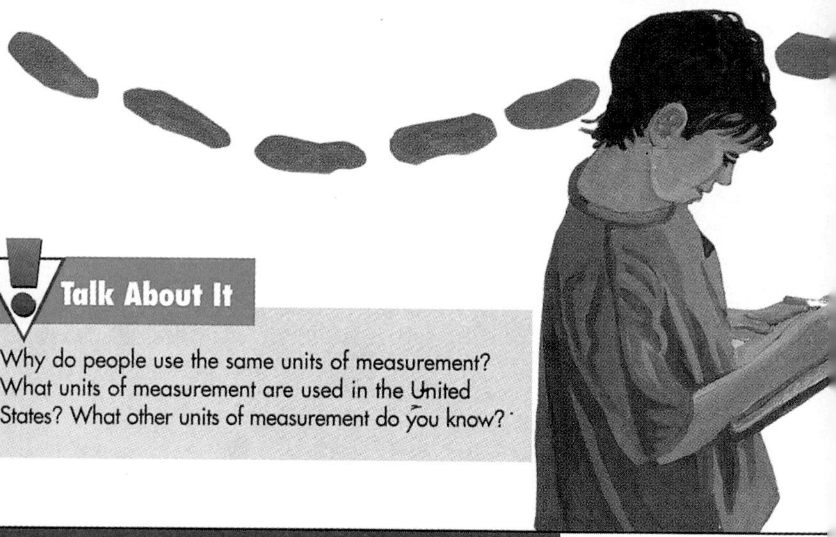

Talk About It

Why do people use the same units of measurement? What units of measurement are used in the United States? What other units of measurement do you know?

10 CONNECT LANGUAGE • HEALTH/MATH

Options for Reaching All Students

Beginning

Math: "Measure" Hunt

Give groups of students cards on which three different measurements in inches or centimeters are listed. Ask each group to find items in the classroom that are closest in length to the three listed measurements. Provide rulers for their searches.

Advanced

Math: Research Measurements

Have pairs research one of the following units of measure: carat, cubit, furlong, knot, league, light-year. Have students begin by identifying relevant reference sources to consult. Ask students to write a brief report in which they tell what the unit is used to measure. Have them present their findings to the class.

Mixed Ability

Math: Measure and Compare

Extend the Try It Out activity. Ask pairs of students to measure the length of each object in the chart on page 10 in standard feet and inches. Have students compare those figures to the measurements they obtained when they used their own feet.

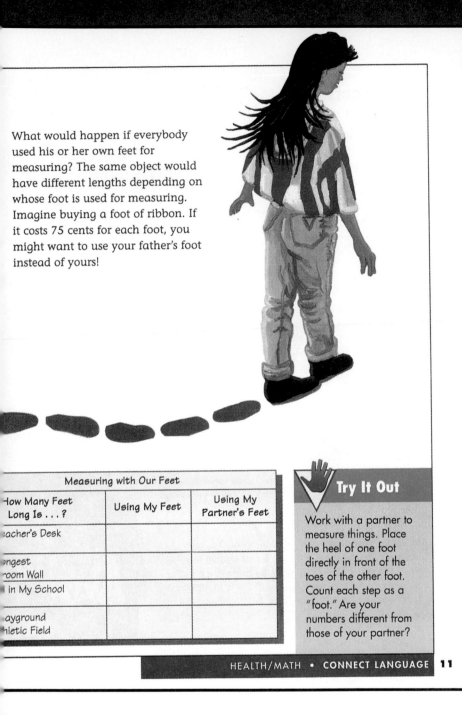

What would happen if everybody used his or her own feet for measuring? The same object would have different lengths depending on whose foot is used for measuring. Imagine buying a foot of ribbon. If it costs 75 cents for each foot, you might want to use your father's foot instead of yours!

Measuring with Our Feet		
-low Many Feet Long Is . . . ?	Using My Feet	Using My Partner's Feet
:acher's Desk		
›ngest -oom Wall		
in My School		
ayground hletic Field		

Try It Out

Work with a partner to measure things. Place the heel of one foot directly in front of the toes of the other foot. Count each step as a "foot." Are your numbers different from those of your partner?

Language Awareness

Grammar
Possessive Adjectives

Create a two-column chart on the board. In column 1, write the subject pronouns *I, you, he, she, it, we, you, they.* In column 2, write *my* across from *I.* Model its use by pointing to your eyes and saying: *My eyes are brown. I have brown eyes.* and so on. Progress through the subject pronouns in the chart, asking students to find the corresponding possessive forms on pages 10 and 11. Have students use each possessive adjective in sentences describing their own traits and those of class members.

Assess ✓

Use the questions in Talk About It for assessment. Students should be able to

- explain the importance of standard units of measurement

LOOK**AHEAD**

In the next section, students will read about some extraordinary measurements.

Home Connection

Read Labels

Bring in a variety of containers (food items, cleaning products, and so on) that show a unit of measure on the label. Help students locate and compare the different units of measure. You might point out which units of measure are used to measure liquid amounts and which ones measure solid amounts. Then encourage students to look for and record units of measure on the labels of products at home. Ask them to make a list of four or more items that have different units of measure, such as a two-*liter* bottle of soda, a *gallon* bottle of milk, a four-*ounce* bag of nuts, and a one-*pound* bag of sugar. They can work with family members to compare amounts. Invite students to share their findings with the class.

Connect

Activate Prior Knowledge

Review Vocabulary

Help students think of physical traits that can be measured. Ask what units of measure can be used to quantify those traits. Ask which student in the class has the longest hair, the oldest family member, can run the fastest, or do the most push-ups. Discuss the notion of setting a record. Ask questions such as: *Have you ever set a record? Do you know anyone who has ever set a record?*

Develop Language and Concepts

Present Pages 12 and 13

Have students look at the pictures on pages 12 and 13 and identify things that can be measured. Ask what units would be used to measure them.

Read each paragraph with students. Relate each record to a more average occurrence and to students' personal experiences.

Prepare students to do the Try It Out activity by helping them create a plan. Ask them what they need to consider before they begin. Tasks might include determining the number of entries to include, brainstorming a list of categories, and deciding how to verify the information. If possible, have students use desktop publishing software to create the book.

When the Book of Records is well under way, but before it is finished, discuss the questions in Think About It with the class.

Fun Facts

People like to measure things and keep records. Here are some interesting facts about people. They are from *The Guinness Book of Records*.

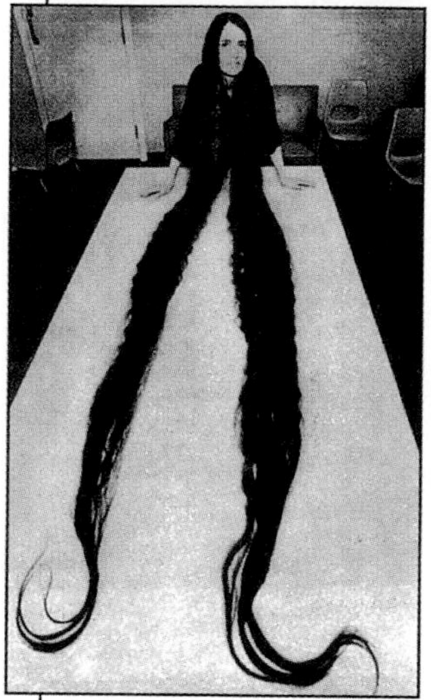

The Longest Feet

Matthew McGrory from the state of Pennsylvania has the longest feet. He wears size 23 shoes. His shoes are about 15 inches (40 centimeters) long. How much longer is his foot than yours?

The Longest Hair

Diane Witt has the longest hair in the United States. In 1993, her hair was more than 12 feet 8 inches (3 meters 86 centimeters) long. Usually hair grows only up to 3 feet (1 meter) long.

The Oldest Family

Do you know your great-great-great-grandparents? A family in China can name members of its family back to 2,800 years ago.

Try It Out

Make a "Book of Records" for your class. You can include information like this: the oldest student in your class, the student who can jump the farthest, the student who has the most cousins. Be sure to include photos or drawings in your book.

Options for Reaching All Students

Beginning

Art: Create Wacky Records

Have students divide a sheet of paper into four panels. Ask them to draw pictures of improbable or silly records, such as the "World's Ugliest Shoes." Help students write a caption describing the illustration in each panel. Have students share their work and choose which record is the "wackiest."

Advanced

Language: Television Interview

Have pairs role-play a television interview with one of the record holders mentioned in the text. Ask one student to act as the reporter and the other student to act as the interviewee. Remind the interviewer to prepare *what, when, where,* and *why* questions. Have the pairs present their interviews to the class, and encourage the audience to ask additional questions.

Cooperative Language Experience

Math: Measure and Visualize Lengths

Use the following activities to illustrate some of the records cited in the text:

- Give students a ball of string and help them cut a piece 3 meters 86 centimeters long to show the length of Diane Witt's hair.

The Oldest Person

The oldest person lived to be more than 120 years old. She was Jeanne Calment of France. She was born in 1875 and was still living in the 1990s.

The Fastest Runners

In 1994, Leroy Burrell ran the fastest 100-meter race. He ran the race in 9.85 seconds. This is about 23 miles (37 kilometers) per hour. Florence Griffith Joyner has run the fastest in the women's 100-meter race. Her time was 10.49 seconds.

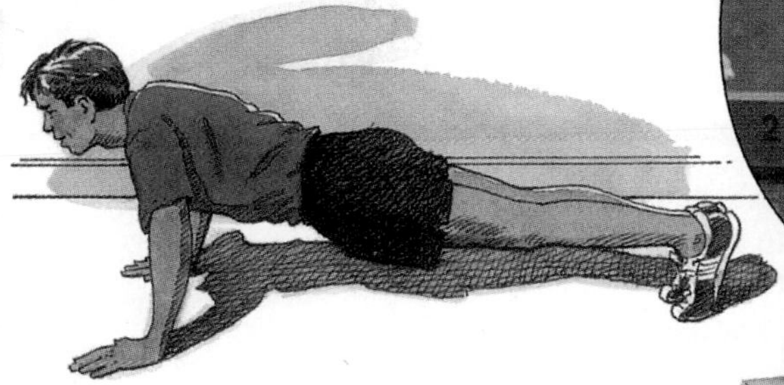

The Most Push-ups

Charles Servizio of the United States did 46,001 push-ups in one day.

The Longest Gum Wrapper Chain

Gary Duschl of Canada made the longest chain from gum wrappers. It was 12,105 feet (3,690 meters) long.

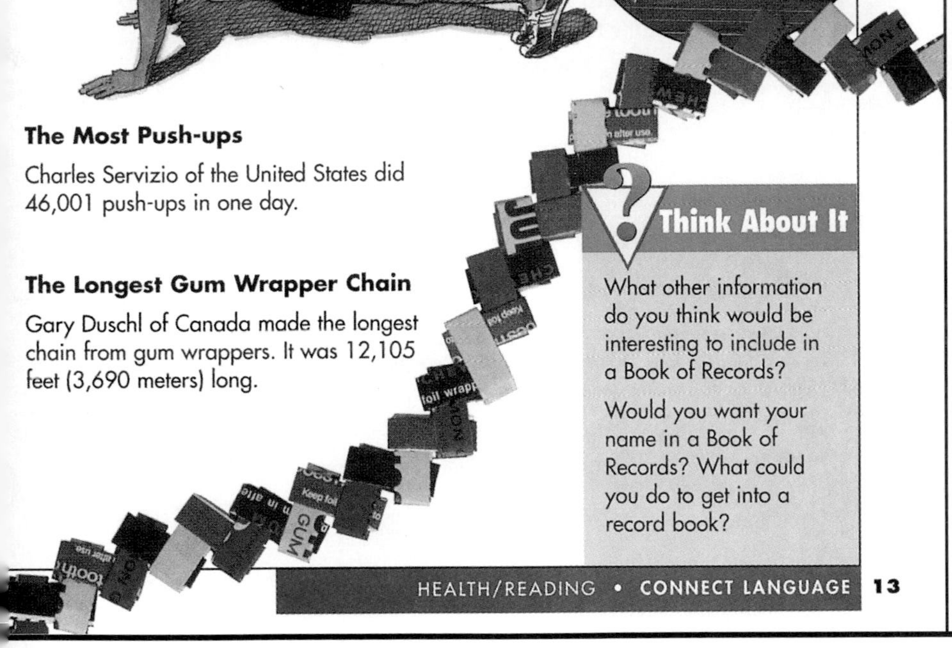

Think About It

What other information do you think would be interesting to include in a Book of Records?

Would you want your name in a Book of Records? What could you do to get into a record book?

Language Awareness

Grammar
Superlatives

ACTIVITY BOOK

Write the following sentences on the board:

Diane Witt has the longest hair in the United States.
The oldest person lived to be more than 120 years old.

Underline the *-est* in *longest* and *oldest* and tell students that the ending *-est* means "the most." Ask students to find other examples of superlatives on pages 12 and 13. Have them suggest other words to which they could add *-est*. (*shortest, tallest, slowest, nicest*) Write their suggestions on the board and ask them to use the words in sentences. Use Activity Book page 8.

FYI More About *The Guinness Book of World Records*

The Guinness Book of World Records **has been published annually since 1955. It lists records for sports, stunts, and natural phenomena. Every record must be verified by an investigator before it is included in the book.**

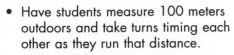

- Have students measure 100 meters outdoors and take turns timing each other as they run that distance.
- Lead a walk outdoors that is half as long as Gary Duschl's gum wrapper chain.
- Have students collect gum wrappers and see how long it takes to make a one-foot chain.

Connect

Activate Prior Knowledge

Review Concepts

Review the meaning of *cycles.* Make a circling gesture with your hand.

Develop Language and Concepts

Present Page 14

RED TAPE

Read the words of the song. Use pantomime to clarify vocabulary. Ask students how it relates to the unit title, Cycles of Life. Play the song on Side 2 of the Red Tape several times, encouraging students to sing along. Additional verses are provided under Mixed Ability below. Ask students if they like the song.

FYI More About the Song

The lyrics are from Ecclesiastes, a book in the Old Testament of the Bible. The song became a number-one hit in 1965–66 for the folk-rock group The Byrds.

Language Awareness

Vocabulary Opposites

ACTIVITY BOOK

Point out that the song contains many opposites: *A time to be born, a time to die.* Ask students to find other opposites in the song. Then invite them to think of opposites from the chapter: *tall/short, young/old, begin/end, earlier/later,* and so on. Use Activity Book page 9.

Turn! Turn! Turn!

by Pete Seeger

To everything, turn, turn, turn,
There is a season, turn, turn, turn,
And a time for every purpose under heaven.

A time to be born, a time to die;
A time to plant, a time to reap;
A time to kill, a time to heal;
A time to laugh, a time to weep.

A time to build up, a time to break down;
A time to dance, a time to mourn;
A time to cast away stones;
A time to gather stones together.

Think About It

The song has many words that are opposites. Can you find them? Does looking for opposites help you understand the meaning of words?

Why do you think the song uses opposites? What is the song saying about the changes in life?

Options for Reaching All Students

Beginning

Language: Pantomime Opposites

Have students pantomime opposites as their classmates try to guess the concepts or actions portrayed (for example, a smile for *happy* and a frown for *sad*). Help students brainstorm a list of opposites to use, such as *run/walk, tall/short.*

Advanced

Writing: Create a Song Variation

Have students work in pairs. Ask them to write an alternative version of the song by substituting different verbs in the second and third verses. Have students evaluate their word choices to make sure they duplicate the rhythm of the original.

Mixed Ability

Music: Sing More Verses

RED TAPE

Help students learn these verses of "Turn! Turn! Turn!"

A time of love, a time of hate;
A time of war, a time of peace;
A time you may embrace;
A time to refrain from embracing.

A time to gain, a time to lose;
A time to rend, a time to sew;
A time to love, a time to hate;
A time for peace. I swear it's not too late.

CHAPTER 1

Tell what you learned.

1. What is a "growth spurt"? How does it make teenagers feel awkward?
2. What is heredity? What are some traits that are determined by heredity?
3. Explain why using your foot to measure length is, or is not, as good as using a ruler.
4. Make the chart with the food groups. Write the names of foods from each group that you ate yesterday.

Food Group	*Examples*
Grains	
Vegetables	
Fruit	
Dairy products	
Meat, poultry, dry beans, fish, eggs, nuts	
Fats, oils, sweets	

5. Which of the facts from *The Guinness Book of Records* did you find most interesting?
6. If you could set a record, what would it be?

Assess ✓

Activity 1: Determine whether students understand the meaning of *growth spurt*.

Activity 2: Evaluate whether students understand the connection between traits and heredity. Students should cite terms from the Word Bank on page 2 as examples.

Activity 3: Determine whether students understand that differences in foot size make a real foot a poor measure of length.

Activity 4: Students should correctly classify foods.

Activity 5: Evaluate students' reasons for their choices.

Activity 6: Check students' use of superlative terms such as *highest* and *most* in their responses.

Have students complete the Chapter Self-Assessment, Blackline Master 31. Have students choose the product of one of the activities to place in their portfolios. Add the results of any rubrics, checklists, self-assessments, or portfolio assessments, Blackline Masters 2–18 and 31.

Listening Assessment

BLACKLINE MASTER

Make sure that each student has a copy of Blackline Master 41 from the Teacher's Resource Book. Play the tape several times and have students mark answers.

WHITE TAPE

See Chapter 1 Resources, page T1c, for the Listening Assessment tapescript.

Options for Assessment

Vocabulary Assessment

Sort by Categories

Write the following categories on the board: *growth, traits, food, measurements*. For each category, give students two minutes to list associated terms. Enter in a class Book of Records the names of students who list the most terms in a category. You can modify this activity as needed by supplying terms students can match to each category.

Writing Assessment

Journal

Have students describe ways they have grown and changed in the past five years. Have students start the writing process by brainstorming a list of changes. Then have them expand the list into sentences and paragraphs. The tone can be informal. Remind them to write in the first person and to use verbs that agree with the pronoun *I*.

Language Assessment

BLACKLINE MASTER

Use Blackline Master 40 in the Teacher's Resource Book.

Standardized Test Practice

ACTIVITY BOOK

Use Activity Book pages 10 and 11. Answers:
1. $1.25 + 5 ($0.45)
2. 107 inches **3.** 48
4. $187.45 - $30 – $45 = A

Preview

Activate Prior Knowledge
Start a K-W-L Chart

Start a discussion of the Chapter 2 topic, life cycles of plants, by helping students discuss plants they know. Bring plants to class and/or show pictures of various plants, including trees, bushes, flowering plants, and plants that produce food, and help students identify them. Allow students time to examine the plants or pictures. Help them identify plant names, plant parts, ,or descriptive words for the plants. Have students use the information to create a K-W-L chart.

K: What We Know	There are many different kinds of plants. Different plants grow in different areas of the world.
W: What We Want to Find Out	What role do plants play in the lives of people?
L: What We Learned	

Have students add to the chart throughout the chapter.

CHAPTER 2

Life Cycles of Plant

Word Bank

flower
fruit
leaf
roots
stem
trunk

Tell what you know.

These plants grow in different regions of the world. Can you name any of the plants? Can you identify their parts?

16

Options for Reaching All Students

Beginning

Art: Draw a Favorite Plant

Have students draw their favorite plant and label its parts using words from the Word Bank. Some students may want to locate a drawing or photo of the plant in a reference source or in a computer database of clip art to use as a model for their drawing. Have students take turns displaying their drawings to each other.

Advanced

Science: Do a Research Project

Have students work in groups to find information about one of the following topics: How Plants Make Their Own Food, How Plants Protect Themselves, Creeping and Climbing Plants, Meat-Eating Plants, Water Plants, Desert Plants, Plants Used for Medicine. Ask each group to present an oral report on its topic. Remind students to speak loudly, slowly, and clearly.

Mixed Ability

Critical Thinking: Categorize

Have groups cut out pictures of plants from magazines. Have them create categories for the plants (such as Plants We Eat, Plants Used for Medicine, Flowering Plants) and paste them on art paper. Ask students to describe their categories and the plants in them. More proficient students can write labels and help beginners attach them.

Talk About It

What plants grow where you live? Which plants grow in other places where you have lived?

17

Develop Language and Concepts

Present Pages 16 and 17

Read the text with the students. Introduce the words in the Word Bank. Help students associate the words with the parts of the plants shown in the pictures. Discuss the functions of the plant parts listed in the Word Bank. Then help students use the Word Bank words to form sentences about the pictures.

The plants shown on the pages are desert cactuses, strawberries, and tropical flowers.

Have students work in groups of three or four to discuss the questions in Talk About It. Ask them to make a list of all the plants they can think of. Beginning learners can contribute by drawing pictures. Provide illustrated reference sources if students need help identifying plant names. Then have the groups present their lists to the class. On the board, create a master list of the plants students mention. Emphasize the diversity of the plants in size, shape, use, and so on.

FYI Plant Categories

The two basic plant categories are flowering plants and nonflowering plants. Mosses, ferns, and conifers are examples of nonflowering plants. Nearly 250,000 species of flowering plants exist in the world today.

Cooperative Language Experience

Field Trip

Take students for a walk around the neighborhood to identify local plants. Try to observe as wide a variety as possible, including trees, shrubs, vines, mosses, wild flowers, and so on. If possible, bring along a guidebook of plants or enlist the aid of a knowledgeable parent or family member.

As a class, write a language experience story about the trip. Help students generalize about the kinds of plants they saw. Have them start by listing the features of the plants they saw and organizing the plants into categories. Have them use reference sources to identify specific plant names.

Home Connection

Plant Inventory

Have students work with family members to take an inventory of the plants growing in and around their homes. Ask students to consult family members or neighbors for plant names that are unfamiliar. Encourage students to draw pictures of the plants for display in the classroom.

Present

Activate Prior Knowledge

Make Observations

Bring a variety of flowers or pictures of flowers to class. Have students examine them and determine what traits they have in common. Ask students how many of their senses they might use to experience the flowers. Ask students what they think the purpose of flowers is. Emphasize that flowers are important for plant reproduction.

Develop Language and Concepts

Present Pages 18 and 19

Have students study the illustrations and read the labels. Read the text with students. Introduce the words in the Word Bank, using the pictures in the book and objects in the classroom.

Review colors. Then have students do the Talk About It activity.

Model a Strategy

Use Pictures for Meaning

Model using pictures for meaning:

When pictures appear with a text, I use them to improve my understanding. For example, on page 18, when I read "The sepals cover and protect the flower buds until the flowers open," I look at the picture to see what sepals look like. The picture helps me understand and remember what sepals are.

Parts of a Flower

Plants are important. They make food for themselves. They make food for animals and people.

Most plants have flowers. These include tall trees and the vegetables that grow in gardens.

Flowers have four main parts. Each part has a different function.

The **sepals** cover and protect the flower buds until the flowers open.

Options for Reaching All Students

Beginning

Language: Plant Words

TPR

Give each student a card with one of these words: *sepal, petal, stamen, pistil.* Read the poem and ask students to hold up their card when they hear the word:

Sepals cover flowers
Until petals open wide,
To show stamens and a pistil,
Tucked away inside.

Advanced

Science: Plan a Garden

Give students seed catalogs and ask them to plan a garden with a variety of plants suitable for your area's climate. Have students sketch a diagram of their garden. Then have them draw or paste pictures on their diagram to show where each type of plant would go. Have students label the plants and write brief descriptions.

Mixed Ability

Art: Draw a Flower

Bring several kinds of fresh flowers and a magnifying glass to class. Have students use the magnifying glass to examine the flowers' structures, including the stems and leaves. Ask students to draw one of the flowers in detail. Have them label the parts and use words from the Word Bank to describe the petals.

Petals protect the parts of the flowers that make seeds. They are often very colorful.

Stamens make pollen. Pollen grains are the male cells of the flower. The stamens are inside the petals.

The **pistil** makes and holds the egg cells. Egg cells are the female cells of the flower. A seed develops when an egg cell and pollen combine.

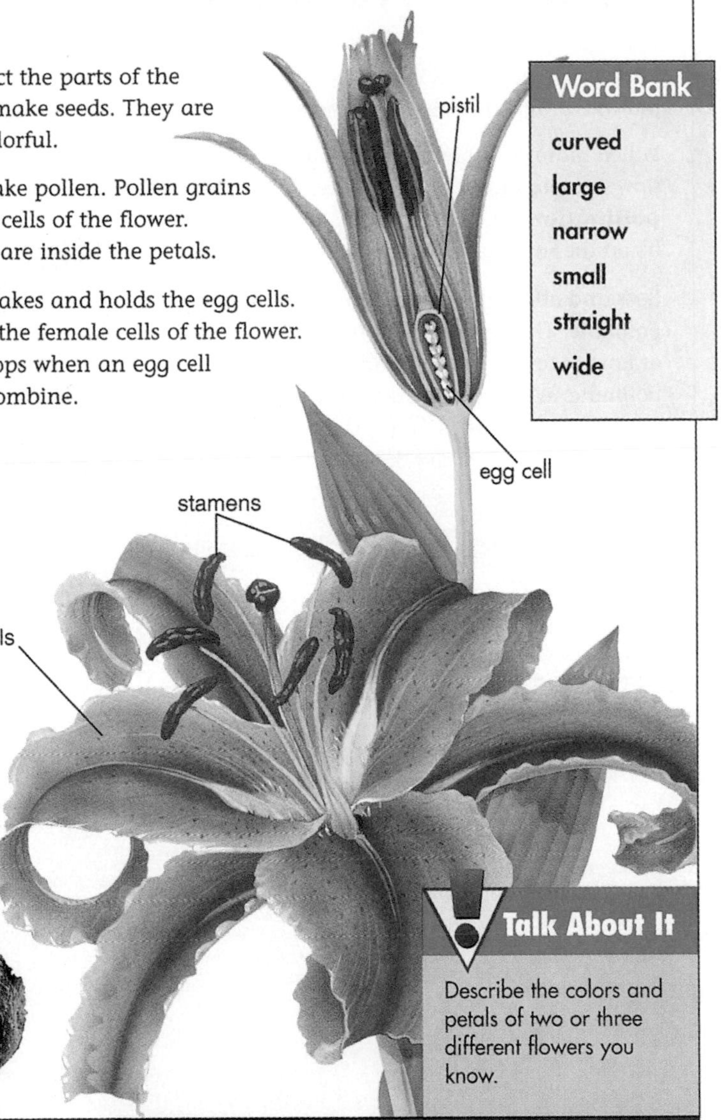

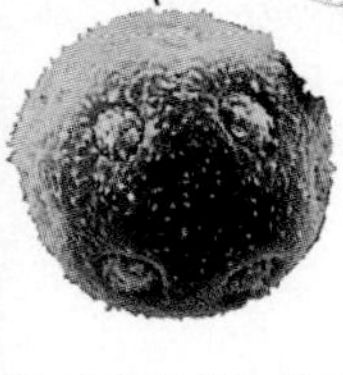

Word Bank

- curved
- large
- narrow
- small
- straight
- wide

Talk About It

Describe the colors and petals of two or three different flowers you know.

Language Awareness

Language Function
Words That Describe

ACTIVITY BOOK Explain that the words in the Word Bank are used to describe, as are color words. Play a guessing game in which students describe objects by size, color, shape, and so on. Use Activity Book page 12.

Assess

Use class discussion for assessment. Students should be able to

- name the parts of a flower
- talk about the function of each part

LOOK AHEAD

In the next section, students will learn what roles plant parts play in the life cycle of a plant.

Cooperative Language Experience

Field Trip

Take students to visit a local botanical garden or nursery. If possible, arrange for someone at the garden or nursery to lead the tour and explain how to grow and care for flowering plants.

As a class, write a language experience story about the trip on chart paper. Students may draw and caption pictures of what they saw. Have students retell their experiences in the correct sequence. Help them punctuate the story correctly. Students can dictate sentences to you or write their own. If you are writing, pause often to prompt responses about word choice and sentence structure.

QuickCheck

Colors

Students should be able to describe colors of objects. Take advantage of the opportunity to present less common color terms such as beige, maroon, and so on. You may want to bring in boxes of crayons or watercolors labeled with the names of colors.

Practice

Activate Prior Knowledge

Demonstrate and Discuss

Show the class seeds of various sizes and shapes and have students discuss the function of seeds in the life cycle of plants. Then ask students if they have ever noticed the "dust" or powder inside a flower. Introduce the word *pollen*.

Develop Language and Concepts

Present Pages 20 and 21

Read the text with students. Use the diagram on page 21 to help students follow the sequence of events as they read. Then help students use the diagram to describe the life cycle of a plant in their own words. Record and number these steps. Then have them answer the Think About It questions.

Model a Strategy

Follow a Sequence

Model tracking the sequence in a process:

When I read about a process, words such as after, now, and then help me follow the sequence of events. For example, these words at the top of page 21 help me follow what happens after pollination. Drawings can also help me. The arrows in the drawing show the order of the steps.

Life Cycle of a Flowering Plant

Flowers are important in the life cycle of most plants. Flowers help the plants reproduce.

Pollen grains combine with the eggs in a flower to produce seeds. This process is called **pollination.** The flower that is pollinated can be on the same plant or on a different plant.

Bees and other insects help some plants pollinate. They carry pollen from the stamens of flowers to the pistils. Wind helps other plants pollinate. Wind carries the pollen through the air. The pollen moves from the stamen of one plant to the pistil of another plant.

20 USE LANGUAGE • SCIENCE

Options for Reaching All Students

Beginning

Art: Draw the Plant Life Cycle

Ask students to draw an outdoor scene that includes plants at different stages of their life cycles. Provide illustrated reference materials that students can use as models. Tell students to show two or three insects and animals that help pollinate flowers and spread seeds. Help students label each stage.

Advanced

Science: Research How Seeds Travel

Have small groups of students seek more information about how seeds travel. Some might investigate plants such as the coconut tree, dandelion, thistle, milkweed, and maple. Others might study more about the role of bees and animals in spreading seeds. Have the groups draw illustrations and present their findings to the class.

Mixed Ability

Art: Create a Seed

Give pairs of students glue, tape, cotton balls, pins, paper, scissors, and other materials that they can use to create an imaginary seed that can move by wind, water, animal, or other natural forces. Have students describe their seeds for one another. They can act out how the seeds can be moved.

After pollination, the flower dries up and falls off. Now the plant produces seeds. These seeds might fall to the ground. Wind or animals might carry them to another place. The seeds then grow into new plants. These new plants then produce flowers. And the life cycle of the plant repeats.

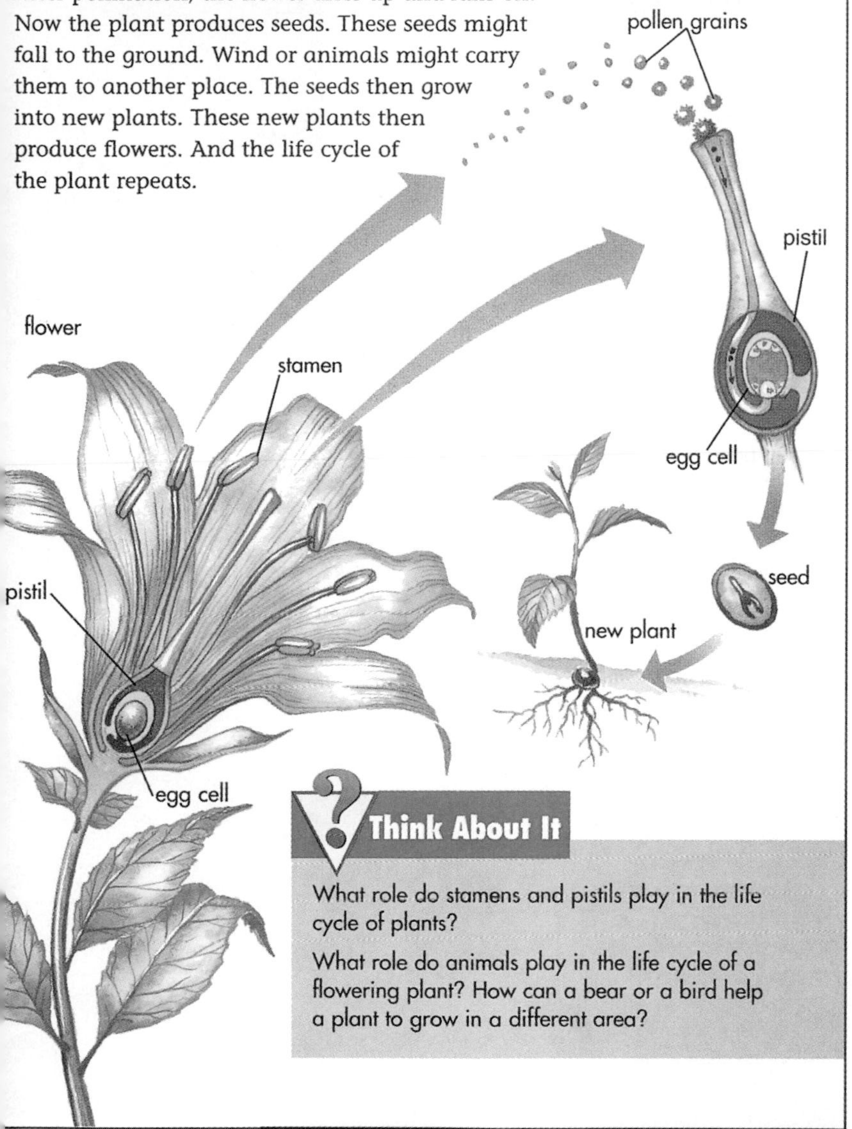

Think About It

What role do stamens and pistils play in the life cycle of plants?

What role do animals play in the life cycle of a flowering plant? How can a bear or a bird help a plant to grow in a different area?

Language Awareness

Phonics
Initial Consonant *p*, Consonant Blends *pl* and *pr*

ACTIVITY BOOK

Write the following words on the board and model their pronunciation:

pollen   plant   produce

Point out that to make the sounds students should close their lips, push air forward in their mouths, and then open their lips. Ask students to find other words that contain *p, pl,* or *pr* in the text and pronounce the words. Then ask them to think of other words that contain those sounds. They can also look up words in a dictionary. Write their suggestions on the board. Use Activity Book page 13.

Assess

Use answers to the Think About It questions for assessment. Students should be able to

- briefly describe the process of pollination

LOOK**AHEAD**

In the next section, students will identify the parts of plants people eat.

Peer or Cross-Age Tutoring

Language: Summarize

Have students work in pairs of mixed ability to write a summary of the life cycle of a flowering plant. Beginning learners could draw a diagram, and more proficient students can write numbered summary statements.

Cooperative Learning

Write Instructions

Have small groups of students look through print or electronic reference sources about plants to find a plant that interests them. Ask them to write a short description of the plant and make a numbered list telling how to grow and care for it. If possible, have students use their instructions as the basis of a simple instructional video on how to grow the plant.

Practice

Activate Prior Knowledge

Use Pictures

PICTURE CARDS

Use Picture Cards 2 (apple), 8 (bread), 14 (carrots), 27 (eggs), 33 (grapes), 36 (hot dog), 38 (juice), 42 (lettuce), 52 (pizza), 57 (rice), and 67 (strawberries). Display the Picture Cards and ask students to identify the foods and plants by naming or pointing to them. Then have students tell what parts of the plant they would not want to eat and why.

Develop Language and Concepts

Present Pages 22 and 23

ACTIVITY BOOK

Read the text with students. As you read, ask students to match the food names with the pictures. Pause while reading to record the name of each plant part and list examples for each part. Help students brainstorm other examples.

Ask students which plants they eat at meals, which they eat as dessert, and which they eat as snacks. Have them name the plants or plant parts they might drink as juice. Have students work in small groups to complete the Try It Out activity.

Students can use Activity Book page 14 to complete the activity on page 23.

Eating Plants

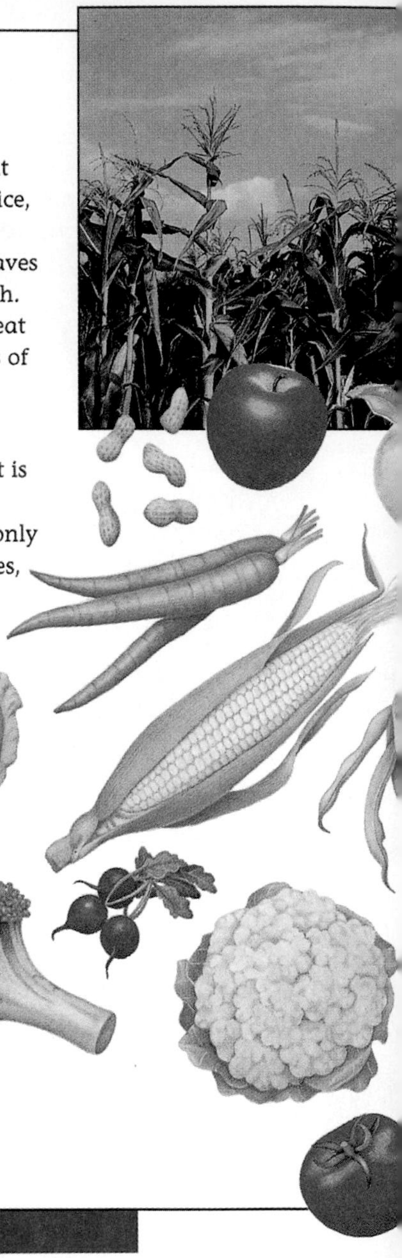

What parts of plants do you eat? You eat the seeds of plants when you eat corn, rice, or peanuts. You eat the stems of plants when you eat asparagus. You eat the leaves of plants when you eat lettuce or spinach. You eat the flowers of plants when you eat cauliflower or broccoli. You eat the roots of plants when you eat radishes or carrots.

You eat the fruit of plants when you eat apples, tomatoes, and peaches. The fruit is the part of a plant that contains seeds. Some fruits, such as avocados, contain only one seed. Other fruits, such as raspberries, contain many seeds.

Try It Out

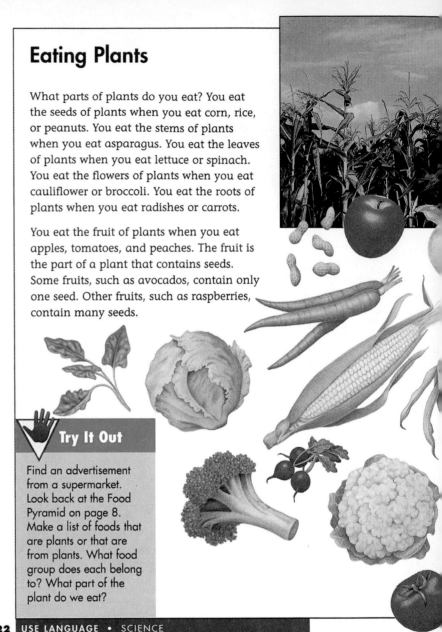

Find an advertisement from a supermarket. Look back at the Food Pyramid on page 8. Make a list of foods that are plants or that are from plants. What food group does each belong to? What part of the plant do we eat?

22 USE LANGUAGE • SCIENCE

Options for Reaching All Students

Beginning

Math: Calculate the Cost of Food

Have students plan menus for a week of lunches for themselves and create a list of the foods they would need to buy. Then have them use supermarket ads to calculate the cost of their lunches or ask them to visit a supermarket to research food prices firsthand. You can simplify the activity by having some students plan and price a single lunch.

Advanced

Language: Make an Advertising Poster

Have students make a poster about their favorite fruit or vegetable. The poster should convince people to eat that food. Suggest they include information on ways that the food can be prepared and on its nutritional value. Encourage students to use both logical and emotional arguments to persuade. Brainstorm a list of persuasive words.

Mixed Ability

Health: Analyze Eating Habits

Ask students to list, using words and/or pictures, all the foods they eat in one day. Then have them circle the foods from plants and underline the foods from animals. Have them determine if they eat more food from plants or from animals. Discuss the results and compare them to the suggestions of the Food Pyramid on page 8 in the Student Book.

Make a chart. Write the names of the plants you eat for a week. Write each name under the correct column. Do you eat the seeds, stems, leaves, flowers, roots, or fruit of the plant?

The Plant Parts I Eat Every Day

	Seeds	Stems	Leaves	Flowers	Roots	Fruits
Monday						
Tuesday						
Wednesday						
Thursday						
Friday						
Saturday						
Sunday						

Write About It

What parts of plants do you eat the most often? What parts of the plants do you like the best?

Language Awareness

Grammar
Count and Noncount Nouns

ACTIVITY BOOK

Write the following sentences on the board:

Carrots are roots.
Spinach is a leaf.
Broccoli is a flower.

Tell students that some things, such as carrots, are easy to count. The names for such things are made plural in most cases by adding *-s* or *-es*. Other things, such as broccoli, are not easy to count. The names for those things do not have a plural form. Present spelling rules for plural forms: for nouns ending in *-y*, the *y* is changed to *i* and then *-es* is added; nouns ending in *-sh*, *-ch*, *-s*, or *-x*, and some nouns ending in *o*, have plurals with *-es*. Use Activity Book page 15.

Assess

Use the questions in Write About It for assessment. Students should be able to

- name edible parts of plants

LOOK **AHEAD**

In the next section, students will learn about the numbered sequences in which some plant parts grow.

Multicultural Connection
Research a Culture

Have students work in groups to research the importance of particular food plants to cultures around the world. Possible choices include rice, corn, potatoes, and coconuts. Ask students to prepare a brief report on topics such as places where the plant is a major crop and how it is used. Brainstorm ways students might locate appropriate information.

Home Connection
Plan a Healthy Menu

Have students work with an adult at home to plan a week of dinners for the family. Encourage students to include dishes from their home countries while keeping in mind the information in the Food Pyramid on page 8. Have students decorate their menus with drawings of the dishes. Create a bulletin board display with the results.

Writer's Workshop
Write About Food

Have students write about a favorite dish made with food from plants. Have them create webs of sensory words to describe how the dish looks, smells, and tastes. Then have them write a paragraph about their dish and edit it for grammar, punctuation, and spelling.

Connect

Activate Prior Knowledge

Think About Patterns

Write the following sequences on the board and have students tell or write the missing numbers:

2, 4, 6, __, 10

1, 4, 7, 10, __

5, 9, 13, __, 21

2, 4, 7, 11, __, 22

Discuss the patterns in each series. Have students who answered correctly explain how they determined their answers. The missing numbers are 8, 13, 17, 16.

Develop Language and Concepts

Present Pages 24 and 25

ACTIVITY BOOK

Read the text with students. After students substitute the correct numbers for the question marks in the Fibonacci sequence, write the sequence on the board in this way:

1, 1, 2, 3, 5, 8, 13, 21

Help students see that the equation for 21 is (13 + 8) and that the next number in the sequence would be 34 (21 + 13).

Help students complete the Think About It. The Fibonacci sequence answers are (1) the number 21 is missing; (2) the numbers 21 and 233 are missing and 375 should be 377. The non-Fibonacci sequence answers are (1) 47, numbers are sum of the previous two; (2) 45, each increment increases by one; (3) 255, each increment is doubled. Use Activity Book page 17.

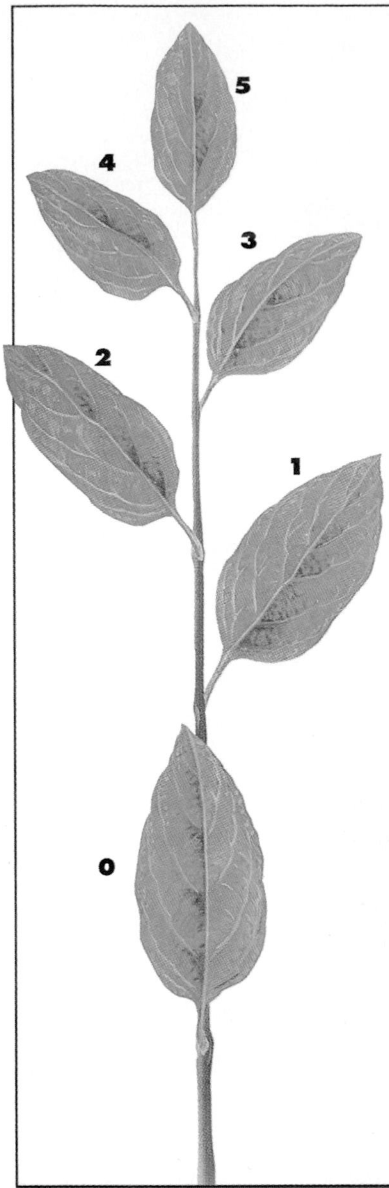

Numbers in Plants

In 1225, an Italian mathematician named Leonardo Fibonacci developed a series of numbers. The series is called the Fibonacci sequence. The series of numbers starts with two 1s. Each number following is the sum of the two numbers before it.

Here is the start of the Fibonacci sequence. Can you fill in the missing numbers?

1	
1	(0 + 1)
2	(1 + 1)
3	(2 + 1)
5	(3 + 2)
8	(5 + 3)
?	(8 + 5)
?	(? + 8)

What do these numbers have to do with plants?

The leaves of some plants grow in Fibonacci sequences. Find a plant in which the leaves grow out of the stem. Find two leaves directly above one another. Count the leaves. Count the bottom leaf as zero. Stop counting at the top leaf. The number is a Fibonacci number.

Options for Reaching All Students

Beginning

Math: Draw a Graph

Bring in pods of fresh beans or peas (usually available in the produce section of the supermarket). Give several pods to each student. On the board (as a group) or on paper (individually), have students graph the number of seeds per pod. Then decide which number of seeds occurs the most and which occurs the least.

Advanced

Math: Create a Sequence

Have students create a number sequence and name it for themselves (for example, *1, 2* ([1 x 1] + 1), *5* ([2 x 2] +1), *26* ([5 x 5] + 1), and so on). Ask them to demonstrate the series and to challenge others to complete part of it.

Mixed Ability

Language: Describe Position

Choose an object in the classroom and use position words to give clues to its identity. *It's on top of the desk. It's next to the eraser.* and so on. Give one clue at a time until students guess which object it is. Then have students take turns using position words to describe and guess other objects in the classroom.

The seeds on a sunflower grow in two sets of spirals. There are usually 21 spirals that grow in one direction, and 34 that grow in the other direction. These are Fibonacci numbers.

When you count parts on many other plants, the numbers are in the Fibonacci sequence.

Think About It

What is wrong in the following Fibonacci sequences?

1, 1, 2, 3, 5, 13, 34, 55

1, 1, 2, 3, 5, 8, 13, 34, 55, 89, 144, 375, 610

Continue these sequences.

1, 3, 4, 7, 11, 18, 29, ___

1, 3, 6, 10, 15, 21, 28, 36, ___

1, 3, 7, 15, 31, 63, 127, ___

Language Awareness

Vocabulary
Position Words

ACTIVITY BOOK

Write this on the board:

Find two leaves directly above one another.

Ask students which word in the sentence tells where one thing is in relation to another. Underline *above*. Use classroom items to demonstrate these position words: *below, in front of, in back of, on top of, at the bottom of, inside*. Have students make up sentences with position words. Use Activity Book page 16.

FYI Leonardo Fibonacci

Fibonacci was the first great mathematician of the Middle Ages. He helped introduce the mathematics of India and Arabia to Europe.

Assess ✓

Use class discussion for assessment. Students should be able to

- explain how Fibonacci numbers relate to plants

LOOK **AHEAD**

In the next section, students will read about an American folk hero who planted apple seeds.

Connect

Activate Prior Knowledge

Think About Heroes

Show students a comic book about Superman or another superhero. Start a discussion about heroes by asking questions such as the following:

- What makes a hero?
- Why is Superman called a hero?

Have students name heroes, real or fictional, with whom they are familiar. Write the names on the board. Ask what traits all heroes have in common.

Introduce the Selection

Have students preview the pictures on pages 26 through 29. Have students use this information, plus their background knowledge to make predictions about the selection. Ask questions such as the following:

- What can you tell about the man?
- Where do you think the story takes place?
- When do you think the story takes place?

Read the Selection

RED TAPE

Read the selection with students. Then read it again, presenting the Reader's Tips.

Play the taped version of the selection on Side 1 of the Red Tape several times. Invite students to listen to the selection as often as they wish.

Language Awareness

Spelling

Capitalization of Place Names

On the board, write the following examples: *United States, Ohio, Illinois.* Underline each capital letter. Explain to students that specific place names are always capitalized in English. Ask students to find other place names on pages 26 through 29. Then have students suggest more place names and tell you which letters to capitalize as you write the terms on the board. You can prompt responses by suggesting common noun categories, such as rivers, states, cities, and so on.

Model a Strategy

Make Inferences

Model making inferences while reading:

When I read a story, I look for details that help me understand the characters. For example, on page 27, the story says that Jonathan Chapman wore a gunnysack coat and a stewpot hat. He ate mush for dinner and rarely wore shoes. From these details, I can infer that Jonathan Chapman had very simple needs, was not interested in material possessions, and probably did not care what people thought of him.

Options for Reaching All Students

Beginning

Language: Recognize Words

PICTURE CARDS

Distribute the following Picture Cards: 2 (apple), 17 (coat), 18 (cook), 21 (cry), 27 (eat), 36 (house), 70 (tree). Review the words. Have students skim the story to find them. Then have students listen to the tape and raise their cards when they hear the same, or nearly the same, word.

Advanced

Language: Research Report

Have students work in small groups to write and illustrate Apple Facts booklets. Encourage students to include information about varieties of apples; places where apples are commercially grown; nutritional information; and songs, poems, and sayings about apples. Model how to take notes from source information.

Cooperative Language Experience

Describe Types of Apples

Bring to class several types of apples. Have students compare and contrast their colors and sizes. Then cut open the apples so that students can taste each one. Ask them to discuss the tastes and textures. Have students ask each other questions to clarify their comments and observations.

The Story of Johnny Appleseed

by Meridel Le Sueur

It was lonely making America. It was a big, big country. It was a deep, wide country. And there were no apple trees, no big round apples, no little bright, tart apples. No apples at all!

It would have been very sad, but there was a man who thought it would be very lonely making America without any apple trees blooming early in the spring, without red apples hanging on the trees in Ohio, Illinois, and Iowa, in the frosty fall. This man's name was Jonathan Chapman.

Reader's Tip
Jonathan Chapman was born in 1774 in Massachusetts (in the eastern part of the United States). Jonathan Chapman decided to travel and plant apple trees in the West. Over the years, people told many stories about this folk hero called "Johnny Appleseed."

My grandmother in Ohio saw him going by her house in the spring, in the fall. The geese flying in a wedge in the sky looked down and saw him traveling along, wearing his gunnysack coat, his books stuffed in the front of it, and on his head his stewpot hat to keep him cool in the heat of the day. When night came, he cooked his mush in it. He never wore any shoes if he could help it.

Strategy Tip
Use Pictures for Meaning
The story tells about the kind of clothes that Johnny wore. You can use the picture on the page to help you understand the words.

Strategy Tip
Locate Places
Find the states named in the story on a map. People from the East were beginning to move west in large numbers during the 1800s. Locating places should help you understand the story better.

Jonathan Chapman was a lean and lonesome man who loved apples. He was a man who never threw an apple core away in his life. When he was a young man, he was walking in Pennsylvania. Beyond was the wilderness.

Jonathan stopped to get something to eat and he heard a child crying from a covered wagon which was going on into the wilderness.

The child was crying to his mother, "I don't want to go. I want to stay here."

The child's mother was angry. She said, "You can't stay here. Your father is going west. And you must go west too."

The child cried, "I don't want to leave the apple trees."

Reader's Tip
When settlers moved out west, they put everything they owned into a wagon. They covered the top of the wagon with canvas to hold everything in and protect it. They used horses or oxen to pull these covered wagons.

Connect

Develop Language and Concepts

Present Pages 30 Through 33

Have students retell the story to this point. List on the board all the facts that they can tell about Johnny Appleseed.

Model a Strategy

Recognize Cause and Effect

Model how tracking cause and effect can improve reading comprehension:

When I read, I find that keeping track of causes and effects helps me see how events are related to each other. For example, because of his meeting with the crying child, Jonathan Chapman decides to plant apple trees throughout the wilderness. And because of his promise to the child, Jonathan decides to pick the apple seeds from the piles of apple mash. Connecting causes and effects helps me understand what happens in a story and why.

Some special needs students may benefit from making or viewing simple cause → effect diagrams such as:

Chapman sees crying child. → *Chapman decides to plant trees.*

Language Awareness

Language Function

Expressing Intention with *going to* or *will*

Have a student read aloud Johnny Appleseed's words on pages 30 to 33. Point out that in many cases, Johnny uses the words *will* or *going to* to state a promise or a plan of his. Highlight the comments that express intention:

I will plant thousands of tiny seeds.
I am going to fill this sack.
I am going to follow the covered wagons.
I am going to plant them.

Ask students to create statements that use phrases such as *I will* and *I am going* toto express intention. Have them discuss their plans for the week, for the next year, and for their future studies. Demonstrate how orally stressing *will* or *going to* makes the speaker sound very determined.

Teachable Moment

Infer Character from Action

Explain to students that people's actions tell a great deal about their characters. For example, Jonathan Chapman's reaction to the crying child tells us that he is kind and compassionate. In contrast, when the man laughs at Jonathan for gathering apple seeds, he reveals himself as mean and short sighted.

Options for Reaching All Students

Beginning

Social Studies: Use a Map

Have students locate Illinois, Indiana, and Kentucky on a map. Compare those states' locations with that of Pennsylvania, where Jonathan meets the crying child. Reread the text on page 31. Then have students draw pictures of the wilderness described in the text.

Advanced

Writing: Point of View

Have students rewrite the scene with the crying child or the events at the cider mill from Jonathan Chapman's point of view. Remind students that the personal pronoun *I* is always capitalized, whereas the pronouns *me, my,* and *mine* are not. Students can exchange drafts and give one another feedback for revisions.

Home Connection

Create an Apple Festival

Bring to class a variety of fresh apples, dried apples, applesauce, apple juice, and other apple products. Encourage students to bring in favorite fruit dishes or beverages from home to share with the class. Have students display the food and make labels for each dish. Invite family members or another class to the festival.

Strategy Tip
Understand Character
What do you learn about Johnny when he tells the child not to cry?

Jonathan said to the crying child, "I love apple trees too. They are my children. I love apples because they have such kind hearts. The trees are so generous. A tree has not one blossom but thousands. If God made no other fruit but the apple, His work would have been well done. Don't cry, child. I will plant thousands of tiny seeds in the wilderness where you are going, in Illinois, in Indiana, in Kentucky, and the apple trees will spring up and bloom in the spring."

So the child stopped crying and smiled at Jonathan and waved from the back of the covered wagon as they went into the wilderness, into the land of the Indian and the snake, of the buffalo and the deep grass.

The land that had no apple trees.

Language Tip
Vocabulary
A *cider mill* is a place where apples are crushed to press out their juice. *Cider* is a drink that is made from the apple juice. *Apple mash* is the crushed part of the apple.

Jonathan was standing by a cider mill. He saw big piles of apple mash and in the mash were all the tiny brown apple seeds. He had a bright idea.

Jonathan got a sack and sat down and began to pick each seed out of the apple mash and put it into the sack.

A man came along and said, "What are you doing?"

Jonathan said, "I am going to fill this sack with apple seeds."

The man said, "And what are you going to do with a sack of apple seeds?"

"I am going to follow the covered wagons out of town toward the sun," Jonathan said. "I am going to plant them. The soil must be good there and the children are crying for apples."

And the man laughed. "What an idea, carrying seed like a bird!"

Connect

Develop Language and Concepts

Present Pages 34 Through 37

ACTIVITY BOOK

Have students retell the story to this point. After they read the story, have them complete Activity Book page 18.

Model a Strategy

Visualize Story Details

Model how to visualize details in a story:

The descriptions in the text help me "see" certain details in my mind, just as pictures do. As I read, I picture Johnny walking through the forest with the animals looking at him. I picture the children running to Johnny as he walks through their small villages with wooden houses.

Language Awareness

Grammar

Past Tense

Point out that the verbs in the story describe events that happened in the past. On pages 34 and 35, call students' attention to *gathered, laughed, answered, was called, told, ran, came, saw,* and *knew.* Review the present tense forms of those verbs. Ask students to retell the story of Johnny Appleseed in the past tense.

FYI More About Johnny Appleseed

The seeds that Jonathan Chapman planted helped build the orchards of the Midwest. Chapman also planted the seeds of many healing herbs such as catnip, horehound, and pennyroyal. He died of pneumonia in 1845 while visiting an orchard in Indiana.

Response Activities

Personal Response

Ask students if they think Jonathan Chapman was a hero. Encourage them to explain their responses. Then ask who their personal heroes are and why.

Critical Response

Ask students what "The Story of Johnny Appleseed" tells them about U.S. history. Encourage them to draw conclusions about the settlers' living conditions, the landforms and animals of the Midwest, methods of transportation, important tools, and the role of individuality.

Creative Response

Have students create their own heroes. Ask them to describe their hero's appearance, character, and heroic acts. Encourage them to draw pictures of their heroes in action.

Options for Reaching All Students

Beginning

Geography: Use Directions

Post signs for *north, south, east,* and *west* on classroom walls. Have students use the signs to refer to classroom objects and people by indicating their direction (for example, "The desks on the north side" or "The students at the south table"). Give pre-productive students instructions involving these directions (for example, "sit at the south table").

Advanced

History: Research Folk Heroes

Have small groups of students research other American folk heroes, such as Calamity Jane (Martha Canary), Davy Crockett, John Henry, Casey Jones, and Annie Oakley. Encourage students to distinguish legend from reality. Have them present their findings to the class orally. Remind them to speak loudly and clearly.

Multicultural Connection

Folk Heroes from Other Cultures

Have students ask adults at home to tell them about folk heroes from their native lands. Have students write short stories or draw pictures about these heroes.

Strategy Tip
Stop and Think
How did Johnny Appleseed get his name?

Others had gathered by this time, and they were all laughing at Jonathan squatting in the mash, putting apple seeds into a sack.

"Ho!" they laughed. "Look! What's your name?"

"Johnny," he answered them.

"Ho!" the men laughed. "Johnny Appleseed!"

So that was what he was called after that, my grandmother told me—Johnny Appleseed.

The children ran out, when he came into the village clearings in the wilderness, shouting, "Here comes Johnny Appleseed."

The deer came with him to the edge of the forest and said, "Good-bye, Johnny Appleseed."

The little round eyes of the robin, the wren, the marsh birds and the swans saw him walking with his pack of apple seeds on his back and they knew Johnny Appleseed was going by.

Strategy Tip
Series
A series is a list of words joined by the word *and*. Often the words in a series are related. All the words in this series are names of birds.

Language Tip
Vocabulary
People use a shovel to dig, an ax to cut trees, and a hoe to prepare the ground for planting seeds.

Study Tip
Understand Character
In many stories, characters' actions tell you about the kinds of person they are. Other peoples' reactions to a character also give clues to a character's personality.

He followed the sun every day, lying down in the fields at night; rising, walking west with the sun. And on his back he carried a gunnysack, and in the sack thousands of apple seeds went with him, which would be great trees along the valley by the time you were born.

And all the animals knew, all the birds and the buffalo and the deer and the bear knew that he carried a shovel, an axe, and a hoe, but never a gun.

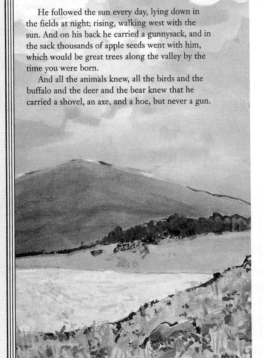

My grandmother, too, told me that he never carried a gun. My grandmother said that he was the friend of all the beasts and birds of America.

It was early spring in Licking Creek, Ohio, my grandmother said, when she first saw Johnny Appleseed coming through the forest with his pack of apple seeds in a sack over his shoulder.

He was tall, she said, skinny, with long black hair falling to his bony shoulders. But it was the eyes, she said, you couldn't forget.

Connect

Activate Prior Knowledge

Brainstorm Vocabulary

Lead students to see how varied salads can be by asking them to name foods that are found in salads. Show pictures from cookbooks to prompt responses.

Develop Language and Concepts

Present Page 38

Bring the ingredients and cooking tools for Waldorf salad to class. Read the recipe with students. Help them understand the quantities of each ingredient. Have students name the cooking tools and containers needed. Then guide two or three students as they demonstrate how to prepare the salad. As students prepare the salad, repeat and reinforce the names of the cooking tools and ingredients with the rest of the class.

Language Awareness

Spelling
Punctuation

Have students find the end punctuation marks of period, question mark, and exclamation mark on page 38 and briefly explain their functions. Help students read aloud sentences with different ending punctuation, using intonation to distinguish between marks.

Recipe for Waldorf Salad

This famous salad was first made at the Waldorf Astoria Hotel in New York City. It is very tasty, and it is made with apples!

Serves 6

1 pound of apples (red and green)
2 tablespoons lemon juice
3 stalks celery, chopped
1/2 cup walnuts, chopped
1/2 cup mayonnaise
Salt and pepper

Wash and cut the apples. Slice them into a bowl. Add the celery, walnuts, lemon juice, and mayonnaise. Season with salt and pepper. Then mix. Keep the salad in the refrigerator until you are ready to serve it. (Mayonnaise can spoil easily if it is not kept cold.)

Talk About It

Which food groups are in a Waldorf Salad? Is it a healthful choice for a snack? Why or why not?

38 CONNECT LANGUAGE • SCIENCE/READING

Options for Reaching All Students

Beginning

TPR: Pantomime

TPR

As you read the recipe, have students pantomime the following actions: washing an apple, slicing an apple, chopping celery and nuts, mixing ingredients together, eating a salad. Encourage them to describe their actions: *We're washing an apple.*

Advanced

Language: Create Recipes

Give students grocery ads and magazines, and have them cut out pictures of a variety of foods. Place the clippings in a paper bag. Then ask each student to draw out five or six pictures and use them to create an imaginary salad. Encourage students to think of creative names for their salads. Have students write out their recipes and read them aloud.

Mixed Ability

Language: Recipes

Have students work in pairs and demonstrate making favorite recipes or simple ones they find in books as if they were cooks on television. Students can pantomime actions as they speak, or, if feasible, they could actually prepare a dish. If possible, videotape students' presentations.

Tell what you learned.

CHAPTER 2

1. Draw a flower. Label the four main parts. Tell what each part of the flower does.
2. Describe the life cycle of a flowering plant.
3. Do you think Johnny Appleseed was a hero? Why or why not?
4. What is the most interesting fact you learned about plants? What else would you like to learn about plants?

Assess √

Activity 1: Make sure students label the *sepal, petals, stamen,* and *pistil* and identify their functions.

Activity 2: Evaluate students' responses to see if they understand the sequence of the life cycle of plants.

Activity 3: Check that students support their reasoning with information from the story.

Activity 4: Check for an understanding of plants' life cycles, structure, or nutritional value.

Have students complete the Chapter Self-Assessment, Blackline Master 31. Have students choose the product of one of the activities to place in their portfolios. Add the results of any rubrics, checklists, self-assessments, or portfolio assessments, Blackline Masters 2–18 and 31.

Listening Assessment

BLACKLINE MASTER

Make sure each student has a copy of Blackline Master 43 from the Teacher's Resource Book. Play the tape several times and have students mark the items.

WHITE TAPE

See Chapter 2 Resources, page T1d, for the Listening Assessment tapescript.

Options for Assessment

Vocabulary Assessment

Personal Word Bank

Have students of mixed abilities work in groups of three. Ask one student in each group to write the following categories on a sheet of paper: *Plant Parts, Life Cycle of Plants, Plants That Are Food.* Have students pass the paper around so that each person can list words in the categories. Give students a time limit. Then decide which group listed the most words over all and in each category.

Writing Assessment

Create a Book

Have students create a picture book about the life cycle of plants and the plants they eat. Have students begin the writing process by determining what information they will put on each page. Allow students to illustrate their books with original drawings or with pictures from magazines. Each picture should be accompanied by an explanatory caption.

Language Assessment

BLACKLINE MASTER

Use Blackline Master 42 in the Teacher's Resource Book.

Standardized Test Practice

ACTIVITY BOOK

Use Activity Book pages 20 and 21. Answers: **1.** (2+3) **2.** 13

Wrap-Up

Activities

Leaves of Language

Instruct students to cut leaves of all shapes and sizes from colored construction paper. Have them write English words they learned in the unit on one side, and the translation into their home languages on the other side. Students may need to work with family members or a dictionary to translate scientific vocabulary.

Plant Product Chart

Have students make large pictorial charts that describe one plant and its products. Have students show a picture (drawing or photo) of the plant growing and the products that come from it. Encourage them to include uses of plants for other than food; for example, cotton for cloth, and rice for paper. Have them label their charts. Visually impaired students may supply verbal descriptions of their chosen plants instead of pictures.

An Abundant Garden

Collect catalogues from nurseries. Include flower, fruit, and vegetable catalogues. If possible, also collect the pictures from bags of seeds. You might also be able to locate images on the Internet or a gardening CD-ROM. Have students cut out pictures of the plants that would grow in the area where you live. Have students arrange the pictures into a "garden" and label the plants.

Discussing the Theme

Have students work in small groups to discuss what they have learned about the changes that occur in both plants and human beings as they progress through the cycles of life. Choose from the following activities to show students how much they have learned, how the information gives them a new perspective on their growth experiences, and how they can apply the concepts and language of the unit to their everyday lives.

- Have students tape-record a list of new words learned.
- Have students draw or find pictures that represent words they have learned. Divide the bulletin board into two sections, and have students work in small groups to label the pictures and place them on one half of the bulletin board.
- Have students draw or find pictures of ideas that are related to the ideas discussed in the chapter. (For example, a drawing of a puppy and a dog, or a tractor in a field of corn.) Encourage students to be creative, for they may find connections where they do not expect them. Place these pictures on the other half of the bulletin board.
- Discuss with students that there are contemporary tree-planting projects such as the one Johnny Appleseed completed during his lifetime. Help them research such projects in the community. Encourage them to plant a tree or a plant in their own home environments. You might want to find out where and when local Arbor Day activities take place.
- Have small groups of students exchange memories and stories about the experience of growing up in their home countries. Encourage them to compare their experiences with those of other students.

Sharing the Project

Use the invitation form, Blackline Masters 32 and 33, to invite family members to school for a visit to the "Garden of Change."

Use the projects created during the unit to transform the classroom as much as possible. For example, scatter the "leaves of language" from the Wrap-Up on the floor. Have students hang their family trees and arrange their drawings of models of plants around the classroom according to the countries in which they grow.

To offer refreshments, ask volunteers to bring native foods from their home countries to share. Suggest that they prepare dishes that use a part of a plant. Have them identify the part of the plant they used and put the name of the dish on a card. For beverages, serve apple cider and apple juice. Be sure the ingredients of all refreshments are displayed to alert visitors with food allergies or dietary restrictions.

Signs of Success!

Duplicate a copy of this checklist for each student.

Name: ____

Refer to the checklist below for a quick determination of how a student is progressing toward transitioning out of ESL instruction.

Objectives

Discuss factors that influence growth

- ☐ Names physical characteristics family members share
- ☐ Describes the human growth spurt
- ☐ Tells how heredity influences growth
- ☐ Names foods from the different groups
- ☐ Describes the parts and life cycle of a plant
- ☐ Tells how plants and animals are interdependent
- ☐ Identifies parts of plants that people can eat

Language Awareness

Understands/Uses:

- ☐ comparatives
- ☐ present tense: *has/have, is/are*
- ☐ plural forms
- ☐ possessive adjectives
- ☐ superlatives
- ☐ opposites
- ☐ words that describe
- ☐ count and noncount nouns
- ☐ position words
- ☐ capitalization of place names
- ☐ expressing intention with *going to* or *will*
- ☐ past tense
- ☐ punctuation

Hears/Pronounces/Reads:

- ☐ initial consonant *p*, consonant blends *pl* and *pr*

Learning Strategies

- ☐ Understands key words
- ☐ Uses a chart
- ☐ Understands directions
- ☐ Uses pictures for meaning
- ☐ Follows a sequence
- ☐ Makes inferences
- ☐ Recognizes cause and effect
- ☐ Visualizes story details

Comments

____

Planning Guide

CHAPTER 3

Changing Weather

Objectives

Name kinds of weather.

Tell what makes weather change.

Tell how we know that air has weight.

Tell what causes storms.

Use weather idioms and sayings.

Vocabulary Focus

Kinds of weather, such as *cold, stormy, windy.*
Weather words, such as *air mass, dry, humid.*
Words about storms, such as *air pressure, low pressure area, front.*
Weather idioms and sayings, such as *raining cats and dogs.*

Lesson	Content Focus	Language Awareness Objectives	Learning Strategies
Preview pp. 40–41 Tell what you know.			
Present pp. 42–43 What makes the weather change?	Science	**Grammar** Conjunctions *and* and *or*	
Practice pp. 44–45 Does air have weight?	Science	**Grammar** Imperatives	Follow directions.
Practice pp. 46–47 Air Pressure and Storms	Science	**Grammar** Present Tense	Track cause and effect.
Connect pp. 48–49 Weather Idioms and Sayings	Science/ Language Arts	**Grammar/Spelling** Adjectives That End in *-y*	Infer word meaning.
Connect pp. 50–57 *Why the Monsoon Comes Each Year*	Science/ Literature	**Grammar** Pronouns *He, She, They* **Grammar** Past Tense	Understand story elements. Read on to get meaning.
Connect p. 58 "Lotsa Winds"	Science/ Literature	**Phonics** *ou* and *ow*	
Assess p. 59 Tell what you learned.			

CHAPTER 4

Predicting the Weather

Objectives

Name the ways we get information about weather.

Tell about meteorologists.

Tell about the tools meteorologists use.

Tell who uses weather forecasts.

Read a weather map.

Vocabulary Focus

Ways we get information about weather, such as *newspapers, observation, forecast.*

Weather tools, such as *anemometer, barometer, radar.*

Weather map words, such as *temperature, predict, key.*

Weather forecast words, such as *breezy, overcast, wind speed.*

Lesson	Content Focus	Language Awareness Objectives	Learning Strategies
Preview pp. 60–61 Tell what you know.			
Present pp. 62–63 The Work of Meteorologists	Science	**Grammar** Future with *Will*	Use a graphic organizer.
Practice pp. 64–65 What tools do meteorologists use?	Science	**Grammar** Expression *Use (It) To*	Understand specialized vocabulary.
Practice pp. 66–67 Who uses weather forecasts?	Science	**Grammar** Clauses with *So* to Express Purpose	Recognize text organization.
Connect pp. 68–69 You can measure wind speed.	Science/Math	**Grammar** *There Is/There Are*	
Connect pp. 70–73 Reading Weather Maps, A Stormy Weather Forecast	Science/ Reading	**Grammar** Future with *Going To*	Use a map key.
Connect pp. 74–75 "Weather"/"Raindrop"	Science/ Literature	**Phonics** The Letter *l*	
Connect p. 76 "Good Day Sunshine"	Science/ Literature	**Phonics** Long *a*	
Assess p. 77 Tell what you learned.			

Resources

Chapter 3

Support Materials

ACTIVITY BOOK — Pages 22–31

DISK — Writer's Notebook

ORANGE TAPE — Side 1: *Why the Monsoon Comes Each Year,* pages T50–T57

Side 2: "Lotsa Winds," page T58

LET'S TALK CARD — 96 cards to start conversations.

STORYTELLING — Storytelling Anthology: *Worlds Together*

Phonics

PHONICS — *Newcomer Phonics,* pages 47, 55, 85–86

Assessment Materials

BLACKLINE MASTER — Language Assessment, Blackline Master 50

Listening Assessment, Blackline Master 51

WHITE TAPE — Side 1: Listening Assessment, page T59

Listen carefully. The weather forecaster is describing weather conditions in the United States. On the map, write *high* or *low* to show where there high and low pressure areas are. Then write *front* to show where a thunderstorm is expected.

Today we have three air masses over the United States. The high pressure area over the western part of the country has brought cold weather to that region. That cold air mass is moving toward the center of the country.

There is a low pressure area in the center of the country. It has brought warm weather to the central states. But thunderstorms could occur along the front where the cold air mass from the West pushes into the warm air mass over the center of the country.

On the East Coast, we have another high pressure area and cold temperatures. No change in weather is expected on the East Coast today.

Support for Newcomers

Newcomer Book C, Survival language for absolute beginners. For overview, see pages xxviii–xxix.

Newcomer Teacher Suggestion Book, Chapter 3, pages 12–13

HomeLink Penguin Readers

The Call of the Wild

For Extended Reading

El Niño: Stormy Weather for People and Wildlife by Clarion Books, 1998. This introduction to the El Niño current describes what it is, theories about what causes it, and how it disrupts weather all over the world. **Level: Advanced**

Hurricanes: Earth's Mightiest Storms by Patricia Lauber, Scholastic, 1996. Dramatic photos, eyewitness accounts, and scientific facts reveal the power and destruction of hurricanes. **Level: Average**

Lightning! and Thunderstorms by Mike Graf, Simon Spotlight Books, 1998. What happens when a plane is hit by lightning? Questions like this one are answered in a book that is full of facts, personal accounts, and safety tips. **Level: Average**

Looking at Weather by David Suzuki and Barbara Hehner, John Wiley & Sons, 1991. This book describes how weather changes and how it affects people's lives, and includes safe and exciting experiments and activities. **Level: Beginning**

Tornadoes Can Make It Rain Crabs: Weird Facts About the World's Worst Disasters by Melvin Berger and Gilda Berger, Scholastic, 1997. A collection of strange facts about natural disasters. **Level: Advanced**

The Weather Sky by Bruce McMillan, Farrar, Straus, & Giroux, Inc., 1991. A study of weather patterns and clouds that occur in the earth's temperate zones. **Level: Average**

Related Technology

Ocean Explorations: El Niño, Tom Snyder Productions, 1997. This interactive software allows students to investigate global weather, focusing on El Niño weather patterns.

Resources

Chapter 4

Support Materials

PICTURE CARDS

Numbers 3, 7, 13, 17, 18, 23, 24, 32, 33, 37, 43, 47, 53, 60, 61, 67, 68, 71

ACTIVITY BOOK

Pages 32–41

ORANGE TAPE

Side 2: "Weather," page T74; "Raindrop," page T75; "Good Day Sunshine," page T76

DISK

Writer's Notebook

Phonics

PHONICS

Newcomer Phonics, pages 30–37

Assessment Materials

BLACKLINE MASTER

Language Assessment, Blackline Master 52

Listening Assessment, Blackline Master 53

WHITE TAPE

Side 2: Listening Assessment, page T77

Listen carefully. Write down the weather forecast. You will hear it once. Then you will hear it again more slowly. Begin to write. Then you will hear it one more time. Check what you wrote.

The weather tomorrow is going to be very bad. It is going to snow all day. The temperature is going to be very cold. It is not going to be a good day to be outside, so stay inside if you can.

Support for Newcomer

Newcomer Teacher Suggestion Book, Chapter 4, pages 14–15

For Extended Reading

Eye of the Storm: Chasing Storms With Warren Faidley by Stephen Kramer, Paperstar, 1999. Incredible photos by storm chaser and photographer Warren Faidley highlight this exiting text. **Level: Advanced**

Janice VanCleave's Weather: Mind-Boggling Experiments You Can Turn Into Science Fair Projects by Janice Pratt VanCleave, John Wiley & Sons, 1995. Experiments and projects help students understand how weather works and how meteorologists predict it. **Level: Average**

The Weather Tracker's Kit by Gregory Aaron, Running Press, 1991. Readers learn what causes different kinds of weather and how to track and forecast weather conditions. **Level: Average**

Weatherwatch by Valerie Wyatt, Addison-Wesley Publishing, 1990. Weather wisdom, fun facts, and activities help readers understand what makes weather and why it changes. **Level: Beginning**

Weather Watch: Forecasting the Weather by Jonathan D. W. Kahl, Lerner Publications, 1996. A history of meteorology and explanation of tools used to develop weather forecasts. **Level: Average**

Related Technology

Compton's Interactive Encyclopedia 1999 Deluxe, Mindscape, 1998. Enriches students' understanding of meteorological research.

Project

Create a Class Weather Center

This optional project can be completed over the next two chapters. Students will be creating a class weather center to measure basic temperature patterns. See the Unit Wrap-Up, page T77a, for more ideas on sharing the project with family members.

What You'll Need

Reference sources: almanacs, encyclopedias, simple books on weather, weather websites

Measuring instruments: anemometer (wind gauge), barometer, rain gauge (or measuring cup), thermometer

Other Materials: local daily newspapers (should be available in class each day), overhead projector, screen, regional map on an overhead transparency, chart paper, poster board, rulers, felt-tipped markers

Strategies You'll Use

- Use reference sources
- Use graphic organizers
- Confirm predictions

Beginning the Project

Designate a corner of the classroom to serve as a simple weather center during the unit. The area should have a window, outside of which the anemometer, barometer, rain gauge, and thermometer can be placed or hung. If there is no appropriate window, an area of the roof or the school grounds might be used instead.

The overhead projector and screen can be set up in the weather center, and the reference sources, daily newspapers, art supplies, and other materials should be readily available on a nearby table or shelves. If your school has Internet access, determine the most convenient way to use it for this project.

Invite students to create and hang a sign reading "Weather Center."

Tell students that in this unit they will participate in activities that will teach them to discuss, measure, record, and predict the weather. They will present the results of these activities at the weather center.

Home Involvement

Send the Letter to the Family, Blackline Masters 44–49, to families, telling them that the class will be studying weather in the weeks to come and that students may be asking family members to share information about weather conditions, as well as stories and folk tales, about weather in their home countries.

Using the Weather Center

Divide students into pairs. Each day partners will check the temperature, air pressure, and amount of rainfall. They will record findings in a weather notebook they keep. Later in the unit, students will be able to add wind speed and direction to these data. In addition, suggested unit activities—such as comparing radio or TV predictions to actual weather, giving special weather reports, graphing a week's temperatures, recording and graphing minimum and maximum temperatures from the newspaper, drawing weather maps, and charting relationships between temperatures and wind speeds—can be presented at the weather center as part of the daily discussion.

Finally, you might want to assign each student a day on which to present a brief oral report on the weather conditions in his or her home country. These could include informative or humorous stories involving weather. Parents and family members could be invited to attend their children's special presentations.

Daily Discussion

Take a few minutes each day to gather the class at the weather center. At this time, each pair of students will report their meteorological readings, commenting, if they wish, on any of the following: how the findings compare to the information reported in the local newspaper or on the local news; how the findings compare to predictions made the previous day; and what they might indicate for the following day's weather.

Next, the designated students may present their reports on weather in their home countries.

As the unit progresses, students will use the center as a forum for presenting their charts, graphs, and special reports. Presentations should become progressively more informed and detailed as students read and study the unit material.

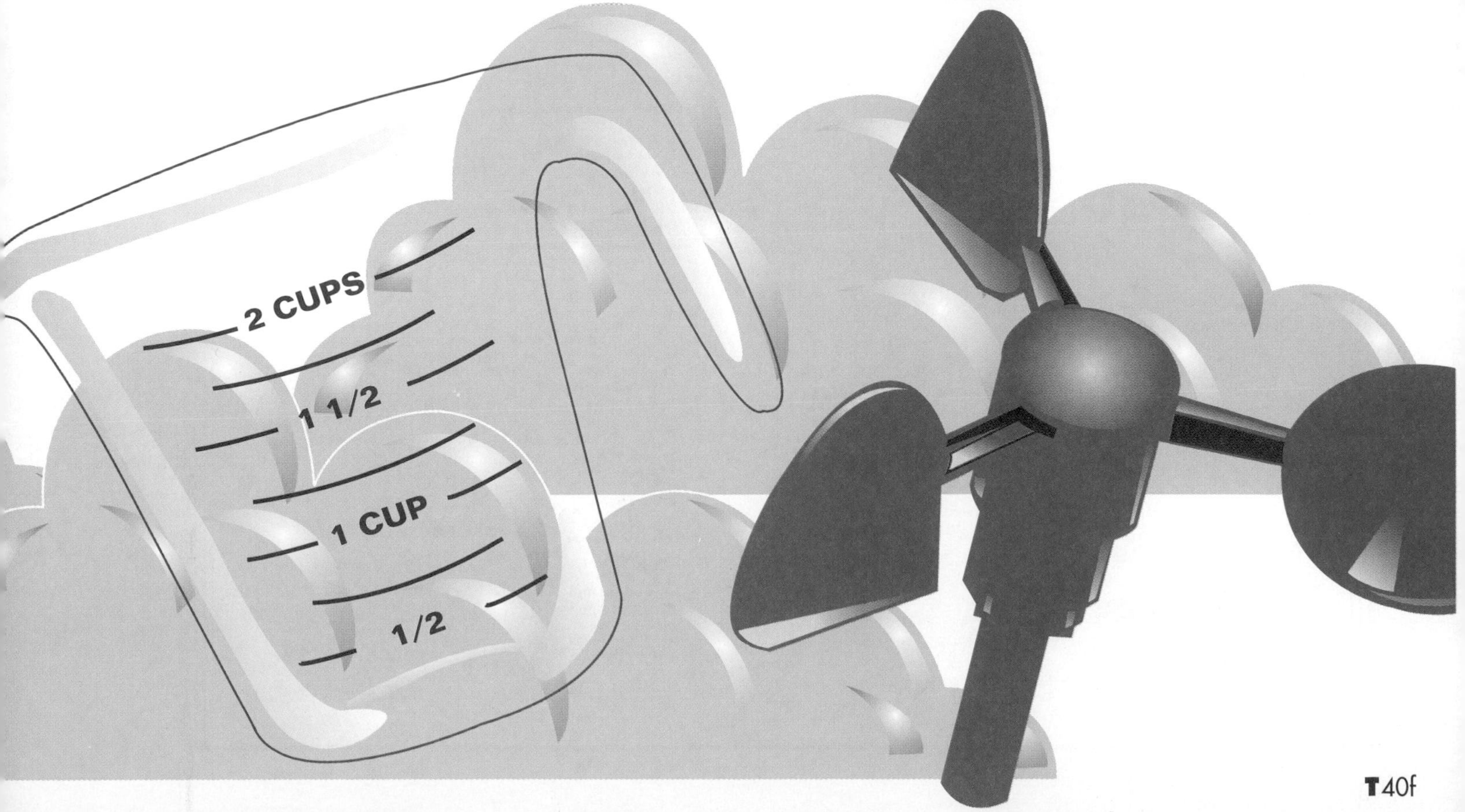

Activity Book Chapter 3

Name ____________________

Air Masses

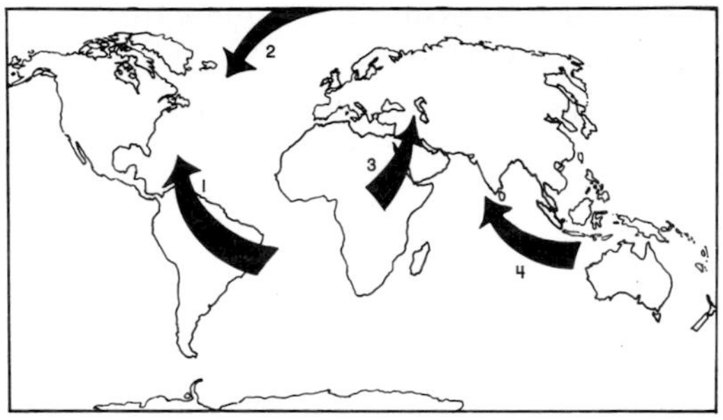

Describe each air mass on the map. Choose from the following combinations. You may use a choice more than once.

hot and dry	cold and dry
hot and humid	cold and humid

1. ___hot and humid___
2. ___cold and humid___
3. ___hot and dry___
4. ___hot and humid___

Now draw an air mass on the map over the area where you live. What kind of air mass is it most likely to be?

___Answers will vary.___

Name ____________________

An Amazing Air Trick

Read the following story.

Yesterday our science teacher, Ms. Fujima, showed us a surprising trick. She used only a sink, a drinking glass, and a paper towel.

First, she filled the sink with water. Next, she crumpled the paper towel into a ball. She pushed the paper towel into the bottom of the glass. Next, she turned the glass upside down and pushed it straight into the sink of water. Then she lifted the glass straight out of the water. When she was done, we studied the results.

What a surprise! The paper towel stayed dry. Ms. Fujima explained that there was air in the glass. The air took up space and kept the water from going into the glass. So the towel did not get wet.

Now rewrite the second paragraph as a numbered list of steps.

Things you need: a sink, a drinking glass, a paper towel

Follow these steps:

1. ___Fill___ the sink with water.
2. ___Crumple___ the paper towel into a ball.
3. ___Push___ the paper towel into the bottom of the glass.
4. ___Turn the glass upside down and push it straight into the sink of water.___
5. ___Lift the glass straight out of the water.___
6. ___Study the results.___

Name ____________________

Describing a Process

Describe what is happening in the pictures. Use the correct forms of the words in the box. You may use some words more than once.

fall	form	push	rise

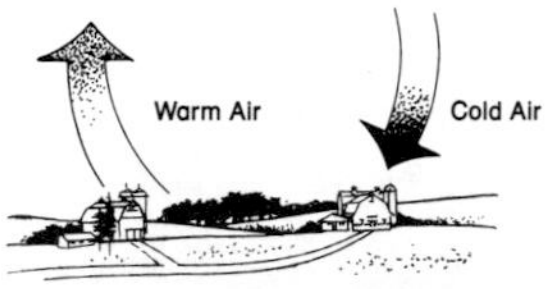

1. Warm air ___rises___.
2. Cold air ___pushes___ down.

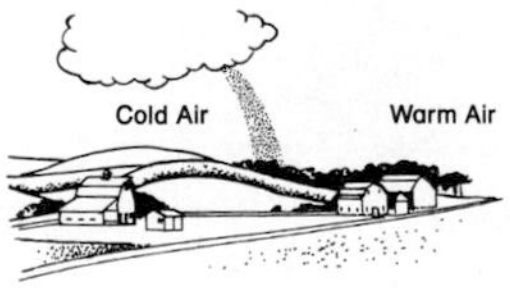

3. A front ___forms___ where two different air masses meet.
4. The cold air mass ___pushes___ into the warm air mass.

5. The warm air ___rises___ very fast.
6. Water in the air ___forms___ clouds.
7. Then the water ___falls___ to the earth as rain.

Name ____________________

Weather Words

Rewrite the sentences using words that end in *-y*.

1. In San Francisco, there is often a lot of fog.
   In San Francisco, it is often ___foggy___.
2. At the top of a high mountain, there is often snow.
   At the top of a high mountain, it is often ___snowy___.
3. Where two different air masses meet, there may be a storm.
   Where two different air masses meet, it may be ___stormy___.
4. When warm air rises and cools, the sky fills with clouds.
   When warm air rises and cools, the sky becomes ___cloudy___.
5. Do you prefer a day when the sun shines or a day when it rains?
   Do you prefer a ___sunny___ day or a ___rainy___ day?

Here are four new idioms with weather words. Can you guess what they mean by studying the words around them? Draw a line from each idiom to its meaning. (Hint: A breeze is a soft wind.)

1. Marta has such a **sunny** personality. She's always happy and in a good mood.
2. Luis **is snowed under.** He has two tests tomorrow and he has to help the science teacher after school.
3. Kim studied hard every day, so she thought the English test was a **breeze.**
4. Stan is very shy. When he goes to a party where he doesn't know many people, he finds it hard to **break the ice.**

- easy
- talk to people he doesn't know
- has a lot of work to do
- cheerful

Name ______________________

A Husband for the Princess

Fill in the blanks to tell the story of Princess Mi Noung. Use the pronouns in the box.

he	she	they

Princess Mi Noung was sad. She was growing old, and she didn't have a husband. Her father, the Emperor, did not like any of her suitors. He wanted Mi Noung to marry a powerful person.

Then one day two suitors came to the palace. They both wanted to marry Mi Noung. The Emperor liked them both. He told them to bring gifts for Mi Noung.

The two suitors left quickly. The Spirit of the Sea went back to the ocean. He got pearls and fish for Mi Noung. The Spirit of the Mountain went back to the mountain. He got jewels and fruit for Mi Noung.

Who would marry the Princess?

Name ______________________

The Battle of the Spirits

Finish telling the story of Princess Mi Noung by filling in the missing words. Use the correct past tense forms of the verbs in parentheses.

The next morning came (come). The Spirit of the Mountain arrived (arrive) first. He showed (show) his gifts. The Emperor liked (like) the gifts. He felt (feel) the Spirit of the Mountain would be a good husband. So he sent (send) Mi Noung off to live with the Spirit of the Mountain.

Then the Spirit of the Sea arrived (arrive) at the palace. When the Spirit of the Sea saw (see) that he was (be) late, he became (become) angry. He started (start) a big storm. The wind blew (blow), the rain fell (fall), and the ocean rose (rise).

The battle between the Spirit of the Sea and the Spirit of the Mountain continued (continue) day and night. The Spirit of the Mountain used (use) magic to make his mountain higher. He took (take) Mi Noung to the very top.

At last the Spirit of the Sea saw (see) that he could not defeat the Spirit of the Mountain. The big storm ended (end). And Mi Noung stayed (stay) with her husband on the high mountain near the sea.

Name ______________________

Who am I?

Characters
Princess Mi Noung
The Emperor
The Spirit of the Sea
The Spirit of the Mountain

Read the descriptions of the characters in the story "Why the Monsoon Comes Each Year." Then write the name of each character by his or her description.

1. I brought the princess perfect pearls and tasty crabs.
   The Spirit of the Sea
2. I have only one daughter, so I want the best for her.
   The Emperor
3. I married the princess and took her off to live in my home.
   The Spirit of the Mountain
4. I finally let my daughter marry a powerful man. But there has been nothing but trouble since then.
   The Emperor
5. I had many suitors, but my father did not like any of them.
   Princess Mi Noung
6. I arrived too late and the princess had already married someone else.
   The Spirit of the Sea
7. I will never give up. I will keep fighting until the princess is my wife.
   The Spirit of the Sea

Name ______________________

Sound Search

Circle each word that contains the vowel sound as in the word sound. Remember, this sound may be spelled *ou* or *ow*.

1. Air is all around the earth. It pushes down on you all the time.
2. Warm air doesn't push down very hard. An area with a warm air mass over it is called a low pressure area.
3. A front forms a boundary between two different air masses. Powerful storms may happen at fronts.
4. Water in the air forms clouds. Then the water falls to earth as rain or snow.
5. We know that rain is important to our survival. Some people hate to go outside when in rains. But they should remember that April showers bring May flowers.

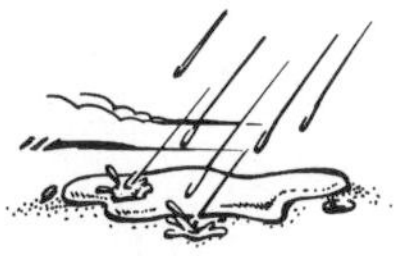

Activity Book

Chapter 4

Name ______________________________

What should I wear?

Read the weather forecasts. Choose clothing to fit with the weather. Use the words in the box. Write your choices on the lines.

boots	hat	shorts	T-shirt
coat	jacket	sunglasses	umbrella
gloves	scarf	sweater	

1. The weather tomorrow will be sunny and hot.

shorts ______ sunglasses ______ T-shirt ______

2. The weather tomorrow will be snowy and cold.

boots ______ coat ______ gloves ______

hat ______ jacket ______ scarf ______

3. Tomorrow will be rainy, windy, and cool.

hat ______ jacket ______ scarf ______

sweater ______ umbrella ______

4. Tomorrow will be breezy and cool. It might rain in the afternoon.

hat ______ jacket ______ scarf ______

sweater ______ umbrella ______

Name ______________________________

What is it used for?

Match the weather tools with how meteorologists use them. Draw lines.

1. Meteorologists use an anemometer

2. Meteorologists use a thermometer

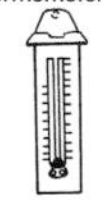

3. Meteorologists use a barometer

4. Meteorologists use a rain gauge

to measure air pressure.

to measure wind speed.

to measure rainfall.

to measure temperature.

Write sentences about why you use gloves, coats, boots, and umbrellas.

1. gloves I use gloves to keep my hands warm.
2. boots I use boots to keep my feet warm.
3. coat I use a coat to keep warm.
4. umbrella I use an umbrella to keep dry.

Name ______________________________

What's the reason?

Complete the sentences. Use the choices in the box.

- so they can protect their crops.
- so they know when it is unsafe to fly and what weather will be like in the air.
- so they can wear the right clothes to keep them warm or cool.
- so they know when to have snow plows ready.
- so they can plan their construction work.
- so they know when to cancel school.

1. People need to know about the weather so they can wear the right clothes to keep them warm or cool.
2. Airports need to know about winter storms so they know when to have snow plows ready.
3. Farmers need to know about the weather so they can protect their crops.
4. Builders need to know about the weather so they can plan their construction work.
5. Pilots need to know about the weather so they know when it is unsafe to fly and what the weather will be like in the air.
6. Schools need to know about the weather so they know when to cancel school.

Name ______________________________

Wind Speed

Use this chart to complete the activity on pages 68 and 69 in the Student Book.

My Record

Date	Wind Speed

Name

What's the weather going to be?

This is what the weather will be in four cities. Write a weather report for each city.

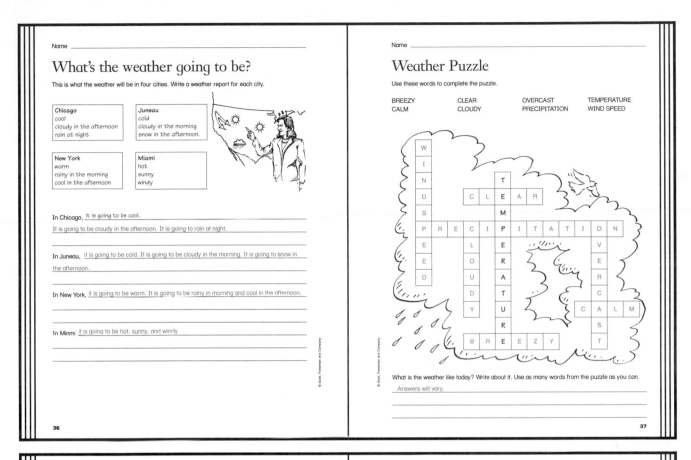

Chicago cool cloudy in the afternoon rain at night	**Juneau** cold cloudy in the morning snow in the afternoon.
New York warm rainy in the morning cool in the afternoon	**Miami** hot sunny windy

In Chicago, it is going to be cool.
It is going to be cloudy in the afternoon. It is going to rain at night.

In Juneau, it is going to be cold. It is going to be cloudy in the morning. It is going to snow in the afternoon.

In New York, it is going to be warm. It is going to be rainy in morning and cool in the afternoon.

In Miami, it is going to be hot, sunny, and windy

Name

Weather Puzzle

Use these words to complete the puzzle.

BREEZY CLEAR OVERCAST TEMPERATURE
CALM CLOUDY PRECIPITATION WIND SPEED

What is the weather like today? Write about it. Use as many words from the puzzle as you can.

Answers will vary.

Name

Weather Patterns

Put weather words in the pictures of the sun, the cloud, and the raindrop to write your own concrete poem.

Ideas:

1. You might fill in the drop with different words about rain.
2. You might write words that tell about your favorite kind of weather.

Name

Long a Sound

The sound of long *a* can be spelled these ways:
say
rain
ate
they

Circle the words with long *a* sounds.

and	(way)
(day)	(pane)
ask	(they)
(make)	(daily)
(rain)	math
ran	(state)

Circle the words with long *a* sounds.

1. One (way) meteorologists study weather is to study the amount of (rain.) (They) also keep track of wind and air pressure.
2. (Hail) and (rain) are forms of water.
3. One (place) in the United (States) got 390 inches of snow in one month.
4. Many people listen to (daily) weather forecasts. It helps them know what kinds of clothes they will need for the next (day.)
5. People who want to be meteorologists (take) courses in math. (They) also study science.
6. Forty-three inches of (rain) fell in one (day) in a town in Texas in 1979.

UNIT 2

Preview

Activate Prior Knowledge

Brainstorm Vocabulary

Start a discussion of the unit topic, weather, by asking students to describe today's weather. For students who are just beginning to speak English, you may present options such as: *Is today sunny or cloudy?* Use pictures, weather maps, symbols, and so on to introduce the words from the Word Bank and help students think of other weather words. Write the words mentioned on the board.

Develop Language and Concepts

Present Pages 40 and 41

Have students examine the photos and read the title and text. Encourage them to use words from the Word Bank when answering the questions on page 40. Record the answers on the board and help students orally summarize class preferences.

Help students use the words in the Word Bank and those they brainstormed earlier to describe the photos. Supply vocabulary as needed: *tornado, drought, flood, snowstorm, hurricane.* Ask students to tell what they know about these and other weather conditions. Invite them to share any personal experiences related to severe or unusual weather conditions. If possible, you might show videotaped footage of severe weather conditions.

Discuss the questions in Talk About It. Have students work in groups of four to prepare lists of "good" and "bad" weather. Remind them to use words from the Word Bank.

UNIT 2 • CHALLENGES

Weather

Word Bank

cold
dry
hot
snowy
stormy
sunny
wet
windy

Tell what you know.

What kind of weather do you like? Why?

What kinds of problems can weather cause?

40

Options for Reaching All Students

Beginning

Art: Illustrate Weather Vocabulary

List the Word Bank words on the board and read them with students. Then have small groups illustrate the words. Encourage them to include people doing weather-related activities and wearing appropriate clothing. Have them use the Word Bank words to label their art.

Advanced

Language: Weather Extremes

Have students talk about the most severe weather they have ever experienced: the hottest, the coldest, the wettest, the driest, the most pleasant, and the worst. Have students use a thesaurus to locate a variety of descriptive words and include intensifiers such as *very* or *really*.

Cooperative Learning

Weather Word Collage

Have students make a collage to illustrate basic weather words that they know or are learning. They can cut pictures from magazines or download them from the Internet, label them, and put them on a bulletin board display. Encourage students to continue to add to the display throughout the study of the unit.

Talk About It

What is the weather like today?

What is the weather usually like on your birthday?

What kind of weather is "bad"?

What kind of weather is "good"?

THEME/KEY CONCEPTS

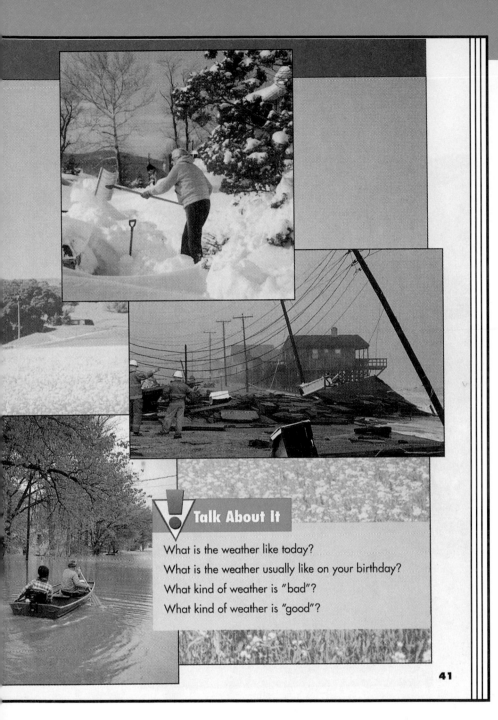

Weather often presents challenges. People have no control over the weather, but they can predict it to some degree and prepare for it.

Chapter 3

- Air masses cause changes in temperature and weather.
- Storms happen when different kinds of air masses meet.

Chapter 4

- Meteorologists, scientists who study the weather, use many tools to collect information.
- Weather forecasts help people make plans and cope with difficult situations.

Multicultural Connection

Science: Compare the Weather

Have students make posters showing the major types of weather in their home countries. Help them find relevant information using an almanac or other reference source. Remind them to use the Word Bank words to describe the weather. Ask them to compare that weather to the weather where they live now. Encourage them to discuss the similarities and differences. (Some students may want to use Venn diagrams to compare and contrast the two sets of weather conditions.) Ask students which weather they prefer and why. Use the posters to create a bulletin board display.

Present

Activate Prior Knowledge
Use Pictures

Show students pictures of tropical beaches and snowy mountains, and help them describe the scenes and the weather. Give beginning learners directions such as: *Point to the place that is cold.*

Develop Language and Concepts
Present Pages 42 and 43

ACTIVITY BOOK Ask students to look at and describe the two regional pictures on page 42 and tell how the air would feel in those areas. Write *dry air, humid (wet) air, cold air, hot air* on the board, and help students use them to tell how the air feels in summer and winter.

Read the text with the students and study the illustration on page 43. Use it to help students understand that air is cold in the polar regions of the far north and south, and hot near the equator, around the center of the earth.

Have students work in small groups to answer the questions in Talk About It. Have them complete Activity Book page 22 for review.

Discuss the difference between climate and weather. Climate is the type of weather a place usually experiences. Help students locate the three basic climate zones: tropical, temperate, and polar. Use diagrams that show the sun and the earth. Help students understand the connection between the angle at which the sun's rays hit the earth and the climate zones.

CHAPTER 3

Changing Weather

What makes the weather change?

Air is all around the earth. The air is hot in some places on the earth and cold in other places. What makes air hot or cold? What makes the weather change? Large bodies of air called **air masses** control changes in the temperature and the weather.

The air above the earth's surface is not the same everywhere. The air above a cold place gets cold and forms a cold air mass. The air above a hot place gets hot and forms a hot air mass. So the air above snow and ice is cold. Is the air above a desert hot or cold?

Options for Reaching All Students

Beginning
TPR: Demonstrate Conjunctions

TPR Give students practice with *and* and *or* by using them in commands that ask students to perform specific actions. Sample commands: *Touch your nose and your ear. Raise your right hand or your left hand. Stand up and turn around.* Modify the directions as necessary for students with motor difficulties.

Advanced
Geography: Hot and Cold Cities

Have students study a globe or world map and make two lists of cities. One list should include cities around the world that often have cold weather. The other list should include cities that often have hot weather. Students can check an almanac or a weather website to get specific temperature data.

Mixed Ability
Language: Weather Debate

Have students debate what areas of the world are the best places to live because of the weather. Suggest students think about the desirability of changing seasons, the possibility of severe weather, and so on. Tell students to plan what they will say, using information and persuasive techniques to make their points.

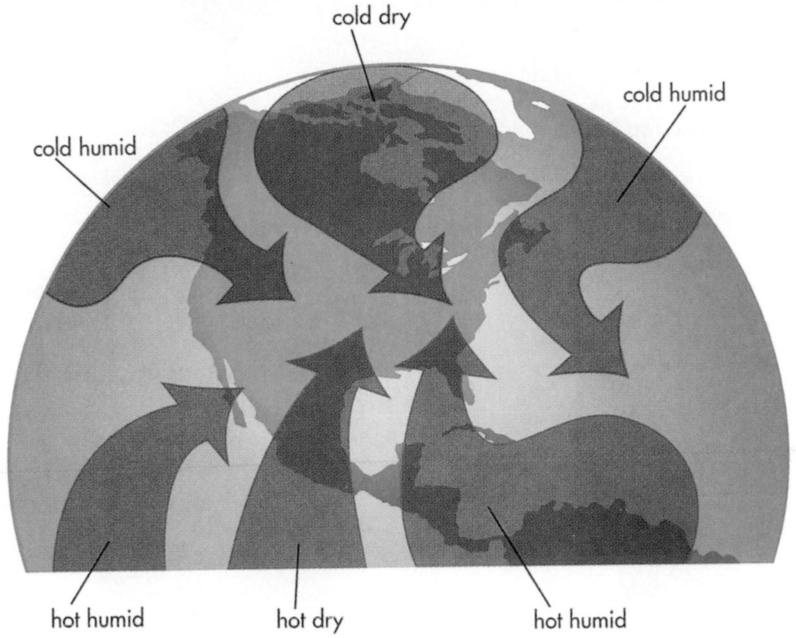

The air in an air mass can be hot or cold. The air in an air mass can also be dry or humid (wet). An air mass that forms above land has mostly dry air. An air mass that forms above water has mostly humid air.

Talk About It

An air mass is forming over your school. Is it hot or cold? Is it dry or humid? Why do you think so?

Language Awareness

Grammar

Conjunctions *and* and *or*

Write the following on the board:

Air above snow and ice is cold.
The air in an air mass can be hot or cold.

Explain that the word *and* is used to tell about two things: both snow and ice are present. In the second sentence, the word *or* is used because the air can be only hot or cold, not both.

Help students create their own sentences like the following to illustrate the difference in use.

I am going to have soup and a sandwich for lunch. I am going to have orange juice or milk for lunch.

Assess

Use the class discussion and Talk About It questions for assessment. Students should be able to

- describe the role of air masses in determining weather

LOOKAHEAD

In the next section, students will do an experiment to determine if air has weight.

Cooperative Language Experience

Field Trip

If feasible, take the class outside on a cloudy day to observe the movement of clouds. When you return, have the class work together to write a language experience story about the shape, color, and movement of the clouds. Ask students to draw pictures to illustrate the story.

Encourage each student to add something to the story, even if it is a single word. Beginning learners or students with other special needs may benefit from being given a cloze sentence to complete.

Practice

Activate Prior Knowledge

Demonstrate

Introduce the concept of weight by having students handle various classroom objects and have them guess which ones are heavier than others. If possible, have a scale available to weigh the objects. Use a pan scale to compare the weights of two objects. Ask students if they think that air has weight. Encourage them to explain their answers.

Develop Language and Concepts

Present Pages 44 and 45

Read the text with the students. Make sure they understand that the point of the experiment is to find out if air has weight. Review each step of the directions. Then divide the class into groups of three or four to perform the experiment. Discuss the questions in Talk About It.

Introduce various systems to measure weight, such as pounds, grams, and kilograms.

Model a Strategy

Follow Directions

Model following directions:

When I must follow instructions for a project, I first read the entire text to get a general idea of what is involved. Then I reread the list of things I need to find out what materials I have to get. Then I carefully reread each step to make sure I know what I have to do.

Does air have weight?

Do this experiment to find out if air has weight.

Things You Need

- string–about 12 to 18 inches (30 to 46 centimeters) long
- ruler–12 inches (about 30 centimeters) long
- two balloons–exactly the same size
- tape (clear)

Follow these steps.

1. Tie the string to the exact middle of the ruler.

Options for Reaching All Students

Beginning

Language: Make Comparisons

Give small groups of students objects of various weights. Ask them to consider the objects two at a time to determine which is heavier. Help them write comparative sentences like: (*The chair*) *is heavier than* (*the book*). Have them put the objects in rank order. Students can use scales to find exact weights and check their ordering of objects.

Advanced

Writing: Write Directions

Have students work in small groups and write directions for an everyday activity, such as how to operate a vending machine. Provide help with vocabulary and make sure that the various steps are described in chronological order. Then have the groups orally read directions to other groups, who try to guess what they are doing.

Mixed Ability

Science: Weather Experiment

Here is another experiment to show that air has pressure and can hold up water. Have students work in pairs over a sink. Give them directions verbally. Students should fill a glass with water and wet the rim. Then put a card on top of the glass, hold it firmly in place with one hand, and turn the card and glass

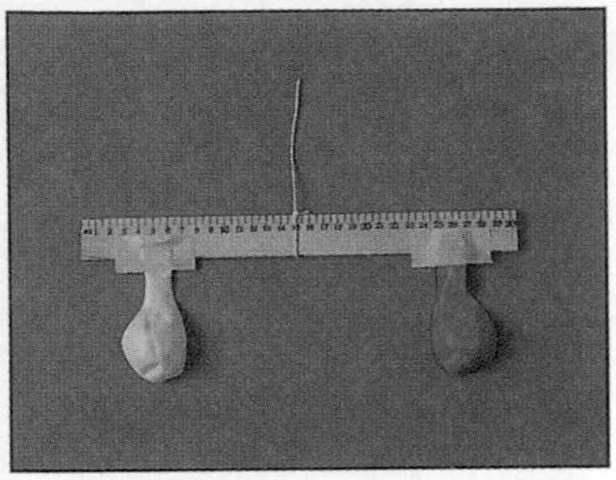

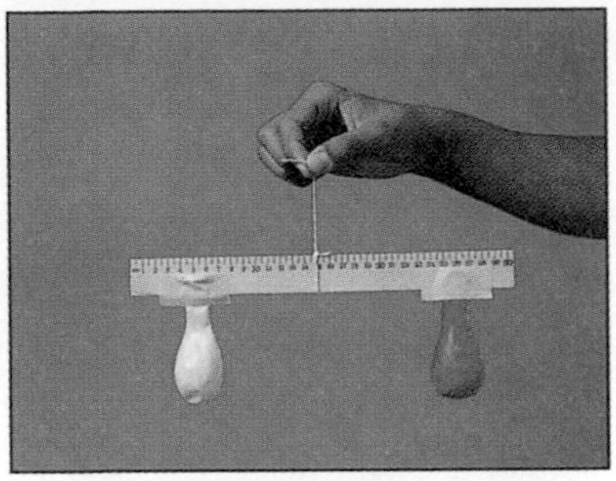

2. Do not blow up the balloons. Tape each balloon exactly 2 inches (5 centimeters) from each end of the ruler.

3. Pick up the loose end of the string. Hold the end of the string up in the air so that the ruler is not touching the table. What happens?

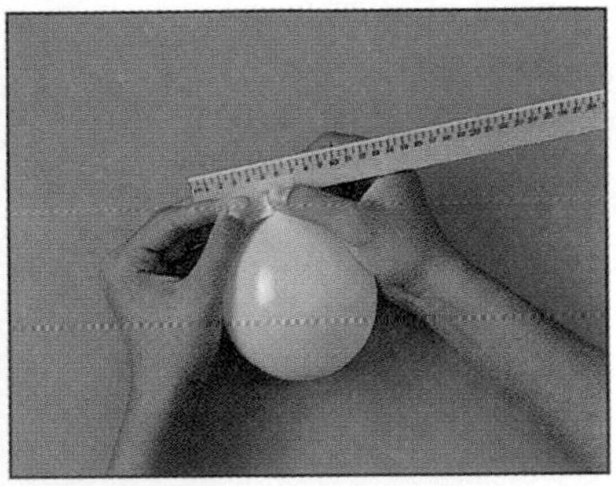

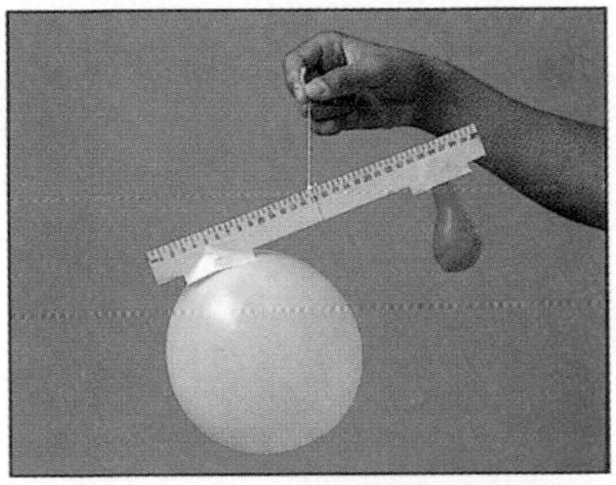

4. Remove one balloon. Blow it up. Tie it tightly. Tape the balloon with air in it back onto the ruler at the place where it was before. If you picked up the string now, which side of the ruler will go down? Why do you think so?

5. Now pick up the ruler by the string. What happens to the ruler? Which balloon is heavier?

Talk About It

Does air have weight? How do you know?

Language Awareness

Grammar
Imperatives

ACTIVITY BOOK

Point out that the instructions for the experiment are given in the imperative. The verb is used without a subject, but the subject is understood to be *you*. Write the following examples on the board:

(You) Tie the string to the exact middle of the ruler.
(You) Do not blow up the balloons.

Ask students to find other examples of imperatives on pages 44 and 45. Show examples of other materials that use imperatives such as recipes and directions for operating machines. Have students bring in examples and discuss them. Use Activity Book page 23.

Assess

Use the questions in Talk About It for assessment. Students should be able to

- tell that air has weight
- demonstrate how they know this

LOOK**AHEAD**

In the next section, students will learn how the weight of air relates to air pressure and storms.

upside down. They should then remove their hands. The water should stay in the glass because of the upward push of the air. Note: For the experiment to work, there should be a good seal between the glass and the card.

Some students may need you to run through the experiment once, performing the steps as you say the directions, before they try.

Home Connection

Directions

Have students find directions and recipes at home. Suggest they discuss the steps and act them out with family members. Invite students to share their examples of directions and recipes, translating or summarizing steps for other students. Beginning learners can use pantomime or illustrations to explain steps.

Practice

Activate Prior Knowledge

Relate Personal Experiences

Show a photograph or a videotape of a thunderstorm. Ask students to describe, using words or pantomime, what they see, hear, and feel during a thunderstorm. Encourage them to talk about storms they have experienced.

Develop Language and Concepts

Present Pages 46 and 47

Read the text with the students. Demonstrate pressure by pushing on students' hands. Use hand gestures or recorded graphics from a TV weather report to help you explain the movements of different air masses. Help students relate each part of the text to the accompanying illustration. Talk about when and where storms happen.

Model a Strategy

Track Cause and Effect

Model how tracking causes and effects can improve reading comprehension:

When I read, I find that keeping track of causes and effects helps me understand a process. For example, on page 47, I learned that when a cold air mass pushes into a warm air mass, it makes the warm air rise very fast. As it rises, it cools. That causes the water in the air to form clouds. The water falls as rain. When I connect all the causes and effects on pages 46 and 47, I can understand why storms happen.

Air Pressure and Storms

Do you feel air pushing all around you? Air pushes down on the earth and on you all the time. This push is called **air pressure**.

Warm air and cold air have different weights. Warm air is lighter than cold air. Warm air rises. So warm air doesn't push down very hard on the earth. An area with a warm air mass over it is called a **low pressure area**.

Cold air pushes down very hard on the earth. So an area with a cold air mass over it is called a **high pressure area**.

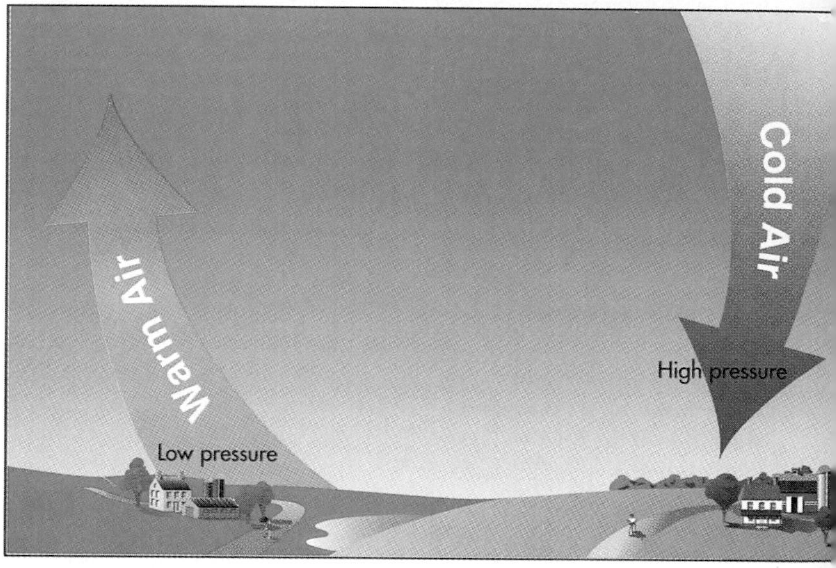

Options for Reaching All Students

Beginning

Science: Label Diagrams

Give students unlabeled diagrams of air pressure systems and forming storms. Ask students to label the diagrams. Then help them describe what is happening in the diagrams. Encourage them to finger-trace along the arrows to show how air masses move.

Advanced

Language: Summarize

Have students work in pairs to summarize the content of the pages, including the process of the formation of thunderstorms. Students may find it helpful to restate information as numbered steps and use drawings to illustrate each step.

Mixed Ability

Science: Study Fronts

Ask students to watch TV weather reports and look at newspaper weather maps for four consecutive days and to focus on air masses and fronts. Provide daily videotapes of local TV weather reports or ones from the Weather Channel that students can view repeatedly. Ask students to take notes about the fronts as they pass through and then tell what weather change resulted.

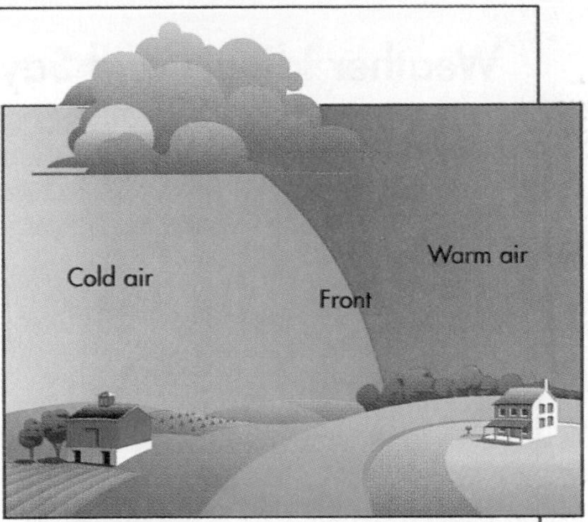

The place where two different air masses meet is called a **front.** The front forms a boundary between the two air masses.

Storms often happen at fronts. A cold air mass pushes into a warm air mass. It makes the warm air rise very fast. The moving air causes wind. As the warm air rises, it cools. Water in the air forms clouds. Then the water falls to the earth as rain or snow.

A cold air mass pushing into a warm air mass can cause a thunderstorm. A thunderstorm has wind, rain, thunder, and lightning!

Write About It

What causes a storm? Draw a diagram and explain.

Language Awareness

Grammar
Present Tense

ACTIVITY BOOK

Write the following sentences on the board:

Water <u>forms</u> into clouds.
Warm air <u>rises.</u>
Air <u>pushes</u> down on the earth.

Point out that the underlined verbs are in the present tense. The present tense can be used to talk about events that are always true. It is often used in scientific explanations. Point out that present-tense verbs often end in *-s* or *-es* when the subject is singular. Ask students to find other examples of such verb forms in the text on pages 46 and 47.

Use Activity Book page 24.

Assess

Use the questions in Write About It for assessment. Students should be able to

- tell that storms happen at fronts where hot and cold masses meet
- draw and explain a simple diagram showing what causes a storm

LOOK**AHEAD**

In the next section, students will learn weather-related idioms and sayings.

Cooperative Learning

Science: Research Storms

Have small groups of students research either an actual tropical storm or an actual winter storm. Tell them to find out where the storm originated, what areas were affected, and how. As they conduct their research, check periodically to make sure that they understand the scientific vocabulary. Have students present the information on posters, using both words and graphics.

Multicultural Connection

Literature: Read Greek Myths

Read students some Greek myths about Zeus and his bucketful of thunderbolts. Invite them to find other myths about thunder and lightning. Talk with students about some of the things that thunderstorms represented to ancient peoples. Discuss why ancient peoples made up myths about natural phenomena such as thunder, wind, and earthquakes.

Writer's Workshop

Write About a Bad Weather Experience

Have students write about something that happened to them or someone they know on a day with bad weather, such as a stormy day. Remind them to use a narrative format, presenting events in sequential order.

Connect

Activate Prior Knowledge

Make Associations

Write on the board: *Today is a sunny day.* Ask students to tell or show their reactions to a sunny day. Ask students if they think people like sunny days and if most people feel happier on sunny days. Then write: *Maria has a sunny personality.* Have students speculate about the kind of personality Maria has. Lead them to conclude that her personality is pleasant. Then use other examples, such as *green thumb,* to explain what an idiom is.

Develop Language and Concepts

Present Pages 48 and 49

On the board, write the expressions that appear in boldface on pages 48 and 49. Ask students to identify the weather words in each and guess what the expressions mean. Then read the text with the students. Help them use the pictures to determine meaning. Ask them to use the expressions to describe people they know. Have students do the Think About It questions.

Model a Strategy

Infer Word Meaning

Model how to infer word meaning:

When I'm not sure what an expression means, I see if it contains a word I know. Thinking about the meaning of the word I know often helps me figure out what the new expression means. For example, when I read that a person runs like the wind, I remember the wind can move very fast.

Weather Idioms and Sayings

English has many idioms with weather words. In the idioms, the weather words take on special meanings. Here are some weather idioms to describe people.

A person who gets angry easily is **stormy.**

A person who is a bit sick is **under the weather.**

A person who is always daydreaming has his or her **head in the clouds.**

A person who can run fast can **run like the wind.**

Options for Reaching All Students

Beginning

Language: Guess Idioms

Ask each student to make an original illustration of one of the idioms or sayings on pages 48 and 49. Then have other students guess which idiom or saying each illustration depicts. If they prefer, some students may act out an idiom or saying.

Advanced

Writing: Create a Context

Have pairs of students brainstorm and then write a short story about the two characters below. The story should explain the characters' behavior and mention something funny that happened as a result.

"Last week Adam had his head in the clouds . . ."

"This morning I saw Rosie and I ran like the wind . . ."

Mixed Ability

Language: Expand Vocabulary

Use other idioms, such as *snowed under, it's a breeze, break the ice,* in context and encourage students to guess their meanings. In addition to providing verbal context clues, use gestures, facial expressions, and vocal cues to convey meaning.

People also can use weather words to talk about life in general.

When it rains hard, people say it is **raining cats and dogs.**

People know that bad things may also have something good related to them. People say, **April showers bring May flowers.**

People also try to be ready for a bad time. Sometimes people save money for this reason. People say, **save for a rainy day.**

Think About It

What do you think this weather saying means? "Everybody talks about the weather, but nobody does anything about it."

Do you know any sayings about the weather in your native language? What are they? What do they mean in English?

Language Awareness

Grammar/Spelling
Adjectives That End in -y

ACTIVITY BOOK

Write noun-adjective pairs, such as *rain—rainy* and *storm—stormy* on the board in context sentences such as: *There was a storm yesterday. It was a stormy day.* Ask students what words describe a day with snow, with clouds, and with sun. Point out that the *n* in *sun* is doubled to create *sunny.* Help students generalize about adding *-y* to nouns to create adjectives.

Use Activity Book page 25.

Assess

Use class discussion and the Think About It questions for assessment. Students should be able to

- understand the nature of idioms
- use weather idioms and sayings

LOOK **AHEAD**

In the next section, students will read a tale from Southeast Asia that explains the origin of monsoons.

Peer or Cross-Age Tutoring

Weather Idioms

Have students dictate the sentences with weather idioms to one another. Have them check their work against the text. Monitor their progress and check whether they are having difficulties saying and/or writing word endings such as plurals with *-s,* adjectives with *-y,* or present progressive's use of *-ing.*

Multicultural Connection

Weather Sayings

Have students write and illustrate a multilingual class book of weather sayings from their home countries and from the United States. Have students collect their sayings, translate or paraphrase them, if needed, and then determine a consistent format for presenting them.

QuickCheck

Plural Forms

Check whether all students are forming and pronouncing plural forms correctly. Have them identify plurals on pages 48–49. Make sure they can distinguish between plural nouns and present-tense verbs.

Connect

Activate Prior Knowledge

Use Pictures to Predict Reading

Ask students to look at the content and style of the pictures on pages 50 through 57. Ask questions such as: *Where do you think this story takes place? Is this a story about today or long ago? Do you think the story is true? How can you tell?*

Introduce the Selection

Explain that this story tells about a kind of seasonal wind called a monsoon. Ask students if they have ever experienced a monsoon. If so, encourage them to tell what it was like. Ask students if they know names of other seasonal winds (e.g., Santa Ana) and list them on the board. Invite students to talk about high winds and their effects on people and property.

Explain that this is a traditional tale from Vietnam retold in this English version.

Read the Selection

ORANGE TAPE

Read the story with students. Then read it again and discuss the Reader's Tips at the appropriate points.

Play the tape of the story on Side 1 of the Orange Tape for students several times.

Discuss characteristics of folk tales and record them in a word web on the board. Point out that the theme, or big idea, of many folk tales focuses on the lessons that characters learn. Discuss some lessons learned in familiar folk tales, and encourage students to read to discover the lesson of this folk tale.

Language Awareness

Grammar

Pronouns *He, She, They*

ACTIVITY BOOK

Write the following sentences on the board:

She sat quietly. He opened his book. They arrived at the same time.

Ask students which word refers to one female, which refers to one male, and which refers to two or more people, either male or female. Point out that pronouns are used instead of the names of people or things. Have students find other uses of *she, he,* and *they* on pages 50 through 53, and identify to whom the pronouns refer. Then have students use the pronouns in original sentences and do Activity Book page 26.

Model a Strategy

Understand Story Elements

Model how to understand story elements:

When I read a story, I first try to learn the basic story elements: Where does it take place? Who are the main characters? What problems do they have? I can guess this story's setting and time from the picture. In the first paragraph, I learn that Princess Mi Nuong is a main character. And the author tells me her problem: she is getting older and she wants to get married.

Options for Reaching All Students

Beginning

Language Arts: Story Elements

BLACKLINE MASTER

Pass out copies of the Story Elements Chart on Blackline Master 25 in the Teacher's Resource Book. Have students begin to fill out the story elements and complete the chart as they read the story. If students have difficulty with this chart, allow them to draw a series of pictures to describe important story events.

Advanced

Social Studies: Research Vietnam

Have students work in small groups to research today's Vietnam. Ask students to locate the country on a map and find out about its government, language, weather, natural resources, foods, and clothing, using printed and electronic information sources. Encourage students to create posters and present their findings to the rest of the class.

Home Connection

Learn About Marriage Customs

Ask students to interview adults at home about marriage customs in their home countries. Help them brainstorm a list of interview questions. Have students report their findings to the rest of the class. Encourage students to illustrate their reports with photos or drawings.

Why the Monsoon Comes Each Year

Retold by Dorothy Lewis Robertson

Language Tip
Vocabulary
A *monsoon* is a seasonal wind that brings heavy rains to South Asia every year. This folk tale is from Vietnam, a country in Southeast Asia.

The Princess Mi Nuong was sad. She sat quietly with downcast eyes while a handmaiden combed her glossy, black hair and idly smoothed a fold in the silk of her gown. When the last jade pin was fastened in her hair and the handmaiden held up a mirror, she pushed it away without even glancing in it. She already knew what the mirror would show her: a tiny new wrinkle between her eyes. It was this new wrinkle that made her sad. She was growing old and she was husbandless.

It wasn't that she was ugly or lame or bad tempered. She had had many suitors. Some were handsome and many had come from foreign lands, but not one had gained the consent of her father, the Emperor. Like many fathers with only one child, he believed that no one was good enough for his charming daughter. For her he wanted someone rich and distinguished and, above all, powerful. Years had passed since the last suitor had proposed and been declined, and it looked as though the Princess would remain single forever.

Language Tip
Vocabulary
A *suitor* is someone who wants to marry someone. Mi Nuong needed her father's *consent* to be married. She needed her father to say yes.

Strategy Tip
Recognize Main Characters
When you read a story, ask yourself, "Who is important in this story?"

Language Tip
Vocabulary
Betrothal means engagement to be married.

Then one day two strangers appeared at the Emperor's court. Both were very handsome, both were very rich, and one was the powerful Spirit of the Sea and the other was the equally powerful Spirit of the Mountain. Since both suitors arrived at exactly the same time, and met with equal favor in the eyes of the Emperor, he was hard put to choose between them. So he told them that whoever first brought his betrothal gifts the next day would have the hand of the Princess and could leave with her immediately.

The Spirit of the Sea rushed back to the ocean and summoned his men. He commanded them to search for the most perfect pearls, the tastiest crabs, and the juiciest squid. The Spirit of the Mountain climbed to the highest peak and gathered his men about him. Then he opened his magic book and wished for the gifts he wanted to present to the Princess. He wished for his men to find a chest of diamonds and emeralds that had been hidden in a dark cave in the mountains for hundreds of years, and he wished for them to fill baskets with rare fruits that couldn't be grown at the Emperor's court.

Strategy Tip
Understand Detail
In this story, both the Spirit of the Sea and the Spirit of the Mountain want to marry Mi Nuong. Each needs to show how strong he is. What does each spirit do to meet the challenge?

Connect

Develop Language and Concepts

Present Pages 54 Through 57

ACTIVITY BOOK

Have students retell the story to this point and complete Activity Book page 28.

Have students dramatize the story. Students may play roles themselves or use stylized puppets to represent the characters. Students can write dialogue for the story or pantomime actions as narrators read it.

Language Awareness

Grammar

Past Tense

ACTIVITY BOOK

Point out the sentences that contain *appeared* and *arrived* on page 54. Discuss that the past tense often ends in *–ed*. Ask students to find other examples of regular past-tense verbs on pages 54 through 57. Then point out the sentences that contain the words *sent* and *came* on pages 54 and 55. Tell students these are the past-tense forms of *send* and *came.* Ask students to find other examples of irregular past-tense forms on pages 54 through 57. Use Activity Book page 27 for practice.

Model a Strategy

Read On to Get Meaning

Model using reading on to get meaning:

When I see an expression I don't know, I keep on reading to see if something that appears later will help me guess the meaning. For example, let's say I'm not sure what dawn was breaking means on page 54. I keep on reading, and I read the sun was barely over the horizon. Then I understand that dawn was breaking means "the sun was just coming up."

Response Activities

Personal Response

Have students tell how they think the Princess felt about the kind of person the Emperor wanted her to marry and how students would feel about such a strict demand.

Critical Response

Ask students what the story tells them about traditional Vietnamese values and life. Encourage students to talk about the roles of women and men, marriage, family, a monarchical government, and weather.

Creative Response

Remind students that since this story takes place in Vietnam, the Princess's suitors bring gifts from that country. Ask students what kinds of gifts the Princess might have received if she lived in the United States. Have them draw pictures of the gifts.

Options for Reaching All Students

Beginning

Language: Who Am I?

Have students write one-sentence descriptions of the characters in the story on index cards. For example, *I wanted to get married* or *I brought gifts of fruit.* Some students may only be able to provide one- or two-word descriptions of their characters. Have students work in small groups and share their cards and guess the characters from the descriptions.

Advanced

Writing: Create a Folk Tale

Have small groups work together to find weather myths from other lands and other times. Have them use those myths as models for writing their own myths explaining a weather phenomenon. Have students begin the writing process by creating a story map, indicating their tale's setting, characters, and plot.

Home Connection

Weather Tales

Have students get information from their families about any weather folk tales that come from their home countries. Also encourage students to bring in examples of other types of folk tales in their home languages, or in English, and share them with the rest of the class. As a class, note common characteristics and themes.

Language Tip
Vocabulary
A *casket* is a small box for holding valuables.

Presently the men appeared before the Spirit of the Mountain with the casket of jewels and baskets of strawberries, peaches, and grapes. Then, while the Spirit of the Sea was still searching the depths of the ocean for his gifts, the Spirit of the Mountain with his men was on his way down the mountainside to be first at the gates of the Emperor's palace. He arrived there just as dawn was breaking, and claimed Mi Nuong as his bride. The Emperor was delighted with the gifts of jewels and fruit, and felt that surely he had made a good match for his daughter. He sent her off with the Spirit of the Mountain and promised to visit her in her new home as soon as she was settled.

Mi Nuong and her husband were barely outside the gates of the Emperor's palace when along the road from the sea came the Spirit of the Sea with his men bearing great trays of pearls and dishes of delicious sea food. When the Spirit of the Sea saw that he was late by just a few minutes and that the sun was barely over the horizon, he was very angry. He suspected that the Spirit of the Mountain had used some tricks to get there first and so he commanded his followers to pursue the Spirit of the Mountain and take Mi Nuong away from him.

Language Tip
Vocabulary
Bearing means carrying.

Strategy Tip
Understand Plot
In a competition, one person wins and the other is defeated. The Spirit of the Mountain won, and got Mi Nuong as his bride. What did the defeated Spirit of the Sea do then?

With that, the wind began to blow and the rain fell and the ocean rose higher and higher. Soon foaming waves were breaking over the land, and the people had to flee for their lives. All of the creatures of the sea turned into soldiers of the Spirit of the Sea and ran screaming up the road to overtake the Spirit of the Mountain before he could get to the high ground where he ruled. Wherever they passed, the rivers rose into floods, houses were washed away, and whole cities were left in ruins. The water rose higher and higher, until waves were breaking at the foot of the mountain, but still the Spirit of the Sea had not caught up with Mi Nuong. Now the Spirit of the Mountain ordered his men to throw huge logs and boulders down on the Spirit of the Sea and his forces.

The battle between the two most powerful spirits continued both day and night, and the poor people of the villages prayed for them to stop. Many had been drowned in the flood; some had been struck by lightning. Their crops had been washed away, as well as their homes. Finally, the Spirit of the Mountain used his magic wishing book to wish his mountain to grow higher. Then he took Mi Nuong and his men to the very highest peak, well out of reach of the Spirit of the Sea.

When the Spirit of the Sea saw that his attempt to overcome the Spirit of the Mountain was in vain, he retreated with his soldiers back to the ocean, taking the flood waters with him. But so angry was he at his defeat that every year he tries again to defeat the Spirit of the Mountain and win the Princess Mi Nuong to be his own wife. Every year he sends storms and floods up the river valleys to the very foot of the mountain where Mi Nuong still lives with her husband. And each year he is again defeated and forced to withdraw to his home in the ocean. And that is why the monsoon comes each year in Viet Nam.

Study Tips
Characters' Problems
In life, people have problems. In stories, characters have problems, too. At the beginning of the story, what problem does the princess have? What problems do the two suitors have? At the end of the story, what problem does the Spirit of the Sea have?

Strategy Tip
Understand the Big Idea
Folk stories are often used to explain why something happens in nature. What does this folk tale explain?

Connect

Activate Prior Knowledge

Review Vocabulary

Review the list of winds that students compiled earlier. Invite students to say any words they know related to winds or make any wind sounds. Tell students that in this poem they will "hear" many winds.

Develop Language and Concepts

Present Page 58

ORANGE TAPE

Read the poem with students. Remind students that poets convey meaning through devices such as word choice, rhyme, and rhythm. Ask why the poet repeats some letters in the names of the winds. Then play the poem on Side 2 of the Orange Tape several times. Invite students to read along.

Lotsa Winds

by Sonja Dunn
with Lou Pamenter

How many sounds
do the four winds make?

Hundreds and hundreds
for goodness' sake

Listen listen
to the sound
As they whoosh
around and 'round

Missssssssssssstral
SSSSSSSSSSSSSSirroco
ChChChChChChChChChChinooooooooook
Monssoooooooooooooooooooooon
Doldruuuuuuuuuuuuuuuuum
Traaaaaaaaaaaade wiiiiiiiind
Northsouthwesteast wiiiiiiiiinds
ZZZZZZZZZZZZZZZZZZZephyr

If you make those sounds again
You may start a HURRICANE!

Think About It

This poem contains the names of many types of winds. These names come from different parts of the world. What do all these different names say about the importance of wind in many different cultures?

Why does the poem's author repeat some letters in the names?

Language Awareness

Phonics

ou and *ow*

ACTIVITY BOOK

Model the vowel sound in the word *sound* and have students pronounce it. Then follow the same procedure with *down.* Point out the letter/sound correspondence in the words *sound* and *down.* Ask students to find or suggest other words that contain *ou* or *ow* pronounced as the vowel in *sound.* Write their suggestions on the board. Use Activity Book page 29.

Options for Reaching All Students

Beginning

Art: Draw the Wind

Ask students to draw a picture of what the wind looks like to them. Help them describe their pictures and their feelings about the wind. They can add describing words and feeling words to the borders of their pictures.

Advanced

Geography: Research Winds

Have small groups research one of the winds in the poem. Model how to do a subject search. Ask them to find out what kind of wind it is, where it blows, and any myths connected to it. (For example, the Mistral is said to drive people insane.) Have groups present their findings. Encourage them to use a world map to locate their winds.

Multicultural Connection

Words for Types of Winds

Have students look up the names of the winds in the poem in a dictionary. Point out that English has adapted words for phenomena from other languages: *mistral* is from French. English also uses the Spanish term *El Niño* to describe a warm current in the Pacific Ocean off South America that can cause widespread weather changes in North America.

CHAPTER 3

Tell what you learned.

1. Explain how you learned that air has weight. Draw pictures of your experiment.
2. What challenge did the Emperor give to the two suitors for Princess Mi Nuong? How did they meet that challenge?
3. Make a list of the way weather challenges people in your town. How do people try to meet that challenge?
4. How do changes in the weather affect you?

Assess ✓

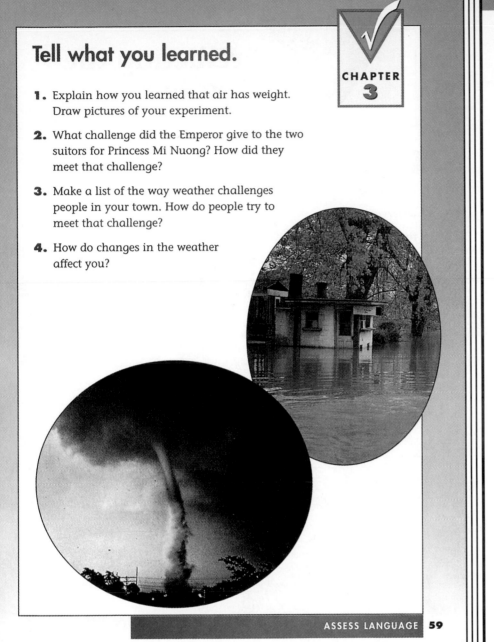

Activity 1: Check that students can explain the experiment and draw accurate pictures of it.

Activity 2: Check that students can explain the Emperor's challenge and how the suitors responded.

Activity 3: Check that responses refer to your community.

Activity 4: Check that responses describe the physical and emotional reactions to various kinds of weather.

Have students do the Chapter Self-Assessment, Blackline Master 31. Have students choose the product of one of the activities to place in their portfolios. Add the results of any rubrics, checklists, self-assessments, or portfolio assessments, Blackline Masters 2-18 and 31.

Listening Assessment

BLACKLINE MASTER

Make sure each student has a copy of Blackline Master 51 from the Teacher's Resource Book. Play the tape several times and have students complete the activity.

WHITE TAPE

See Chapter 3 Resources, page T40c, for the Listening Assessment tapescript.

Options for Assessment

Vocabulary Assessment

List Weather Terms

Have students work in groups of three or four. Give each group a paper with columns. The columns in the top row should each have one of the letters in the word *weather*. Have students pass the paper around so that each can list all the weather words and expressions he or she can think of that begin with the letters at the top. The group with the longest list wins.

Writing Assessment

Tell What You Learned

Ask students to write a paragraph telling what new information they learned about weather from this chapter. Have them review their paragraphs for accuracy of information, correct spelling of weather terminology, complete sentences, and correct punctuation.

Language Assessment

BLACKLINE MASTER

Use Blackline Master 50 in the Teacher's Resource Book.

Standardized Test Practice

ACTIVITY BOOK

Use pages 30 and 31. Answers: **1.** A princess did not have a husband because her father wanted a powerful one for her. **2.** the Spirit of the Sea is angry.

Preview

Activate Prior Knowledge

Use Newspapers

Bring newspapers to class and ask students to identify the weather section. Read the forecast with them. Ask them how and why they might use weather information.

Develop Language and Concepts

Present Pages 60 and 61

Have students study the illustrations on the spread. Help students identify them as related to weather forecasting. They include a TV weather forecaster, a newspaper article on bad weather, radar (which is used to track storm and front movements), and a satellite (which can photograph and track weather movements over large areas).

You may wish to present realia, such as newspapers, recorded TV and radio weather reports, and outdoor thermometers to help students understand the Word Bank words and to prompt responses to the question on page 60. Encourage students to use the Word Bank words in their answers.

Then have students work in small groups and answer the Talk About It questions. Have students share their answers with the rest of the class.

CHAPTER 4

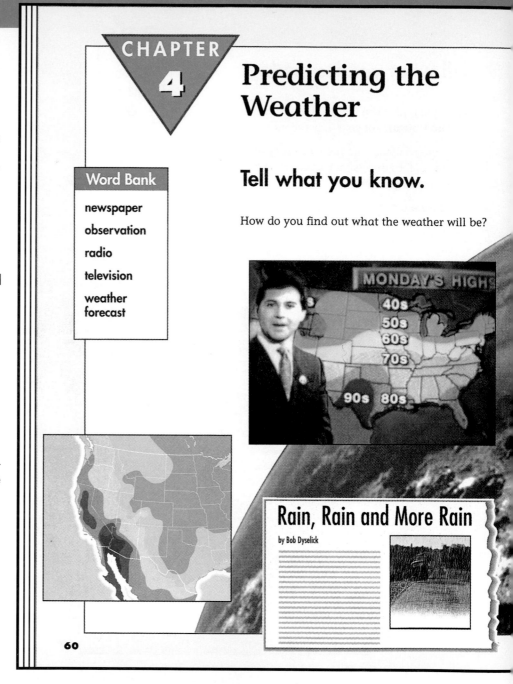

Predicting the Weather

Word Bank

- newspaper
- observation
- radio
- television
- weather forecast

Tell what you know.

How do you find out what the weather will be?

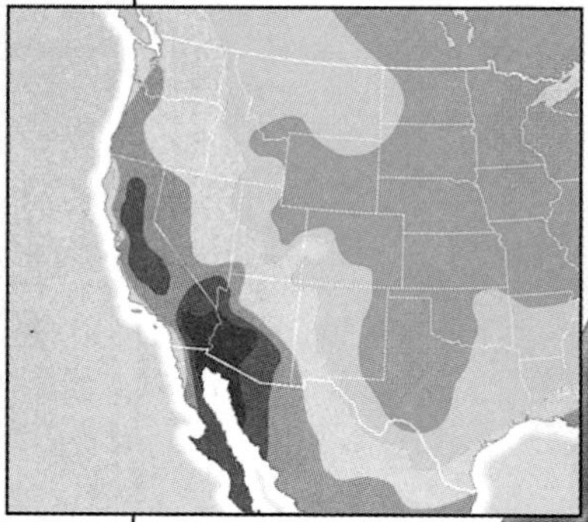

Rain, Rain and More Rain

by Bob Dyselick

Options for Reaching All Students

Beginning

Writing: Describe the Weather

Have students review weather words by describing the weather for every day of the last week. Have students work in groups. See if the lists of different groups match. You may need to simplify this activity for some students by giving them sentences to complete such as: *On Monday, the skies were cloudy/sunny.* Have them circle the correct answer.

Advanced

Science: Research Meanings

Have groups each choose one of the pictures on the page, research what it is and how it is used to report the weather, and then write short paragraphs describing their findings. Suggest they begin by matching their chosen picture with a Word Bank word. They can then look up this word in a dictionary or encyclopedia, or ask others about how it relates to weather.

Mixed Ability

Science: Record Daily Weather

Have students work in small groups. Ask them to read the weather report in the newspaper for a week. Tell them to record each day's high temperature and to write *sunny, hot, cold, rainy,* or *cloudy* under the day of the week. Have students present their findings to the rest of the class in this format: *On Monday, the high temperature was ____. The day was ____.*

Talk About It

Why is it important to know what the weather will be?

Where can you get daily weather information?

Cooperative Learning

Weather Report Words

Tape-record TV and radio weather reports and play them for students. Have students work in pairs and write down all the weather-related words that they hear. Have pairs compare lists and come up with a comprehensive class list. You may want to simplify this activity for beginning learners by giving them lists of weather-related words and instructing them to circle the ones they hear.

Present

Activate Prior Knowledge

Relate Personal Experiences

Ask students whether they regularly listen to or watch weather forecasts. Ask them to relate cases where knowing the weather has helped them: for example, by knowing to take an umbrella or not to plan outdoor activities on a rainy day.

Develop Language and Concepts

Present Pages 62 and 63

ACTIVITY BOOK

As you read the pages with students, organize the information it contains into three columns on the board labeled *What meteorologists do, What meteorologists study, Where meteorologists work.* Help students understand the names of academic subjects. With the class, brainstorm a list of academic subjects and talk in general about what is studied in each. Guide students in answering the Talk About It questions. As a follow-up, brainstorm a list of jobs that students would like.

Talk with students about how the weather causes them to wear certain kinds of clothes. Talk about winter and summer and about special clothes, such as boots, for wet or snowy weather. Make a list on the board of pieces of clothing. Have students complete Activity Book page 32.

The Work of Meteorologists

A **meteorologist** is a scientist who studies the weather. A meteorologist studies the weather to help people plan their activities. A meteorologist can help people plan for the next day or for the next season. People want to know what kind of clothes to wear tomorrow or if they should prepare for an especially cold winter.

A meteorologist can help people plan what to wear by predicting if it will snow tomorrow. ▶

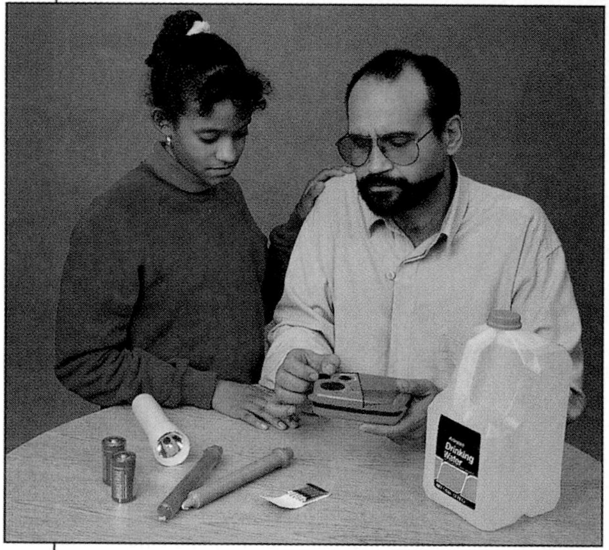

▲ A meteorologist can tell people when to get ready for a bad storm.

Options for Reaching All Students

Beginning

Language: Occupations

PICTURE CARDS

Use Picture Cards 3 (artist), 13 (carpenter), 18 (cook), 23 (dentist), 24 (doctor), 43 (mail carrier), 47 (musician and nurse), 53 (police officer), and 61 (secretary) to introduce names for various occupations. Use the cards as an opportunity to expand vocabulary. For example, help students tell what the person does *(A secretary types letters and answers the phone.)* and where the person works. *(A secretary works in an office.)* Some students may choose to draw pictures of or act out the tasks the various workers perform.

Advanced

Careers: Interviews

Have students prepare a list of questions that they would like to ask a meteorologist. Questions should ask for information about the meteorologist's job, what that person studied in school, what that person likes and does not like about the job. Then have students contact a local radio or TV station to conduct an interview via mail, e-mail, or, if possible, in person.

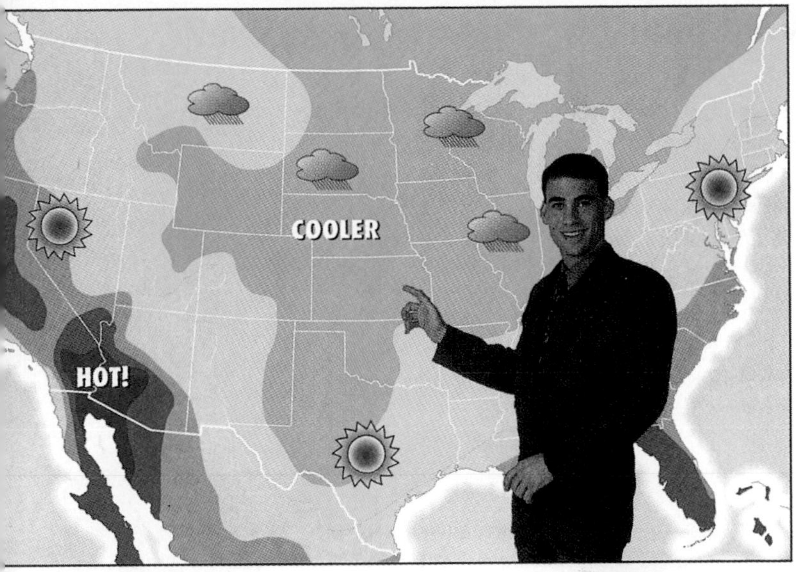

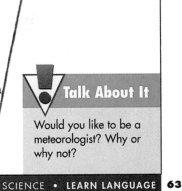

▲ A meteorologist can tell people what kind of weather their friends and relatives are having in faraway places.

People who want to be meteorologists take courses in math, statistics, computer science, chemistry, and physics in college. As meteorologists, they study information on air pressure, temperature, wind speed, and other factors. They use computer models of the world's weather to say what they think will happen.

In 1994, there were about 6,600 meteorologists in the United States. About half of them worked for the government. Others worked for TV or radio stations, universities, and private companies.

Talk About It

Would you like to be a meteorologist? Why or why not?

Language Awareness

Grammar
Future with *Will*

Read the last sentence of the first paragraph on page 63 with students. Help them understand the role of the word *will* in describing a future event. Explain that *will* is often used in weather forecasts and it is also used to discuss personal future plans. Have students create sentences using *will*.

Model a Strategy

Use a Graphic Organizer

Model using a graphic organizer:

When I am reading about a new topic, I can keep track of information and organize it in a graphic organizer, such as a chart or a word web. For example, decide what the main categories are, and write them in a chart. Then I can list the details under the appropriate heading. Graphic organizers like this can help me understand and remember key points.

Assess ✓

Use class discussion and Talk About It for assessment. Students should be able to

- briefly describe the training and work of meteorologists

LOOK**AHEAD**

In the next section, students will learn about the tools that meteorologists use.

Peer or Cross-Age Tutoring

Language: Clothing and Weather

PICTURE CARDS

Have students work in pairs with these Picture Cards: 7 (boots), 17 (coat), 32 (gloves), 34 (hats), 37 (jacket), 60 (scarf), 67 (sunglasses), 68 (sweater), 71 (umbrella). Ask each pair to draw six columns and label them *Cold, Hot, Sunny, Cool, Rainy,* and *Snowy.* Then have students take turns categorizing each piece of clothing according to the weather during which it would be worn. Remind students that some clothes may fit into more than one category.

You can modify this activity for beginning students by adding a graphic symbol to each label (e.g., a sun for *sunny*).

Cooperative Learning

Career Selection

Have students discuss their career plans and research what types of schooling they will need to achieve their goals. A guidance counselor or school librarian may be able to supply students with appropriate career information or suggest reference sources. Ask students to organize the information on charts and share their findings.

Practice

Activate Prior Knowledge

Demonstrate a Thermometer

Show students a thermometer and ask them to describe or show how to use and read it. Have them tell some things that can be measured with it.

Develop Language and Concepts

Present Pages 64 and 65

ACTIVITY BOOK

Read the title and the text with students. Point out that the terms *thermometer, barometer,* and *anemometer* all contain the word part *meter,* meaning "a device for measuring." Remind students that looking for familiar word parts is a good strategy for clarifying the meaning of new words.

Create a two-column graphic organizer on the board. Title the graphic organizer *Meteorology Tools.* Label the left-hand column *Tool*; label the right-hand column *What It Does.* After each text paragraph is read, write the names of the tools on the board in the left-hand column. In the right-hand column, write a phrase that tells what each instrument measures. You may wish to bring some of these tools to class so students can examine them closely. Point out the different units of measure that each tool uses. Have students complete Activity Book page 33 for practice with this specialized vocabulary.

Have students do the Think About It activity. Emphasize the variability of weather and the number of factors that influence it.

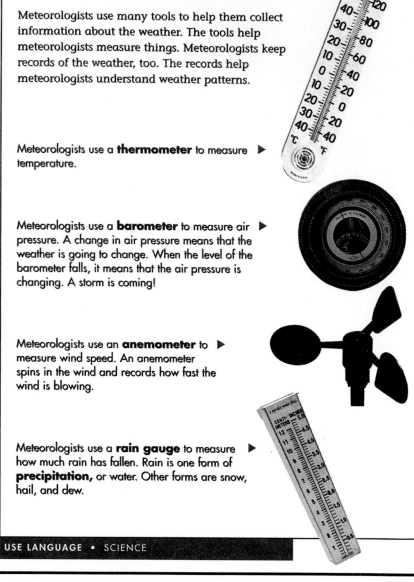

What tools do meteorologists use?

Meteorologists use many tools to help them collect information about the weather. The tools help meteorologists measure things. Meteorologists keep records of the weather, too. The records help meteorologists understand weather patterns.

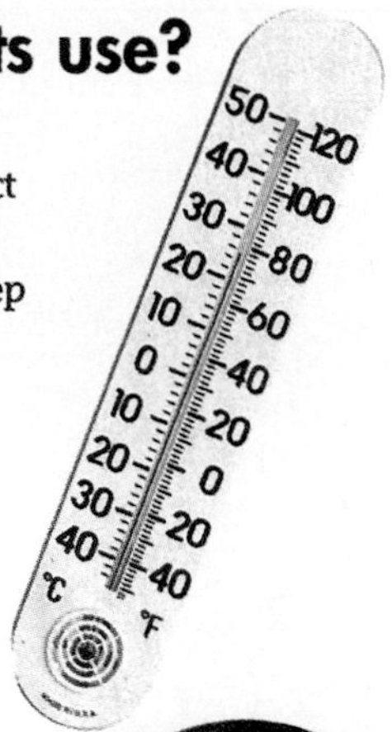

Meteorologists use a **thermometer** to measure temperature. ▶

Meteorologists use a **barometer** to measure air pressure. A change in air pressure means that the weather is going to change. When the level of the barometer falls, it means that the air pressure is changing. A storm is coming! ▶

Meteorologists use an **anemometer** to measure wind speed. An anemometer spins in the wind and records how fast the wind is blowing. ▶

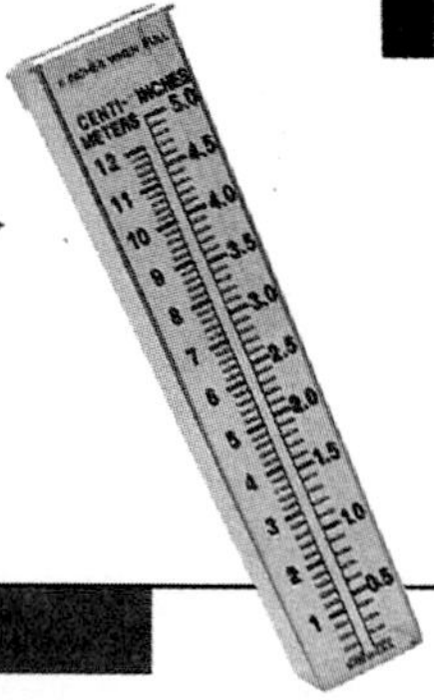

Meteorologists use a **rain gauge** to measure how much rain has fallen. Rain is one form of **precipitation,** or water. Other forms are snow, hail, and dew. ▶

Options for Reaching All Students

Beginning

Math: Record Temperatures

Have pairs use thermometers to record morning and afternoon temperatures for one week. Then have them make bar or line graphs of their daily results and describe any trends. Make sure all students know how to read a thermometer and are using the same unit of measure (Celsius or Fahrenheit degrees).

Advanced

Critical Thinking: Assess Weather Reports

Have students prepare a three-column chart. Tell them to label Column 1 *Prediction,* Column 2 *Actual,* and Column 3 *Accurate?* Ask students to listen to the same weather forecaster's reports on the radio or TV for one week. For each day, have students record the prediction and the actual weather on the chart. Then have them compare the two and decide if the prediction was accurate. At the end of the week, ask students to analyze the results for the entire week and assess the forecaster's overall accuracy.

You may wish to record weather reports for students so they can listen to them repeatedly and take notes about the predictions made.

Meteorologists use **radar** to watch a storm that is far away. Meteorologists use this information to help them predict what direction a storm is going and how fast it is moving. ▶

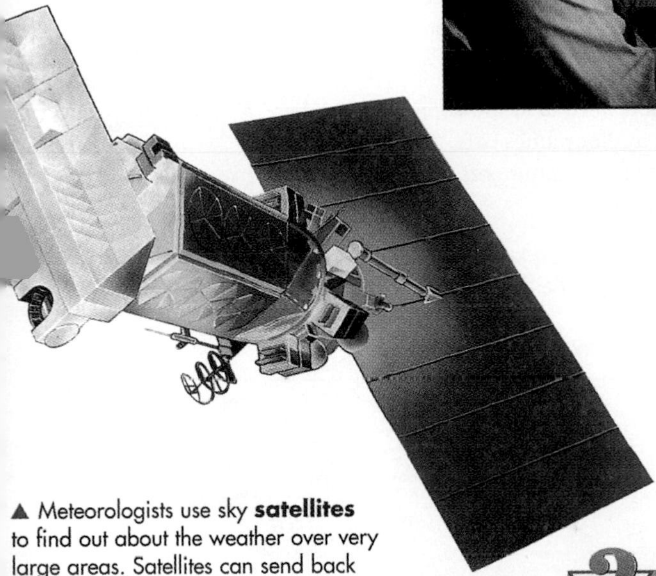

▲ Meteorologists use sky **satellites** to find out about the weather over very large areas. Satellites can send back information and photographs to the meteorologists on the ground. Meteorologists use this information and the photographs to learn more about storms and other kinds of weather all over the earth.

Think About It

Meteorologists use many tools to predict the weather, but their predictions are not always correct. Why not?

Language Awareness

Grammar
Expression *Use (It) To*

Point out sentences that employ the format of *Meterologists use (tool name) to . . . .* Discuss how this construction tells what an object will be used for. Make up several classroom-oriented sentences that contain this construction.

Model a Strategy
Understand Specialized Vocabulary

Model understanding specialized vocabulary:

When I have to understand and remember the meaning of special words, like the names of the tools in this section, I reread the names several times and then write them in my vocabulary log or on index cards with a clue word or definition next to each one. For example, I write: barometer—air pressure. That helps me study and remember the words.

Assess ✓

Use class discussion for assessment. Students should be able to

- identify and explain the uses for some of the tools for predicting weather

LOOK **AHEAD**

In the next section, students will learn about the importance of weather forecasts.

Cooperative Learning
Weather Experiments

Have students work in small groups of mixed abilities. Provide the groups with weather-related experiments and hands-on activities available in textbooks or books of experiments. Help them collect needed materials and preview the steps of the activity with them. Allow students to choose a group leader and decide who will do specific tasks.

Have groups perform one of the experiments and write the results in a report. Invite groups to present their findings to others. Encourage them to include visual aids, such as drawings, charts, and graphs, in their reports.

Practice

Activate Prior Knowledge

Review Prior Learning

Ask students to summarize what they have learned about weather prediction and to describe aspects of their lives that are affected by the weather. You might bring in items related to different types of weather (e.g., warm hats, umbrellas, sunglasses, sunsceen), and have students tell when they are worn.

Develop Language and Concepts

Present Pages 66 and 67

Read the text with students. As you read, complete a concept chart with two columns labeled *Who* and *Why* to explain why weather forecasts are important and to whom. Help students link the illustrations to the text to ensure comprehension.

Help students plan how to complete the second part of the Talk About It.

Model a Strategy

Recognize Text Organization

Model how to recognize text organization:

When I read a selection, I look for the information I need to answer a question. This section is titled "Who uses weather forecasts?" So I carefully read each paragraph and see that each describes a different group of people who use forecasts and why. Looking for main ideas and answers to questions helps me better understand and remember what I am reading.

Who uses weather forecasts?

Many TV news programs tell about the weather. Radio stations tell about the weather, too. Newspapers print weather **forecasts** and weather maps.

Why is there so much talk and writing about the weather? People want to know about the weather so they can make plans. People need to know about the weather so they can prepare for dangerous situations.

Airport managers need to know about the weather to keep people and airplanes safe. A weather forecast will let airport managers know when to have snowplows ready.

Airline companies need to know about high winds and storms that might be dangerous for their airplanes in the sky.

Farmers need to know about the weather so they can plan their work. A weather forecast can tell farmers when they need to do special things to protect their crops. For example, a forecast may say that there will be low temperatures that will damage unprotected crops.

Options for Reaching All Students

Beginning

Language: Vocabulary

Help students display and list tools that they use in a day as a student; for example, a pencil, a notebook, a watch, a ruler, a computer. Then give students names of occupations and provide reference pictures, if possible. Help them list tools for those workers.

Advanced

Science: Make Preparations

Have students tell how they would prepare if the forecast predicted a major snowstorm, or a tropical storm, as appropriate for your locale. Students may work with family members to come up with a plan. Have them list their ideas as a series of steps using imperative sentences.

Mixed Ability

Social Studies: Service Organizations

Have students find out about organizations such as the Red Cross that help people during and after devastating weather events such as hurricanes. Students can make posters highlighting the information they learn. Stress that the poster should convey the basic facts about the organizations in a clear, succinct way.

Builders need to know about the weather so they can know when it will be too cold to do some kinds of construction work.

School principals need to know about the weather so they can cancel school if it will be too cold, snowy, or icy for students and teachers to get to school safely.

Talk About It

Do you use weather forecasts? How do weather forecasts help you?

Talk with some people where you live. Find out how they use weather forecasts.

Language Awareness

Grammar
Clauses with *So* to Express Purpose

ACTIVITY BOOK

Talk with students about the word *so* and how it can be used to express what the purpose of some thing or some action is. Write some examples on the board:

Meteorologists use thermometers so they can measure temperature.
Satellites send back photographs so meteorologists can learn more about storms.

Provide additional examples and have students use Activity Book page 34.

Assess ✓

Use class discussion and students' answers to Talk About It for assessment. Students should be able to

- tell how different people use weather forecasts
- say why forecasts can be important

LOOK**AHEAD**

In the next section, students will do an experiment to measure wind speed.

Cooperative Learning
Social Studies

Have students work in small groups to find out about the prediction of, preparation for, and the effects of hurricanes in the Caribbean in a recent year. Suggest students contact the National Hurricane Center in Florida for information or help them find suitable websites on the Internet.

Student groups should prepare and deliver short oral presentations on their findings to the rest of the class. Be sure all students in each group participate in the presentation in some way. Remind students that sufficient volume, good pacing, and clear pronunciation will positively affect the presentation.

Connect

Activate Prior Knowledge

Review Prior Learning

Ask students to tell about experiments they have conducted. Remind them of the one they did to measure the weight of air. Elicit the general steps that must be taken before conducting an experiment. Tell students that they will be doing another experiment.

Develop Language and Concepts

Present Pages 68 and 69

ACTIVITY BOOK Read the text with the students, being careful to check that they understand the directions. Discuss the practicality of knowing about wind speed. Review the meaning of the word *anemometer* with students.

Have pairs perform the experiment. Make sure they have the necessary materials for this experiment. Have students use Activity Book page 35 to record their results. Ask students to record any problems they experience during the experiment and how they solved these problems.

Guide students in doing the Try It Out experiment. As a preliminary activity, ask students to look at the sky and notice how clouds move. (Warn them not to look directly into the sun with their eyes or through the camera.) Discuss with students what they saw and how the Try It Out experiment will help them record this effect. If possible, have students use a tripod to keep the camera's position fixed.

You can measure wind speed.

Airline pilots and other people need to know how fast the wind is blowing. You can measure the speed of the wind by doing this experiment. Work with a partner.

Things You Need

- strong thread or fine nylon fishing line—about 12 inches (30 centimeters) long
- tape
- a ping-pong ball
- a protractor—the biggest one you can find

Follow these steps.

1. Tape one end of the string to the ping-pong ball. Tape the other end to the exact center point on the base of the protractor. Now you have made an anemometer.

2. Test your anemometer. Hold it level and away from your body. The flat side of the protractor should be up. Make sure the ball can swing freely.

3. Test your anemometer. There is no wind in your classroom, so the ball should hang straight down. The string will hang at the 90 degree mark on the protractor.

4. Now go outside on a windy day. Hold your anemometer so the narrow side points into the wind. Hold the anemometer away from your body. The ping-pong ball will swing. Ask your partner to read and record the angle on the protractor.

Options for Reaching All Students

Beginning

Writing: Vocabulary

Have students observe other weather phenomena as they do this experiment and use words and/or pictures to record their findings in a Weather Log. Some students may need help focusing on particular phenomena within the complex mixture of weather-related stimuli.

Advanced

Science: Research Clouds

Have small groups prepare a report on three basic kinds of clouds: cirrus, cumulus, and stratus. Suggest that students outline their findings before writing their reports. (Allow students who have a special interest in this topic to go into greater detail.) Have the groups illustrate their reports and present them to the rest of the class. Encourage them to include visuals in their reports.

Mixed Ability

Math: Speed Relationship

Review with students that "miles per hour" and "kilometers per hour" indicate different systems of measurement. Have students study the numbers on the chart on page 69 to gain some understanding of the mathematical relationship between the two measurement systems. One mile is equivalent to about 1.6 kilometers.

5. Use the chart that follows to determine how fast the wind was blowing when you measured it.

How fast is the wind blowing?

Angle	0	85	80	75	70	65	60	55	50	45	40	35	30	25	20
Miles Per Hour	0	5.8	8.2	10.1	11.8	13.4	14.9	16.4	18.0	19.6	21.4	23.4	25.8	28.7	32.5
Kilometers Per Hour	0	9.3	13.2	16.3	19.0	21.6	24.0	26.4	29.0	31.5	34.4	37.6	41.5	46.2	52.3

Try It Out

Try this experiment on several days that are windy and cloudy. Take pictures of the sky. Point the lens of the camera up towards the clouds. Take several pictures about two minutes apart of the same area of sky. When you look at the finished pictures, you will be able to see the movement of the clouds.

Language Awareness

Grammar

There Is/There Are

Write several sentences on the board that use *there is/there are* constructions. Point out the use in the text: *There is no wind.* Explain that *there is/there are* can be used to describe a scene. Also explain the uses of singular and plural verbs in this construction: *There is a window in my room. There are two windows in my room.* Ask students to make up sentences that use this construction, such as describing a favorite place or their rooms.

Assess

Use the completed anemometer and the recording of the results of wind speed for assessment. Students should be able to

- conduct the experiment
- say how they resolved difficulties during the experiment
- tell what they learned as a result of the experiment

LOOK **AHEAD**

In the next section, students will learn how to read a weather map and write a radio script.

Cooperative Learning

Chart Weather Statistics

Have students use old newspapers to find out a week's daily temperatures and wind speeds. Then have students prepare a chart for both temperature and wind speed. Encourage them to look for a relationship between the two sets of figures. If students have trouble grasping the relationship, tell them to first breathe out gently and then to blow air quickly on one of their hands. Ask: *Which is colder?*

QuickCheck

Numbers with Decimals

Check that students can easily read the numbers in the chart. Talk about how to read decimals aloud: *nine and three-tenths.* Also point out that many people also say *nine point three.* Give them sets of decimals, and have them order them from least to greatest.

Connect

Activate Prior Knowledge

Relate Personal Experience

Ask students to think of times they have used maps and to tell the rest of the class what they used the maps for and when.

Develop Language and Concepts

Present Pages 70 Through 73

ACTIVITY BOOK Have students study the map and map key on pages 70 and 71 and read the text with you. Have pairs answer the Try It Out questions. Then have the whole class think up and answer more weather questions based on the map. Help with the pronunciation of place names as needed.

Read the words in the Word Bank on page 73 with the class and check that students understand them. Relate the words to concepts learned in prior lessons. You might also show pictures of outdoor scenes that match the adjectives in the Word Bank. Then read pages 72 and 73 with students. Make sure they understand the use of boldfaced names in scripts. For additional vocabulary practice, have students use Activity Book page 37.

As necessary, help students prepare and present the activity in the Write About It section. Students might use props such as microphones and maps, and they may want to videotape or tape-record their reports.

Language Awareness

Future with *Going to*

ACTIVITY BOOK Point out the use of *going to* on pages 72 and 73 to indicate the future. Review the sentences on page 72, paragraph 2 that use this form. Give students several more examples. Then have them make up their own examples based on the weather map on pages 70 and 71. Use Activity Book page 36.

Model a Strategy

Use a Map Key

Model how to use a map key:

When I read a map, I look carefully at the map key. The key explains what the colors, signs, and symbols mean on the map itself. The map key tells me what information the map itself contains. I study the map key every time I look at a map because different maps use different colors, signs, and symbols.

On this map, I see that Tampa, Florida, is in a light red part of the map. I match this color to the color in the map key and find out that it means that Tampa had temperatures in the nineties. I look closely at Tampa and see the number 91, this is the high temperature for the day. The map key tells me that the letters pc mean it was a partly cloudy day.

Options for Reaching All Students

Beginning

Language: Use Location Words

Make sure that students understand *north, south, east,* and *west* and their locations on a map. Have students work in pairs and take turns describing and guessing places on the map in the text by giving clues such as *It's north of Chicago, It's south of Omaha.* Help students with pronunciations.

Advanced

Science: Regional Weather

Have each student select a state and use an encyclopedia to research that state's weather patterns: average temperature for each season, amount of rainfall, and other recurring weather phenomena. Have each student make a poster that shows the relative location of the state on an outline map of the United States and the weather statistics.

Multicultural Connection

Weather Patterns

Have students research and report on the general weather patterns of their home countries. Teach students different strategies for locating information on this subject (e.g., by starting their search with reference sources about their home country or region or with sources about weather). Encourage them to consider and evaluate a variety of print and electronic sources.

Reading Weather Maps

A weather map like the one on this page shows what weather is forecasted for the United States. The map uses colors, numbers, and letters. The map key tells what these colors, numbers, and letters mean.

United States Weather Map

Numbers (in degrees Fahrenheit): today's forecast high, tomorrow morning's forecast low.

Below 10 | 10s | 20s | 30s | 40s | 50s | 60s | 70s | 80s | 90s | 100s

c	Cloudy	sh	Showers
pc	Partly cloudy	sn	Snow
r	Rain	sf	Snow flurries
s	Sun	t	Thunderstorms

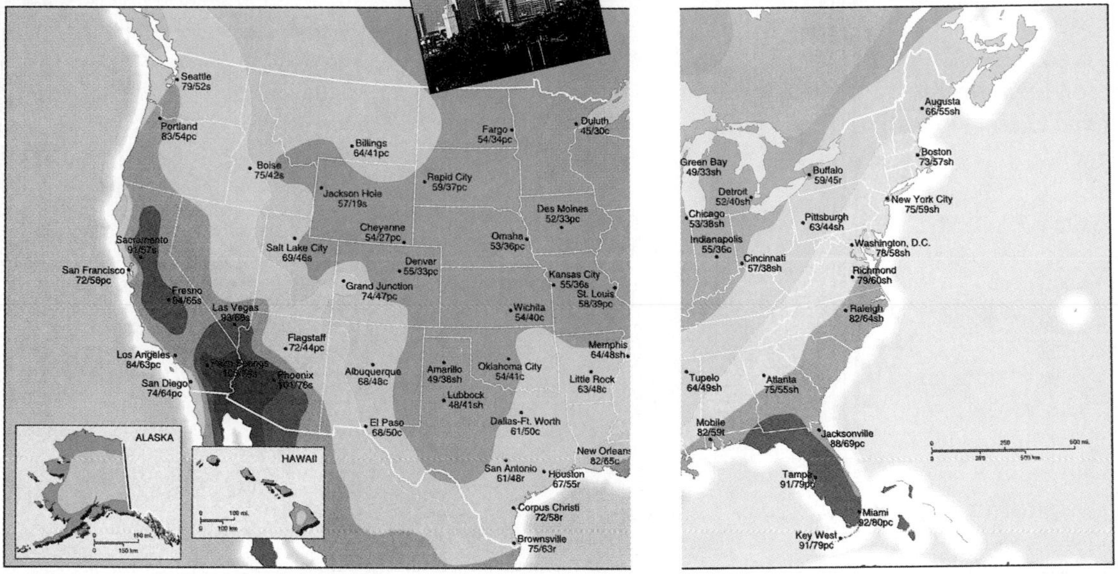

Try It Out

Work with a partner. Use the map to answer these questions. Then make up your own. Ask your partner the questions you make up.

What two states are predicted to have the highest temperatures?

What temperature range does the color yellow stand for?

What is the high temperature predicted to be in Brownsville, Texas?

Is it predicted to be cooler in New York City or in Miami, Florida?

What is the weather predicted to be like where you live?

A Stormy Weather Forecast

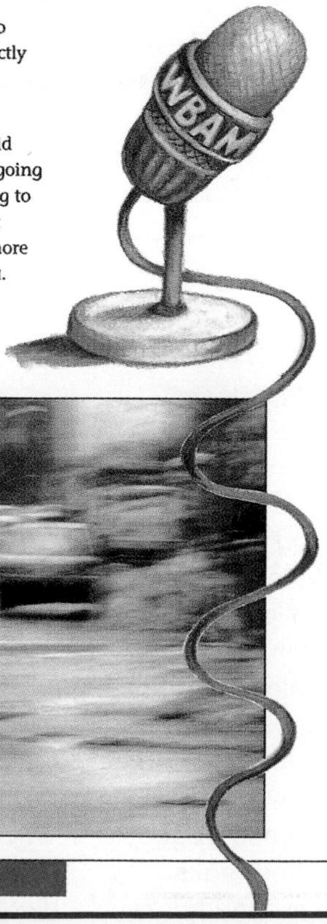

Nancy: It's noon—time for the WBAM Radio Midday Weather Report. So now let's go directly to meteorologist Keith Baker at the WBAM weather center.

Keith: Good afternoon, Nancy. . . . I'm afraid that the heavy rain storms of last night are going to continue. The severe weather front is going to be stalled in our area until at least midnight tonight. So far, we have officially recorded more than 9 inches of rain since yesterday at 7 P.M. As most of you know, this large amount of precipitation has caused flooding in many city neighborhoods.

Word Bank

- **breezy**
- **calm**
- **clear**
- **cloudy**
- **overcast**
- **precipitation**
- **temperature**
- **wind speed**

Within the last hour, the wind has increased in speed. We are recording gusts of up to 40 miles per hour on the WBAM anemometer right now. Because of these high winds, the state police have closed our freeways to all truck and bus traffic for the rest of the day.

At noon, the official temperature at City Hall was 48 degrees. That temperature, along with the heavy precipitation and high winds, will give us a pretty lousy afternoon and evening. So stay indoors if possible folks!

Nancy: Thanks, Keith, for bringing us up to date on this continuing situation. . . . And now to the national news. . . .

Write About It

Work with a partner to write and perform your own radio station weather forecast. Talk about the temperature, wind, clouds, and precipitation for today and tonight.

Connect

Activate Prior Knowledge

Relate Personal Experiences

Ask students to discuss their favorite kinds of weather. Encourage them to discuss their reactions to good and bad weather. Beginning learners can respond by using pantomime and facial gestures to react to weather conditions you name.

Develop Language and Concepts

Present Pages 74 and 75

ORANGE TAPE

Direct students' attention to the illustrations. Then read the poem on page 74 with students several times. Talk about the authorship and explain that *Anonymous* means the author is unknown. Call attention to the word *whether* and say it indicates a choice between two outcomes. Explain to students the play on words in the title and tell them that it is a technique used by writers in English to use words with similar pronunciations but different meanings. Use paraphrasing to clarify any confusing phrases. Then play Side 2 of the Orange Tape and invite students to join in the recitation.

Direct students' attention to page 75. Point out the shape of the poem called "Raindrop." Discuss the Think About It question. Follow the same procedure for presenting this poem as for the one on page 74.

ACTIVITY BOOK

Have students write their own concrete poetry by completing Activity Book page 38.

Weather

Anonymous

Whether the weather be fine,
Or whether the weather be not,
Whether the weather be cold,
Or whether the weather be hot,
We'll weather the weather
Whatever the weather
Whether we like it or not.

Think About It

What idea about weather does this poem suggest? Do you think that the idea is right?

Options for Reaching All Students

Beginning

Language: Read Poetry

Read "Weather" with students. Say each line and have students repeat it after you. Have several students read the poem aloud. It's a tricky poem—make sure students realize that reading it is an accomplishment. Repeat these steps for the poem "Raindrop." Then ask students which poem they personally prefer.

Advanced

Language: Read Poetry

Have students use indices to find other weather poems they like. Have students practice reading them aloud before making oral presentations to the class. Remind speakers to use appropriate gestures, facial expressions, and speaking techniques to convey the meanings of their poems. Encourage listeners to ask questions and make comments about the poems they hear.

Mixed Ability

Language: Homonyms

Explain that there are many homonyms like *weather/whether* in English—words that are pronounced the same way but that are spelled differently. Have students work in pairs to look through the unit and try to come up with pairs of homonyms and use them in context sentences. Examples would be *right, write; our, hour; know, no; to, two; be, bee.*

Raindrop

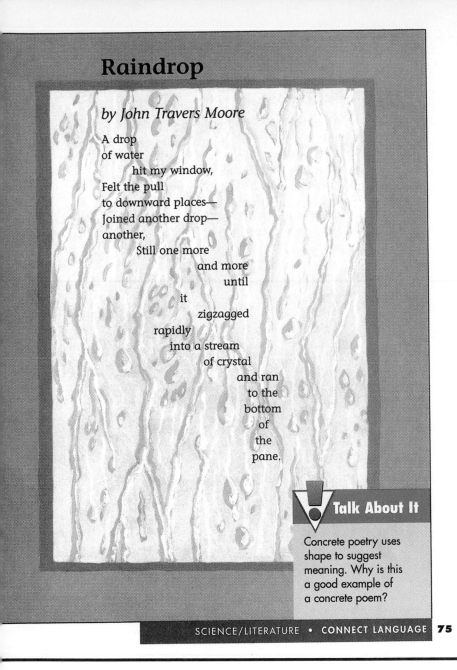

by John Travers Moore

A drop
of water
hit my window,
Felt the pull
to downward places—
Joined another drop—
another,
Still one more
and more
until
it
zigzagged
rapidly
into a stream
of crystal
and ran
to the
bottom
of
the
pane.

Talk About It

Concrete poetry uses shape to suggest meaning. Why is this a good example of a concrete poem?

Language Awareness

Phonics
The Letter *l*

Write these words on the board: *cold, like, felt, until, crystal.* Work with students on the pronunciation of each, focusing on the various pronunciations that the letter *l* takes. Then talk about how words that end in an *l* sound often are spelled with double letters. Point out *pull* and *still* as examples. Also point out *we'll* as a contraction for *we will,* another example of a doubled final *l.* Play a letter-exchange game where students take turns substituting one or more letters in one of the words on the board to create a new word with an *l* sound. For example, they can change *cold* to *colt* or *felt* to *fell.*

Home Connection

Read at Home

Have students read the poems in English to their families and ask their family members to read or recite poems to them in their home languages. Students can bring to school examples of poems in their home languages and explain what these poems mean in English.

If appropriate, students can try to explain ways in which their poems reflect the culture of their home country. More proficient students might point out any poetic devices (rhyme, rhythm, word play, and so on) that might be missed in the translation.

Writer's Workshop

Weather Preferences

Have students write about differences in the weather between where they live now and other places where they lived in the past. As a prewriting strategy, they can record ideas in a T-Chart. Remind them to use present tense for scientific statements that are always true.

Connect

Activate Prior Knowledge

Relate Personal Experiences

Ask students to tell or act out what they like to do on a sunny day. Have a volunteer make a list of these activities on the board.

Develop Language and Concepts

Present Page 76

ORANGE TAPE

Read the title and the author's name with students. Tell them that this is a song written in the 1960s by one member of the famous singing group called the Beatles. Read the song with students. Then play Side 2 of the Orange Tape and invite students to sing along. Discuss how the lyrics describe one person's idea of a "good day."

Language Awareness

Phonics
Long *a*

ACTIVITY BOOK

Write the following words on the board:

d<u>ay</u>   th<u>ey</u>   r<u>ai</u>n

Point out that all have the sound of long *a*, but are spelled differently. Have students look through the unit and find other examples of these pairs of letters standing for the long *a* sound. For practice, use Activity Book page 39.

Good Day Sunshine

by Paul McCartney

Good day sunshine, good day sunshine,
good day sunshine.
I need to laugh, and when the sun is out,
I've got something I can laugh about.
I feel good in a special way,
I'm in love, and it's a sunny day.
Good day sunshine, good day sunshine,
good day sunshine.
We take a walk, the sun is shining down,
burns my feet as they touch the ground.
Good day sunshine, good day sunshine,
good day sunshine.

Options for Reaching All Students

Beginning

Language: Total Physical Response

TPR

Brainstorm with students actions or gestures that can represent words or phrases. Then have students pantomime as you read selected lines. Tell students they can also repeat the lines as your echo. Play the tape several times and then have students sing along.

Advanced

Writing: A Good Day

Have students write about what makes a "good day" for them. Have them start by brainstorming words or phrases that come to mind when they think of a "good day." Then have them expand a few of these ideas into a one- or two-paragraph description. Have them review their drafts for clarify of ideas and correct any errors in grammar, spelling, and punctuation. Then have them prepare a final copy. If possible, encourage students to use word processing software when drafting and finalizing their work.

Tell what you learned.

CHAPTER 4

1. Why do people listen to weather forecasts? How do you use weather forecasts?
2. Make a weather dictionary for the students who will study weather next year. Put in all the words you think are important, and draw pictures to help explain them.
3. What other information would you like to learn about weather forecasting?

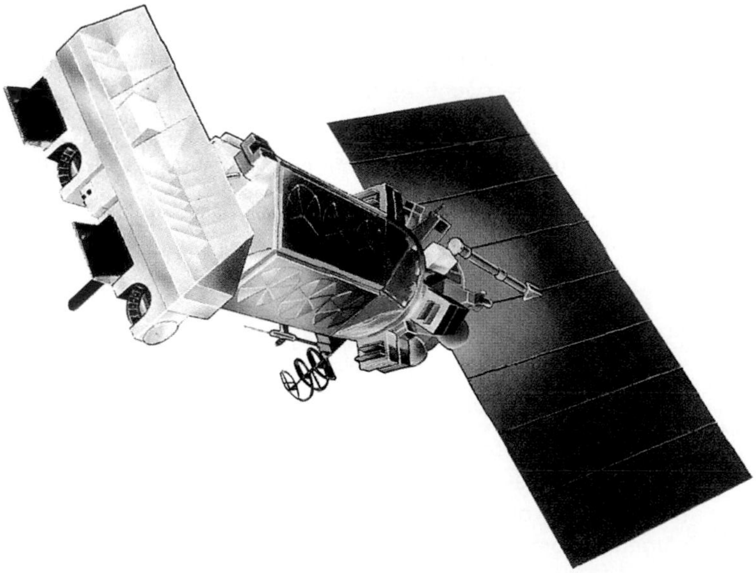

Assess ✓

Activity 1: Check that responses indicate both why people listen to weather forecasts and personal ways students use them.

Activity 2: Evaluate the number of entries and the clarity of students' responses.

Activity 3: Evaluate whether students' responses show understanding of what has been learned.

Have students complete the Chapter Self-Assessment, Blackline Master 31, and choose the product of one of the activities to place in their portfolios. Add the results of any rubrics, checklists, self-assessments, or portfolio assessments, and Blackline Masters 2–18 and 31.

Listening Assessment

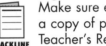

BLACKLINE MASTER

Make sure each student has a copy of page 53 from the Teacher's Resource Book and is ready to listen. Play the tape several times and have students write down what is dictated.

WHITE TAPE

See Chapter 4 Resources, page T40d, for Listening Assessment tapescript.

Options for Assessment

Strategy Assessment

Use a Graphic Organizer

Have students use a graphic organizer to summarize key information that they learned about meteorologists. Check that students use appropriate categories in an idea web or a multicolumn chart. You may need to assist some students by creating a blank web or chart for them to fill in.

Writing Assessment

Weather Report

Have students write a typical weather report for a place they know. Provide examples of reports they can use for models. Discuss the characteristics of a good report and develop a checklist of elements to include. Remind them to use *will* or *going to* to describe any predictions of weather in the future. Partners can proofread each other's work, using the checklist as a guide.

Language Assessment

BLACKLINE MASTER

Use Blackline Master 52 in the Teacher's Resource Book.

Standardized Test Practice

ACTIVITY BOOK

Use pages 40 and 41.
Answers: **1.** gasometer **2.** The weather will change. **3.** east **4.** Washington, D.C.

Wrap-Up

Activities

Class Trip or Visit

Plan a class trip to a local science museum. Call ahead of time to see if there are special presentations on meteorology. Or arrange a guided visit to a local weather station, where students can view professional meteorological equipment.

Alternatively, contact a local radio or TV station and invite the staff meteorologist to come to class to talk with students. Encourage students to compare the meteorologist's equipment to the tools in the weather center they created for the unit project.

Weather Map

Using a large outline map of the country, have students create a weather map that shows the conditions for an average day during the month, as computed for the charting activity. Instruct them to use the symbols and colors they learned during the lesson on weather maps to complete their project. They can hang the map at the weather center.

Folk Tales

Folk tales about the weather are common in many cultures. Have students write or illustrate one such story they know. As a complementary activity, have students look for English versions of folk tales from their home countries.

Weather Charts

Have students compute average temperature, air pressure, wind speed, and cumulative rainfall, based on their records for a period of two weeks to one month. Then, on a sheet of poster board, help them create a bar graph that compares their averages to (1) those in local papers, and (2) almanac statistics for the previous year during the same month. The chart can be displayed at the weather center. If possible, encourage students to use graphing software to create their bar graphs.

Discussing the Theme

Review with students how weather is important to a region, affecting everything from clothing worn to types of housing, popular sports, and even music and art. Choose from the following activities that will demonstrate to students how much they have learned about weather and how useful this information can be to them.

- Have students tape-record a list of new words learned.
- Have students draw or find pictures representing the weather conditions they have discussed, label the pictures, and display them in the weather center.
- Discuss with students how the special weather conditions in their home countries and regions affect the ways of life there.
- Have students discuss situations in which the words they have learned will be useful—from talking to an acquaintance to planning a trip.

Sharing the Project

Use the invitation form, Blackline Masters 32 and 33 in the Teacher's Resource Book, to invite family members to school for a "Special Report from the Class Weather Center."

Have students prepare an oral presentation that will include a daily weather report, an explanation of a weather map projected on a screen, and one or two reports on weather in students' home countries.

After the presentation, encourage visitors to view the charts, graphs, maps, and pictures exhibited in the weather center.

Serve refreshments featuring regional crops. A sign on the table could explain how local weather conditions enable the growing of various foods. For example, a class in Florida or California might use a sign saying: *Oranges need warm temperatures all year round.*

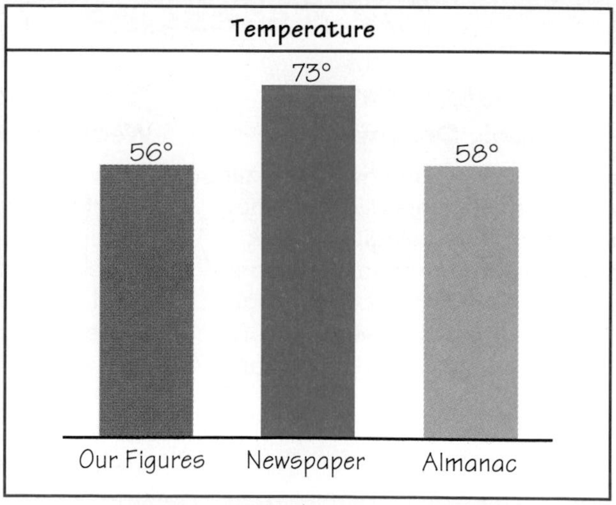

Signs of Success!

Duplicate a copy of this checklist for each student.

Name: ______________________________

Refer to the checklist below for a quick determination of how a student is progressing toward transitioning out of ESL instruction.

Objectives

☐ Names kind of weather
☐ Tells what makes weather change and what causes storms
☐ Tells how air has weight
☐ Uses weather idioms and sayings
☐ Tells how people get weather information
☐ Tells about meteorologists and their tools
☐ Tells who uses weather forecasts
☐ Reads a weather map

Language Awareness

☐ conjunctions *and* and *or*
☐ imperatives
☐ adjectives that end in *-y*
☐ pronouns *he*, *she*, and *they*
☐ past tense
☐ future with *will*
☐ expression *use (it) to*
☐ clauses with *so* to express purpose
☐ *there is/there are*
☐ future with *going to*

Hears/Reads/Pronounces:

☐ *ou* and *ow*
☐ the letter *l*
☐ long *a*

Learning Strategies

☐ Follows directions
☐ Tracks cause and effect
☐ Infers word meanings
☐ Understands story elements
☐ Reads on to get meaning
☐ Uses a graphic organizer
☐ Understands specialized vocabulary
☐ Recognizes text organization
☐ Uses a map key

Comments

____

Planning Guide

CHAPTER 5

The United States Before the Civil War

Objectives

Describe the economies of the North and South before the Civil War.

Discuss slavery and the abolitionist movement.

Talk about Harriet Tubman and the Underground Railroad.

Vocabulary Focus

Words relating to the pre-Civil War era, such as *abolitionist, slavery, North, South, states.*

Words to describe economics, such as *factory, plantation, railroad, canal.*

Words about the Underground Railroad, such as *conductor, risks, escape.*

Lesson	Content Focus	Language Awareness Objectives	Learning Strategies
Preview pp. 78–79 Tell what you know.			
Present pp. 80–81 A Nation Divided	Social Studies	**Vocabulary** Words That Contrast	
Practice pp. 82–83 Slavery	Social Studies	**Grammar** Passive Voice	Recognize main ideas and supporting details.
Practice pp. 84–85 Those Who Opposed Slavery	Social Studies	**Spelling** Italics for Titles	Use encyclopedias.
Connect pp. 86–87 Working on the Erie Canal	Social Studies/ Math	**Grammar** Expressions for Comparison	
Connect pp. 88–89 Harriet Tubman	Social Studies/ Reading	**Grammar** Past Tense	Understand textbook explanations.
Connect p. 90 "Nobody Knows the Trouble I've Seen"	Social Studies/ Literature	**Grammar** Contractions	
Assess p. 91 Tell what you learned.			

CHAPTER 6

War Between North and South

Objectives

Tell how people were affected by the war.

Describe the results of the war.

Name the leaders and some famous people of the war.

Tell how songs of the era describe the times.

Tell how literature describes the war.

Vocabulary Focus

Words relating to war, such as *soldier, wounded, bloodiest, medical supplies.*

Words describing people related to the war, such as *president, lawyer, general, nurse.*

Words used in the Gettysburg Address, such as *freedom, government, dedicated.*

Words describing people, such as *brave, caring, honest, hard-working.*

Lesson	Content Focus	Language Awareness Objectives	Learning Strategies
Preview pp. 92–93 Tell what you know.			
Present pp. 94–95 The Nation's Bloodiest War	Social Studies	**Vocabulary** Use Commas in Numbers	
Practice pp. 96–97 Leaders of the War	Social Studies	**Language Function** Stating Opinions	Understand chronology in biographies.
Practice pp. 98–99 Famous People of the War	Social Studies	**Grammar** Occupation Words ending in *-er* and *-ist*	
Connect pp. 100–101 Songs of the Civil War	Social Studies/ Music	**Grammar** Future Tense with *Will* and *Going to*	
Connect pp. 102–113 *Thunder at Gettysburg*	Social Studies/ Literature	**Grammar** Action Words **Vocabulary** Words That Paint Pictures **Grammar** Position Words	Understand characters' feelings. Summarize events.
Connect p. 114 "The Gettysburg Address"	Social Studies/ Literature	**Grammar** Prefix *un-*	
Assess p. 115 Tell what you learned.			

Resources

Chapter 5

Support Materials

ACTIVITY BOOK

Pages 42–51

YELLOW TAPE

Side 2: "Nobody Knows the Trouble I've Seen," page T90

DISK

Writer's Notebook

LET'S TALK CARD

96 cards to start conversations.

STORYTELLING

Storytelling Anthology: *Worlds Together*

Assessment Materials

BLACKLINE MASTER

Language Assessment, Blackline Master 60

Listening Assessment, Blackline Master 61

WHITE TAPE

Side 2: Listening Assessment, page T91

Listen carefully. Complete the chart. Write down the dates in the chart.

Harriet Tubman was born in 1820. She was one of eleven children. Her parents were slaves, and she herself was a slave. But she escaped in 1849 and she went to live in the North. The next year, in 1850, she made her first trip back to the South to help slaves escape. She made many trips back to the South. During the Civil War, she helped the North. She lived a long life. She died in 1913, when she was over ninety years old.

Support for Newcomers

Newcomer Book C, Survival language for absolute beginners. For overview, see pages xxviii–xxix.

Newcomer Teacher Suggestion Book, Chapter 5, pages 16–17

HomeLink Penguin Readers

A White Heron and Other American Short Stories

For Extended Reading

Escape from Slavery: Five Journeys to Freedom by Doreen Rappaport, HarperCollins, 1999. Five accounts of slaves who escaped to freedom during the period before the Civil War. **Level: Average**

If You Traveled on the Underground Railroad by Ellen Levine, Scholastic Inc., 1993. A question-and-answer format introduces readers to the Underground Railroad and how it helped slaves escape. **Level: Beginning**

Freedom Train by Dorothy Sterling, Scholastic, 1991. Learn about the life and deeds of a remarkable young woman in this wonderful biography. **Level: Advanced**

Our Song, Our Toil: The Story of American Slavery as Told by Slaves edited by Michele Stepto, Millbrook Press, 1994. Slave autobiographies and documents tell the story from African captivity to emancipation. **Level: Beginning**

A Picture of Freedom: The Diary of Clotee, a Slave Girl by Pat McKissack, Scholastic, 1997. A twelve-year-old Virginia slave recounts her year in this fictional diary. **Level: Average**

The Underground Railroad by Raymond Bial, Houghton Mifflin Co., 1999. This photo-essay recreates the experience of the brave runaways and conductors using first-person accounts and photographs. **Level: Average**

Related Technology

African American History: Slavery to Civil Rights, Queue Inc., 1995. Checks for understanding and keeps a record of completion for each student.

Resources

Chapter 6

Support Materials

ACTIVITY BOOK

Pages 52–61

YELLOW TAPE

Side 1: *Thunder at Gettysburg*, pages T102–T113

Side 2: "Tramp! Tramp! Tramp!," page T100; "When Johnny Comes Marching Home," page T101; "The Gettysburg Address," page T114

DISK

Writer's Notebook

Assessment Materials

BLACKLINE MASTER

Language Assessment, Blackline Master 62

Listening Assessment, Blackline Master 63

WHITE TAPE

Side 2: Listening Assessment, page T115

Listen to this story about Clara Barton. Write the dates in the chart.

In 1821, Clara Barton was born in Massachusetts. She was a teacher for many years. In 1861, she began helping wounded Civil War soldiers. She helped get them supplies, food, and medicines. In 1881, she started the American Red Cross. This organization helps people with food, clothing, and shelter during bad times. Clara Barton died in 1912.

Support for Newcomer

Newcomer Teacher Suggestion Book, Chapter 6, pages 18–19

For Extended Reading

Civil War by Martin W. Sandler, HarperCollins, 1996. An overview of the Civil War is brought to life with historical photographs, prints, speeches, and songs, **Level: Average**

The Battle of Gettysburg by Neil Johnson, Simon & Schuster, 1989. Photographs of a reenactment of the famous Battle of Gettysburg accompany this informative text. **Level: Average**

The Boys' War: Confederate and Union Soldiers Talk about the Civil War by Jim Murphy, Clarion Books, 1993. Actual letters and diaries of boys, sixteen and younger, tell of their experiences as soldiers in the Civil War. **Level: Average**

The Emancipation Proclamation by Brendan January and R. Conrad Stein, Children's Press, 1998. Learn about the document that led to the passage of the Thirteenth Amendment. **Level: Beginning**

A Light in the Storm: The Civil War Diary of Amelia Martin by Karen Hesse, Scholastic, 1999. A Newberry Medal author crafts the diary of a Union girl living in the divided state of Delaware during the first year of the Civil War. **Level: Average**

Lincoln: A Photobiography by Russell Freedman, Clarion Books, 1989. This Newberry Medal Book combines text and photos to tell about the life and career of the man who was President during the Civil War. **Level: Average**

A Separate Battle: Women and the Civil War by Ina Chang, Puffin Books, 1996. Describes the deeds of the strong women who fought their own battle during the Civil War. **Level: Advanced**

Related Technology

The Civil War Experience, South Peak Interactive, 1999. A good research tool about the Civil War filled with biographies, images, and videoclips taken from the History Channel.

Project

Civil War Dioramas

This optional project can be completed over the next two chapters. In the project, students will be making Civil War dioramas. See the Unit Wrap-Up, pages T115b, for more ideas on sharing the project with family members.

What You'll Need

Collect the following items:

Art Materials: small cardboard boxes; clay, or play dough; colored construction paper and white paper; glue; pieces of fabric and yarn; stones, pebbles, gravel, twigs, and so on; scissors; paints; magic markers

Research Materials: print and/or electronic resources that show drawings and photographs of the United States during the Civil War

Strategies You'll Use

- Use reference resources
- Use a diorama
- Visualize

Beginning the Project

Divide students into small groups and have them study the Civil War pictures in the Student Book and in resource materials that you have collected. Tell students that, as they study this unit, they will be building dioramas, or small three-dimensional scenes, of events of the Civil War era. Tell students they will be using various art materials to build these scenes, as well as real items such as pebbles and twigs, and that the dioramas will be constructed inside of small cardboard boxes.

Home Involvement

Send the Letter to the Family, Blackline Masters 54–59, to families, explaining that the class will be studying the Civil War during the next few weeks. The letter encourages family members to share their knowledge of wars with students and to help them collect small boxes for the project. Be sensitive to the fact that some families may have fled from civil wars or similar situations and may not wish to discuss their experiences.

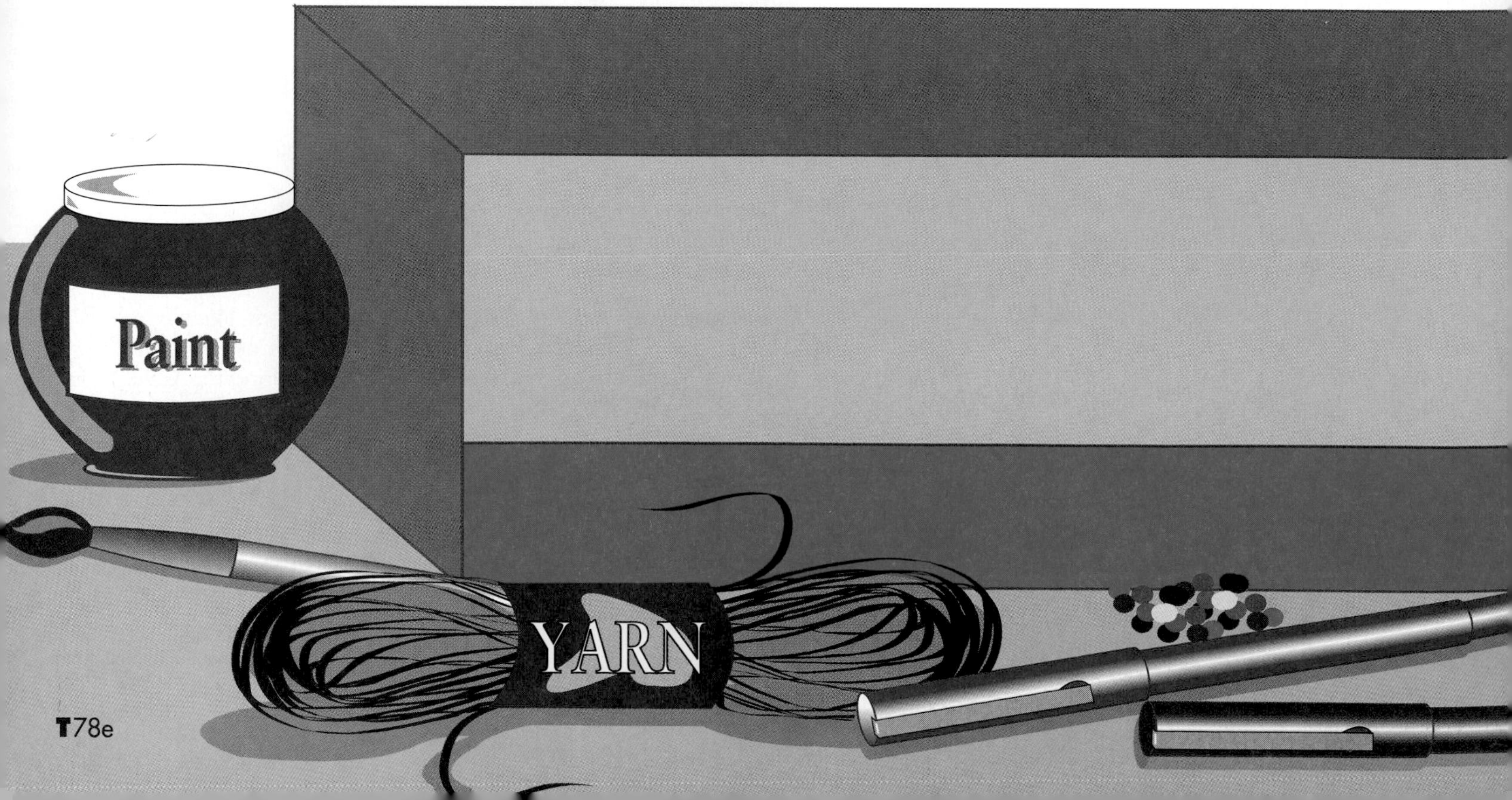

Presenting the Project

Show examples of dioramas that previous classes may have done or that are available in the school. Discuss with students how a diorama is like a scene from a play, using a central area to present an event and a backdrop to enhance its authenticity. Suggest that groups explore both foreground and background in their dioramas, building key figures and items from cardboard and clay, and painting or drawing additional elements on the sides of the boxes.

Help groups brainstorm and choose their subjects. You might suggest the following:

- a southern plantation
- workers and travelers on the Erie Canal
- soldiers at camp
- soldiers in battle
- a photographer taking pictures of a battle
- a nurse treating wounded soldiers
- slaves escaping via the Underground Railroad
- Lincoln delivering the Gettysburg Address

Tell students that, if they prefer, they may develop their own ideas. Remind them to pay particular attention to their chosen subjects as they appear in the unit, and encourage students to do further library research.

Daily Discussion

Take a few minutes each day to talk about the dioramas. Talk about how each diorama will be in one of the cardboard boxes, with three-dimensional figures representing the people. The inside of the box and bottom should be decorated to "set the scene." Help groups brainstorm what to include in their scenes. Encourage them to be as detailed as possible, researching the appropriate nineteenth century clothing, technology, and architecture. Suggest they look for sensory details in their research materials and visualize scenes in their minds as they read. Allow class time for students to work on their dioramas. Have students label the scenes in the dioramas and arrange them for display.

Activity Book

Chapter 5

Name

What is it made of?

Use this page to write down what some of your clothes are made of. Look at the labels.

Word Bank

cotton
leather
nylon
polyester
wool

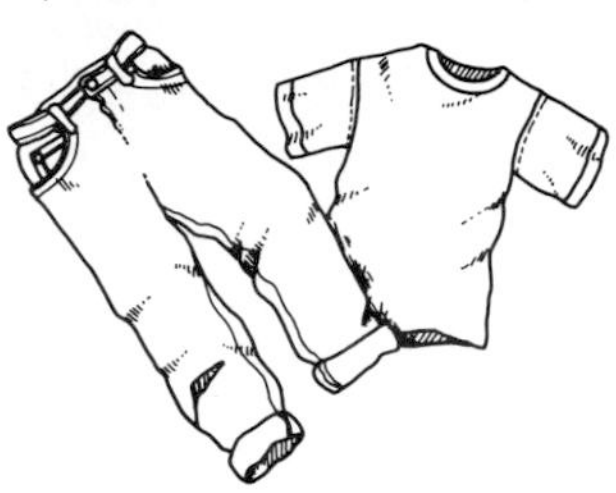

My Record		
Piece of Clothing	What It Is Made Of	Where It Was Made

Name

Supporting Details

Read the sentences below. Then circle the main idea sentence. Write the supporting details on the lines below.

Most slaves worked in farm fields, but some slaves did other jobs. Some slaves worked as servants in their owners' homes. Some slaves cooked the food. Some slaves cared for their owners' children. Some slaves built and repaired buildings from brick and wood. Some slaves made horse shoes. Slave owners often hired out these skilled slaves for wages. Some slaves earned enough money to buy their own freedom.

Answers: lorked as servants
cooked the food
cared for their owners' children
built and repaired buildings
made horse shoes

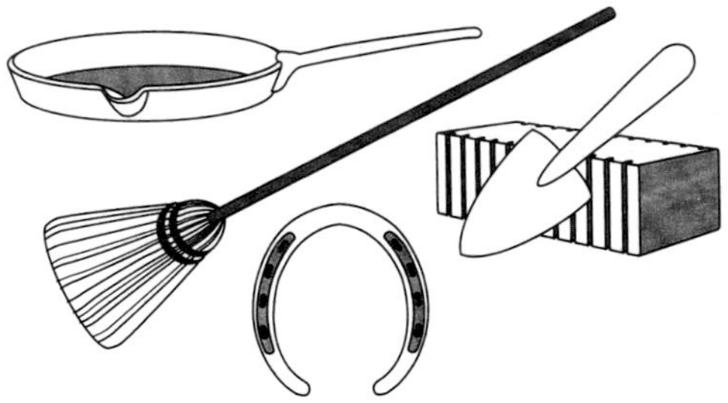

Name

Using Italics

Read the sentences. Circle the names that should be in italics.

Many people have written books about the Civil War. One of these books is Gone with the Wind. It was written by Margaret Mitchell, who lived in Atlanta, Georgia. The book talks about a woman named Scarlett O'Hara, her family, and a man named Rhett Butler. In the story, Scarlett's father owns a large plantation called Tara. After the Civil War, Scarlett tries to make Tara a great plantation again. In 1939, Gone With the Wind was made into a movie starring Vivien Leigh and Clark Gable. Both the book and movie versions of Gone with the Wind were very popular.

Another book about the Civil War was written by Stephen Crane. The book is called The Red Badge of Courage. It talks about a young northern soldier named Henry Fleming. The Red Badge of Courage is often read by students in Grade 8.

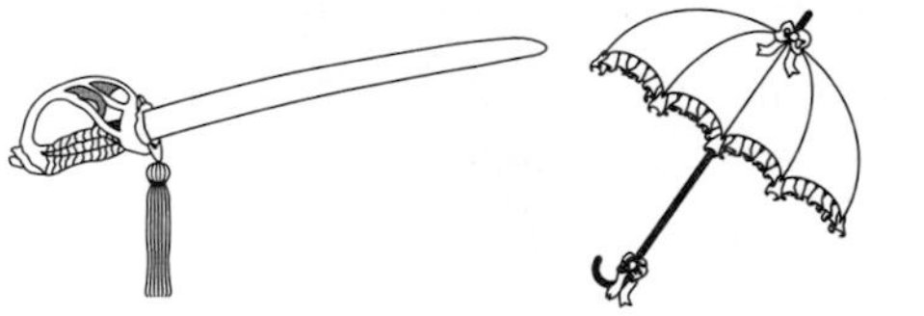

Use the lines below to write the names of three books or newspapers that would need to be underlined or written in italics.

Answers will vary

Name

Reading Graphs

Study the graph and answer the questions.

Bushels of Wheat and Corn Grown on the Gordon Family Farm, 1831–1835

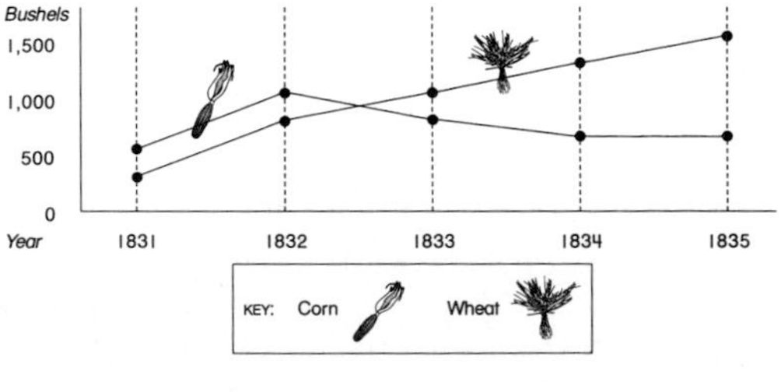

1. In what year did the Gordon family grow the most corn? 1832
2. About how many bushels of wheat did the Gordon family grow in 1833? about 1000 bushels
3. In what year did the Gordon family grow about 250 bushels of wheat? 1831
4. About how many bushels of wheat and corn together did the Gordon family grow in 1834? about 1,850 bushels
5. In what year did the farm produce the most crops? 1835

Name ______________________

Important People and Places

Use the clues to complete the crossword puzzle.

Across

2. woman who wrote *Uncle Tom's Cabin*
5. man who started *The Liberator*
6. woman who was the Underground Railroad's most famous conductor

Down

1. man who started *The North Star*
3. southern sisters who freed their own family's slaves
4. the part of the United States where most slaves lived

				1 D							
		2 S	T	O	W	E		3 G			
				U				R		4 S	
				5 G	A	R	R	I	S	O	N
				L				M		U	
6 T	U	B	M	A	N			K		T	
				S				É		H	
				S							

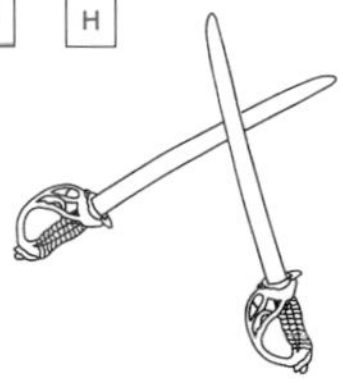

Name ______________________

Writing About the Past

Write the correct form of the words to talk about things that happened in the past.

Most slaves __lived__ (live) in the South. They __worked__ (work) in farm fields. Some slaves __escaped__ (escape). They __traveled__ (travel) north at night in secret. In the day, they __hid__ (hide). Slaves who got caught __returned__ (return) to the South. Usually their owners __punished__ (punish) them.

Harriet Tubman was an escaped slave. She __led__ (lead) many escaping slaves to safety on the Underground Railroad. She __returned__ (return) to the South many times. She __helped__ (help) hundreds of people escape.

Frederick Douglass was an escaped slave. He __opposed__ (oppose) slavery. He __started__ (start) a newspaper he __called__ (call) *The North Star*. He __became__ (become) a strong leader of the abolitionist cause.

Name ______________________

Vocabulary Review

Circle these words in the puzzle.

Canals	Slavery
Factories	Plantation
Rights	South
Civil War	Conductor
North	Underground Railroad

A	Y	V	K	L	W	S	L	A	V	E	R	Y	K	F	C	F	A	I
W	P	C	I	V	I	L	W	A	R	C	O	N	D	U	C	T	O	R
S	L	J	K	E	Z	X	W	U	P	L	A	N	T	A	T	I	O	N
R	I	G	H	T	S	S	A	L	X	R	X	A	V	Z	Q	V	C	Y
U	N	D	E	R	G	R	O	U	N	D	R	A	I	L	R	O	A	D
Z	H	O	O	O	J	M	J	U	W	H	P	E	Q	B	T	O	N	B
T	F	L	R	P	K	L	S	F	T	J	B	E	R	B	V	K	A	P
Q	W	R	X	T	M	I	Q	A	B	H	K	V	L	T	C	N	L	T
T	U	H	O	V	H	X	J	F	A	C	T	O	R	I	E	S	S	V

Name ______________________

Using Contractions

Circle the correct contraction in each sentence.

(I'm)/I've a student in this school. This year (I'm)/I've in Grade 8. Next year, (I'm)/I've going to be in Grade 9. Sometimes, I'm/(I've) got a lot of homework. Most of the students I'm/(I've) talked to think there should be no homework on the weekends, but I study a lot on the weekends. Sometimes, I'm/(I've) got to study hard to keep up with the class. But (I'm)/I've working hard to learn English.

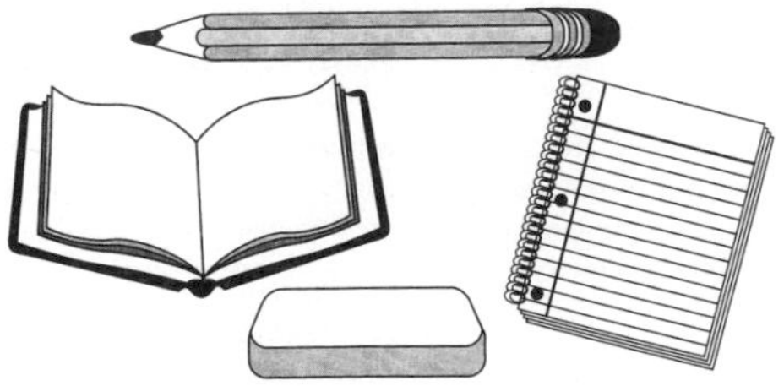

Write about yourself. What grade are you in? How are you doing in school? Use the contractions *I'm* and *I've*.

Answers will vary.

Activity Book

Chapter 6

Name ______________________________

Causes of the Civil War

Put the correct number from Column B in the blank in Column A to make true sentences.

Column A	Column B
The North had __5__	1. many large farms.
In the South, there were __1__	2. slavery was needed.
Slavery was legal in __4__	3. elected President of the United States.
Abolitionists believed __7__	4. the South.
Many southern plantation owners believed __2__	5. many railroads and factories.
Abraham Lincoln was __3__	6. seceded from the United States.
Some southern states __6__	7. slavery was bad.

Name ______________________________

Using Commas

Read the sentences. Add commas to the numbers that need them.

In 1860, Abraham Lincoln was elected President of the United States. He got 1,8 6 5,5 9 3 votes. His main opponent, Stephen A. Douglas, got 1,3 8 2,7 1 3 votes. Other people got 1,4 4 1,2 6 2 votes.

At the start of the war, Lincoln called for 7 5,0 0 0 soldiers to serve for 90 days. The South called for 1 0 0,0 0 0 men to serve for 12 months. In all, about 1,0 0 0,0 0 0 men served in the South's armies. About 5 0 0,0 0 0 men served in the North's armies.

Use the lines below to write three numbers that do need commas and three numbers that do not.

Answers will vary.

____

____

Name ______________________________

Stating Opinions

Choose a word from the group below to complete each sentence. More than one choice may be correct.

Answers will vary.

believed	respected	thought	trusted

When the Civil War began, many people ____________ it would not last long. They ____________ that not many soldiers would be hurt or killed. They ____________ that the war would be over in a few weeks. People in both the North and the South ____________ this. Within a few months, people on both sides ____________ differently.

People in the North ____________ Abe Lincoln. They ____________ that he would do a good job as President. They ____________ that he could help win the war for the North. People in the South ____________ that Robert E. Lee was such a good general that they would win easily. They ____________ him as a person and as a soldier.

Use the lines below to write a sentence using one of these four words: *believe, respect, think, trust*. Give your ideas about Civil War events and people.

____

____

____

____

Name ______________________________

Abe Lincoln

Number the facts about Abe Lincoln so they are in the order in which these things happened to him.

__2__ His mother died when Abe was 9 years old.

__4__ In the 1840s, Abe Lincoln married Mary Todd.

__6__ In 1864, Abe Lincoln was reelected President of the United States.

__1__ Abe Lincoln was born in a log cabin in 1809.

__3__ In 1830, the Lincoln family moved to Illinois.

__7__ Six months later, Abe Lincoln was shot and killed as he watched a play.

__5__ Abe Lincoln became President in 1861, and the family moved to Washington, D. C.

Name ______________________________

Using *-er* and *-ist* Words

Add the correct word from the list to each of the sentences.

abolitionist
conductor
founder
leader
novelist
photographer
owner
soldier

1. Matthew Brady was a photographer who took many pictures of the Civil War.
2. Harriet Tubman was the most famous conductor on the Underground Railroad.
3. Clara Barton was the founder of the American Red Cross.
4. Robert E. Lee was a soldier before the Civil War.
5. Frederick Douglass was an abolitionist and started a newspaper called *The North Star*.
6. Abe Lincoln was the leader of the North during the Civil War.
7. Harriet Beecher Stowe was a novelist who wrote *Uncle Tom's Cabin*.

Name ______________________________

Civil War People

Choose two people you have learned about in this unit. Complete the charts about them.
Answers will vary.

Name of Person
What I Learned About the Person
What I Would Like to Learn About the Person
What I Would Like to Ask the Person
Why I Am Interested in the Person

Name of Person
What I Learned About the Person
What I Would Still Like to Learn About the Person
What I Would Like to Ask the Person
Why I Am Interested in the Person

Name ______________________________

Vocabulary

Use the clues to do the crossword puzzle.

Across
2. escaped slave who started *The North Star*
4. part of the United States that was mostly farms
7. man who led the North during the Civil War
8. man who started *The Liberator*
10. what the United States was involved in from 1861 to 1865
11. woman who wrote *Uncle Tom's Cabin*

Down
1. part of the United States where most of the railroads and factories were
3. someone who opposed slavery
5. what connected Lake Erie to the Hudson River
6. how most African Americans in the South lived
9. name of the man who led the South's armies

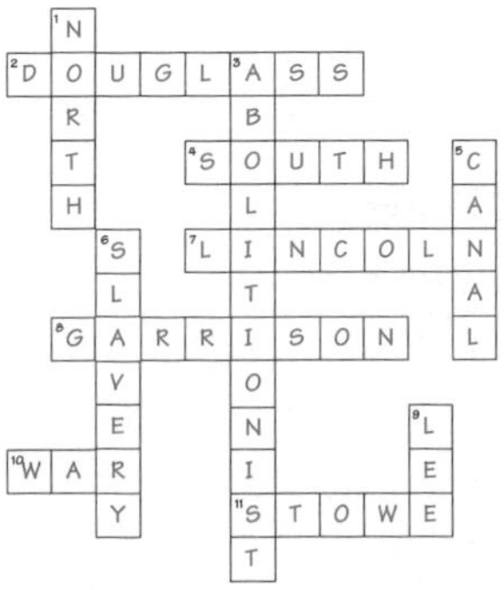

Name ______________________________

Thunder at Gettysburg

Tillie did many things in the story *Thunder at Gettysburg*. Number the events in the order they happened in the story.

3 Tillie left the Weikerts' farm in a wagon when officers told people to go to a safe place.

1 Early in the morning Tillie went to take tea to the wounded soldier she had met the night before.

4 Tillie stopped at a gray farmhouse that was crowded with people.

2 Tillie learned that General Weed, the wounded solider, was dead.

5 Tillie started to help by carrying water and making bandages.

8 Tillie sat on the grass and thought about what had happened in the battle and what war meant.

7 Tillie learned that the North had won the battle.

6 There was a sudden silence.

Write what you thought of this story. It is based on the true story of a young girl who lived in Gettysburg.

Preview

Activate Prior Knowledge

Brainstorm Vocabulary

Ask students to tell what they already know about war. Be sensitive to students' feelings, especially those of students who may have lived through such a conflict. Show pictures of current conflicts from news magazines. Ask students to say any war-related words they may already know, such as *soldier, battle, gun, bullet, fight,* or to point to pictures that demonstrate these concepts.

Develop Language and Concepts

Present Pages 78 and 79

Have students study the pictures on pages 78 and 79. Ask them to describe what the pictures show. Read the text on page 78 and use picture details to help students understand that these pictures represent a time long ago. Help students answer the questions on page 78. You may wish to model some descriptive statements such as:

The soldiers were young.
The soldiers rode horses.

Present the Talk About It activity. Talk with students about the meaning of a civil war. Help them understand that a civil war is a war that is fought between groups within the same country. Use historical and contemporary maps to help students describe who was fighting in the civil wars they mention.

UNIT 3 • CONFLICT

The Civil War

Tell what you know.

What is war?
These pictures are from the 1860s, during the U.S. Civil War. What things do the pictures tell about the war?

78

Options for Reaching All Students

Beginning

Language: Contrast

Have students make posters that show life in the United States now and life in the United States at the time of the Civil War. Have students use large pieces of butcher paper that they divide vertically into two sections, with one labeled *Then* and one labeled *Now*. Then students should add illustrations of comparative objects. For instance, students can put a car on the *Now* side and fill in the *Then* side with a buggy or wagon. Students can draw their own pictures, photocopy them from encyclopedias, or paste in images from magazines. Help students name and label the items on their charts if they need assistance. You may simplify this activity for some students by allowing them to place *any* old-fashioned items in the *Then* column.

Advanced

Critical Thinking: Talk About War

Have students write answers to this question: *Why do people fight wars?* Write the question on the board. Have students write three or more sentences that answer the question. Model how to use infinitive phrases to list reasons. Then discuss students' statements and determine which are facts and which are opinions.

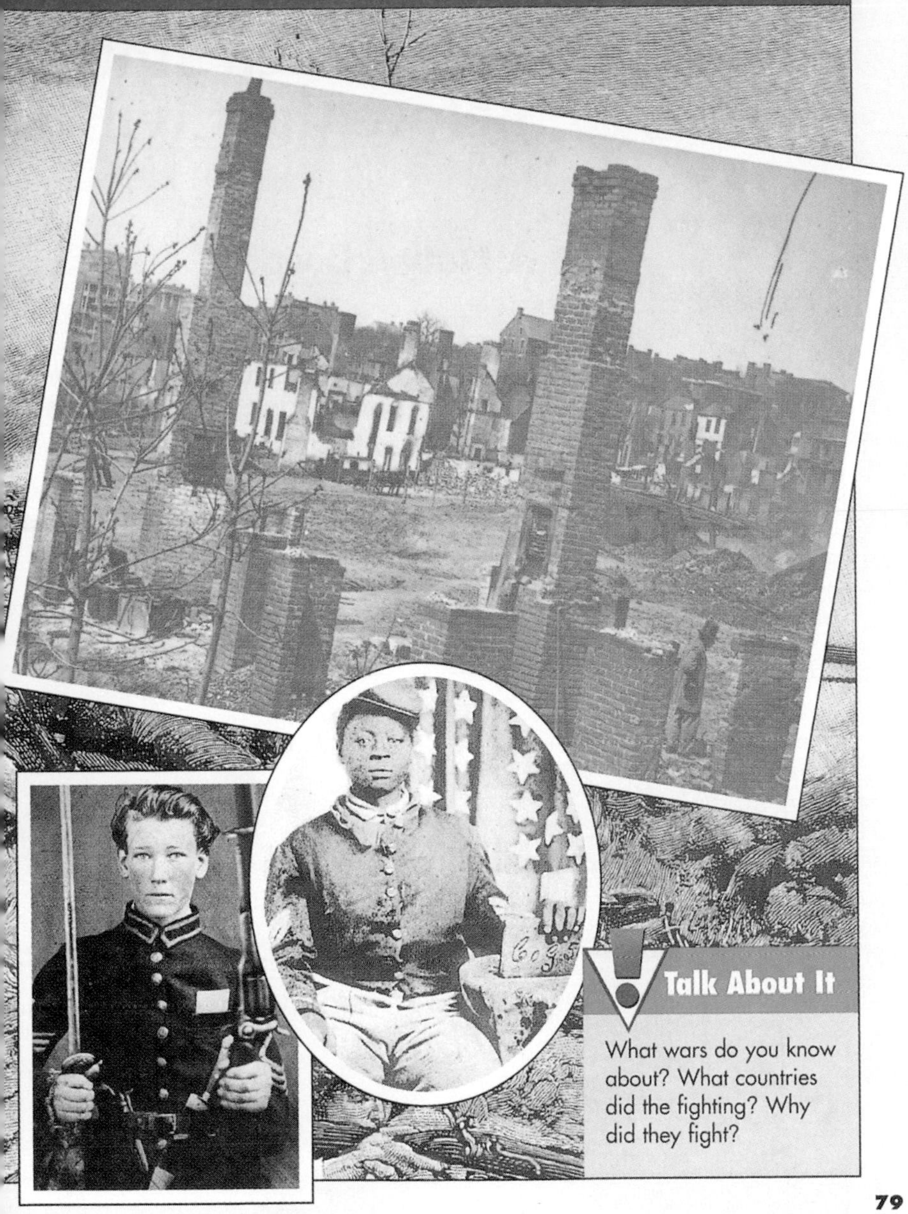

Talk About It

What wars do you know about? What countries did the fighting? Why did they fight?

79

THEME/KEY CONCEPTS

In this unit, students will learn about the U.S. Civil War as the major conflict of the 1800s in the United States. Students will also learn the causes of the war and some of the events that led up to it.

Chapter 5

- The United States became economically divided.
- Slaves had no rights and were badly treated.
- Abolitionists tried to end slavery while the Underground Railroad helped people escape from their lives as slaves.

Chapter 6

- The Civil War was the bloodiest war in United States history.
- Lincoln, Lee, Brady, and Barton were some of the famous people of the war era.
- The war affected ordinary people as well as soldiers.

Cooperative Language Experience

Learning About the Past

If possible, have students visit a historic site or building in your area. Otherwise, have students look at pictures of life in your area in the past. With the class, write a story about what you saw and learned. Encourage each student to contribute something.

Home Connection

Historical Events

Invite students to ask family members about major historical events in their home countries' political history, including wars, changes in government, and causes of conflicts. Students can record information using a chart or time line. Encourage them to share any information they have gathered and feel comfortable talking about. You may wish to use pictures, maps, or other visuals to support students' information.

Present

Activate Prior Knowledge

Relate Personal Knowledge

Ask students to name things that are against the law, such as stealing or hurting another person. You may need to use pantomime or chalkboard sketches to clarify these action words. Then introduce the words *legal* and *illegal*. Be sure that students understand that illegal means "not legal, or against the law."

Develop Language and Concepts

Present Pages 80 and 81

Have students look at the pictures on page 81. Name and act out some of the elements in each picture. Explain that they illustrate life in the United States more than one hundred years ago. Invite students to predict the contents of the lesson. Read page 80 with students. Clarify and discuss the meaning and concept of slavery.

Direct attention to the map and map key. Discuss with them the division of *North* and *South*, leading them to the concept of *A Nation Divided*.

Read page 81 with students. Use the pictures to contrast the differences between the industry in cities in the North and the farm and plantation life in the South.

Draw a T-Chart on the board. Label one side *North* and the other side *South*. Then ask volunteers to come to the board and

(Continued on page T81.)

CHAPTER 5

The United States Before the Civil Wa

A Nation Divided

In 1861, the states in the United States were divided into two kinds. In the North, slavery was mostly **illegal,** or against the law. In the South slavery was **legal.** It was not against the law.

The states were different in other ways, too. In the northern states, people had left farms to work in factories. They made many kinds of products. There were many roads, canals, and railroads. These made it possible to move people and goods quickly and cheaply.

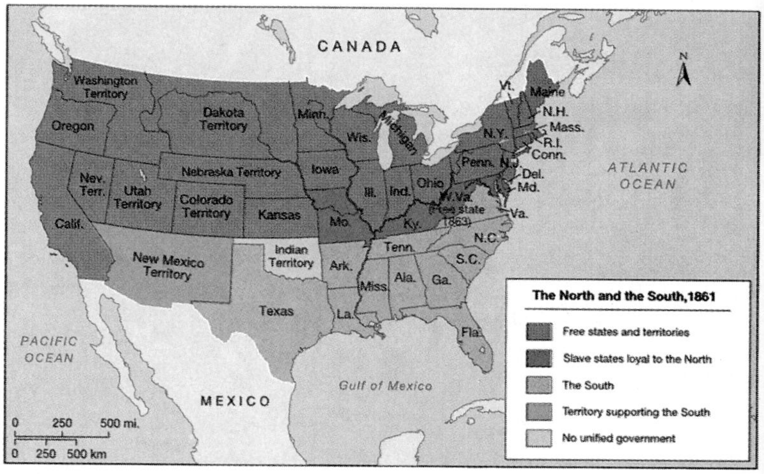

Options for Reaching All Students

Beginning

Language: T-Charts

BLACKLINE MASTER

Have students make a T-Chart in which they list words relating to farms such as animal names, crops, and agricultural tools versus words relating to cities and factories, such as machines, products made, and transportation. Students can use Blackline Master 22 in the Teacher's Resource Book.

Advanced

Social Studies: Study States

Have students study the map and each select one state to find out more about. They should find out these facts about their state: the state capital, about how many people live in the state, the governor, the names of the two largest cities, and the names of all states that share borders with this state. Then point to individual states and have volunteers stand and recite their facts.

Peer or Cross-Age Tutoring

Critical Thinking: Categorize North and South

Have pairs make word cards using the words they have learned in this section. Students should mix the cards together and then sort them into North or South categories. Have students continue using the cards until both students in a pair can correctly categorize all the words.

In the southern states, most people still lived on farms. There were few railroads, canals, roads, or factories.

These differences caused problems between the North and the South. Each side was afraid of the other getting too much power. Every time a new state became part of the nation, people asked the same questions: Would slavery be legal or illegal in the new state? Who had the right to decide—the state government or the federal government in Washington?

Talk About It

Talk about where you were born. Were most people there farmers or factory workers or some of both?

write or draw an appropriate item on the chart, such as *railroads* for North and *farms* for the South.

Invite students to discuss personal experiences and understandings about farms versus factories in the Talk About It.

Language Awareness

Vocabulary
Words That Contrast

Say to students, *Some words here help us contrast and compare things. Often, these words are used in pairs. Two of the words used like that here are* legal *and* illegal. *A similar set is* possible *and* impossible. *Two other words are* many *and* few. Then say sentences that use these pairs of words so that students can have additional examples of the meanings. Have students look through the text to find examples of contrasting words, such as *farmers* and *factory workers* and explain the basis of the contrast.

Assess

Use class discussion for assessment. Students should be able to

- name differences between the North and South at the time of the Civil War

LOOK AHEAD

In the next section, students will learn about slavery and what it meant to be enslaved.

Mixed Ability

Social Studies: State Locations

Help students use a map to name and locate states. Then have them work in pairs to play a guessing game in which one student gives a location or state fact, such as a capital name, and the other student guesses the state being named. Model possible clues that can be given about various states before students begin playing the game. Review the directions *north, south, east,* and *west* as needed.

Writer's Workshop

A Place to Live

Have students write about where they live now or lived in the past. Brainstorm categories with students; for example, kinds of houses and transportation, schools, and jobs that people have. Have each student exchange his or her first draft with a classmate and make revisions based on this peer review.

Practice

Activate Prior Knowledge

Relate Experiences

Show pictures of farms around the world. Then ask students to tell about any farms they visited or lived on, including what crops were grown there and whether a few or a lot of people worked there.

Develop Language and Concepts

Present Pages 82 and 83

ACTIVITY BOOK

Bring a picture of a cotton plant to class along with a piece of clothing made of cotton. Let students touch the garment. Point out the label that tells that the item is cotton. Explain that in the past, much clothing was made of cotton because synthetic materials, such as polyester, had not been invented yet. Use Activity Book page 42.

Read the text with students. Make sure they understand what *rights* mean in this context.

Model a Strategy

Recognize Main Ideas and Supporting Details

ACTIVITY BOOK

Model recognizing main ideas and supporting details:

When I read, I read carefully the first sentence in a paragraph because it

(Continued on page T83.)

Slavery

By the 1800s, growing cotton was an important business in the South. Farmers grew cotton on farms and large **plantations.** Farmers needed more and more workers for their cotton fields.

When the Civil War began in 1861, about 3.9 million African American slaves lived in the United States. Almost all of them lived in the South and worked on the farms and plantations of white families.

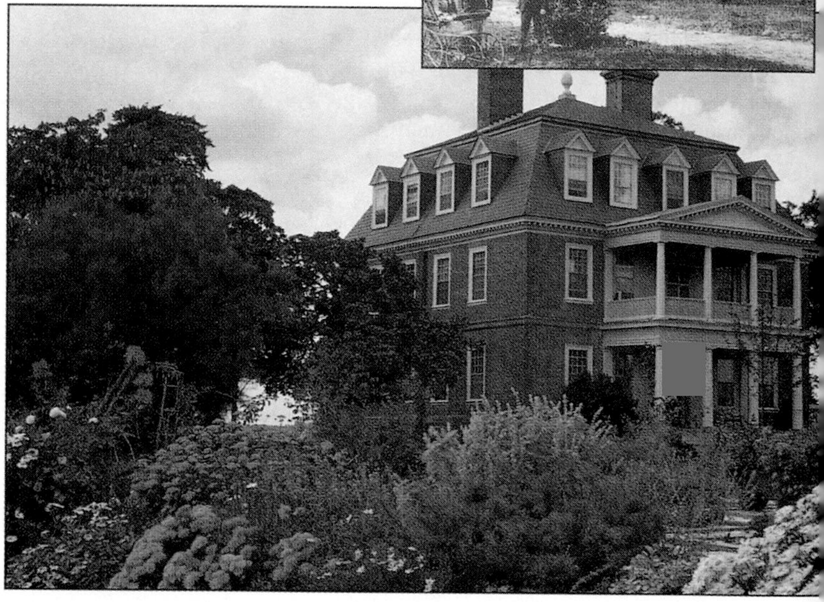

Options for Reaching All Students

Beginning

Social Studies: Use Pictures

Search print and electronic resources to find pictures of how crops are planted and harvested today. Have students photocopy or print out the pictures and make a bulletin board display under the heading of "Growing Crops Today." Help them write labels or captions for their pictures.

Advanced

Social Studies: Slave Codes

Have students look in other textbooks and in library sources to find out about the slave codes that were in place by the late 1600s in North America and that regulated all aspects of the institution of slavery from then on. Students should compile lists of three or more things the codes regulated such as the outlawing of marriage between blacks and whites, the requirement that slaves carry passes if they left their plantations, and the forbidding of slaves to congregate.

Encourage students to check the validity and accuracy of their findings by locating information in more than one source.

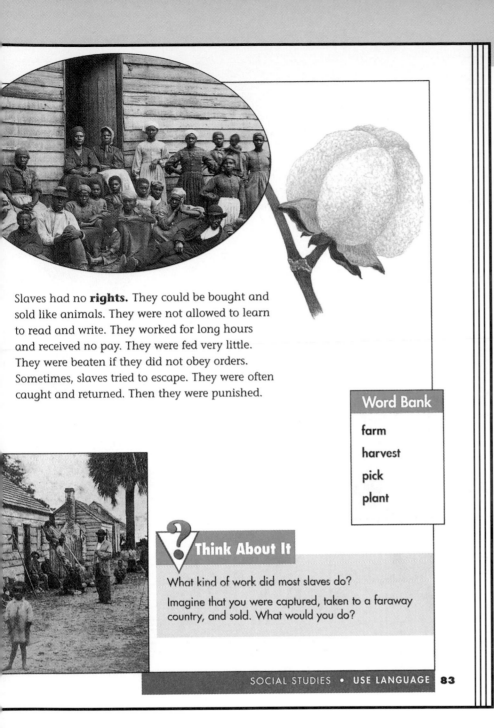

Slaves had no **rights.** They could be bought and sold like animals. They were not allowed to learn to read and write. They worked for long hours and received no pay. They were fed very little. They were beaten if they did not obey orders. Sometimes, slaves tried to escape. They were often caught and returned. Then they were punished.

Word Bank

- farm
- harvest
- pick
- plant

Think About It

What kind of work did most slaves do?

Imagine that you were captured, taken to a faraway country, and sold. What would you do?

often tells what the whole paragraph is about. The sentences that follow explain that main idea. Look at page 83. The first sentence tells what the paragraph is about. The next sentences give examples that show that the slaves had no rights.

Have students do Activity Book page 43.

Language Awareness

Grammar
Passive Voice

Write these sentences on the board: *They could be bought. They were punished.* Beside each sentence, write another version such as *Owners could buy slaves. Owners could punish slaves.* Help students see that the passive form implies that someone did something to the slaves. Point out other examples of the verb *to be* plus the past participle on page 83: *were fed, were beaten, were caught,* and so on.

Assess

Use students' responses to Think About It for assessment. Students should be able to

- tell what kind of work most slaves did
- relate to some degree what it would be like to be enslaved

LOOK **AHEAD**

In the next section, students will learn about the abolitionist movement.

Home Connection

Clothing Labels

Show students where to locate clothing labels and to find out from what materials clothing is made. (You may want to point out to students that clothing items often have several labels that tell such things as the brand, size, and cleaning instructions. Help students recognize what labels tell fabric contents.) Then tell students to go home and look at the labels of five pieces of clothing that belong to them or someone in their families. Tell them to write down what each fabric label says. When students come back to class, make a list on the board of all the different materials that clothes are made of. Help students recognize that clothing today is made from many different types of fabrics.

QuickCheck

Plurals

Check whether students can recognize and form simple plurals. Use the plurals on the page, including *farmers, farms, workers, fields,* and so on. The point out the word *families* and discuss how the *y* becomes an *i* when the plural form is created.

Practice

Activate Prior Knowledge

Review Prior Learning

Have students describe the lives of slaves. Ask students' reactions to such a practice in present-day society and if they would accept a society in which there are slaves or if they would be against such practices.

Develop Language and Concepts

Present Pages 84 and 85

Read the text with students. Point out that being an abolitionist was not popular or particularly safe in the mid-1800s. Ask students why they think a person would take such a dangerous position. Make a chart on the board that compares and contrasts the abolitionists. Students should come to conclude that all kinds of people were against slavery.

Model a Strategy

Use Encyclopedias

Display an encyclopedia volume for *S,* and model how to find out about people in encyclopedias:

If I want to find out more about Harriet Beecher Stowe, a good place to look is in the encyclopedia. I know I must look in the volume that has the letter printed on it that starts her last name—S. Now I have the right book, but I still must find the right page. To do this, I look for the part that has words that start with the letters ST then STO, and so on until I find the right part.

Those Who Opposed Slavery

By the mid-1800s, many people in the United States opposed slavery. These people were called **abolitionists.** They wanted to abolish, or end, all slavery. William Lloyd Garrison was an abolitionist. He started a newspaper called *The Liberator.* It opposed slavery.

Frederick Douglass was another abolitionist. Douglass was an escaped slave. He made abolitionist speeches and started an abolitionist newspaper called *The North Star.* He became a major leader of the abolitionist cause.

William Lloyd Garrison

Frederick Douglass

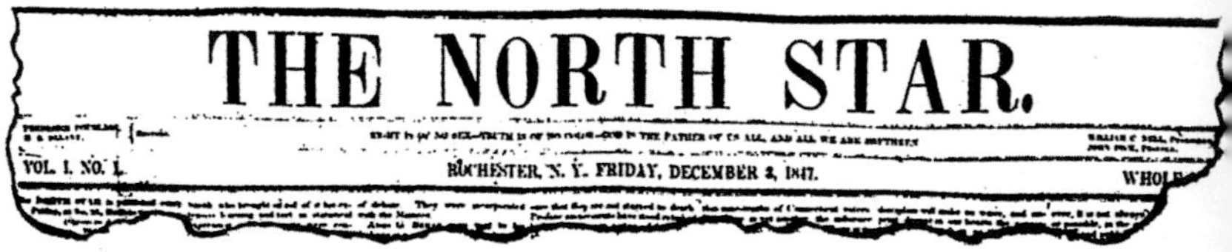

Options for Reaching All Students

Beginning

Study Skills: Use Encyclopedias

Have students find William Lloyd Garrison, Frederick Douglass, and Sarah and Angelina Grimké in one or more encyclopedias. Have students write down the numbers of the volumes in which the information was found. If your school has more than one set or type of encyclopedias, discuss with students why the correct information might not be found in the same volume number of each encyclopedia set. Also encourage students to use picture encyclopedias to find basic information. If possible, demonstrate the use of electronic encyclopedias.

Advanced

Social Studies: Biography

Have students go to the library and use the Internet or any online service to find out more about the abolitionists mentioned in this section. Demonstrate how to search by subject using key words. Ask students to bring the additional information to class and report to other students on what they found and what sources they used.

In 1852, northerner Harriet Beecher Stowe wrote a novel opposing slavery. It was called *Uncle Tom's Cabin*. Stowe's book sold more than 300,000 copies in the first year. It made many people think that the abolitionists were right.

Not all abolitionists were northerners or slaves. Angelina and Sarah Grimké were from South Carolina. These two sisters freed the slaves on their own family's plantation. The sisters also traveled around the country speaking against slavery.

Harriet Beecher Stowe

Angelina Grimké

Sarah Grimké

Think About It

Many of the abolitionists lived in the North. Why was this so?

What would you do if you believed something was very wrong and wanted to change it?

Language Awareness

Spelling
Italics for Titles

ACTIVITY BOOK

Tell students that English sometimes uses italics—letters that slant—to indicate titles. Help students find the three italic titles on pages 84 and 85. Here italics are used to indicate newspapers and books. Tell students that when they write, such titles would be underlined. Point out that the first letter of most words in such titles is capitalized. Have students do Activity Book page 44 for practice.

Assess

Use students' responses to Think About It for assessment. Students should be able to

- name some abolitionists
- tell why many of the most active abolitionists lived in the North
- speculate about what they might do if they wanted to right a wrong

LOOK**AHEAD**

In the next section, students will learn about the Erie Canal, one of the transportation systems that helped the North become more economically developed.

Cooperative Language Experience

Social Studies: Create a Newspaper

Students may enjoy creating their own abolitionist newspaper, using a computer and desktop publishing software, if available. Begin by creating a name for the newspaper. Then have small groups of students work together to write headlines for articles. Tell students they may write headlines about the facts they learned in this section or they could write editorials about the importance of the abolitionist movement. Articles might include "Slavery Should be Abolished Because . . . ", and "Harriet Beecher Stowe's Novel Sells 300,000 Copies." Beginning learners might help by drawing pictures that could go with various articles. Before students begin, discuss the purpose, audience, and language style of each article. Point out that most newspapers use formal language and facts. Editorials may use facts and opinions as well as persuasive words to convince readers to think or act a certain way.

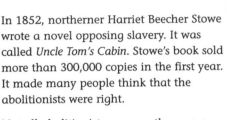

Connect

Activate Prior Knowledge

Recall Information

Ask students to recall information about the importance of transportation routes of the North and the South that they read about earlier in the chapter. Review *roads, canals,* and *railroads* as terms. Point out that each of these required special workers. Discuss with students the kinds of jobs workers did to build and to use a canal. Prompt students to include trench diggers, materials haulers, brick layers, and so forth, as well as people who loaded and unloaded the barges. If possible, show reference pictures of the different stages of building the Erie Canal or any other canal.

Develop Language and Concepts

Present Pages 86 and 87

ACTIVITY BOOK

Read the text with students. Have the class study the painting and the map.

Remind students that building such things as canals is a huge project even today. Point out that hundreds of workers were needed to build the Erie Canal and to maintain it later. Help students use the map and scale to determine about how long the canal was. Point to the line graph, and use finger-tracing to model how to read it. Talk about the four types of workers listed there and what they probably did every day. For example, point out that teamworkers drove the horses and mules along the banks of the canals. Have students do Activity Book page 45 for practice.

Working on the Erie Canal

People in the South mostly continued to work as farmers. In the North, people had many more work opportunities, such as the Erie Canal. Laborers, carpenters, and masons built and later repaired the canal. Teamworkers drove the animals that pulled the ships along the canal.

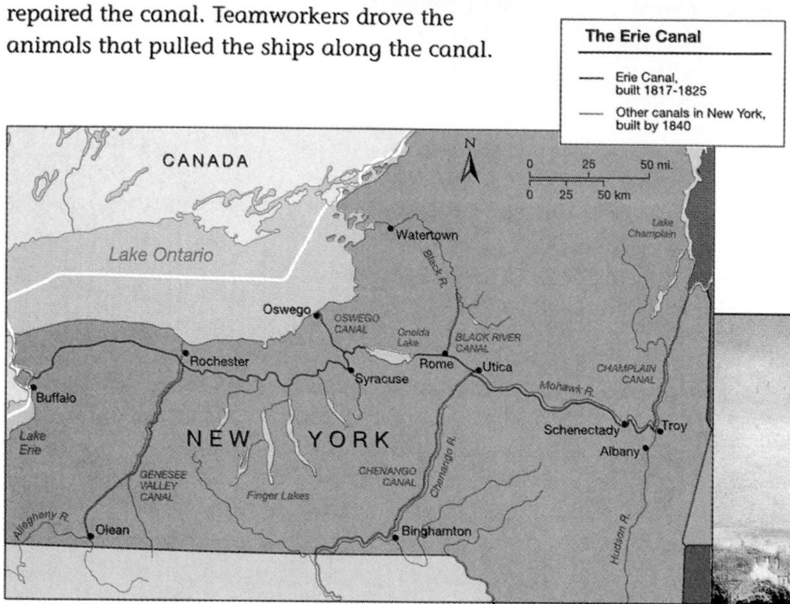

▲ The Erie Canal was one of the major transportation routes in the North before the Civil War.

86 CONNECT LANGUAGE • SOCIAL STUDIES/MATH

Options for Reaching All Students

Beginning

Language: Odd One Out

Divide students into pairs. Then write these lists on the board and ask students to copy them and circle the word in each group that does not belong:

- factories, canals, farms, railroads
- pay, work, job, business, war
- legal, illegal, wrong, right, cotton
- canal, water, ocean, lake, abolitionist
- plantation, slave, cotton, farm, factories

Help pairs form sentences that tell why each wrong word does not belong. For example: *These four words are all related to water. An abolitionist is someone who worked to end slavery. It does not belong in this group of words.* Then ask volunteers to say their sentences aloud.

Advanced

Math: Graph Wages

Have students work in groups of three or four to make their own charts of present-day workers' wages. Almanacs, online services, and government publications such as the *Occupational Outlook Handbook* have listings of wages by industry or job title. Remind students to check the validity of the information by checking the publication date of the source.

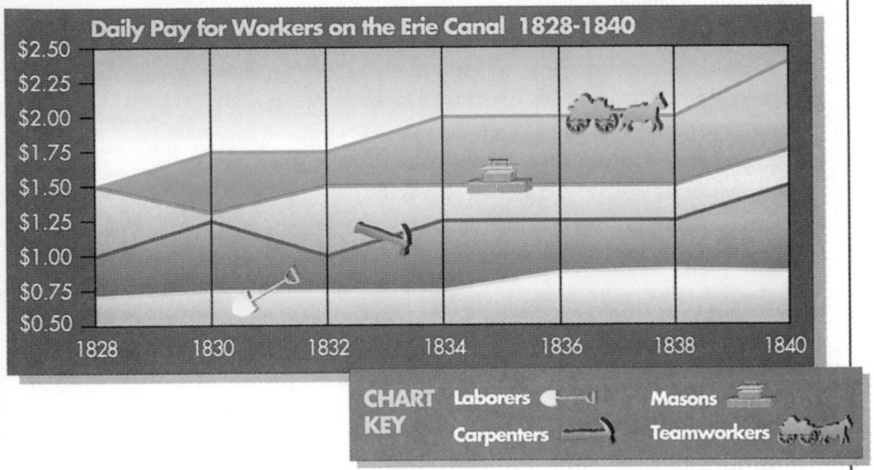

Write About It

Which group of workers was always paid the least?

Which group of workers earned $2.00 a day in 1834?

Which groups of workers saw their pay fall in some years?

Why do you think that teamworkers were paid more than other types of workers?

Language Awareness

Grammar
Expressions for Comparisons

Write the words *most, least, less than,* and *more than* on the board. Tell students that these words help us compare two or more things or ideas. (You may want to use concrete objects, such as pencils or coins, to demonstrate these words.) Ask a volunteer to read the first question in Write About It aloud. Then point out that *the least* means the group of workers who got paid less than any other. Relate the sentence to the line graph. Continue in the same way to explain *most, less than,* and *more.*

Assess ✓

Use the Write About It for assessment. Students should be able to

- interpret the line graph and answer questions based on it
- understand the map and graph keys as sources of information

LOOK**AHEAD**

In the next section, students will learn about the Underground Railroad and the exploits of Harriet Tubman.

Cooperative Language Experience

Field Visit

Take a class trip to a museum or restored home in your area that will give students a sense of what life might have been like in the mid-1800s. Prior to the visit, have students make a list of questions to ask. You might want to suggest that students ask about transportation, farming, and local industry.

Assign several students to act as note-takers during the visit and/or obtain permission to videotape the visit.

After the visit, have students write a class story about what they learned. Help with vocabulary and spelling as needed, but encourage each student to contribute something. Note-takers can help their classmates remember specific facts about the trip.

Connect

Activate Prior Knowledge

Recall Information

Have students recall the description of what it was like to be a slave. Remind them of what happened if a slave tried to escape. Ask them if they think any slaves succeeded in escaping.

Develop Language and Concepts

Present Pages 88 and 89

ACTIVITY BOOK

Read the text on pages 88 and 89 with students, reviewing and clarifying information as needed. Invite students to dramatize events and help them form suitble dilogue to say.

Ask students why they think the secret routes of escaping slaves came to be called the Underground Railroad. Help them recognize that the Underground Railroad was a way of moving people—like the railroads, which were expanding in the 1850s and 1860s.

Discuss the danger that the people who helped with the Underground Railroad were in. Tell students that Harriet Tubman is considered by many to be a heroine of the pre–Civil War era. Ask students why they think Tubman and others were willing to take great risks to help free slaves.

To review important people and places from this chapter, have students do Activity Book page 46.

Harriet Tubman

Harriet Tubman was an escaped slave. She became famous because of her work on the Underground Railroad. The Underground Railroad wasn't really a railroad. It was a system that helped slaves travel to the North in secret and become free.

People in both the North and South hid escaped slaves during the day. At night, the slaves walked to the next safe place. The slaves kept walking north until they did not fear being caught and returned to their owners.

Options for Reaching All Students

Beginning

Art: Summarize Visually

Have students work together to create a wall mural that shows Harriet Tubman in her role as a conductor on the Underground Railroad. Be sure to position the mural so all students can access it easily.

Advanced

Social Studies: Research

Have pairs research Harriet Tubman, the Underground Railroad, or slavery in the South. Have them list five additional facts not found in the Student Book and the sources in which they located their facts. Model how to take notes about key information and where to find bibliographic information about a source (title, author, publisher, copyright date, and page number).

Home Connection

Heroes

Invite students to ask family members about famous heroes from their home countries. Students can work with family members to write a few sentences about each hero. They can then share their information with the class and create an encyclopedia of heroes.

arriet Tubman (far ▶
ft) helped these
eople escape
om slavery.

Tubman had escaped from slavery by using the Underground Railroad. But after her escape, she could not forget that her family was still living in slavery in the South. So she took great risks returning in secret often to the South to help others escape. Over the years, Tubman helped more than 300 people escape from slavery. For this, she is known as the most famous conductor on the Underground Railroad.

◀ This farm was a stop on the Underground Railroad.

Talk About It

What kind of people do you think helped African Americans escape from slavery?

Language Awareness

Grammar
Past Tense

ACTIVITY BOOK Review the past tense with students, discussing how adding *-ed* to verbs creates the past tense. Point out *helped, escaped, returned,* and *walked* as examples of such words. Then point out the irregular words *hid* and *led* as past-tense words that do not fit the model. Write *hide, hid, lead,* and *led* on the board. Ask students to tell what they learned in this chapter by creating sentences that use the past tense. Have students complete Activity Book page 47 for written practice.

Model a Strategy
Understand Textbook Explanations

Model how to understand textbook explanations:

Often when I see new words in textbooks, I read on to get meaning. In this section, the author uses the term Underground Railroad. When I read the sentences and following paragraph, I find out what it means. I learn that it was really a system of people who helped slaves as they traveled to freedom in the North. Textbooks often introduce new terms and then explain them in the next sentences.

Connect

Active Prior Knowledge

Review Prior Learning

Ask students for examples of physical work they have done (e.g., housework, lawn work, gardening). Ask how long they usually work at a stretch. Remind students that slaves worked long hours and did back-breaking tasks.

Develop Language and Concepts

Present Page 90

YELLOW TAPE

Read through the song with students. Discuss what the title means. Explain that being *up* means being happy, while being *down* means being sad. Help students draw the conclusion that being *almost to the ground* means being very sad. Play Side 2 of the Yellow Tape and invite students to sing along.

ACTIVITY BOOK

Have students do Activity Book page 48 for vocabulary practice.

Language Awareness

Grammar

Contractions

ACTIVITY BOOK

Point out and discuss the terms *I'm* and *I've*. Tell students that these are contractions. List other contractions on the board and have students use them in sentences. Use Activity Book page 49 for further practice.

Nobody Knows the Trouble I've Seen

This song describes the feelings of many African Americans before the Civil War.

Nobody knows the trouble I've seen,
Nobody knows but Jesus.
Nobody knows the trouble I've seen,
Glory, Hallelujah!

Sometimes I'm up, sometimes I'm down,
Oh, yes, Lord;
Sometimes I'm almost to the ground,
Oh, yes, Lord.

Options for Reaching All Students

Beginning

Language: Practice with Contractions

Have students work in groups. Have them talk about things that they have and have not seen by making up sentences that use the contraction *I've* plus *seen*. Prompt the activity with words such as *giraffe, skyscraper, ocean, baseball game, soccer game.*

Advanced

Music: Express Moods

Have students bring in examples of music they like and tell what moods and feelings each example expresses. Help students focus on specific words or phrases that indicate feelings, as well as use of instruments and tempo. Invite others to agree or disagree with a speaker's analysis.

Mixed Ability

Music: Spirituals

Play some other spirituals for students. Include a variety of styles. Ask them whether the songs sound happy or sad. Encourage students to realize that even if they don't understand all the words, the tempo and mood of the song can help them understand the general meaning.

Tell what you learned.

CHAPTER 5

1. Have you ever traveled on a canal or a railroad? Tell about it.
2. Where were the differences between the North and South? How did they lead to conflict?
3. Why did Harriet Tubman risk her life again and again?
4. The abolitionists opposed slavery. What are some of the things that groups of people oppose today? How are these people like the abolitionists? How are they different?

Assess

Activity 1: Evaluate students' ability to talk about their travels.

Activity 2: Evaluate students' ability to talk about how industrialization and slavery led to conflict.

Activity 3: Check that students understand the value Tubman placed on being free.

Activity 4: Evaluate students on their ability to list some of the things that people oppose today.

Have students complete the Chapter Self-Assessment, Blackline Master 31. Have students choose the product of one of the activities to place in their portfolios. Add the results of any rubrics, checklists, self-assessments, or portfolio assessments, Blackline Masters 2–18 and 31.

Listening Assessment

BLACKLINE MASTER

Make sure that students have copies of Blackline Master 61 from the Teacher's Resource Book. Play the tape several times and have students complete the activity.

WHITE TAPE

See Chapter 5, page T78c, for the Listening Assessment tapescript.

Options for Assessment

Strategy Assessment

Main Idea and Supporting Details

Ask students to identify the main idea and supporting details for paragraphs on pages 80 and 81, 82 and 83, and 84 and 85. For beginning learners, you may wish to simplify the activity by having students circle the main idea from a choice of three possible answers.

Writing Assessment

What I Learned

Have students write the most important things they learned in this chapter. Encourage them to write in complete sentences and to use past-tense verbs when writing about things that happened long ago.

Language Assessment

BLACKLINE MASTER

Use Blackline Master 60 in the Teacher's Resource Book.

Standardized Test Practice

ACTIVITY BOOK

Use pages 50 and 51. Answers: Score composition according to criteria listed on page 51.

Preview

Activate Prior Knowledge

Use Pictures

Bring in pictures from news magazines about wars and the effects of wars. Help students see that war affects people beyond just the soldiers who are fighting. Talk about some of the effects of war, such as political refugees, destroyed buildings and farms, and so on.

Develop Language and Concepts

Present Pages 92 and 93

Have students look at each picture on pages 92 and 93. Help them understand what each shows. Then discuss the question on page 92 with students. Encourage students to tell or point out the soldiers and civilians in each picture and tell or use facial expressions to show how individuals feel.

Discuss with students how these pictures relate to war in general and specifically to the Civil War. Discuss the things families do regardless of war, such as cooking food, mending clothes, and so on. Give students the option of not relating personal experiences in the Talk About It section. They might talk about general effects instead.

CHAPTER 6

War Between North and South

Tell what you know.

Wars affect many people besides soldiers. What do these pictures show about the effects of the Civil War?

92

Options for Reaching All Students

Beginning

Language: Describe a Picture Orally

Have pairs choose one of the pictures on pages 92 and 93 and then work together to prepare and present an oral description of it. Help students with vocabulary and pronunciation. Ask students to think of a sentence that describes the picture. Then they might name details in the picture that tell more about this main idea.

Advanced

Writing: Create a Written Description of a Picture

Have students work in pairs to write descriptions of one of the pictures. Help students with vocabulary and syntax. Have students put their descriptions on the bulletin board. Have the rest of the class read each description and identify which picture it describes.

Mixed Ability

Social Studies: Current Events

Tape TV news programs that deal with current conflicts in the world. Have students watch the news stories and identify places where the conflicts are taking taking place and issues in the conflicts. Help students use responsive listening skills, including paraphrasing, summarizing, and asking questions, to clarify and demonstrate their understanding of the news stories.

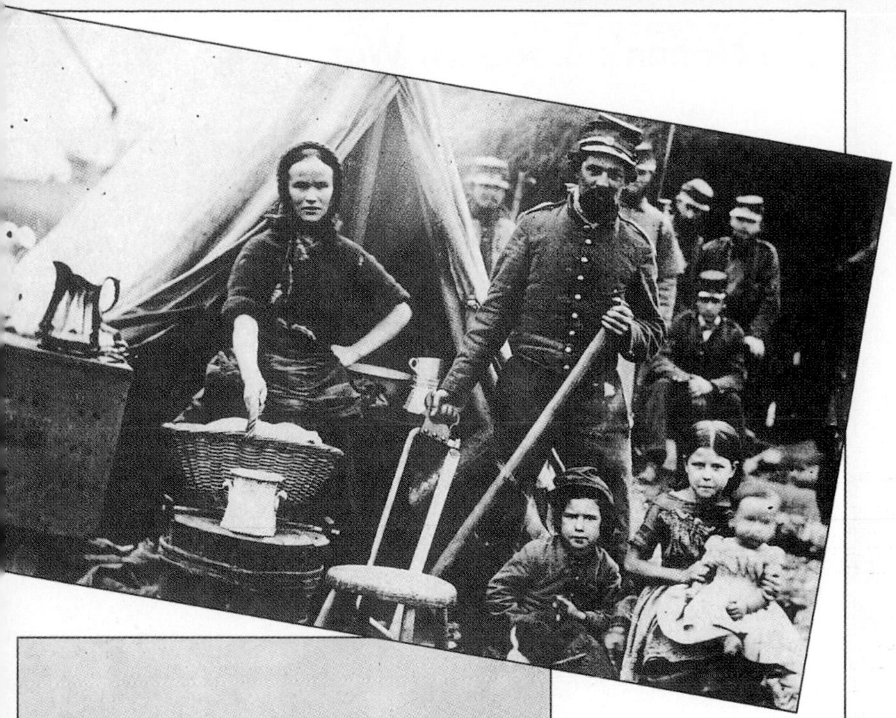

Talk About It

Has a war ever affected you or your family? How?

FYI

- **The top picture on the left-hand page shows residents watching from the housetops of Charleston, South Carolina, during the bombardment of Fort Sumter in April 1861. This was the initial battle of the war.**
- **The picture at the bottom left shows the return of a wounded soldier to his family.**
- **The picture at the top right shows a Union soldier and his family in a northern army camp during the war.**
- **The picture at the bottom right shows a burnt-out area in Richmond, Virginia, the Confederate capital, in April 1865, the month of the Confederate surrender to the Union.**

Home Connection

Talk About War

Have students ask adults at home about any wars they or members of earlier generations may have experienced. Suggest students find out about what family members did during the war, how it affected the family, and so on. These questions may be sensitive, so allow students to respond and participate as they are willing to. Allow students to discuss more general causes and effects if they wish.

Present

Activate Prior Knowledge

Recall and Review Information

ACTIVITY BOOK Have students recall and review what they learned about the causes of the U.S. Civil War in the previous chapter.

Have students complete Activity Book page 52 as a stimulus to recall the causes of the Civil War.

Develop Language and Concepts

Present Pages 94 and 95

Read pages 94 and 95 with students. Explain the disagreements and opposing opinions in the first paragraph. You might have more proficient volunteers role-play arguments of the North and South. Ask students to relate any personal experiences with disagreements that could not be easily resolved. Help students understand that the Civil War was the result of many disagreements over a long period of time, after all peaceful solutions had seemingly been exhausted.

Discuss with students the outcome of the war: the defeat of the South, a reunited nation, and freed slaves. Then discuss other outcomes of the war as mentioned on page 95. With the class, make a T-Chart of the causes and the effects of the war.

Ask students to give verbal answers to the Think About It question as a way of evaluating their understanding of the depth of feeling the war generated.

The Nation's Bloodiest War

Abraham Lincoln became President of the United States in 1861. His political party was against slavery in the new states. The southern states were afraid of this idea. So they **seceded,** or left, the United States. The southern states believed they had the right to leave. Lincoln and others thought that no state had this right.

▲ Union flag (the North)

The Civil War began in 1861 and ended in 1865. The North fought the South and the North won. It had more factories to make guns and uniforms. It had more railroads to move soldiers and supplies. When the war ended, all the slaves were freed.

▲ Confederate flag (the South)

Options for Reaching All Students

Beginning

Math: Commas in Numbers

Have students work individually to find three or more examples of numbers that use commas. Suggest that they look in magazines, newspapers, and math and science textbooks. Have students write the numbers and the sentence or context in which they occur. Then students should share their papers with each other.

Advanced

Social Studies: Cooperative Writing

Have students use the library or an online source to find out three additional facts about the Civil War. Then have students work cooperatively to write a brief report about the Civil War using their new facts. Remind students that their first "writing" task will be to organize their facts into a logical order. Then they should write short expository paragraphs.

Cooperative Language Experience

Field Trip

Have students visit a community library, museum, or local newspaper office to find out if your community was affected by the U.S. Civil War. Find out if anyone from your community was involved in the fighting, if your town was more sympathetic to the North or the South, and where any memorials may be located.

Both sides had thought that the war would be over quickly. People thought that few soldiers would be hurt. In fact, the Civil War was the nation's bloodiest war. About 618,000 Americans died in the war. Hundreds of thousands of others were wounded.

Think About It

In the Civil War, brothers fought against brothers and fathers fought against sons. What does this say about the beliefs held by both sides?

Language Awareness

Spelling
Commas in Numbers

ACTIVITY BOOK

Talk to students about how commas are used in writing large numbers in the United States. Be sure to point out that commas set off groups of three digits and are used in writing numbers of four digits or more. Also mention that no comma is used when writing a year, even though it is more than three digits. Have students do Activity Book page 53 for practice.

Assess ✓

Use class discussion for assessment. Students should be able to

- tell when the Civil War began and ended and which side won
- discuss some of the immediate causes of the start of the fighting
- describe some of the results of the war

LOOK **AHEAD**

In the next section, students will learn about Abraham Lincoln and Robert E. Lee.

For communities that were not involved in the war, this would be an opportunity to talk about chronology and geography as factors in Civil War participation. It could also lead to discussions of when and why your town started, who the founders were, and so on.

Practice

Activate Prior Knowledge

Brainstorm Leadership Words

Talk with students about national leaders. Then have students brainstorm a list of words that describe such leaders.

Develop Language and Concepts

Present Pages 96 and 97

Read page 96 with students. Talk about Abraham Lincoln and clarify students' understanding of his background and leadership. Explain the words *log cabin, lawyer, honest,* and any others that students need to clearly comprehend to gain a fuller understanding of Lincoln. Discuss the meaning of Lincoln's metaphorical phrase about a divided house. Then read page 97 with students and discuss and clarify Lee's choices and leadership during the Civil War. Have students compare and contrast these two leaders.

Model a Strategy

Understand Chronology in Biographies

ACTIVITY BOOK

Model a strategy for understanding chronology in biographies:

When I read about the lives of historical people, I try to think of their lives as being like stories. I try to organize in my mind all the facts in the order in which they happened. That helps me get a better feeling for what that person's life was really like.

Have students do Activity Book page 55.

Leaders of the War

A Northern Leader

Abraham Lincoln was born in a log cabin. His family was poor, but he worked hard, studied, and became a lawyer. He was honest, and people trusted him. In fact, they called him "Honest Abe."

As President, Lincoln led the United States through very difficult times. He believed that the nation would not survive if states could secede. He had said, "A house divided against itself cannot stand." Lincoln worked hard and kept the nation together. Many people think he was the nation's greatest President.

Beginning

Writing: Write About a President

Have students work together in pairs to list words that describe Abraham Lincoln. Have them reread the text on page 96 and make a list of the words used there to describe him. Help clarify vocabulary by giving synonyms or examples, such as: *An honest person tells the truth.*

Advanced

Critical Thinking: Make Decisions

Have students imagine that they had been born in the American South and that their brother said he was going to fight for the North. Have pairs discuss how they would feel and what they would do. You may wish to invite pairs to role-play dialogue that the brothers might have said.

Home Connection

Talk About Leaders

Ask students to talk with adults at home about leaders the adults may have known or know about in their home countries. These could be church leaders, family leaders, and community leaders, as well as national leaders. Ask students to talk with the adults about what qualities made these people the leaders they were. Then have

A Southern Leader

Robert E. Lee was a wealthy army general from Virginia. When the war started, President Lincoln asked Lee to lead the northern troops. But Lee was a southerner. Lee felt it was not right to fight against his home state.

Lee led the southern troops during the war. He was a great general, but the North had more people, railroads, and other things needed to fight a war. After the war, Lee returned to his Virginia home. People in both the North and the South respected Lee as a great leader.

Talk About It

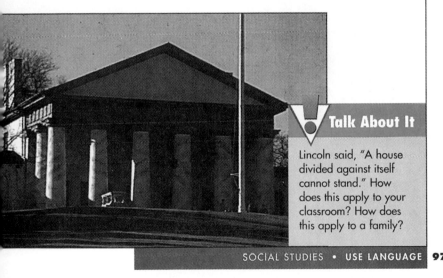

Lincoln said, "A house divided against itself cannot stand." How does this apply to your classroom? How does this apply to a family?

Language Awareness

Language Function
Stating Opinions

ACTIVITY BOOK

Talk with students about words in English that express thoughts and ideas. Point out such words in this section, including *trusted, believed, think, felt,* and *respected.* Help students see that opinions follow these words. For example, *They believed that the war would be short.* Have students do Activity Book page 54 for more practice.

FYI

The house shown on page 96 is in Springfield, Illinois. Lincoln lived there when he was elected President.

Assess ✓

Use class discussion for assessment. Students should be able to:

- describe Lincoln and Lee

LOOK **AHEAD**

In the next section, students will learn about two other famous people from the Civil War era.

the whole class discuss together what they have decided about leaders. Revise and possibly expand the list of human qualities that the class developed at the beginning of this section as part of the Activate Prior Knowledge activity.

Cooperative Learning

Create a Political Advertisement

Bring in printed political advertisements or spots taped from television or radio. Analyze the logical and emotional arguments used in the advertisements. Then have students create a modern mass media campaign for Abraham Lincoln. Help students list and assign tasks for everyone. Beginning learners can draw pictures for campaign posters or plan costumes and sets for TV commercials. More proficient students can write slogans or broadcast scripts. If time allows, have students record a TV or radio advertisement.

Practice

Activate Prior Knowledge

Review Vocabulary

Use simple definitions, examples, or synonyms to introduce the words in the Word Bank. Ask students to suggest times when people display these qualities. Discuss how difficult times often bring out good qualities in many people.

Develop Language and Concepts

Present Pages 98 and 99

ACTIVITY BOOK

Use contemporary pictures to introduce the occupations *photographer* and *nurse*. Help students tell or act out tasks that each type of worker does. Then read pages 98 and 99 with students. Tell them that photography was a fairly new invention at the time of the Civil War. Point out that taking a picture was harder then than it is today and that each photograph then took several minutes to set up and shoot. Students should come to see that taking 3,500 photos would be a difficult feat and that it was a tremendous accomplishment for the times. Students can use inexpensive disposable cameras for the Try It Out project or collect photos or postcards from families or neighbors.

Review Clara Barton's role in establishing medical care for the northern armies. Discuss how leadership ability and organizational skills were required for her to accomplish her work.

(Continued on page T99.)

Famous People of the War

A War Photographer

Mathew Brady was one of the first photographers in the United States. He helped the world learn about the Civil War. Brady and his helpers traveled with the northern army. Their cameras were very heavy and hard to use, but they took about 7,000 photographs of the war. Today these photographs are famous. They are a major part of the record of the war.

▼ Mathew Brady (below) took many photographs of Abraham Lincoln.

Try It Out

Take photographs that describe your neighborhood. What things would you include? What things would you leave out? Why?

Options for Reaching All Students

Beginning

Language: Career Words

Have students photograph adult family members or draw pictures of them and label each person's picture with the work or task that person does. If possible, the pictures should show the person at work. Remind students to include work done in the home, such as cleaning, cooking, and laundry.

Advanced

Language: Helping

Have students work as a group to make a list of ways that people help each another. Have students start by listing service occupations in which people help one another, such as doctors and fire fighters. Have each group member choose two or more of the ways people help and work and write sentences that describe these ways.

Mixed Ability

Writing: Caption Pictures

Have students work together to create and caption a display of the pictures they took for the Try It Out project. Have them write two different types of captions for each picture. One should be a serious, informative caption using formal English. The other should be a casual, perhaps funny, caption using informal English.

A Civil War Angel

In 1861, the northern and southern armies had few doctors, nurses, or supplies. A Massachusetts woman named Clara Barton changed that for the northern armies. She collected medical supplies and took them to battles. Her work helped thousands of wounded soldiers. She earned the respect of the nation. After the war, she founded the American Red Cross, a group that helps people in time of need.

Word Bank

- brave
- caring
- hard-working

Write About It

What kind of person do you think Clara Barton was?

Have students complete Activity Book page 57 to review information about people at the time of the Civil War.

Language Awareness

Vocabulary
Occupation Words Ending in *-er* and *-ist*

ACTIVITY BOOK

Write the words *photography, photographer, lead,* and *leader* on the board. Tell students that the *-er* ending is used to describe people.

Thus, a *leader* is one who leads; a *photographer* is one who takes photographs. Have students look back through this unit to find more words such as *owner* and *farmer* that have the *-er* ending. Repeat the same procedure for *-ist* words such as *novelist* and *abolitionist.* Use Activity Book page 56.

Assess

Use class discussion for assessment. Students should be able to

- discuss Brady and his accomplishments
- describe Barton's pioneering efforts

LOOK**AHEAD**

In the next section, students will be introduced to some songs of the Civil War.

Multicultural Connection

Exchange Information

Talk with students about the Red Cross and any experiences they may have had with the group or have read and heard about. Point out that in Islamic nations, the group is called the Red Crescent. If possible, check online databases for recent mentions of the Red Cross in news stories.

Cooperative Learning

Interviews

Have groups of four or five develop interviews between two or three of the Civil War people they have read about and modern TV reporters. Have students present their interviews to the class. Students may want to use a panel format to present the interviews. Remind the "reporters" to use follow-up questions to clarify answers given by the "interviewees."

Writer's Workshop

Write About a Famous Person

Ask students to select a historical person and then write about the person's life and the kind of person they think she or he was. The report should have a clear main idea and should use strong supporting details. It should be edited for spelling, punctuation, and grammar.

Connect

Activate Prior Knowledge

Discuss Music

Have students discuss ways in which music can express emotions and feelings. Demonstrate with both historic martial music and current lyrical music.

Develop Language and Concepts

Present Pages 100 and 101

YELLOW TAPE

Read the head note and lyrics of each song aloud as students follow along in their textbooks. Discuss the repetitive feeling of marching and why both songs talk about coming home.

Play "Tramp! Tramp! Tramp!" on Side 2 of the Yellow Tape several times and encourage students to join in the singing. The tape begins with this verse:

In my prison cell I sit
Thinking Mother, dear, of you
And our bright and happy home so far away;
And the tears, they fill my eyes
'Spite of all that I can do
Though I try to cheer my comrades and be gay.

Then play the second song several times and encourage students to sing along. (There are two additional verses on the tape.) Explain that Southern soldiers were often called *Johnny Reb*, *Hurrah!* is a cheer, and *gay* means happy. Then do the Talk About It section as a class.

Songs of the Civil War

Tramp! Tramp! Tramp!

Many soldiers were taken prisoner and held in prison camps during the Civil War. This song talks about a captured northern soldier who hopes he will soon be set free.

Tramp! Tramp! Tramp! the boys are marching;
Cheer up, comrades, they will come.
And beneath the starry flag,
We shall breathe the air again,
Of the free land in our own beloved home.

Options for Reaching All Students

Beginning

Language: Build Vocabulary

Have students study the artwork on these two pages. Then have them draw pictures of the objects and label each object with its name: *drum, sword, star, flag, horn, tent,* and *eagle.*

Have students practice *marching*. Use a thesaurus to identify other words related to *walking* and demonstrate the differences in meaning.

Advanced

Language: Practice Plurals

Have advanced students review plurals by studying these two pages and making a list of all the words that are plurals. Help them identify irregular plurals, such as *people* and *men.* Make sure they can distinguish between plurals and present-tense verbs that end in *-s.*

Cooperative Language Experience

Study and Perform Songs

Have students listen to recordings of other Civil War songs. Encourage students to find similarities in what the songs are about. Help students identify old-fashioned words or phrases and remind them that language changes over time. Ask students to perform the songs for the rest of the class.

When Johnny Comes Marching Home

This song was sung to southern soldiers at the start of the war. Many people then believed that the war would be short and wonderful.

When Johnny comes marching home again,
Hurrah! Hurrah!
We'll give him a hearty welcome then,
Hurrah, Hurrah!
Then men will cheer, and the boys will shout,
The ladies they will all turn out,
And we'll all feel gay,
When Johnny comes marching home!

Talk About It

These two songs tell about life in the United States during the Civil War. They have been sung for many years. Do you know any songs that tell about life in the nation where you were born or that have been sung there for many years?

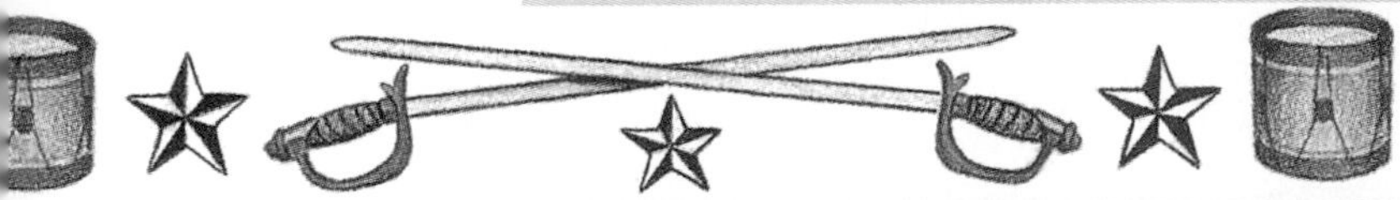

Language Awareness

Grammar
Future Tense with *Will* and *Going to*

Tell students that the songs talk about hopes and dreams for the future. Point out that *we'll* is often used to talk about the future. Have students find instances of *will* and the contraction *we'll* in the text. Review other ways to talk about the future, including *be + going to.* Invite students to talk about their hopes and plans for the future by making up appropriate sentences using *will* and *going to.*

ACTIVITY BOOK

Use Activity Book page 58 to review Civil War vocabulary.

Assess ✓

Use class discussion and the Talk About It question for assessment. Students should be able to

- describe the two Civil War songs and their meanings
- talk about similar songs from other countries

LOOK **AHEAD**

In the next section, students will learn the true story of a young Civil War participant.

Cooperative Learning

Newspaper

Have students put together a newspaper about Civil War events. It could include news reports of battles and profiles of famous people, as well as interviews with ordinary people. Have students use word processing software to publish their final work. Before they begin, review what they know about newspapers and different types of articles in newspapers.

Home Connection

Songs

Ask students to take their textbooks home and sing one or both of these Civil War songs for other family members. Then have students talk to those family members about traditional songs that tell about life in their home countries. Invite students or family members to share these songs with the class, summarizing their main ideas in English.

QuickCheck

Verb Tenses

Check that students are clear about using past tense to describe historical events. Point out that the songs here use the future tense to tell about what people at the time believed was yet to happen.

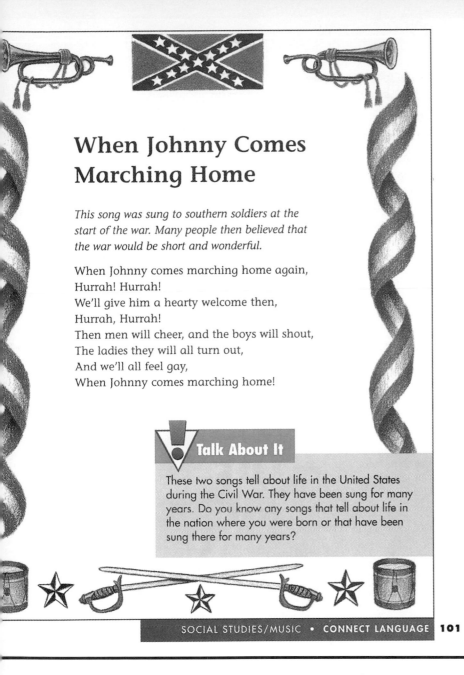

Connect

Activate Prior Knowledge

Use Pictures to Predict

Have students look at the pictures in the story. Ask them to predict what they think it will be about and guess when they think the story took place.

Introduce the Selection

Present Pages 102 through 105

Help students find and read the title of the story. If necessary, explain the word *thunder* and its use here. Tell students that Gettysburg is in the state of Pennsylvania. Have students locate Pennsylvania on the map on page 80. Ask students whether Pennsylvania was part of the North or the South in the Civil War.

Read the introduction to the story with students. Be sure students understand the setting of the story before they begin to read. Explain that this selection is the end of a longer story.

Read the Selection

YELLOW TAPE

Read the story through once aloud to students. Then read it again and discuss the Reader's Tips at the appropriate points.

Play the story on Side 1 of the Yellow Tape for students several times. Invite them to listen to the story as often as they wish.

Language Awareness

Grammar

Action Words

Point out that in narrative stories, action words are important. Go through the story with the students and help them locate words that identify Tillie's actions. Have students act out these words. Sets of actions would include taking the tea to the soldier, following people into the wagon, seeing the soldiers on the road, and helping at the farm.

Model a Strategy

Understand Characters' Feelings

Model a strategy for students about understanding characters' feelings in a story:

In this story, I know that Tillie is the main character, so I know that her feelings are an important part of the story. As I read through the story, I try to understand what Tillie is thinking and how she is feeling. I can use picture clues and word clues to figure out how she feels. I can also think about how I would feel if I were Tillie. For example, when Tillie can't wake the "soldier" up by shaking him, her stomach starts to hurt. This tells me that she is very upset.

Options for Reaching All Students

Beginning

Art: Illustrate Ideas

Put a large piece of butcher paper on the bulletin board and divide it vertically into several sections. After the whole class has read the story several times, have small groups choose incidents in the story they wish to illustrate. Suggest students use the illustrations in the story as guides for ideas. Help them write captions for their illustrations.

Advanced

Social Studies: Find Additional Information

Have small groups use print and electronic resources to find out more about the Battle of Gettysburg. Have each small group find out two or more "new" facts. Model how to take notes on note cards and include bibliographic information about sources. Then have groups organize and present their new information to the class.

QuickCheck

Quotation Marks

Review with students the meaning of quotation marks. Point out the sentences and phrases on pages 102 and 103 that use quotation marks as being examples of the specific words that various characters say. If students need practice, write sentences that include dialogue on the board. Have volunteers add quotation marks to indicate a speaker's exact words.

Thunder at Gettysburg

by Patricia Lee Gauch

Introduction

This is the true story of Tillie Pierce, age 14. In July, 1863, the bloodiest battle in U.S. history took place at her hometown of Gettysburg, Pennsylvania. Tillie was looking for a safe place, but she got caught in the middle of the battle. She is with Henny, a neighbor woman, and Henny's two small girls. They have spent the night in the Weikert family's farm house where Tillie talked with a wounded northern soldier. Tillie supports the North.

NO RUMBLING / NO SHOOTING

July 3, 1863

First thing in the morning
Tillie took Mrs. Weikert's big blue cup
filled with steaming tea downstairs.
The soldier would like that,
she knew.
Tillie was happy to see him
still sleeping near the doorway.
"Sir!" she said quietly.
But he didn't move.
It was as if he were frozen.
"Sir?" Tillie said again, louder.
Her stomach started to hurt.

"General Weed's dead, miss,"
a soldier said.
"He died some time in the night."
The hurt wouldn't go away.

Reader's Tip
General Weed was the soldier that Tillie had talked to the night before.

When the officers put the two cannons
on either side of the house
and told everyone to get to a safe place,
Tillie just followed everyone else
into the wagon.

She could hear the drums
rolling,
the fifes trilling,
and she could hear a low rumble
of voices like leaves in the wind
down Cemetery Ridge way.
But she rode silently,
down Taneytown Road, over the cross road,
toward Baltimore pike.
On the way she saw some prisoners.
They looked plain tired.
Not so bad or so awful
as plain tired.
A lot like General Weed had looked.
The wagon finally stopped
at a little gray farmhouse beyond the pike.
It was full,
packed like a chicken house.
It seemed as though all the farm folk
and wounded near the battleground
had fled there.
And more kept coming,
each telling what he had seen or heard.

Language Tip
Vocabulary
A *fife* is a small musical instrument. People play it by blowing into it and moving their fingers over holes.

Language Tip
Vocabulary
A *pike* is a kind of road.

Reader's Tip
The prisoners were southern soldiers.

Connect

Develop Language and Concepts
Present Pages 106 through 109

Have students retell the story to this point. Encourage them to speculate on how Tillie feels and how they figured this out.

Ask students to study the pictures on these pages. Then have them compare and contrast these pictures with the ones about the war that appeared earlier in the unit. Ask students to name similarities and differences. Have a volunteer write the lists of similarities and differences on the board.

Be sure students understand that this part of the story tells more about the actual battle than about Tillie. Point out the importance of the phrase "American men" on page 107. Discuss with students what this phrase tells about the author's feelings regarding war. Help them see the emotional appeal of this word choice.

Model a Strategy
Summarize Events

Help students model a strategy for summarizing events:

One way I keep track of what is happening in a long story is to make a summary. A summary tells the main ideas or important things that have happened. Summaries are short. I can leave out less important details. Making a summary now will help me better understand what I read as I go on.

Language Awareness

Vocabulary
Words That Paint Pictures

Write these four words on the board: *billowing, burst, quietly, sweeping.* Say to students:

Some words in this part of the story help us paint pictures in our minds about what is happening. Some of these words are billowing, sweeping, quietly, *and* burst. *These words help us get a fuller idea about the story's action.*

Go over each of these four words with students and help them understand the fuller meanings that their use brings to the story. Then have students go back over earlier parts of the story and find additional words that "help paint pictures." Suggest students use a dictionary to get precise definitions.

Teachable Moment
A Dramatic Story Form

Say to students: *Stories usually are written in paragraphs, but this story breaks sentences into short phrases like poetry. This gives the story more of a poetic, dramatic feeling than if it were set in paragraphs.* Invite students to share examples of other stories that use a similar form.

Options for Reaching All Students

Beginning
Language: Retell Experiences

Tell students that in this part of the story, various people relate what they saw in the battle. Ask students to think of some event that happened in the school or the community in which they participated and tell the rest of the group what they remember. Encourage listeners to differentiate between statements of fact and opinion in what they hear.

Advanced
Social Studies: Civil War Life

Have students research and find resources with pictures about the lives of soldiers and others during the Civil War. Have students present orally what they learned to others. Remind them to speak loudly, slowly, and clearly and to use appropriate facial expressions for conveying serious information.

Cooperative Language Experience
War Stories

Find and read to the class additional Civil War stories, both fiction and nonfiction. Have students give oral summaries of the stories and tell how they are alike and different. Help students make a list of common themes that many war stories explore. Invite students to share about any other war stories they have read or viewed.

Reader's Tip
Rebs are a short name for the southern soldiers. *Yanks* are another name for the northern soldiers.

Language Tip
Vocabulary
A *copse* is a group of small trees.

"Well," said one, "all I saw was smoke,
billowing smoke,
but I heard there's some rebel general—
Picket they called him—
sweeping his men across Cemetery
Ridge like . . .
a giant wave.
I do believe nothing will stop those Rebs!"
"Maybe," another said.
"But did you see those Yanks
lining up behind that stone wall
on Cemetery Ridge,
like it was a fortress."
"I did!" a third man yelled out.
"And I saw a gunner there
in a copse of trees just firing
and firing."
A latecomer put in quietly,
"They were fighting hand to hand
when I saw them.

Hand to hand.
Thousands of 'em.
Thousands and thousands of American men,
fighting each other."

Strategy Tip
Stop and Think
The latecomer talks about Americans, not Rebs and Yanks. What point do you think the author is making?

Tillie burst out the back door.
The doctors were setting up straw mats
right outside for the wounded.

She caught up with Henny,
who was carrying water.
Tillie started carrying water, too.
Then she helped the farmer's wife
rip some linen for bandages.
Then she helped a nurse carry blankets.
After that she cut bread
and passed it to the men.
Finally Henny told her, "Sit
for a minute, Till!"
"No, ma'am," Tillie said.
She didn't want to,
and she wouldn't.

Strategy Tip
Understand Character
How was Tillie helping? Why did she want to continue to help?

Connect

Develop Language and Concepts

Present Pages 110 through 113

Have students retell the story up to this point. Then read pages 110 through 113 with students. Tell them that one way to respond to literature is to apply it to your personal life. Ask them how they think they would feel if they were in Tillie's place at the end of the story. Invite them to offer personal experiences that may have affected them strongly. Point out any differences in the emotions that students describe. Help them recognize that powerful situations can cause a variety of emotions. Ask students to name some of the strong emotions Tillie is obviously feeling at the end.

ACTIVITY BOOK Have students complete Activity Book page 59 for practice in sequencing events in the story.

Language Awareness

Grammar
Position Words

Write the words *near, under, behind,* and *by* on the board. Explain that these words tell about position. Use classroom objects to illustrate the specific meanings of the words. Then ask volunteers to follow and give commands to others to position themselves or classroom items *under, near, behind,* or *by* something else.

Response Activities

Personal Response
Point out that Tillie's life was changed by the Civil War. Ask students to think of an event or situation that changed their lives and to write about how they were changed.

Critical Response
Point out that Tillie's story is personal. It doesn't give facts and figures about the Civil War. Ask students to tell why it is good to read both kinds of information and which form they find to be more interesting.

Creative Response
Tell students that the author of the story helped readers feel what Tillie felt during the battle. She used details of what Tillie could see, hear, smell, and feel. Then ask students to think of powerful experiences they have had and use sensory details to describe these experiences.

Options for Reaching All Students

Beginning

Language: Retell the Story

Have pairs take turns retelling the story in their own words. Remind them to use story pictures and to retell events in the order in which they happened.

Advanced

Language Arts: Tell Reactions

As students finish the story, discuss with them their personal reactions to the events that Tillie experienced. Then encourage them to use their overall understanding to retell the story in their own words. Tell students to try to recreate the mood of the story in their retelling.

Mixed Ability

Language: Use Position Words

Have a class treasure hunt. Have one team hide several objects in the classroom and then give oral hints of *near, by, behind, over, under,* and so on, to the other team to help them find the hidden objects. At an appropriate point, have the two teams reverse roles. If necessary, intervene occasionally to give less proficient students time to interpret the clues.

Reader's Tip
At the time of the Civil War, many people in the United States went to church on Sunday morning and did not work. Sunday morning was a quiet time. What does the sudden silence mean?

Language Tip
Vocabulary
Dusk is the time in the early evening just before total darkness.

Even this far away the rumbling
went on and on as though it would finally
split the sky.
But near three o'clock
Tillie felt the air get still.
Sunday morning still.
There was no rumbling or shooting
or shouting.
Nothing.
Some folks started waiting
by the fence or over by the hill,
but the Weikerts and Tillie started
back to the farm.
A misty dusk was settling
when they walked into the yard,
but Tillie could see.

Wounded men,
their arms and legs broken
or bleeding or gone,
lay scattered all over the yard.
Like bits of cloth.

Strategy Tip
Picture the Scene
Tillie sees the wounded and dying soldiers. As you read, picture the scene in the your mind. The author includes the scene to show how terrible war is.

Strategy Tip
Understand Character
What do you think Tillie was thinking about at the end when she sat on the grass? What did she learn about war?

Near the barn. Under the trees.
Everywhere.
Many calling for help.
And behind them near the fence,
a growing pile of long pine boxes.
Coffins.
Nobody could speak. Not Mrs. Weikert
or Henny, not the girls. Not Tillie.
And then a soldier passed them at the well.
"We won!" he said. "General Lee and his Rebels
aren't in retreat yet,
but everyone's saying it's over.
We've won!"
Tillie sat down on the wet grass.
For a long time she sat and thought.
About General Weed's hand
on her arm,
about the men lying outside on the straw mats.
About the smoke, the screaming bullets, bursting shells,
about . . . this yard . . . now.
It was better to win.

But look what had happened.
Dear God, look what happened.

Study Tip
Author's Purpose
An author usually has an important point to make in telling a story. The author chooses details and characters to help make a more important point. In this story, the author tells her ideas about war.

Connect

Activate Prior Knowledge

Recall the Story

Have students review what they know about the Battle of Gettysburg.

Develop Language and Concepts

Present Page 114

YELLOW TAPE

Read the head note and speech excerpt with students. Encourage students to ask questions about the speech. Help them restate sentences in their own words to clarify meaning. Discuss the reason for the speech. Help students understand that it was to honor the soldiers on both sides who had died during the July 1863 battle.

Play the taped version of the speech on Side 2 of the Yellow Tape.

FYI

Lincoln gave his short speech following a now-forgotten two-hour oration by Edward Everett, a very famous speaker of the time.

Language Awareness

Vocabulary
Prefix *un*

Write *unfinished* on the board. Underline the prefix *un-* and point out its meaning as "not." Help them use the prefix to define *unfinished* as "not finished, or not done." Give more examples, such as *unhappy*, *unending*, and *unable*.

The Gettysburg Address

In November, 1863, President Lincoln spoke at the dedication of a cemetery for soldiers at Gettysburg, Pennsylvania. His speech is one of the most famous in U.S. history. Here is part of what he said:

The world will little note, nor long remember what we say here, but it can never forget what they [these soldiers] did here. It is for us the living, rather, to be dedicated here to the unfinished work which they who fought here have thus far so nobly advanced. . . . that this nation . . . shall have a new birth of freedom—and that government of the people, by the people, for the people, shall not perish from the earth.

Talk About It

What do you think the unfinished work was? How can people carry on that work today?

Options for Reaching All Students

Beginning

Language: Description

Have students recall what they know about Abraham Lincoln. Ask them to study the text and look at pictures in the chapter for review. Then have them work in pairs to describe Lincoln to one another. Remind them to include words that describe his appearance, his job, and his character.

Advanced

Social Studies: Compare Versions

Have students look in encyclopedias or other reference materials to find the complete text of the Gettysburg Address and compare it with what is printed here. Challenge students to memorize, recite, and explain parts of the speech that they enjoyed.

Mixed Ability

Speaking: Give a Speech

Have pairs think of an important event that they want people to remember. Have them write and deliver a short (one- to three-minute) speech on the event. Partners can take turns reading sections of the speech. Encourage speakers to speak clearly and use gestures and expressions as appropriate.

CHAPTER 6

Tell what you learned.

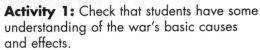

1. What have you learned about the Civil War from studying this unit?
2. What picture in the unit taught you the most about the Civil War? Why?
3. What can the story about Tillie Pierce teach us about war?
4. In this unit, you studied about several people who lived during the time of the Civil War. Which person would you most like to meet? What questions would you ask that person?

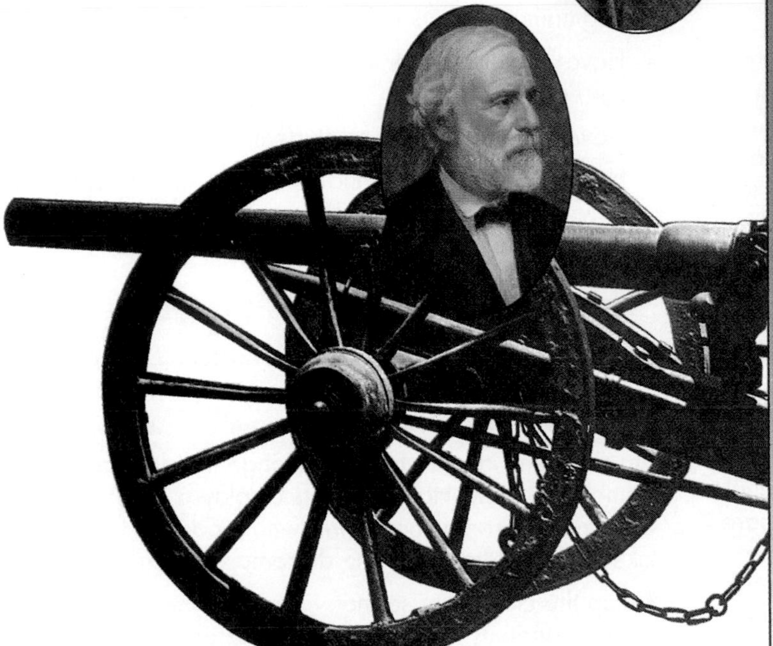

Assess

Activity 1: Check that students have some understanding of the war's basic causes and effects.

Activity 2: After students select a picture, check that they describe it in terms of its importance.

Activity 3: See that students' responses focus on the author's main points, such as the chaos of war.

Activity 4: Give students time to review the unit, select a person, and formulate questions that they would like to ask. Have students present their questions in the format, written or oral, in which they feel most comfortable.

Have students complete the Chapter Self-Assessment, Blackline Master 31. Have students choose the product of one of the activities to place in their portfolios. Add the results of any rubrics, checklists, self-assessments, or portfolio assessments, Blackline Masters 2–18 and 31.

Listening Assessment

BLACKLINE MASTER

Make sure students have copies of Blackline Master 62 from the Teacher's Resource Book.

WHITE TAPE

Play the tape several times and have students complete the activity.

See Chapter 6 Resources, page T78d, for the Listening Assessment tapescript.

Vocabulary Assessment

Make Word Webs

Have students make word webs using some of the core vocabulary from this unit such as *North, South, Lincoln, abolitionist, Civil War, Gettysburg,* and so on. Encourage them to group related words by strand. For instance, one strand could include words related just to life in the North.

Writing Assessment

Civil War Booklet

Ask students to make short booklets about the Civil War. Have them start by making a writing plan. Encourage them to include sections on Causes and Effects, Famous People, and Major Battles and Events. Have them check their work for capitalization, punctuation, spelling, and grammar.

Language Assessment

BLACKLINE MASTER

Use the Blackline Master 63 in the Teacher's Resource Book.

Standardized Test Practice

ACTIVITY BOOK

Use pages 60 and 61.
Answers: **1.** on the Underground Railroad
2. slavery and states' rights
3. leaders during the Civil War.
4. opposed slavery

Wrap-Up

Activities

Civil War Stories

Have the librarian help students find out more about the Civil War. Suggest that advanced students read biographies of famous people and stories about specific battles. (Such books are widely available.) Beginning students can study some of the books that are largely filled with photographs and read the picture captions to understand more about the period.

Other Civil Wars

Invite advanced students to research civil wars in other countries. Demonstrate how to search by subject online or in indices to find relevant resources. Have students take notes summarizing what the conflict was or is about and the main issues involved. Then have students present their findings to one another orally. Help the group find parallels between the conflicts.

Local Economy

Have students find out about local businesses and factories of today and the 1860s. If possible, have students contact a local chamber of commerce to find out about the economy of the area now and in the past. Have students make a poster listing the most important industries, as well as local products of today. Then have students use this information to compare the present-day economy to the economy at the time of the Civil War. Suggest students do this with a two-column chart headed "Then" and "Now" that shows similarities and differences between the two eras.

The Local Economy	
Then	Now

Discussing the Theme

Talk with students about conflicts that result in war. Choose from the following activities that will demonstrate to them how much they have learned and how the information applies to their everyday lives.

- Have students tape-record a list of new words they have learned.
- Have students draw or find pictures that represent words they have learned. Have more proficient students label the pictures and arrange them in alphabetical order. Have beginning students review the labels and pictures.
- Have students relate what they learned about conflicts to current events.
- Have a counselor talk to students about conflict resolution.
- Have groups discuss situations in which the words they have learned will be useful, for example, in social studies classes and in discussions of current events.

Sharing the Project

Use the invitation form, Blackline Masters 32 and 33 in the Teacher's Resource Book, to invite family members to school to see the Civil War dioramas.

Have students decide how to arrange the dioramas for family members to view. Have students display a card that describes what their diorama shows and who made it. Have students take turns standing near the diorama to discuss it with visitors.

Set up the classroom so that visitors can see the other visual projects students have created during unit activities as well as the dioramas.

Signs of Success!

Duplicate a copy of this checklist for each student.

Name: ____

Refer to the checklist below for a quick determination of how a student is progressing toward transitioning out of ESL instruction.

Objectives

- ☐ Describes the prewar economies of the North and South.
- ☐ Discusses slavery and the abolitionist movement.
- ☐ Tells about Harriet Tubman and the Underground Railroad.
- ☐ Describes the results of the war.
- ☐ Names the leaders and some famous pople of the war.
- ☐ Tells how songs and literature describe the war.

Language Awareness

Understands/Uses:

- ☐ words that contrast
- ☐ passive voice
- ☐ expressions for comparison
- ☐ past tense
- ☐ contractions
- ☐ commas in numbers
- ☐ words for stating opinions
- ☐ occupation words ending in *-er* and *-ist*
- ☐ future tense with *will* and *going to*
- ☐ action words
- ☐ words that paint pictures
- ☐ position words
- ☐ prefix *-un*

Learning Strategies

- ☐ Recognizes main ideas and supporting details
- ☐ Uses an encyclopedia
- ☐ Understands textbook explanations
- ☐ Understands chronology in biographies
- ☐ Understands characters' feelings
- ☐ Summarizes events

Comments

____

Planning Guide

CHAPTER 7

The Sun

Objectives

Describe the solar system.

Explain why space appears to be black.

Tell how ancient peoples interpreted the universe.

Cite some literary examples that were inspired by the Sun and moon.

Vocabulary Focus

Parts of the solar system, such as *moon, planet, comet, asteroid.*

Words relating to the solar system, such as *orbit, heat, space.*

Parts of the Sun, such as *gases, yellow dwarf, core.*

Names of ancient peoples, such as *Egyptians, Romans, Greeks.*

Lesson	Content Focus	Language Awareness Objectives	Learning Strategies
Preview pp. 116–117 Tell what you know.			
Present pp. 118–119 The Parts of the Solar System	Science	**Grammar** Prepositions of Position	Read a diagram.
Practice pp. 120–121 What is the sun like?	Science	**Vocabulary** Words for *Big*	
Practice pp. 122–123 Why does space look black?	Science	**Grammar** *Little* Versus *Few*	
Practice pp. 124–125 Ancient Ideas About the Universe	Science/ Social Studies	**Grammar** Nationalities Ending in *-ese* and *-an*	
Connect pp. 126–127 "Here Comes the Sun"	Science/ Literature	**Vocabulary** Homonyms	
Connect p. 128 "Brazilian Moon Tale"	Science/ Literature	**Vocabulary** Synonyms	
Assess p. 129 Tell what you learned.			

CHAPTER 8

The Planets

Objectives

Describe different physical characteristics of the planets.

Describe some major events in the history of space exploration.

Name different idioms that relate to space.

Vocabulary Focus

Different characteristics of planets, such as *atmosphere, size, revolve, rotate.*

Instruments used to study the planets and space, such as *telescopes, spacecraft.*

Idioms that refer to space, such as *to space out, sunny-side up, out of this world.*

Lesson	Content Focus	Language Awareness Objectives	Learning Strategies
Preview pp. 130–131 Tell what you know.			
Present pp. 132–135 Facts About the Planets	Science	**Grammar** Present Tense to State General Facts **Grammar** Comparatives	Use charts to make comparisons.
Practice pp. 136–137 Space Exploration Time Line	Science	**Grammar** Dates; *Before* and *After*	Read a time line.
Connect pp. 138–139 How old would you be on Mars?	Science/ Math	**Grammar** Unreal Conditionals	
Connect pp. 140–147 *The Solar System*	Science/ Literature	**Language Function** Words That Describe **Grammar** Ordinal Numbers	
Connect pp. 148–151 *Exploring the Planets*	Science/ Literature	**Grammar** Superlatives	
Connect p. 152 Space Idioms	Science/ Language Arts	**Vocabulary** Idioms	
Assess p. 153 Tell what you learned.			

Resources

Chapter 7

Support Materials

ACTIVITY BOOK: Pages 62–71

DISK: Writer's Notebook

GREEN TAPE: Side 2: "Here Comes the Sun," page T126–T127; "Brazilian Moon Tale," page T128

LET'S TALK CARD: 96 cards to start conversations.

STORYTELLING: Storytelling Anthology: *Worlds Together*

Assessment Materials

BLACKLINE MASTER: Language Assessment, Blackline Master 70

Listening Assessment, Blackline Master 71

CREAM TAPE: Side 1: Listening Assessment, page T129

Look at the map of the solar system. Listen carefully and follow the instructions.

The Sun is the center of the solar system. The Sun is a star. Write the word *Sun* on the Sun.

Nine planets orbit the Sun. Pluto is the planet farthest from the Sun. Draw a circle around Pluto.

Other objects besides planets orbit the Sun. Asteroids are small rocks. Many asteroids orbit the Sun between Mars and Jupiter. Write an X on the map between the fourth and fifth planets.

We live on Earth. Earth is the third planet from the Sun. Write the name *Earth* on our planet.

Support for Newcomers

Newcomer Book C, Survival language for absolute beginners. For overview, see pages xxviii–xxix.

Newcomer Teacher Suggestion Book, Chapter 7, pages 20–21

HomeLink Penguin Readers

The Red Badge of Courage

For Extended Reading

Astronomy Smart Junior: The Science of the Solar System and Beyond by Michael L. Bentley, Random House, 1997. This book teaches about our solar system while transporting readers to colonies in a twenty-first century. **Level: Advanced**

Close Encounters: Exploring the Universe With the Hubble Space Telescope by Elaine Scott, Disney Press, 1998. Dramatic photos, computer images, and current text convey the information about our Solar System. **Level: Advanced**

Galileo and the Universe by Steve Parker, Chelsea House, 1995. The story of how this mathematician, physicist, and astronomer bravely challenged thousand-year-old ideas and changed the course of science. **Level: Advanced**

Our Solar System by Seymour Simon, William Morrow & Co., 1992. An easy-to-read text takes readers on a tour of the planets, moons, asteroids, meteoroids, and comets that travel around the sun. **Level: Beginning**

Starry Skies: Questions, Facts, & Riddles About the Universe by Mike Artell, GoodYearBooks, 1997. This high-interest book about space includes fascinating facts, riddles, and tongue twisters. **Level: Average**

Stars and Planets by David H. Levy and Gregory Bridges, Time-Life Books, 1996. Information on planets, stars, and other astronomical topics is presented in this attractive book. **Level: Average**

Related Technology

Planetary Taxi, Learn Technologies Interactive, 1993. Students drive a space cab searching for the answers to trivia questions about the solar system.

Resources

Chapter 8

Support Materials

ACTIVITY BOOK

Pages 72–81

GREEN TAPE

Side 1: *The Solar System,* pages T140–147

DISK

Writer's Notebook

Assessment Materials

BLACKLINE MASTER

Language Assessment, Blackline Master 72

Listening Assessment, Blackline Master 73

CREAM TAPE

Side 1: Listening Assessment, page T153

Listen carefully. Fill in the information you hear in the right place in the chart.

Planets rotate or spin. Some planets rotate quickly and others rotate more slowly.

Jupiter rotates the fastest of all the planets. Jupiter rotates once in about 10 hours. Venus rotates the slowest of all the planets. Venus rotates once in 243 days. Earth and Mars rotate at almost the same speed—about once in 24 hours.

Planets also orbit the Sun at different speeds. Mercury orbits the Sun in only 88 days, while it takes Pluto 248 years to orbit the Sun. Earth orbits the Sun in about 365 days.

Support for Newcomer

Newcomer Teacher Suggestion Book, Chapter 8, pages 22–23

For Extended Reading

The Adventures of Sojourner: The Mission to Mars That Thrilled the World by Susi Trautmann Wunsch, Mikaya Press, 1998. An exciting and well-written account of the robotic rover and lander that explored the surface of Mars. **Level: Average**

Journey to the Planets by Patricia Lauber, Crown Publishers, 1993. Journey to the planets with vivid photographs and informative text. **Level: Advanced**

The Moon by Carmen Bredeson, Franklin Watts, Inc., 1998. Meet Earth's closest neighbor in this informative book about the moon. **Level: Beginning**

Seeing Earth from Space by Patricia Lauber, Orchard Books, 1990. A look at Earth from the astronauts' point of view. **Level: Average**

Space Exploration by Carole Stott, Alfred A. Knopf, Inc., 1997. Read about moon landings, space shuttles, rocket launches, space stations, and the future of space travel in this comprehensive book. **Level: Average**

Voyager: Exploring the Outer Planets by Joan Marie Verba, Lerner Publications, 1991. Travel with the space probes Voyager 1 and Voyager 2 and discover how they have expanded knowledge of the solar system. **Level: Advanced**

Related Technology

Beyond Planet Earth, The Discovery Channel, 1994. The Discovery Channel's exciting contribution to astronomy education.

Project

Solar System Model

This optional project can be completed over the next two chapters. In this project, students will make two different models of the solar system. See the Unit Wrap-Up, page T153a, for more ideas on sharing the project with family members.

What You'll Need

Resource Materials: books or other sources with charts, diagrams, and color pictures of the solar system

Art Materials: plastic foam balls of various sizes; balloons; newspaper strips; flour-water paste, tacks, and scissors; colored construction paper, cardboard, and butcher paper; paints, markers, and colored yarn; textured materials, such as plastic wrap, gravel, and sand; cellophane tape and colored masking tape

Strategies You'll Use

- Use reference resources
- Use a chart and a model
- Visualize

Beginning the Project

Because the distances in the solar system are so great and the Sun is so large, it is impractical to make a model of the solar system in which both the sizes of the planets and their distances from the Sun are in proportion. The project should thus be done in two phases: one in which students make proportional models of the planets and one in which students visualize the planets' proportional distances from the Sun.

Invite students to look at the pictures of the solar system in resource materials and the Student Book. Divide the class into nine pairs or small groups. Write the name of each planet on a separate slip of paper. Have groups randomly select a slip of paper to determine which planet they will focus on. (Depending on the size of the class, you may want to add a tenth group to focus on the Sun.)

Instruct students to pay particular attention to their selected part of the solar system as it is mentioned in the unit. Encourage them to study resource materials in the classroom and do library research as well.

Home Involvement

Send the Letter to the Family, Blackline Masters 64–69, to families, explaining that the class will be studying the solar system and encouraging family members to share information with students. The letter suggests that family members discuss the words for the parts of the solar system in their home languages and tell stories about the solar system from their home countries.

Creating Model Planets

Help students use these charts to create their models. The scale is 1 inch = 92,000,000 miles for the distance from the Sun; 1 inch = 12,500 miles for the circumference.

Planet	Distance from Sun
Mercury	1/3 inch
Venus	3/4 inch
Earth	1 inch
Mars	1 1/2 inches
Jupiter	5 1/2 inches
Saturn	9 1/2 inches
Uranus	19 1/2 inches
Neptune	30 inches
Pluto	39 1/3 inches

Body	Circumference
Sun	5.8 feet
Mercury	0.8 inch
Venus	2 inches
Earth	2 inches
Mars	1 inch
Jupiter	22 inches
Saturn	19 inches
Uranus	8 inches
Neptune	7.7 inches
Pluto	0.4 inch

Have each group make a papier-mâché model of its planet using a balloon or plastic foam ball, newspaper strips, and flour-water paste. Once the models have dried, students can complete them by adding appropriate colors, textures, and other significant features (such as the rings around Saturn). To achieve special effects, students may paint their models, paste colored paper to them, draw on them, or cover them with textured substances, such as sand, gravel, or plastic, to represent a craggy surface, ice, or water.

Making a Mural of the Solar System

Hang butcher paper along an entire classroom wall or a school corridor. Have students make a mural depicting the distance of the planets from the Sun. Because the Sun is so big, it would work best to show just a part of it at one end of the mural. Have each group use the chart headed *Planet/ Distance from Sun* to calculate the proportional distance of its planet from the Sun. The list shows how far the planets would be from the Sun if Earth were one inch from the Sun.

Have each group draw its planet in the appropriate place on the mural. Ask them to include a label showing the planet's name, actual circumference, and actual distance from the Sun.

If butcher paper is not available, have students draw their planets on separate pieces of paper and mount them on the wall.

Daily Discussion

Take a few minutes each day to talk about students' planet-related projects. Note that several other planet-based group activities are suggested in the Options for Reaching All Students in Chapters 7 and 8. Start by discussing how the groups will construct their planets. As the unit progresses, point out information that students can use in making their models or the mural. See page T153a for ideas about sharing the models and mural with families and friends when the unit is completed.

Activity Book

Chapter 7

Name

Space Word Search

Complete the words in the sentences.
Then find each completed word in the puzzle.

1. P l a n e t s orbit the S u n.
2. M o o n s orbit the planets.
3. The Sun is a s t a r.
4. The u n i v e r s e contains all stars and all space.
5. C o m e t s are made of rock and ice.
6. A s t e r o i d s are pieces of rock and metal that orbit the Sun.

A	S	O	M	X	R	F	Z	M	H	E	T	I	A	K
D	U	C	E	W	S	Y	U	N	I	V	E	R	S	E
R	N	B	O	E	E	C	A	E	F	P	H	L	T	P
P	L	A	N	E	T	S	G	C	E	S	S	I	E	J
M	Y	T	V	O	I	Z	N	T	O	L	O	A	R	G
S	O	L	S	T	U	E	R	P	Q	M	D	N	O	D
K	X	O	S	J	T	V	Q	N	J	T	E	S	I	S
A	S	M	N	U	R	U	U	R	E	I	M	T	D	S
C	W	N	V	S	T	A	R	Z	S	C	N	C	S	B

Name

Where are they?

Complete the sentences with the words in the box. Use the information on pages 118 and 119 in the Student Book.

Word Bank	
around	from
between	next to
close to	to
far from	

1. Comets are balls of rock and ice. They orbit the Sun. Their orbit takes them far from the Sun and then close to the Sun. When comets are close to the Sun, they form tails.
2. The planet Mercury is close to the Sun. It is also close to Earth.
3. The planet Venus is also close to the Sun. It is next to Earth.
4. The Moon travels around Earth.
5. Light travels from the Sun to the planets in the solar system.
6. Planets that are far from the Sun are colder. Planets that are close to the Sun are hotter.
7. There are many asteroids between Jupiter and Mars.
8. The planet Uranus is between Saturn and Neptune.
9. The Moon orbits Earth. It is close to Earth, and it travels around Earth.
10. Comets, asteroids, and planets travel around the Sun.
11. Ten trips around Earth is equal to one trip to the Moon.
12. The planet Pluto is far from Earth.

Name

Solar System Facts

True or False? Write T or F in the blanks.

If a sentence is false, write a correct sentence on the lines.
Use the information on pages 120 and 121 of the Student Book.

1. F The Sun is a planet like Earth or Mars.
   The Sun is not a planet like Earth or Mars.
2. F Most of the light and heat from the Sun gets to Earth.
   Very little of the light and heat from the Sun gets to Earth.
3. T The planets close to the Sun are very hot, and the planets far away from the Sun are very cold.
4. F The Sun is made of solid rock and metal.
   The Sun is made of burning gas.
5. F The Sun is a star that is much different from other stars in the universe.
   The Sun is a star that is much like other stars in the universe.
6. F The core of the Sun is cooler than the outside of the Sun.
   The core of the Sun is hotter than the outside of the Sun.
7. T The Sun is a yellow dwarf. That means it is not in the hottest group of stars.

Name

The Metric System

Word Bank

Kilometers = Miles x 1.6
Miles = Kilometers x .6

Celsius degrees = (Fahrenheit degrees - 32)/1.8
Fahrenheit degrees = (Celsius degrees x 1.8) + 32

Solve the problems. Convert to the unit of measurement in parentheses. Use the information in the box. Show how you found each answer.

1. 180 miles (kilometers)
   180 miles x 1.6 = 288 kilometers
2. 68 kilometers (miles)
   68 kilometers x .6 = 40.8 miles
3. 98.6 degrees Fahrenheit (degrees Celsius)
   (98.6 degrees Fahrenheit -32) ÷ 1.8 = 37
4. 38 degrees Celsius (degrees Fahrenheit)
   38 degrees Celsius x 1.8 = 68.4 + 32 = 100.4 degrees Fahrenheit

Answer the questions. Show how you found the answers.

1. Winds on Neptune can be to 700 miles per hour. How many kilometers per hour is this?
   700 miles per hour x 1.6 = 1120 kilometers per hour
2. The largest asteroid is about 950 kilometers in diameter. How many miles is this?
   970 kilometers x .6 = 582 miles
3. Mercury is a hot planet. But the side of Mercury away from the Sun can have temperatures as low as -279 degrees Fahrenheit. How many degrees Celsius is this?
   -279 degrees Fahrenheit - 32 = -311 ÷ 1.8 = -172.7 degrees Celsius
4. The highest temperature recorded on Earth was 58 degrees Celsius. How many degrees Fahrenheit is this?
   58 degrees Celsius x 1.8 = 104.4 + 32 = 136.4 degrees Fahrenheit

Name ______

Few or *Little*?

Complete the sentences about space and the solar system. Use the words *few* or *little*.

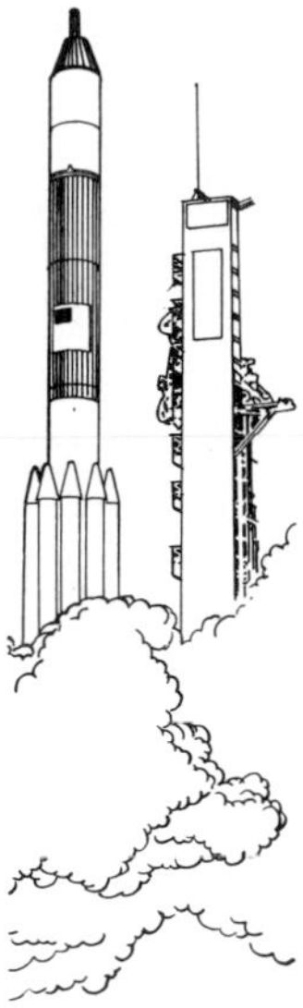

1. There are very few things in space.
2. Little heat from the Sun reaches Earth.
3. Few planets in the solar system have rings around them.
4. In space, there are few things to reflect light.
5. It takes little time for a space ship to leave Earth's atmosphere.
6. Only a few meteors reach the Earth's surface.
7. We have very little information about planets outside of our solar system.
8. Few people have walked on the Moon.
9. We have only a little understanding of how vast the universe is.
10. It takes sunlight only a little time to reach Earth.

Name ______

Names of Nationalities

The Lincoln School did a survey of students who were born in countries other than the United States. Here are the results.

Country	Number of Students	Country	Number of Students
Brazil	2	Ukraine	5
Egypt	2	Mexico	4
China	2	Italy	1
Japan	6	India	2
Greece	1	Colombia	3
Korea	4		

Write sentences that tell the results of the survey. Do not start a new line for each sentence. Use the answers given as a model.

There are 2 Brazilian students. There are 2 Egyptian students. There are 2 Chinese students. There are 6 Japanese students. There is 1 Greek student. There are 4 Korean students. There are 5 Ukrainian students. There are 4 Mexican students. There is one Italian student. There are 2 India students. There are 3 Colombian students.

How many students are there from each continent? Write sentences.

There are 4 North American students. There are 7 European students. There are 2 African students. There are 7 South American students. There are 14 Asian students.

Name ______

Name the planets.

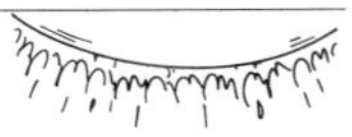

Use the clues to name the planets in the solar system.

1. This planet is farthest from the Sun. Its name has five letters.
   Pluto
2. This planet is closer to the Sun than Earth is. Its name begins with *v*.
   Venus
3. This planet orbits the Sun faster than any other planet. Its name ends with *y*.
   Mercury
4. This planet is closer to the Sun than Jupiter. It has the shortest name of all the planets.
   Mars
5. This planet orbits the Sun every 365 days.
   Earth
6. This planet is the second farthest from the Sun. It is the only planet with two *e*'s in its name.
   Neptune
7. This planet is farther from the Sun than Mars is. The second letter in its name is *u*.
   Jupiter
8. This planet is third farthest from the Sun. You can spell *sun* with the last three letters of its name.
   Uranus
9. This planet is between Jupiter and Uranus. Its name has six letters.
   Saturn

Name ______

Homonyms

Circle the correct homonym to complete each sentence.

1. The (Son / Sun) is the center of the solar system.
   My father is my grandfather's (son / sun).
2. That is the (right / write) answer to the math problem.
   Mark is learning to read and (right / write) in English.
3. I would like to (hear / here) that song again.
   (Hear / Here) she comes!
4. You can (sea / see) the moon at night from Earth.
   Sonia likes to swim in the (sea / see).
5. Adam is studying to (be / bee) an astronomer.
   I yelled when the (be / bee) stung my arm.
6. Earth has only (one / won) moon.
   Lucinda (one / won) the bicycle race.
7. It looks as if someone (ate / eight) a part of the moon.
   When I was (ate / eight) years old, I lived in another country.
8. Did someone eat a (piece / peace) of the moon?
   People want (piece / peace) on Earth. They want all wars to stop.
9. The (main / mane) parts of the Sun are the core, photosphere, and chromosphere.
   The (main / mane) of a horse is the hair on its head.
10. The sun is a yellow star, not a (read / red) one.
    The class (read / red) an article about the solar system.
11. In the experiment, we cut a (whole / hole) in a box.
    The (whole / hole) world could easily fit inside the Sun or the planet Jupiter.
12. The volcano (threw / through) out rock and gases.
    In the experiment, we looked (threw / through) the top of the box.

Activity Book

Chapter 8

Name ______________________

The Solar System

Draw a line from the words on the left to their definitions on the right.

1. asteroids
2. atmosphere
3. comets
4. gas
5. moons
6. orbit
7. planets
8. rotate
9. Sun
10. surface

- move around the Sun
- gases that surround a planet
- nine of these orbit the Sun
- pieces of rock and metal that orbit the Sun
- the outside of a planet
- Earth's air is an example
- balls of rock and ice
- they orbit planets
- turn around (causing day and night on planets)
- the center of the solar system

Find the words listed above in the puzzle. Circle them.

A	S	T	E	R	I	O	D	S	B	P	H	S	M	S	M	O	B	N
I	D	E	C	O	I	T	E	F	S	R	T	F	R	O	R	B	I	T
D	R	O	A	T	M	O	S	P	H	E	R	E	E	E	O	R	O	O
T	I	P	B	A	T	A	G	O	U	A	T	M	N	S	U	N	I	H
C	O	M	E	T	S	E	A	A	S	L	E	E	A	K	R	I	S	J
P	L	A	N	E	T	S	C	L	S	U	R	F	A	C	E	H	G	G

Name ______________________

Comparing the Planets

Use comparatives to complete the sentences about the planets.
Use the chart on Student Book pages 134 and 135 to find the right answers.
Hint: One orbit of the Sun is one year. One rotation of a planet is one day.

1. Mercury is ___smaller___ than Earth. (size)
2. Neptune is ___farther___ from the Sun than Saturn is. (distance)
3. A day on Uranus is ___longer___ than a day on Saturn. (length)
4. Earth is ___warmer/hotter___ than Mars. (temperature)
5. Uranus is ___larger___ than Venus. (size)
6. Jupiter is ___closer___ to the Sun than Neptune. (distance)
7. A year on Mercury is ___shorter___ than a year on Venus. (length)
8. Pluto is ___cooler/colder___ than Mercury. (temperature)
9. Saturn is ___warmer/hotter___ than Pluto. (temperature)
10. A year on Pluto is ___longer___ than a year on Uranus. (length)
11. Mars is ___closer___ to the Sun than Jupiter. (distance)
12. A day on Earth is ___longer___ than a day on Neptune. (length)
13. A year on Jupiter is ___longer___ than a year on Venus. (length)
14. Venus is ___smaller___ than Jupiter. (size)
15. A day on Venus is ___longer___ than a day on Mars. (length)

Make your own comparisons between planets. Which do you find the most interesting?

Answers will vary.

Name ______________________

Read and take notes.

Read the article about Mercury. Then fill in the missing notes.

Mercury

Mercury is the closest planet to the Sun. It is about the size of Earth's moon. The planet was named after the Roman god Mercury. He was the swift messenger for the gods.

Because it is so near the Sun, Mercury can be very hot. The average temperature during the day is 842 degrees Fahrenheit (450 degrees Celsius). The only planet that gets hotter is Venus. Mercury can also be very, very cold. Temperatures on the side of the planet away from the Sun can be as low as -300 degrees Fahrenheit (-184 degrees Celsius).

Mercury orbits the Sun quickly. A year on Mercury lasts only 88 Earth days. However, Mercury rotates much more slowly than Earth. A day on Mercury lasts 59 Earth days. So a Mercury day is almost as long as a Mercury year.

Mercury has a rocky surface covered by craters. Asteroids that hit the planet made the craters. Mercury has a metal core. It has no water and very little air. Unlike Earth, Mercury has no moon.

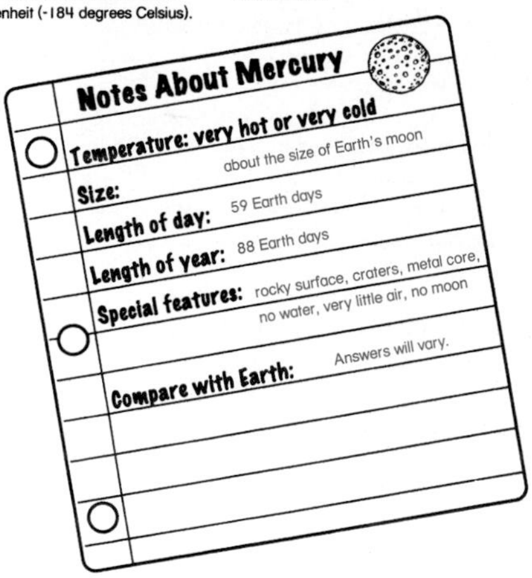

Notes About Mercury
Temperature: very hot or very cold
Size: about the size of Earth's moon
Length of day: 59 Earth days
Length of year: 88 Earth days
Special features: rocky surface, craters, metal core, no water, very little air, no moon
Compare with Earth: Answers will vary.

Name ______________________

An Imaginary Trip

Pretend that you are taking a trip to three other planets in the solar system, such as Mercury, Mars, and Jupiter. What would you see? To write about your imaginary trip, use your notes on Mercury from page 74 of this book. Also use the information in the Student Book.
Be sure to write about how the planets you see are the same and how they are different.

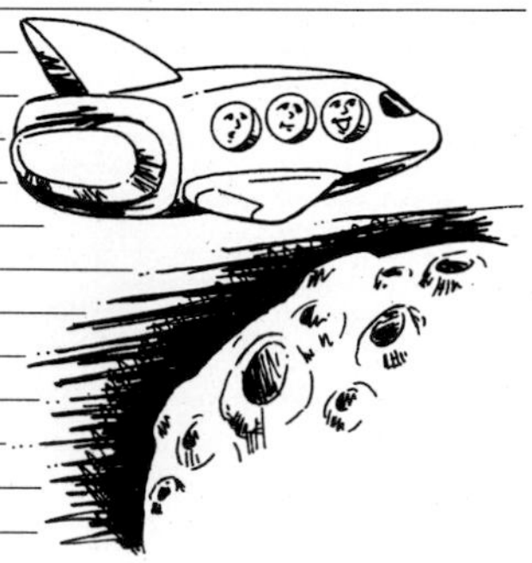

Name ______

If you lived on Mars, . . .

The charts show how much you would weigh and how old you would be if you lived on other planets.

Weight on Earth = 100 pounds	
Mercury	38 pounds
Venus	88 pounds
Mars	38 pounds
Jupiter	265 pounds
Saturn	107 pounds

Age on Earth = 13	
Mercury	54 years old
Venus	19 years old
Mars	7 years old
Jupiter	13 months old
Saturn	5 months old

Use the chart. Write three pairs of sentences like the examples below.

Example:

If you weighed 100 pounds on Earth, you would weigh 107 pounds on Saturn.

If you were 13 years old on Earth, you would be 5 months old on Saturn.

1. Answers will vary.

2. ______

3. ______

Name ______

Facts About the Solar System

Look at the articles about the solar system on pages 140 to 151 in the Student Book. Pick out one or two facts that you think are interesting about each thing listed below. Write sentences with those facts. Answers will vary.

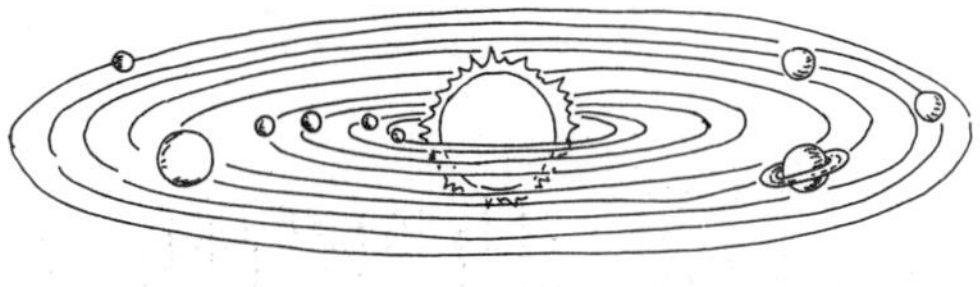

The Solar System

The Sun ______

Mercury ______

Venus ______

Earth ______

The Moon ______

Jupiter ______

Uranus ______

Neptune ______

Name ______

Superlatives

Fill in the sentences with the superlative form of each word given. The superlative form ends in *-est*.

1. Mercury is the closest planet to the Sun. (close)
2. Jupiter is the biggest planet in the solar system. (big)
3. Venus is the closest planet to Earth. (close)
4. Venus has the slowest rotation in the solar system. (slow)
5. The core is the hottest part of the Sun. (hot)
6. Pluto is the smallest planet in the solar system. (small)
7. Pluto is also the coldest planet in the solar system. (cold)
8. Jupiter's moon Europa is the smoothest object in the solar system. (smooth)
9. Neptune's moon Triton is the coldest place in the solar system. (cold)
10. Venus is the hottest planet in the solar system. (hot)
11. Jupiter has the fastest rotation of the planets. (fast)
12. Pluto has the longest year in the solar system. (long)

Name ______

Space Idioms

Complete the sentences with the idioms in the Word Bank. These idioms are on page 152 of the Student Book.

Word Bank

spaced out
sunny-side up
out of this world
sitting on top of the world

1. Angela's new hat is out of this world!
2. Margie didn't hear what I said because she was spaced out.
3. I've been sitting on top of the world since I won the swimming trophy.
4. Why did you scramble my eggs? I like them sunny-side up.

Here are four new idioms with space words. Can you guess what they mean by studying the words around them? Draw a line from each idiom to its meaning.

1. Lobster is expensive. So I only eat it *once in a blue moon*. — rarely, not very often
2. Juan is *starry eyed* over his new girlfriend. — very much in love with
3. That is the best chocolate *under the sun!* — on Earth; anywhere
4. Vanessa hates to lose. She will *move heaven and earth* to win first prize in the spelling contest. — do anything; work very hard

Preview

Activate Prior Knowledge

Relate Personal Experiences

Start students thinking about the unit topic, the solar system, by asking if they enjoy TV programs and movies about space travel. Have them name their favorite programs and movies about space and tell why they enjoy them. Help them decide which shows present realistic information about space and which are fantasies. Work with students to develop a list of space words and/or facts they have learned from these shows.

Develop Language and Concepts

Present Pages 116 and 117

Have students look at the pictures on pages 116 and 117 and make whatever comments they can. Help them use the words in the Word Bank to describe the pictures. Then help students answer the questions on page 116. You may need to suggest possible answers or ask yes/no questions to prompt students' responses.

Have students discuss the question in Talk About It. Help them draw parallels between the popularity of space-related TV programs and movies and people's fascination with space travel.

FYI

The image in the lower left corner is a painting by Steven Hunt.

UNIT 4 • RELATIONSHIPS

The Solar System

Tell what you know.

Word Bank

- moon
- planet
- star
- sun
- universe

What is the solar system?

What would you see traveling in space?

When did people begin to explore space? Where have they been? What have they discovered?

116

Options for Reaching All Students

Beginning

Art: Visualize Space Travel

Ask students to draw a picture or use drawing software to show what they think they would see if they were traveling in space. Encourage them to use words from the Word Bank to label objects in their drawing. Help them add the words they need to label other parts of their drawing. Emphasize that the drawing need not be realistic.

Advanced

Science: Research Astronomers

Have small groups research a famous astronomer, such as Ptolemy, Galileo, Tycho Brahe, Nicolaus Copernicus, Johannes Kepler, or Sir Isaac Newton. Ask students to find out when and where the astronomer lived and what he is famous for. Have students orally present their findings to the class. Remind them to speak loudly and clearly.

Mixed Ability

Critical Thinking: Analyze Science Fiction

Show students two to four selected scenes from a video of a *Star Trek* episode or a similar space adventure. Ask students which, if any, of the events and devices seemed realistic and which seemed unrealistic. Discuss why this type of entertainment is called *science fiction*.

Talk About It

Why do people want to travel in space?

THEME/KEY CONCEPTS

The solar system is vast. Like the elements of any system, the elements of the solar system are highly interdependent.

Chapter 7

- The Sun is a gigantic star at the center of the solar system that produces light, heat, and energy.
- Since ancient times, people have recognized the importance of the Sun and tried to explain the workings of the universe.

Chapter 8

- Nine very different planets orbit the Sun.
- Through space exploration, scientists have learned much about the solar system and Earth itself.

Present

Activate Prior Knowledge

Start a K-W-L Chart

Start a discussion of the Sun and the solar system by asking students what they see in the sky during the day and what they see at night. Have them tell what they know about the Sun and other parts of the solar system. Use the information to create a K-W-L chart:

K: What We Know	The Sun is the center of the solar system.
W: What We Want to Find Out	What are the other parts of the solar system?
L: What We Learned	

Complete the chart at the end of the chapter.

Develop Language and Concepts

Present Pages 118 and 119

ACTIVITY BOOK Tell students that a system is a set of parts that affect each other. Help students name some systems (for example, digestive system, river system). Read the text with students. Help them use the diagrams on these pages to describe the relationships of the elements of the solar system (for example, Earth orbits the Sun and the moon orbits Earth). Finger-trace the orbital paths. Discuss the questions in Talk About It. Use Activity Book page 62.

CHAPTER 7

The Sun

The Parts of the Solar System

The Sun is the center of the solar system. The Sun is a star. It produces light, heat, and energy. Nine planets **orbit,** or move around, the Sun. Earth is one of the planets that move around the Sun.

Other objects orbit the Sun. They are **asteroids** and **comets.**

Moons orbit planets, just as planets orbit the Sun. The Earth has one moon. Some planets have several moons.

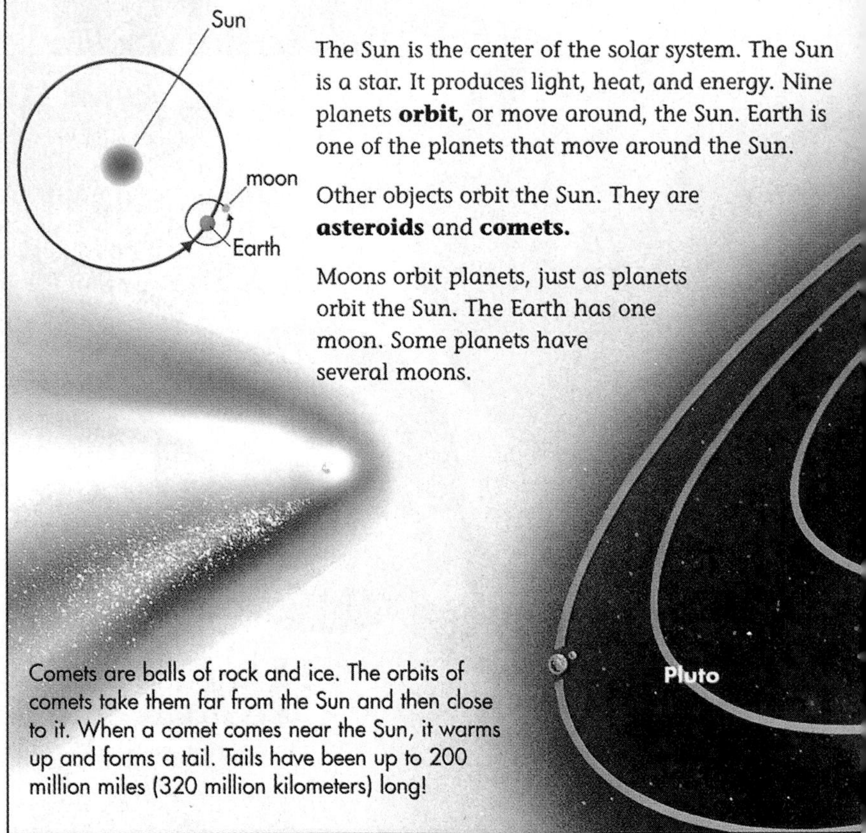

Comets are balls of rock and ice. The orbits of comets take them far from the Sun and then close to it. When a comet comes near the Sun, it warms up and forms a tail. Tails have been up to 200 million miles (320 million kilometers) long!

Options for Reaching All Students

Beginning

Language: Prepositions of Position

Have students make a simple drawing of a real or imaginary place. Ideas would be their rooms or an imaginary classroom. Have them work in pairs and give instructions for a partner to copy the drawing without looking at it by using expressions such as: *There is a chair next to the girl.*

Advanced

Science: Research Parts of the Solar System

Have small groups find more information about one part of the solar system, such as asteroids, comets, or moons. Review how to take notes and list source information on note cards. Encourage each group to draw a poster to illustrate their findings and make an oral presentation to the rest of the class.

Mixed Ability

Language: Give and Follow Commands

Ask three students to go to the board without their books and draw and label the main features of the solar system. Have students in their seats use their books to coach the students at the board. Encourage seated students to give commands using prepositions of place (for example, *near, between, far from*).

The solar system is vast. Thirty trips around the Earth are equal to one trip to the moon. One hundred trips to the moon are equal to one trip to Venus. Beyond the solar system, there are billions of stars and the rest of the universe.

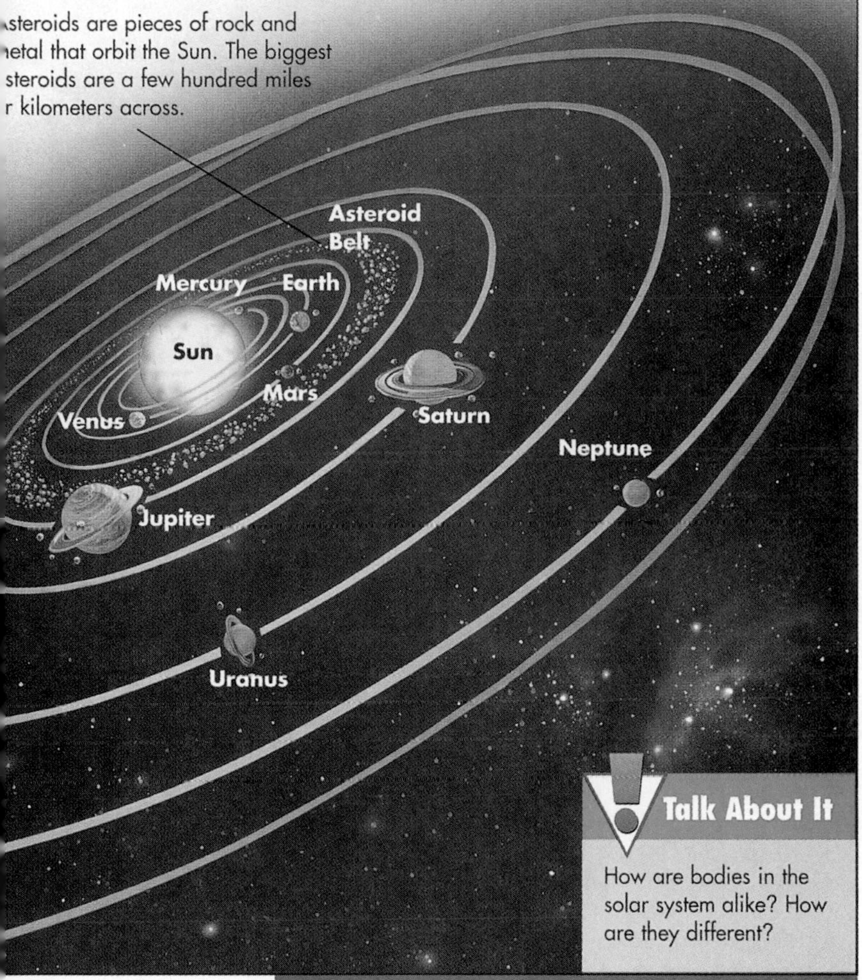
steroids are pieces of rock and
etal that orbit the Sun. The biggest
steroids are a few hundred miles
r kilometers across.
Asteroid Belt
Mercury
Earth
Sun
Mars
Venus
Saturn
Neptune
Jupiter
Uranus

Talk About It

How are bodies in the solar system alike? How are they different?

Language Awareness

Grammar
Prepositions of Position

ACTIVITY BOOK

Explain that words such as *around* tell the position of something. Ask students to find other position words in the text *(beyond, far from, close to, near)*. Present the additional terms *between* and *next to*. Have students use position words to describe the location of classroom objects. Use Activity Book page 63.

Model a Strategy

Read a Diagram

Model how to read a diagram:

When I want to understand a diagram, I start by trying to see the overall picture. For example, this diagram shows the position of each planet in relation to the Sun. Then I look for details. Here I can see the planets are different sizes and colors and travel in different orbits.

Assess ✓

Use class discussion and the Talk About It questions for assessment. Students should be able to

- describe the solar system

LOOK**AHEAD**

In the next section, students will learn what the Sun is like.

Cooperative Learning

Research a Planet

Divide the class into nine groups and assign the name of a planet to each group. Have each group gather as much information as possible about their planet over the course of the unit. The information may come from the text, newspapers, magazines, books, encyclopedias, CD-ROMs, the Internet, and other sources. Tell students that at the end of the unit, they will present an oral report plus a written and illustrated report or a well-organized scrapbook about their planet.

Give students time to meet and plan their research and report. Discuss steps in the research process. Have a school librarian review how to use card catalogs, online databases, and reference materials. Students should gather and evaluate relevant material, take notes on important information, list sources, and organize information logically. Remind them to follow the steps of the writing process (prewrite, draft, revise, proofread/edit, and present/publish). (Note: Depending on the number of students in the class, a tenth group could research the Sun.)

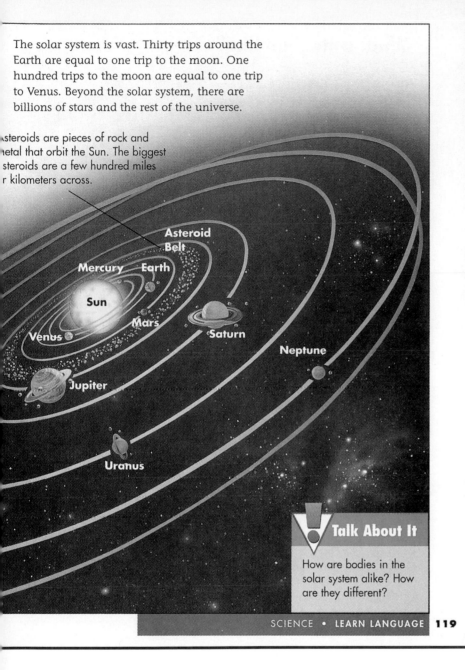

Practice

Activate Prior Knowledge

Make Hypotheses

Ask students to think what Earth would be like if it did not have the Sun to heat it. Help students realize that Earth would probably be too cold for people, as well as most plants and animals, to survive.

Develop Language and Concepts

Present Pages 120 and 121

Read the text with students. Pause often to paraphrase statements and allow students to ask questions. Use a peach or other model to help explain the cross-section diagram of the Sun. To help them picture the size of the Sun and its distance from Earth, take them to a nearby football field. Explain that if the Sun were a 30-inch ball, Earth would be the size of a pea. Place the pea on the 10-yard line of the field. Then walk to the opposite goal line and put down the ball. The 90 yards between the ball and the pea approximate the proportional distance between the Sun and Earth.

To help students understand the immense heat of the core, ask them to think of the hottest day they can remember. Have them describe how hot it felt. Assuming the temperature that day was 100 degrees, help students calculate how many times hotter the Sun's core is (27 million degrees ÷ 100 degrees). Discuss the question in Think About It. Use Activity Book page 64.

(Continued on pate T121.)

What is the Sun like?

The Sun is a star much like other stars in the universe. It is a gigantic ball of burning gas. (**Gases** are materials like air that flow and do not have any shape.) The Sun produces energy. It produces a huge amount of light and heat.

The Sun is about 93 million miles (150 million kilometers) from the Earth. It takes 8 minutes and 20 seconds for the light from the Sun to travel to Earth. Very little of the heat and light from the Sun actually gets to Earth. It is lost in space.

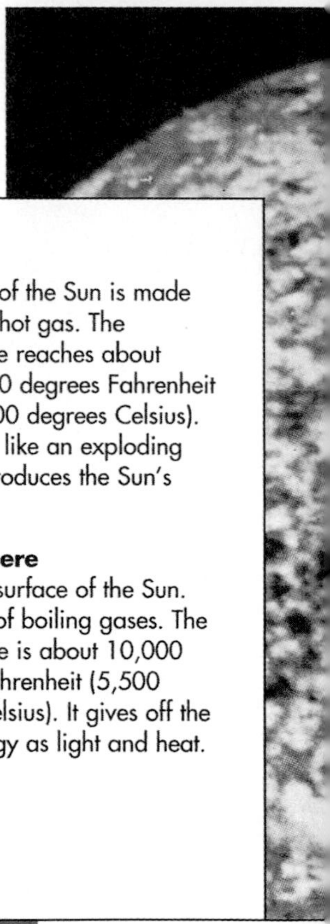

The Sun

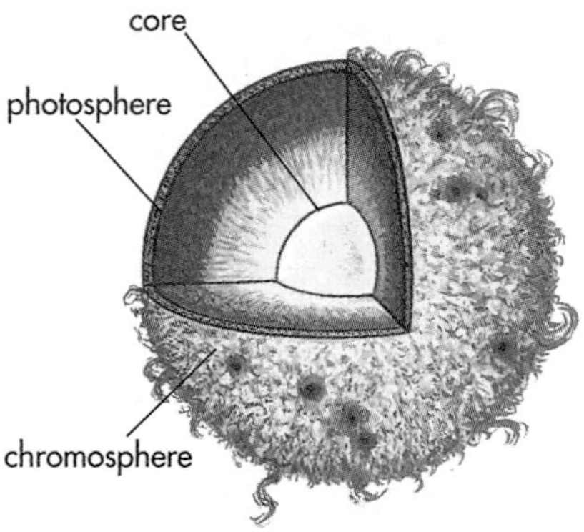

core
The center of the Sun is made up of very hot gas. The temperature reaches about 27,000,000 degrees Fahrenheit (15,000,000 degrees Celsius). The core is like an exploding bomb. It produces the Sun's energy.

photosphere
This is the surface of the Sun. It is made of boiling gases. The temperature is about 10,000 degrees Fahrenheit (5,500 degrees Celsius). It gives off the Sun's energy as light and heat.

chromosphere
This is above the Sun's surface. It is made up of hot gases in motion. Gases often erupt, or burst out, from the Sun's surface into the chromosphere.

Options for Reaching All Students

Beginning

Science: Describe the Sun

On the board, make a word web with the word *Sun* in the center. Have students suggest as many words as possible that describe the Sun. Help students use the words in the web to create sentences about the Sun. You might create cloze sentences for students to complete and recite.

Advanced

Science: Research Stars

Have pairs of students research the differences between the Sun and other stars. Ask them to present their findings in a two-column chart, with one column labeled *Sun* and the other labeled *Other Stars.* Have students take notes or highlight information in the source material they collect. Then have them use each other's notes or highlighted text to check the validity of the facts on the charts.

Mixed Ability

Language: Riddles

Ask students riddles such as the following: *I'm hotter than a red star and cooler than a blue one. What am I?* (Answer: a yellow star) *It takes me 8 minutes and 20 seconds to travel from the Sun to Earth. What am I?* (Answer: light) Tell students to write two riddles of their own based on information in the text. Then allow them to take turns asking and answering each other's riddles.

Compared to other stars, the Sun is medium-sized. Scientists classify it in the group of stars called **yellow dwarfs.** Yellow stars are not as hot as blue stars, but they are hotter than red ones.

The Sun's energy is produced at its center. This energy moves through the Sun's layers to its surface and out into space. The diagram on page 120 shows the main parts of the Sun.

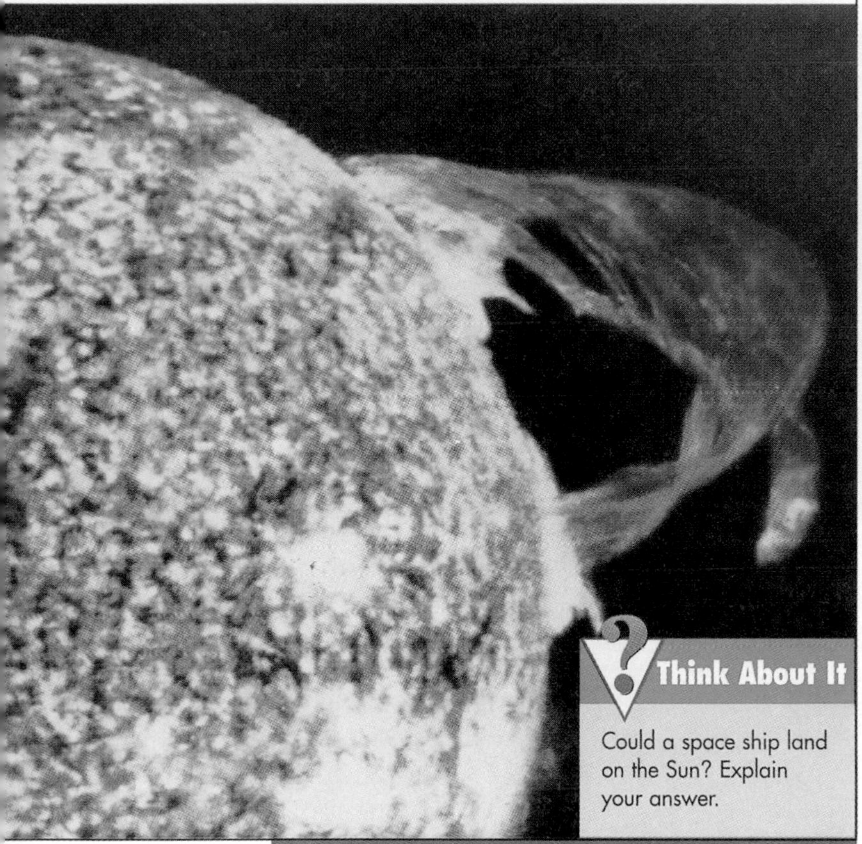

Think About It

Could a space ship land on the Sun? Explain your answer.

ACTIVITY BOOK Present the formulas for converting Celsius to Fahrenheit and vice versa. Use Activity Book page 65.

Language Awareness

Vocabulary
Words for *Big*

Point out that on page 119, the solar system was described as *vast.* On page 120, the Sun is described as a *gigantic* ball that produces a *huge* amount of light and heat. Tell students that *vast, gigantic,* and *huge* all mean "very big." Ask students if they can think of any other words that mean "very big." They may come up with *enormous, great, immense,* and *tremendous.* Provide students with thesauruses to find additional synonyms. Have students make up sentences using words meaning "very big."

Assess

Use class discussion for assessment. Students should be able to

- tell basic facts about the Sun's heat, composition, and distance from Earth

LOOK **AHEAD**

In the next section, students will do an experiment that will help them understand why space looks dark.

Cooperative Learning
Compare Theories of the Universe

Tell students that people in earlier times believed that Earth was the center of the universe and that the Sun revolved around Earth. Have students work in groups of three or four. Ask them to draw diagrams of the earlier idea and the system we now know. Have students compare the two diagrams and make a list of the differences. Ask one person from each group to present their group's diagrams and list to the class. Invite class discussion.

Practice

Activate Prior Knowledge

Develop Theories

Ask students what color they see when they look at the sky at night. Point to the picture of the night sky on page 123, if needed. Encourage students to speculate about why the sky looks black. Write their theories on the board. Then say that the class will test their theories by performing an experiment.

Develop Language and Concepts

Present Pages 122 and 123

Have students work in groups of three or four. Give them the required materials and read the instructions with them. Clarify any points that cause confusion. For example, show students where to cut the holes in the box. Emphasize the importance of working through the list of instructions one by one. Ask students to predict what they will see.

Have students do the experiment. Be sure all groups have finished step 1 and have their flashlights in hand before you darken the classroom. Use window coverings if needed. When the groups have finished, discuss the results with the class and read the text on page 123. Use a flashlight and a hand mirror to demonstrate how light can reflect, or bounce, off a surface. Finally, have students work individually to complete the Write About It activity.

Why does space look black?

When you see photographs of the planets in space, the space around the planets looks black. You can demonstrate why space looks dark.

Things You Need

 scissors 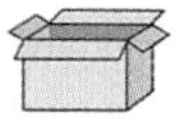 cardboard box  flashlight

Follow these steps.

1. Cut a small circle in one side of the cardboard box. Also cut a small hole in the top of the box for you to look through.
2. Turn out the lights in the room. Turn on the flashlight. Hold it over the hole at the side of the box.
3. Look through the hole in the top of the box. Where can you see the light?

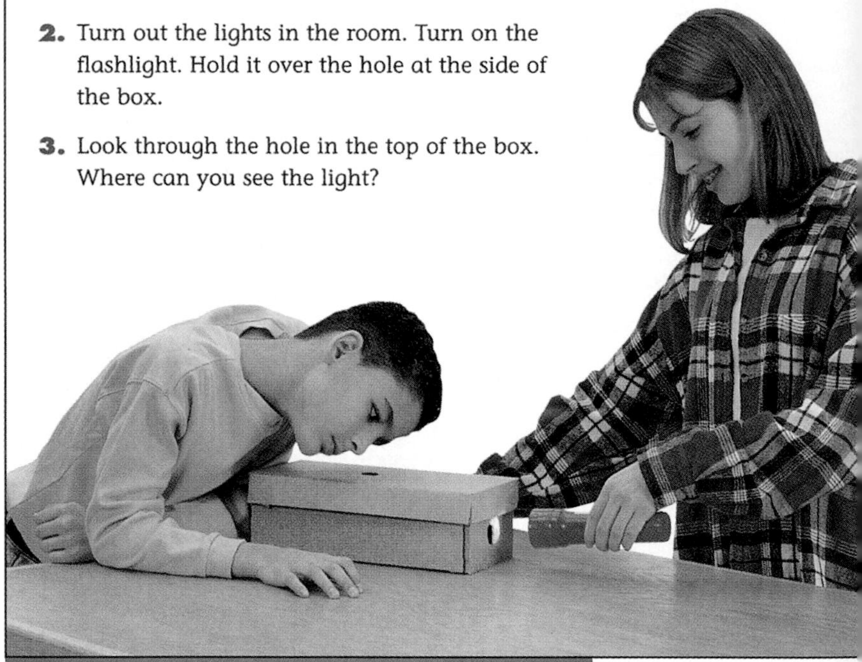

Options for Reaching All Students

Beginning

Language: Follow Directions

TPR

Identify the actions in the directions on page 122 (for example, *cut a small circle, cut a small hole*) and ask students to pantomime or perform those actions. Repeat the commands several times, changing their sequence and speed. Have students take turns giving each other commands.

Advanced

Writing: Describe Space

Have students work in groups of three or four to brainstorm and use a thesaurus to find words that describe space. Then have students work individually to write a description of space and their feelings about it. Have students use creative writing strategies, such as using vivid language and figurative language to convey feelings and ideas about space.

Peer or Cross-Age Tutoring

Language: Practice Shapes

Have students work in pairs of mixed ability. Give each pair five index cards and ask them to draw one of the following shapes on each card: circle, square, rectangle, triangle, oval. Have them identify each shape on the back of its card. Then have them use the cards as flashcards to practice naming

You see a circle of light on the side of the box opposite the flashlight. You see little or no light between the flashlight and the side of the box.

Why is that? You can see light only when something reflects it into your eyes. The light reflects, or bounces, off the side of the box into your eyes. In the middle of the box, there is nothing for the light to bounce off.

There are very few things in space. So light passes through space and it is not reflected. That's why space looks dark.

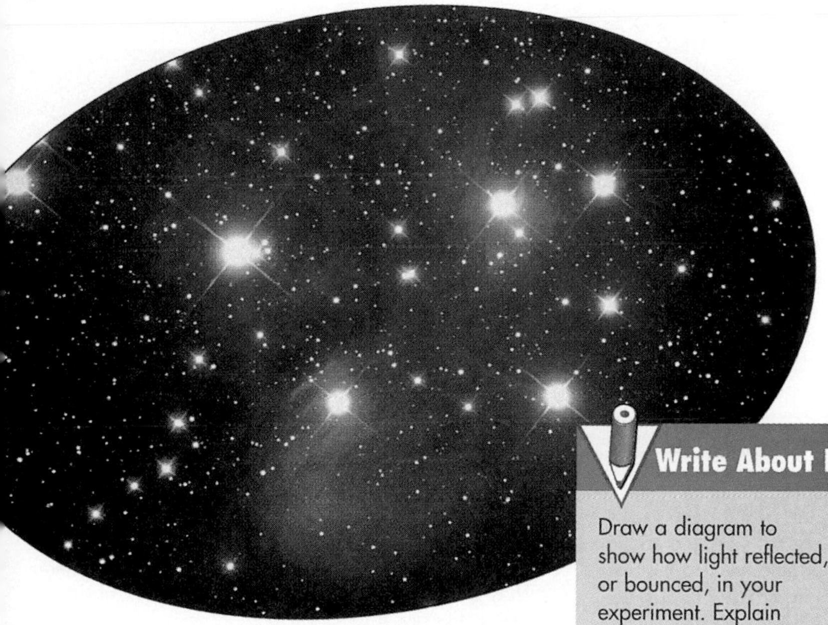

Write About It

Draw a diagram to show how light reflected, or bounced, in your experiment. Explain your diagram.

Language Awareness

Grammar
Little Versus *Few*

ACTIVITY BOOK

Write the following sentences on the board:

You see little or no light between the flashlight and the side of the box.

There are very few things in space.

In the first sentence, underline *little* and *light*. Tell students that here *little* means "a small amount." In the second sentence, underline *few* and *things*. Tell students that *few* means "a small number." Make sure students understand that *little* is used for things that cannot be counted, such as light or heat. *Few* is used for things that can be counted, such as stars or planets. Have students make up sentences using *little* or *few*. Use Activity Book page 66.

Assess ✓

Use class discussion for assessment. Students should be able to

- describe or draw the experiment and explain why space looks black

LOOK**AHEAD**

In the next lesson, students will learn how some ancient peoples viewed the universe.

shapes. As a follow-up, ask each pair to draw five columns on a sheet of paper and to label each column with one of the shapes. Ask them to list or sketch as many everyday objects as possible that fit each shape. The pair with the longest list in each column wins.

Cooperative Language Experience

Field Trip

Take the class to visit a local planetarium, observatory, or museum that has an exhibit about the solar system. Or enlist the help of a science teacher or expert in astronomy to take students on a field trip to observe the night sky. If possible, take along a telescope and allow students to use it to view the sky. When you return to school, have the class write a language experience story about the trip. Encourage each student to contribute something to the story, even if it is just a word or a phrase. Encourage more proficient students to use any specialized vocabulary they have learned. Beginning learners can also contribute by drawing pictures to illustrate the story.

Connect

Activate Prior Knowledge

Demonstrate

Bring in an assortment of personified pictures of the sun. (Children's picture books may be a good source.) Tell students that in the United States, the Sun is sometimes called Old Sol and pictured as a jolly face. Ask students to explain or demonstrate how the Sun is viewed in their home countries in art and in stories. Encourage students to speculate about why the Sun often appears in a culture's art and stories.

Develop Language and Concepts

Present Pages 124 and 125

ACTIVITY BOOK

Read the text with the students. Use simple definitions and paraphrasing to clarify vocabulary. Examine the illustrations and captions, and help students connect them to the appropriate paragraphs. Help students record information about ancient beliefs in a chart and invite them to add any information they know about their home cultures.

Point out that ancient stories like these were intended to explain scientific facts, but they also became subjects for art and literature. Many myth-based stories are still told, even though we now know more about the scientific explanations of natural phenomena. Ask the question in Talk About It. Encourage students to share stories with the class. Use Activity Book page 68 for an activity on planet names.

Ancient Ideas About the Universe

Ancient people knew that the Sun was important. It brought light and heat. Many peoples worshiped the Sun as a great and good god.

Ancient people told stories about the Sun. But the people of long ago did not know how the Sun really worked. They invented stories to explain why the Sun moved across the sky from east to west.

▲ The ancient Egyptians had a Sun god called Ra. They believed that when Ra crossed the sky in a boat, it was day.

▲ The ancient Greeks had a Sun god called Apollo. They believed that when he drove a chariot of fire across the sky, it was day.

Options for Reaching All Students

Beginning

Language: Summarize

Have students summarize the key ideas on the pages. Help students by asking them to review the names of peoples in the text and to tell why each group was mentioned. You may wish to write a paragraph that states a main idea and supporting details. Omit several key words and let pairs work together to complete it.

Advanced

Social Studies: Research Ancient Cultures

Have students work in groups to find out more about one of the ancient cultures mentioned in the text or another culture that revered the Sun. Encourage students to focus on why the Sun was so important to that culture. Have students write reports and illustrate their findings for a bulletin board display entitled *The Sun in Many Cultures.*

Cooperative Learning

Research Myths

Have students work in the planet-based groups that were formed on page 119. Ask students to look up Roman myths about the god for whom their celestial body was named. Model how to do online subject searches or use card catalogs, indices, and table of contents to locate relevant sources. Then have groups summarize and

Astronomers study the universe. Ancient peoples were the first astronomers. The ancient Greeks, for example, made maps of the stars. They gave names to the groups of stars that seem to form patterns in the sky. People still use these groups to talk about the stars.

The ancient Romans named the planets after their gods and goddesses. The names are still used in English. When scientists discovered three more planets in modern times, they named them after the Roman gods Uranus, Neptune, and Pluto.

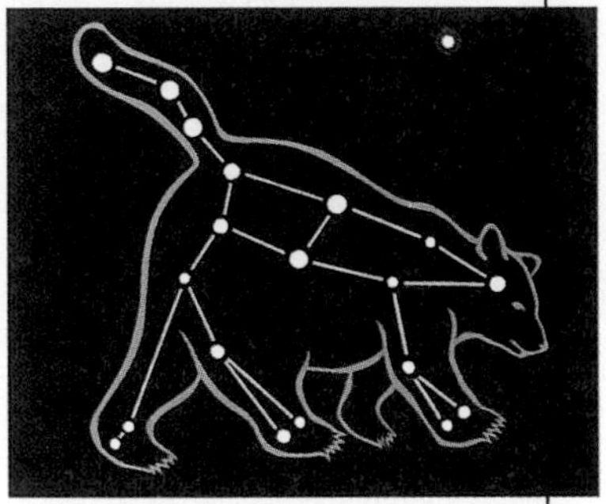

▲ One of the patterns that the Greeks saw in the stars was a big bear.

◀ The Romans named the largest planet after their most powerful god, Jupiter.

Talk About It

Do you know any stories about how the Sun, stars, or planets began? Share them with your classmates.

Language Awareness

Vocabulary/Spelling
Nationalities Ending in *-ese* and *-an*

ACTIVITY BOOK

Write the following names of countries and nationalities on the board:

China Chinese Italy Italian

Tell students that words for nationalities often end in *-ese* or *-an*. Write names of other countries on the board and have students form the nationalities *(Vietnam → Vietnamese, Russia → Russian, Egypt → Egyptian, Mexico → Mexican)*. Then have students tell their families' home countries and nationality by completing the following sentences: *I come from _____. I am _____.* Be sure to help students whose nationality does not end in *-ese* or *-an*. For practice, assign Activity Book page 67.

Assess

Use students' responses to Talk About It for assessment. Students should be able to

- tell why ancient peoples created stories about the Sun
- give some examples of ancient ideas about the universe

LOOK AHEAD

In the next section, students will learn some songs about the Sun.

illustrate at least one myth about its namesake. More proficient students should help beginners read and comprehend the myths. Tell students to include the myths in their final reports about their planets.

Home Connection

Tell Stories About the Universe

Have students ask family members if they know any traditional stories about the Sun or stars from their home countries. Invite students and/or family members to share their stories with the class. Have students summarize and illustrate the stories for a bulletin board display entitled *The Sun in Many Cultures.*

Writer's Workshop

Write a Myth

Have students write their own myths to explain some aspect of the solar system, such as why the Sun moves across the sky or why space looks dark. Discuss the characteristics of a myth, and help students use a plot diagram to list ideas about setting, characters, and story events.

Connect

Activate Prior Knowledge

Review Related Facts

Ask volunteers to relate some of the facts about the Sun they learned earlier in this chapter.

Develop Language and Concepts

Present Pages 126 and 127

GREEN TAPE

Read and discuss the words of the song with students. Draw two columns on the board. Label one column *Sun* and the other *No Sun.* Help students find all the words in the song that are related to *Sun* and all that are related to *No Sun.* Ask students to generalize about the writer's attitude toward the Sun. Play Side 2 of the Green Tape several times, encouraging students to sing along.

Discuss the questions in Think About It. Ask students if they feel the same way about the Sun as George Harrison does.

FYI

"Here Comes the Sun" is one of two Beatles songs in this book. The other, "Good Day Sunshine," by Paul McCartney, appears on page 76.

Here Comes the Sun

by George Harrison

Here comes the sun, here comes the sun,
And I say it's all right.
Little darling it's been a long cold lonely winter
Little darling it feels like years since it's been here.

Here comes the sun, here comes the sun,
And I say it's all right.

Little darling the smiles returning to their faces,
Little darling it seems like years since it's been here,

Options for Reaching All Students

Beginning

Language: Practice Homonyms

TPR

Give students seven index cards. Ask them to write one of the following words on each card: *two, too, to; four, for; eight, ate.* Read sentences containing one of the words and have students hold up the corresponding card. Invite students to make up their own sentences.

Advanced

Music: Study a Song About the Sun

Help students brainstorm a list of songs about the Sun. Have small groups each pick its favorite and write the lyrics or bring a recording to class. The library may have a media center of recordings, and there are websites that specialize in song lyrics. Have each group present its song to the class, summarize the song's message, and tell why they like it.

Peer or Cross-Age Tutoring

Vocabulary: Use Homonym Flashcards

Make flashcards containing pairs of homonyms—one word on each side. Have students work in pairs of mixed ability. Ask them to take turns naming the homonym of the word on each flashcard. Tell them to spell the homonym and use it in a sentence.

Here comes the sun, here comes the sun,
And I say it's all right.

Sun, sun, sun, here it comes.
Sun, sun, sun, here it comes.
Sun, sun, sun, here it comes.
Sun, sun, sun, here it comes.

Little darling I feel that ice is slowly melting,
Little darling it seems like years since it's been clear,

Here comes the sun, here comes the sun,
It's all right, it's all right.

Think About It

When the singer talks about the coming of the Sun, what season does he mean?

How does the Sun affect how the singer feels?

Does the Sun ever affect how you feel?

Language Awareness

Vocabulary
Homonyms

ACTIVITY BOOK

Write the words *sun* and *son* on the board. Ask students to pronounce each word. Then ask them to use each word in a sentence that shows its meaning. Point out that some words in English may be pronounced the same even though they are spelled differently. Write the word *right* on the board. Ask students if they can think of another English word that is pronounced like *right* but is spelled differently. *(write)* Have students use the words in sentences. Follow the same procedure for *here*. Then encourage students to think of other English homonyms. Ask them to spell the words and use them in sentences that show their meaning. Use Activity Book page 69.

Possible homonyms include *here/hear, sun/son, right/write, know/no, one/won, four/for, eight/ate, blue/blew, pair/pear, be/bee, their/there, through/threw.* You may wish to review the meanings of each homonym before pairs start the activity. Encourage more proficient students to help beginning learners form sentences. They could write cloze sentences and have beginners complete them.

Home Connection

Learn Songs About the Sun

Have students ask adults at home if they know any songs about the Sun from their home cultures. Have students work with family members to write the lyrics to one song in their home language or in English and draw a picture to illustrate it. Encourage students to write English summaries for songs written in their home language. Add the lyrics and summaries to the bulletin board entitled *The Sun in Many Cultures.*

Connect

Activate Prior Knowledge

Discuss Phases of the Moon

Show or have volunteers draw pictures of the phases of the moon. Discuss why the moon appears to change shape and size each month. Explain that the phases of the moon depend on how much of the sunlit part of the moon can be seen from Earth. Show or draw simple diagrams that show the relationship between the Sun, the moon, and Earth.

Develop Language and Concepts

Present Page 128

GREEN TAPE

Read the poem aloud. Ask why the moon may look as if an animal has been eating it. Then play Side 2 of the Green Tape several times. Discuss the question in Talk About It.

Language Awareness

Vocabulary
Synonyms

Point out that *nibbled* and *gnawed* are synonyms for *eaten,* although their meanings differ a bit. Explain that *nibble* means "take small bites" and *gnaw* means "wear away by biting." Add that a *gulp* is a big, greedy swallow. Have small groups look through picture thesauruses to find a group of related words to illustrate and use in sentences, such as words for *say, fast,* or *slow.*

Brazilian Moon Tale

by Jane Yolen

Did you hear the one
about the moon
being nibbled, gnawed,
eaten away,
by a rat, a jaguar,
a lion, until
in one great gulp
it was gone?

I didn't believe it
either,
until I looked up
and saw that moon,
the teethmarks
still on it,
growing smaller every night.

Talk About It

Do you know any stories that tell why the moon grows smaller and bigger in the sky? Share them with your classmates.

Options for Reaching All Students

Beginning

Art: Draw the Moon

Ask students to observe the moon and draw what they see. Encourage them to use binoculars or telescopes, if available. Suggest they show the light and dark shadings that indicate mountains, craters, and flat areas. Ask students which word in the poem might refer to the moon's markings. (teethmarks)

Advanced

Literature: Research Writing About the Moon

Have students find literature and songs about the moon. Help students identify adjectives, metaphors, and similes used to describe the moon. Have them compile a list of these words and phrases. Discuss their meanings, and have students decide which ones they find the most interesting or original. Encourage them to add their own ideas to the list.

Tell what you learned.

CHAPTER 7

1. Describe the parts of the solar system.
2. What is the most interesting fact you learned about the Sun?
3. How did ancient peoples' stories about the Sun relate to what they saw in the sky?

Assess √

Activity 1: Make sure that students can name and describe *Sun, star, planet, asteroid, comet, moon* as well as at least some of the planets themselves.

Activity 2: Evaluate students' reasons for their choices.

Activity 3: Evaluate whether students understand that ancient peoples invented myths to explain the workings of the universe, such as the movement of the Sun from east to west in the sky.

Have students complete the Chapter Self-Assessment, Blackline Master 31. Have them choose the product of one of the activities to include in their portfolios. Add the results of any rubrics, checklists, self-assessments, or portfolio assessments, Blackline Masters 2–18 and 31.

Listening Assessment

BLACKLINE MASTER

Make sure that each student has a copy of Blackline Master 70 from the Teacher's Resource Book. Play the tape several times and have students complete the activity.

CREAM TAPE

See Chapter 7 Resources, page T116c, for the Listening Assessment tapescript.

Options for Assessment

Vocabulary Assessment

Definition Quiz

Have students work in pairs to define the following words: *moon, planet, star, sun, universe, orbit, comet, asteroid, gas, yellow dwarf, core, photosphere, chromosphere, astronomer.* If students define a word incorrectly, they should put it on a list for further study. Beginning learners might draw and label pictures, using diagrams in the chapter as models.

Writing Assessment

Create a Book

Ask students to write books of interesting facts about the Sun. Remind them to plan the book's structure before writing. They can exchange drafts with partners and check one another's facts for accuracy, grammar, spelling, and punctuation. Encourage them to illustrate their books with pictures and charts.

Language Assessment

BLACKLINE MASTER

Use Blackline Master 71 in the Teacher's Resource Book.

Standardized Test Practice

ACTIVITY BOOK

Use pages 70 and 71.
Answers: **1.** 87.97 **2.** 40% **3.** 14 **4.** \$2.00 and \$3.00.

Preview

Activate Prior Knowledge

Brainstorm Vocabulary

Start a discussion of the Chapter 8 topic, planets, by asking students to name as many words as possible that are related to space and space travel. List the words on the board. Then help students classify the words into categories, such as *Parts of the Solar System, Names of Planets,* or *Space Travel.*

Ask each student to tell the most interesting thing he or she has learned about the solar system thus far. List the answers on the board to see if they suggest a pattern as to what students find interesting. Then talk with students about how they do or do not share similar interests.

FYI

- **Page 131 shows the Hubble space telescope as it looks deployed in space.**
- **In the mid-1990s, scientists began finding the first evidence of planets in other solar systems. Before this time, the likely existence of such planets had only been theorized.**

CHAPTER 8

The Planets

Word Bank

- size
- surface
- temperature
- spacecraft
- telescope

Tell what you know.

What do you know about the planets?

How is Earth like other planets? How is it different?

How do people learn about the planets?

130

Options for Reaching All Students

Beginning

Art: Draw a Planet

Show students pictures of the nine planets and help them practice saying the planets' names. Then ask each student to draw a picture of the planet that interests him or her most. Help them write captions that tell why their planet interests them. Point out the use of capital letters in planets' names.

Advanced

Writing: Write a Message to Send into Space

Tell students that scientists have been using radio signals to send messages into space for some time. Ask students to each write the message they would send into space if they had the opportunity. Allow students to say anything they like, but encourage them to include a statement about life on Earth and questions about the world of the message's recipients. Have them exchange their messages with classmates and review each other's work clarity.

Talk About It

What planets interest you the most? Why?

131

Develop Language and Concepts

Present Pages 130 and 131

Look at the pictures on pages 130 and 131 with the students. Help students use the words in the Word Bank to describe them. If necessary, make references to more familiar objects to define *size, surface,* and *temperature*. Show pictures of several space crafts and a telescope.

Read the text with students and have them answer the questions. Point out that the first three Word Bank words help them compare planets and the last two words describe ways we learn about planets.

Encourage them to recall what they learned about planets in Chapter 7 and to raise questions about things they would like to learn. Have students discuss the questions in Talk About It. Use students' comments and questions to create a K-W-L chart:

K: What We Know	Planets are one part of the solar system.
W: What We Want to Find Out	What are some special features of each planet in the solar system?
L: What We Learned	

Have students add to the chart throughout the chapter.

Present

Activate Prior Knowledge

Recall Prior Learning

Ask students to look at the diagram of the solar system on pages 118 and 119. Draw the Sun on the board. Then have students tell you each successive planet to draw, moving out from the Sun. Encourage students to describe the color and relative size of each planet and any distinguishing features. Ask students who researched the Roman gods to tell something about the namesake of each planet. Save the diagram for use later.

Develop Language and Concepts

Present Pages 132 and 133

Read the text with students. Use a ball on a string to demonstrate the difference between *rotate* and *revolve*. Hold the string so that the ball is straight down. Give the ball a spin and show students that it is *rotating*, or turning in its own circle, on its axis. Tell students that this is the same motion illustrated at the top of page 132.

Next hold the end of the string and spin the ball in a circle around your hand. Explain that the ball is *revolving* around your hand and that the path it takes around your hand is its orbit. Emphasize that the planets both rotate and revolve.

(Continued on page T133.)

Facts About the Planets

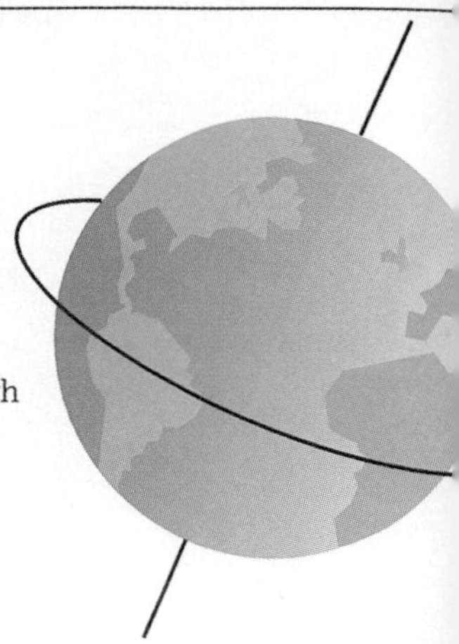

The planets are in motion. They **revolve**, or orbit, the Sun. They also **rotate.** One rotation makes a complete day and a night.

The planets are different in many ways. Some planets are mainly rock with a metal core. Earth is one of these planets. Other planets are made mostly of gases. Each planet is surrounded by an **atmosphere** of gases. Earth's atmosphere is mainly oxygen. It holds in the heat from the Sun.

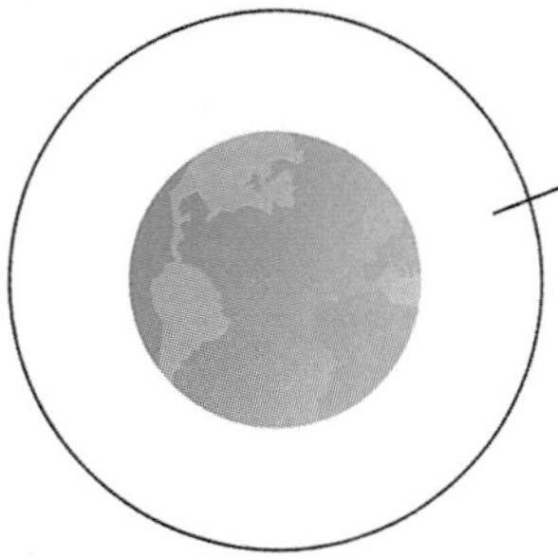

Mercury is about the size of Earth's moon. Mercury has a rocky surface and a core of metal. Because it is so near the Sun, Mercury is very hot. Its temperature can reach 800 degrees Fahrenheit (427 degrees Celsius). It orbits the Sun quickly. ▶

Options for Reaching All Students

Beginning

Language: Revolve and Rotate

TPR

Bring in a basketball, a softball, and a soccerball to class. Have students demonstrate rotation and revolution of Earth and the moon in relation to the Sun. Also have students use a flashlight to demonstrate night and day and the phases of the moon. Provide diagrams from science texts as necessary for help. Help students verbalize the demonstration. Make any necessary accommodations for students with motor difficulties, such as pairing them with classmates who can assist them in the demonstration.

Advanced

Science: Identify Objects That Rotate or Revolve

Have students work in pairs or small groups. Ask them to draw two columns on a sheet of paper, labeling the first column *Revolve* and the second column *Rotate*. Ask students to list as many things as possible in each category (e.g., the brush on an electric toothbrush rotates, baseball players revolve around

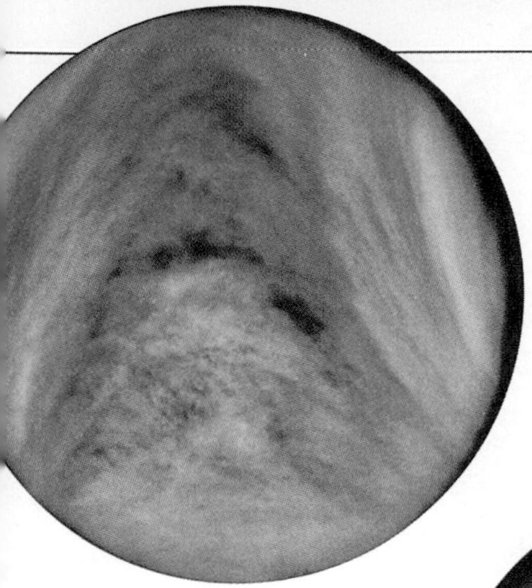

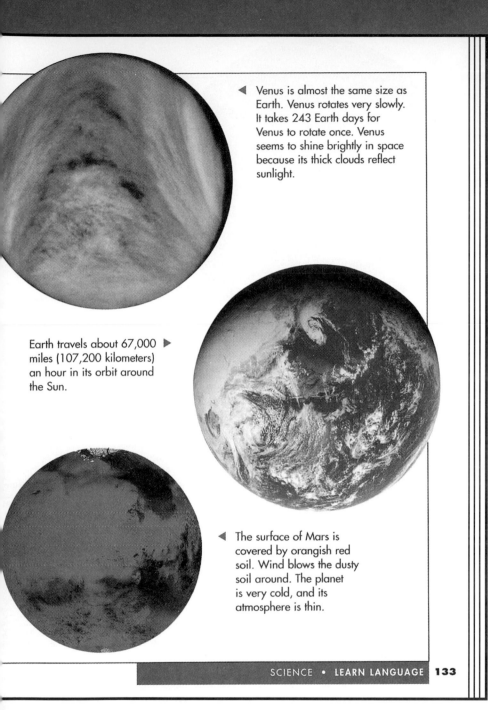

Venus is almost the same size as Earth. Venus rotates very slowly. It takes 243 Earth days for Venus to rotate once. Venus seems to shine brightly in space because its thick clouds reflect sunlight.

Earth travels about 67,000 miles (107,200 kilometers) an hour in its orbit around the Sun.

The surface of Mars is covered by orangish red soil. Wind blows the dusty soil around. The planet is very cold, and its atmosphere is thin.

ACTIVITY BOOK Look at the pictures and read the captions with students. Have students locate each planet in the diagram on the board. Help them describe and compare the planets, using vocabulary from the text and their own words. Use Activity Book page 72 to review key vocabulary.

Language Awareness

Grammar
Present Tense to State General Facts

Write the following sentences on the board:

The planets <u>are</u> in motion.
They <u>revolve</u> around the Sun.

Point out the present-tense verbs and the fact that the present-tense form is used to state things that are always true.

Ask students to find other verb forms on pages 132 and 133 that state something that is always true. Write their answers on the board.

Help students create original sentences containing verbs that tell things that are always true (for example, *The Sun is the center of the solar system*).

the pitcher as they move from base to base). Have the groups compare and discuss their lists. Then decide which group named the most items in each category and overall.

You can simplify this activity as needed by giving students a list of objects that revolve and rotate and seeing if they can assign each object to the correct category. You may need to provide visual support to clarify vocabulary.

Mixed Ability

Science: Atmosphere

Have small groups of students research the layers of Earth's atmosphere. Instruct the groups to make diagrams of the atmosphere. Remind students to label their diagrams. The labels should be brief, accurate, and similar in structure. Have them use the diagram on page 120 as a model.

Cooperative Learning

Art: Diagram Revolving and Rotating

Give small groups a piece of butcher paper and ask them to diagram the rotation and revolution of Earth. Have each group explain its diagram to the class. Give students the option of creating a three-dimensional model instead of a two-dimensional diagram.

Develop Language and Concepts

Present Pages 134 and 135

ACTIVITY BOOK

Look at the pictures and read the captions with students. Have them locate each planet in the diagram on the board.

Use pictures, classroom examples, or pantomime to introduce the terms in the Word Bank. Ask questions that will lead students to use the Word Bank terms to describe the planets For example: *Why does Neptune look blue? Because of a gas in its clouds.*

Have students look at the chart and its heads. Point out that the same kind of information is presented about each planet. Ask questions that will lead students to read and interpret the chart. For example: *How long does it take for Mercury to orbit the Sun?*

Prepare students to do the activity in Write About It by asking the class to choose two planets. Then help them use the information in the captions and the chart to make a comparison of the two planets. Use Activity Book page 74.

Model a Strategy

Use Charts to Make Comparisons

Model a strategy for using charts to make comparisons:

Sometimes information is easier to compare when it is presented in chart form. This chart presents comparative information about the planets. For example, if I look in the "Length of One Orbit" column, I can easily see that Mercury orbits the Sun more quickly than Venus does.

◀ Jupiter is a giant ball of gases. More than 1,000 Earths could fit inside it. Jupiter rotates very fast. A day is less than ten hours long. Swirls of clouds cover the planet. Jupiter has at least sixteen moons. Its biggest moon is bigger than Mercury.

Uranus has rings around it. It looks blue-green because of a gas in the clouds that cover the planet. Scientists think that there is rock and ice under the clouds. Uranus was discovered in 1781. ▶

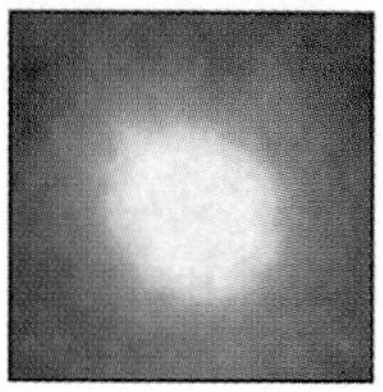

▲ Pluto is the smallest and coldest planet. Astronomers guessed that Pluto existed before they first saw it in 1930. It is a cold ball of gas and rock. Some scientists think that it once was a moon of its neighbor, Neptune.

Planet	Length of One Rotation (in Earth time)	Length of One Orbit (in Earth time)
Mercury	59 days	88 days
Venus	243 days	224.7 days
Earth	24 hours	365.3 days
Mars	24.5 hours	687 days
Jupiter	9.8 hours	12 years
Saturn	10.7 hours	29.5 years
Uranus	17 hours	84 years
Neptune	16 hours	165 years
Pluto	6 days	248 years

Options for Reaching All Students

Beginning

Science: Use a Chart

Have students look at the names of planets in the first chart column on page 134. Ask them to follow the rows across and read the planets' average temperatures. Help students use the words *hotter* and *colder* to compare pairs of planets. Then ask them to compare the planets' diameters using the words *bigger* and *smaller.*

Advanced

Science: Make a Chart

Have students research the following information about each planet: average distance from the Sun in miles, atmosphere (main gases), and one other fact they find interesting. Ask them to present their findings in chart form. Encourage them to use the chart on pages 134 and 135 as a model. Remind them that similar data should use the same unit of measure.

Mixed Ability

Language: Play a Planet Guessing Game

Divide the class into nine teams. Secretly assign each team a planet. Allow each team ten minutes to write down all the information they can about their planet. Then have the teams take turns going to the front of the room and start by giving one hint about their planet. Then the rest

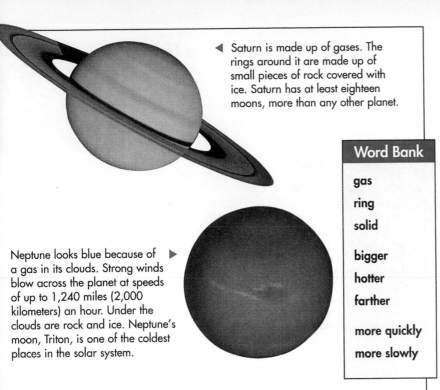

◀ Saturn is made up of gases. The rings around it are made up of small pieces of rock covered with ice. Saturn has at least eighteen moons, more than any other planet.

Neptune looks blue because of ▶ a gas in its clouds. Strong winds blow across the planet at speeds of up to 1,240 miles (2,000 kilometers) an hour. Under the clouds are rock and ice. Neptune's moon, Triton, is one of the coldest places in the solar system.

Word Bank

- gas
- ring
- solid
- bigger
- hotter
- farther
- more quickly
- more slowly

Average Temperature (Daytime)	Diameter at Its Center (km = kilometers)
662 ° F (350° C)	3,024 miles (4,878 km)
869° F (465° C)	7,504 miles (12,103 km)
59° F (15° C)	7,909 miles (12,756 km)
-9° F (-23° C)	4,207 miles (6,786 km)
-238° F (-150° C)	88,648 miles (142,980 km)
-292° F (-180° C)	74,735 miles (120,540 km)
-346° F (-210° C)	31,694 miles (51,120 km)
-364° F (-220° C)	30,709 miles (49,530 km)
-382° F (-230° C)	1,416 miles (2,280 km)

Write About It

Compare two planets. Write how they are alike and how they are different. Which one is bigger than the other? Which one is hotter than the other? Use the information in the captions and chart.

Language Awareness

Grammar
Comparatives

ACTIVITY BOOK

Point out that some words in the text and charts are used to compare two things or actions. Write the following sentences on the board:

One of Jupiter's moons is <u>bigger</u> than Mercury. Mercury revolves around the Sun <u>more quickly</u> than Pluto does.

Explain that comparative words often end in *-er*. Then explain that some comparative words take *more*. These are usually words of two or more syllables. Give examples in sentences that refer to classroom objects or students.

Then have students use information from the chart on pages 134 and 135 to practice making comparisons. For more practice, students can use Activity Book page 73.

Assess ✓

Use Write About It for assessment. Students should be able to

- tell how the planets are alike and different

LOOK**AHEAD**

In the next section, students will use a time line to learn about the history of space exploration.

of the class should ask questions and as quickly as possible determine the planet's identity. A team should answer honestly, but should try to force the class to ask as many questions as possible before guessing the planet's identity. Beginning learners can act as time keepers, keeping track of how long it takes the class to guess each team's planet.

Cooperative Learning

Order the Planets

Teach students the mnemonic *My Very Excited Monkey Just Slid Under Nathan's Piano* to help them recall the order of the planets from the Sun. Then have students work in small groups to devise two other ways to order the planets. Tell students that the chart on pages 134 and 135 may suggest some possibilities (e.g., size, temperature). Have the groups present their systems to the rest of the class. Discuss the various ways that are presented. Then discuss the major ways in which information is usually ordered (e.g., using alphabetical, chronological, and numerical systems).

Practice

Activate Prior Knowledge
Use Pictures/Videotape

Show students pictures or videotaped footage of a space launch, the interior of a manned spacecraft, and the like. Ask such questions as: *Have you ever watched a space launch (either on TV or in person)? What did you see? What problems might you have if you spent a week in a space? Would you like to travel in space?*

Develop Language and Concepts
Present Pages 136 and 137

ACTIVITY BOOK

Explain that a time line shows relationships between events. Read the text with students. Ask students which event they think is the most significant. Discuss the activity in Try It Out. Then divide the class into small groups to prepare recordings. Finally, discuss the questions in Think About It. You might present space events that have occurred since 1990. Use Activity Book page 75 to review information about the planets.

Model a Strategy
Read a Time Line

Model how to use a time line:

When I read a time line from left to the right, I can follow history from earlier events to the most recent. I can also see patterns in the events. On page 136, I can see that before 1962, the Soviet Union seems to have had many space firsts.

Space Exploration Time Line

People wanted to explore space for thousands of years. The time line shows what people have done in half a century of space exploration.

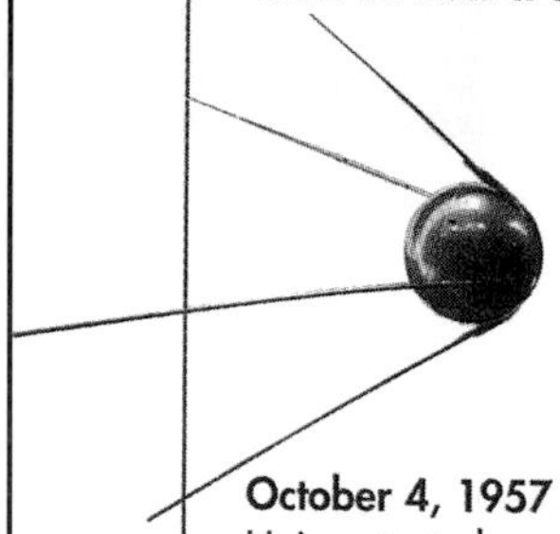

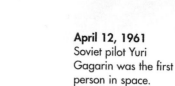

October 4, 1957 The Soviet Union started space flight with *Sputnik 1*, the first human-made satellite in space.

November 3, 1957 *Sputnik 2* went up with a dog named Laika.

1960

April 12, 1961 Soviet pilot Yuri Gagarin was the first person in space.

February 20, 1962 John Glenn was the first person from the United States to orbit the Earth.

1970

July 20, 1969 *Apollo 11* landed on the moon. Neil Armstrong of the United States was the first person to walk on the moon.

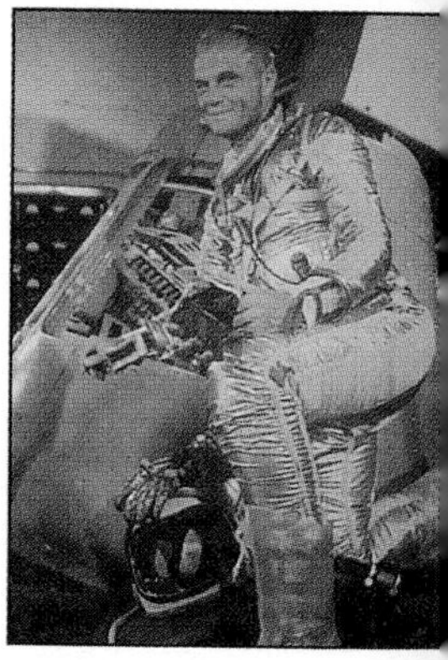

Try It Out

The *Voyager 2* spacecraft is now traveling through space, beyond the solar system. It is carrying a special recording. The recording is a message to any other intelligent life in the universe. The recording has sounds from Earth, including music and the sound of a baby crying.

Work with a group. Prepare a tape recording of sounds that you would like to send to outer space.

Options for Reaching All Students

Beginning
Writing: Space Travel

Have students write about the kind of trip that they would like to take into space. Suggest that they think about whether they would like to walk on the moon, live in a space station, or travel to a planet. Students' writings can include both words and illustrations. You may wish to model sample sentences or supply cloze sentences.

Advanced
Science: Research Famous People in Space

Have each student research and present biographical information about a famous person who has traveled in space. Help students synthesize and/or separate collected information into useful components (e.g., country of origin, dates of trips, and importance of trips). Possible subjects might include Yuri Gargarin, Neil Armstrong, Valentina Tereshkova, and Sally Ride. Have students combine their data into a "Famous People in Space" chart. They might also give a multimedia presentation that includes video or audio sources.

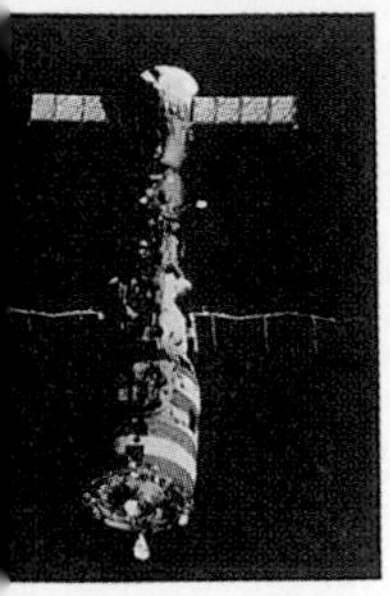

19, 1971 The
ts sent up *Salyut 1*,
rst space station.
e can live and work
space station for
periods of time.

August 20,1977 The United States sent up *Voyager 2* spacecraft. It took photographs of the outer planets in the solar system.

June 18, 1983 Sally Ride was the first woman from the United States in space.

1980

1990

July 20,1976 The U.S. *Viking* spacecraft landed on Mars and took pictures of its surface.

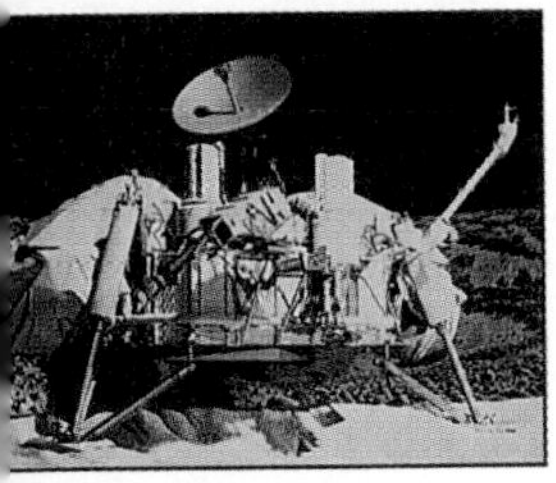

April 24,1990 Europe and the United States sent up the Hubble space telescope. It is taking pictures of space as it orbits around Earth. It gets better pictures because it is above the atmosphere.

Think About It

What should be the next thing we do in space? Should more people go up in space? Explain your choice.

Language Awareness

Grammar
Dates; *Before* and *After*

Write the following dates on the board and ask students to read them aloud: *October 4, 1957; June 18, 1983.* Remind students that dates are usually read as ordinal numbers. Have them read other dates on the time line aloud.

Practice the terms *before* and *after* by asking questions such as *Were you born before the Hubble telescope was sent up? Were you born after Sally Ride went into space?* Have students ask one another questions using *before* and *after*.

Assess

Use class discussion for assessment. Students should be able to

- name and discuss two or three important events in the history of space exploration

LOOK**AHEAD**

In the next section, students will figure out how old they would be on various planets.

Mixed Ability

Science: Plan a Space Mission

Have students work in groups of three or four. Ask them to imagine that they work for NASA and must create a written plan for a space mission. Have each group use collaborative decision making to choose a mission, set goals, and identify procedures. Have each group's "mission director" present its plan to the class.

Multicultural Connection

Research Another Nation's Space Program

Have small groups write reports about another nation's accomplishments in space. Among the possibilities are Russia, Japan, Canada, France, and Germany. Ask students to give an overview of the nation's achievements. Remind them to capitalize proper nouns and use past tense for historical events.

Home Connection

Create a Family Time Line

Have students ask adults at home to help them make a list of significant events in the lives of their families (e.g., births, marriages, arrival in the United States). Have students put the events in chronological order and then use the dates to create time lines showing the history of their families.

Connect

Activate Prior Knowledge

Discuss Age

Ask students their ages. Ask if they would like to be younger or older than they actually are. Encourage them to explain their choices. Ask students how many days there are in a year. Then ask how that number is determined. Elicit the response that it corresponds to the number of days it takes Earth to orbit the Sun.

Develop Language and Concepts

Present Pages 138 and 139

Read the text with students. Ask someone who has had a recent birthday to state his or her age in days. Use the age in days to demonstrate the calculation of age on Mercury. Then use another student's age to demonstrate the calculation of age on Saturn. Give students time to calculate their own ages on those two planets, helping as necessary. Then have them calculate their age on a third planet of their choice. Ask students to explain the messages presented on the two travel posters on page 139. Finally, discuss the questions in Think About It.

How old would you be on Mars?

Years on other planets are longer or shorter than the years on Earth. A year is the amount of time it takes the planet to orbit the Sun. If you have a birthday every planet year, you would have more or fewer birthdays than you have on Earth.

The nearer planets don't take very long to orbit the Sun. You would have many more birthdays. Follow these steps to find out how old you would be:

1. Determine how many days you have lived on Earth. To do this, multiply your age by 365 days. Then add the number of days that have passed since your last birthday.

   For example, if you are 13 years and 33 days old:
   (13 X 365) + 33 = 4,778 Earth days old

2. Next use the chart below. Divide the number of days old you are by the number of days in the planet's year.

   $\frac{4,778}{88 \text{ (days in Mercury's year)}} = 54$ years

   You would be 54 years old on Mercury!

Planet	Length of Year in Earth Days
Mercury	88 days
Venus	225 days
Mars	687 days

Options for Reaching All Students

Beginning

Math: Graph Ages

Help students calculate how old they would be on Mercury, Venus, and Mars. Ask them to make bar graphs of their ages on those three planets plus their age on Earth. Tell them to arrange their four ages according to the planets' distances from the Sun. Help them describe their graphs and explain the pattern that is formed.

Advanced

Math: Calculate School Days

Have students determine how many days they spend in school each year. Then have them calculate what percentage of a year that number represents. If, for example, they spend 200 days in school, they would spend about 55% of a year there (200 ÷ 365 = .548). Have students use your school's percentage and the information from the charts on pages 138 and 139 to calculate how many days they would spend in school in a year on each planet if they attended school the same percentage of the time. Then ask students which planets would they prefer to live on and why. You may wish to present this activity as a series of numbered steps.

The outer planets take much longer to travel around the Sun. You can calculate with years to find your age.

Divide your age by the number of Earth years it takes the planet to orbit the Sun.

For example, if you are 13 years old:

$\frac{13}{29.5 \text{ years (for Saturn)}}$ = .44 year (or about 161 days)

You wouldn't have had your first birthday yet on Saturn!

Planet	Length of Year in Earth Years
Jupiter	12 years
Saturn	29.5 years
Uranus	84 years
Neptune	165 years
Pluto	248 years

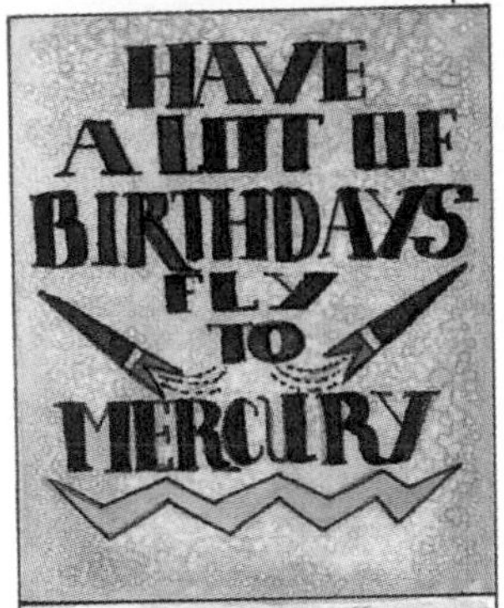

Think About It

Why are years longer on the planets farther from the Sun?

Where in the solar system would you like to have your birthday? Why?

Language Awareness

Grammar
Unreal Conditionals

ACTIVITY BOOK

Write the following sentence on the board:

If you lived on Mercury, you would be 54 years old.

Point out that *if* is followed by the past tense form of the verb and the verb in the next part of the sentence is *would* plus the base form of the verb. Explain that this pattern is used to express situations that are not real. Have students use the information in the charts on pages 138 and 139 to tell how long a year would be if they lived on each planet. For example *If I lived on Mercury, my year would be 88 days long.* For practice, students can complete Activity Book page 76.

Assess

Use class discussion and the Think About It questions for assessment. Students should be able to

- use the tables to calculate what their age would be on several planets
- explain why the years vary in length from planet to planet

LOOK**AHEAD**

In the next section, students will read a description of the solar system.

Mixed Ability

Language: Describe a Space Alien

Have students draw a picture of what they think a space alien would look like. Ask them to use *if* clauses and the conditional to write five sentences about their alien (e.g., *If my alien came to Earth, she would . . .*). Beginning learners could have the option of writing simple labels describing their alien's body parts instead of writing sentences.

Cooperative Learning

Write and Present a Skit

Have students work in the planet-based groups that were formed to work on the activities discussed on page 119. Ask each group to write a skit about a journey to their planet. Have students organize their ideas (i.e., plan the setting, characters, and plot) before writing. Remind them to consider a character's personality when writing dialogue and decide whether formal or informal English is appropriate.

Then have the groups present their skits to the rest of the class. Encourage them to use gestures and expression when performing. After the skits have been performed, ask students to give constructive feedback to the presenters. Remind groups to include their script in their final report about their planet.

Connect

Activate Prior Knowledge

Brainstorm Vocabulary

Tell the students they are going to read an excerpt from a book about the solar system. Have them use their background knowledge of the subject to brainstorm a list of words they think may appear in the selection. List their suggestions on the board. Have a student check off each word as it appears in the selection.

Introduce the Selection

Have volunteers read the first sentence in each paragraph aloud. Have students tell what parts of the solar system are discussed in the selection.

Read the Selection

GREEN TAPE

Read the selection with students. Then read it again and discuss the Reader's Tips at the appropriate points.

Play the selection on Side 1 of the Green Tape several times. Invite students to read along and to listen to the selection as often as they wish.

Language Awareness

Language Function
Words That Describe

Write the following on the board:

On a clear, moonless night the sky seems to be filled with stars.

Ask students to identify the words that describe *night.* Underline *clear* and *moonless* as you explain that such words are used to describe nouns—people, places, and things. Ask students to suggest other words that can be used to describe *night.* List the words on the board. Ask volunteers to use the words in sentences. Help students find other words that describe (adjectives) in the selection.

Teachable Moment

Tone

Point out that the author seems to be speaking directly to the reader as she describes the features of the solar system. She achieves that effect by using the pronoun *you* and addressing the reader directly. Have students compare this style of writing with the writing style on pages 132 and 133. Point out that this selection is more conversational in tone and uses everyday analogies. You might have students share examples of stories they've read that use a similar tone.

Options for Reaching All Students

Beginning

Language: Describe the Planets

On an unlabeled poster of the solar system, point to the Sun and each planet in turn. Have students identify each planet and state one fact about it. Encourage students to use descriptive words in their facts. (You can modify this activity for students with little English by naming the planets and having them point.)

Advanced

Language: Write Descriptively

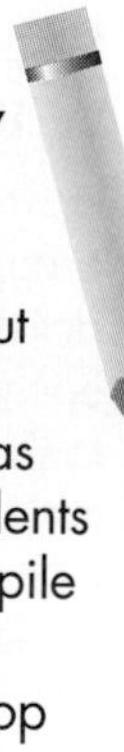

Have students brainstorm a list of adjectives or phrases that describe the planets, not in technical terms but in more colorful writer's terms. For example, Jupiter can be described as *huge, striped,* and so on. Have students first work individually and then compile a master list. Post the list to help students complete the Writer's Workshop activity.

Writer's Workshop

Write About a Planet

Ask students to write a description of the planet they are researching in the planet-based groups that were formed on page 119. Encourage them to use both descriptive and scientific terms. Remind students to use present-tense verbs for statements that are true all the time.

The Solar System

by Maura Gouck

Language Tip
Vocabulary
A *meteor* is a piece of rock traveling in space. Usually meteors burn up when they enter the Earth's atmosphere.

On a clear, moonless night the sky seems to be filled with stars. Watch carefully, and you'll see that those twinkling stars are different colors—yellow, red, bluish white. You'll probably spot the *Big Dipper, Orion*, or another group of stars. If you are lucky, you might even see a meteor streaking across the sky!

Study Tip
Learn Key Vocabulary
This reading describes the solar system. Look for the key vocabulary you learned in this unit to understand the story more easily. When you read books in a subject area, it is helpful to keep a list of important words to remember.

As daylight arrives, the night stars fade from view. At sunrise there is only one star that you can still see. It is the star nearest to our planet. This star is the *Sun*. The Sun is very important because it provides light, heat, and energy to our planet.

To us, the Sun seems to be about the same size as the Moon, but it is really much larger. In fact, the Sun is about four hundred times wider than the Moon. The Sun is also much larger than our own planet Earth. It would take over one million Earths to fill the Sun!

Language Tip
Vocabulary
Eruptions occur when gases, fire, or other materials suddenly rise up from the surface.

You can't stare at the Sun the way you stare at other stars. The Sun is so bright it hurts your eyes. Scientists look at the Sun through special instruments. They see a lot happening on this star! To us the Sun looks like a peaceful, yellow disk floating slowly across the sky. Actually, though, it is a ball of bubbling, churning gases. Powerful storms swirl across its surface, and eruptions of hot gases shoot thousands of miles into space.

The Sun is the center of our *solar system*. The solar system consists of the Sun and the planets, asteroids, and comets that circle it. There are nine planets in our solar system. Each one follows a different path, or *orbit*, around the Sun.

The planet closest to the Sun is *Mercury*. It is a small planet, less than half the size of Earth. Mercury has a hard, rocky surface covered by many *craters*. Craters are circular holes formed when rocks, called *asteroids*, crashed into the planet. The temperature on Mercury ranges from very hot to icy cold. Humans could not survive on this planet because it has no water and very little air.

Strategy Tip
Read On to Get Meaning
The author uses a word you may not know, *crater*. When you read on, the author gives the meaning of the word. What is a crater?

Connect

Develop Language and Concepts

Present Pages 144 Through 147

ACTIVITY BOOK

Read the text with students. Encourage students to ask questions for elaboration and clarification. Ask students to identify the words that describe the planets. List the words on the board. Then have students use the words on the board and their own words to describe the pictures on pages 144–147. To check comprehension, use Activity Book page 77.

Language Awareness

Grammar
Ordinal Numbers

Write the following on the board:

The hottest planet is Venus, the <u>second</u> planet from the Sun.

We live on Earth, the <u>third</u> planet from the Sun.

Explain that ordinal numbers are used to show order or rank. Arrange a group of students in a line, and point out the second and third students. Ask students what the ordinal form of *one* is. (first)

Write these numbers on the board:

four fourth
ten tenth
fifteen fifteenth

Underline the *-th* ending. Then ask students to give the ordinal forms of various cardinal numbers. You can lead a TPR activity by lining up students and naming ordinal numbers. Students should step forward when they hear their position called.

Options for Reaching All Students

Beginning

Science: Use Ordinal Numbers

Use an unlabeled map of the solar system to practice ordinal numbers. First use ordinal numbers in sequence to ask students to identify the planets (e.g., *What is the second planet from the Sun?*). Encourage students to repeat the ordinal number in their answers. Finally have students use ordinal numbers to quiz each other.

Advanced

Science: Compare Earth and Venus

Have students work in pairs to find information about Earth and Venus. Ask them to create a chart that compares the two planets' features. Have students use the information they find to explain why Earth and Venus are sometimes called sister planets and to tell whether they think that characterization is justified.

Mixed Ability

Art: Create an Animal

Ask students to choose a planet and create an animal that could survive there. Emphasize that the animal should have ways of adapting to its planet's specific environment. Ask them to draw their animal and write a short description of it. Students might use the planet that was the focus of their planet-based group from page 119.

Strategy Tip
Understand Comparisons
Authors often compare things you don't know with things you do know. The author uses the expression "hotter than a pizza oven" to help you understand how hot Venus is.

The hottest planet is *Venus*, the second planet from the Sun. The temperature on Venus is hotter than a pizza oven! Venus is about the same size as Earth. Sometimes these two are called sister planets, but they have really very little in common. Venus is covered by thick, yellow clouds—but they're not rain clouds. They're made of poisonous acid! Venus and Earth even spin in opposite directions. If you lived on Venus, you would watch the Sun rise in the west and set in the east!

We live on *Earth*, the third planet from the Sun. Earth is about 93 million miles from the Sun. It would take more than fifteen years to fly from Earth to the Sun in a jet plane!

Photographs taken from space show us that Earth is a beautiful blue ball surrounded by a layer of air—our *atmosphere*. The blue, of course, is caused by all the water in Earth's oceans. About three-fourths of Earth's surface is covered by water. Earth's water and air, along with light and heat from the Sun, make it possible for plants and animals to live. As far as we know, Earth is the only planet on which life exists.

Even Earth's nearest neighbor, the Moon, has no life. There is no water on the Moon and no air to breathe. Astronauts who landed there found a cratered landscape covered with gray, powdery dirt. The Moon is beautiful to look at from Earth, but you wouldn't want to live there!

Reader's Tip
To read about the rest of the planets, get the book *The Solar System* by Maura Gouck.

Connect

Develop Language and Concepts

Present Pages 148 Through 151

Read the text with students. Show students a map of the solar system and have them trace the sequence of *Voyager 2*'s trip. Help students match the text to the photographs. Have students use descriptive words to tell what they see in the photos.

Language Awareness

Grammar
Superlatives

ACTIVITY BOOK

Write the following on the board:

The icy moon Europa is the smoothest object in the solar system.

Underline the *-est* in *smoothest* as you explain that the ending *-est* means "the most." Ask students to suggest other words they could add *-est* to in order to mean the most of something. (*shortest, tallest, slowest*) Write their suggestions on the board and ask them to use the words in sentences.

Then write the following on the board:

The most unusual moon may be Hyperion.

Point out that the word *most* may also be used to form the superlative. Have students scan pages 148 and 149 to find examples of superlatives formed with *most.* Use superlatives to ask questions such as: *Which planet is the smallest?* (Pluto) Use Activity Book page 78.

Response Activities

Personal Response
Ask students to think about what would be appropriate information to tell a younger brother or sister about the solar system. Discuss how you might change a presentation depending on the audience. Ask students what they think the most important facts are. Encourage them to tell why they think the facts are important.

Critical Response
Ask students if they think it is important for scientists to continue to gather information about other planets. Have students justify their responses by judging and evaluating the benefits and drawbacks of the U.S. space program. They could list their ideas in a T-Chart.

Creative Response
Ask students to imagine that they could visit any planet in the solar system. Have them each tell which planet they would like to visit and to explain their choices. Encourage them to include factual information to support their choices.

Options for Reaching All Students

Beginning

Science: Planet Facts

Have students draw pictures of each planet that *Voyager 2* passed, using information from the Student Book to determine color, size, and the like. Ask students to label each picture with the planet's name and one interesting piece of information that *Voyager 2* provided. Help them check their spelling and the accuracy of their information.

Advanced

Science: Research Space Missions

Have students work in small groups to research a specific U.S. space mission from the Mercury, Gemini, or Apollo program. Ask students to use cards to list the dates of the mission, names of the astronauts, and mission highlights. Have students display their cards under pictures of the spacecraft or the mission crew.

Cooperative Learning

Science Experiment

Have students do this experiment. To show why Earth is a blue planet, shine a flashlight through a glass of water in a dark room. Then add a drop of milk to the water. The light will pass through clear water unaffected, but will turn a pale blue gray color through the milky water. This is because the milk particles block out blue light. Earth's gases act like the milk.

Exploring the Planets

Strategy Tip
Locate Places
This article describes the trip of the *Voyager 2* spacecraft. Use your knowledge about the order of the planets to follow the order in which they are described.

How do people learn about the planets? Of course, people have used telescopes for centuries. Modern-day telescopes are very powerful, but their ability to show the planets is still limited.

That's why over the last thirty years scientists have sent small spacecraft on trips to the planets to take close-up pictures. For example, spacecraft have landed on Venus and Mars and taken pictures of their surfaces.

The most interesting of all these spacecraft was *Voyager 2*. It was launched by the United States on August 20, 1977, to explore the outer planets. It took *Voyager* two years to reach its first destination, the planet Jupiter.

Voyager took pictures of Jupiter's clouds and measured their temperatures. But the most amazing pictures were the close-ups that Voyager took of Jupiter's moons. The icy moon Europa is the smoothest object in the solar system. Some people call Jupiter's moon Io a pizza pie because of its reddish-yellow colors. Voyager showed that Io had active volcanoes, mountains that throw out fiery gases.

The next destination was Saturn. There *Voyager* found eleven new moons. The most unusual may be Hyperion. Because so many objects have hit into it, it is not round.

Uranus was disappointing to the scientists. *Voyager* did find ten new moons circling the planet. But *Voyager* was not able learn much about Uranus because of the thick clouds that cover it.

Twelve years after its launch, *Voyager* reached its final destination, the planet Neptune. After Uranus, Neptune was a surprise. *Voyager* found stormy clouds moving around the planet. *Voyager* also proved that Neptune, like Jupiter, had rings.

Voyager explored Neptune's large moon, Triton. Voyager found several active volcanoes on Triton, but the volcanoes throw out water, not hot rock.

After *Voyager* passed Neptune, it left the solar system and entered outer space. It will continue sending information to Earth until about 2010.

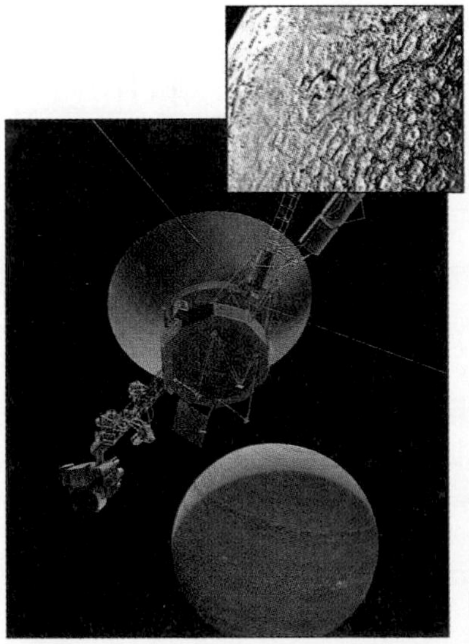

Strategy Tip
Stop and Think
What does this article tell you about what scientists know about the planets? Why is it hard for scientists to get information about the planets?

Connect

Activate Prior Knowledge
Make Associations

Write the following on the board: *I like my eggs sunny-side up.* Ask students to draw a picture of what they think a sunny-side-up egg looks like. Use other examples, such as *green thumb,* to remind students of what an idiom is.

Develop Language and Concepts
Present Page 152

On the board, write the expressions that appear in boldface on page 152. Ask students to guess what they mean. Then read the text with students. Help students use the pictures to determine meaning. First ask students to restate each italicized sentence, replacing the idiom with a more formal equivalent. Next ask students to use each idiom in an original sentence.

Language Awareness
Vocabulary
Idioms

ACTIVITY BOOK

Explain that an idiom is an expression whose meaning cannot be understood from the ordinary meanings of the words in it. Point out that idioms often fall in categories, such as idioms with color, weather, or space. Give examples. Have students think of idioms in their home languages. Ask if those idioms have counterparts in English. Use Activity Book page 79.

Space Idioms

Here are some English idioms that have words related to space. Can you find the words?

To space out —to not pay attention, to be thinking about something else. ▶
"I'm sorry. Could you tell me that address again? I spaced out while you were talking."

Sunny-side up —a way to cook an egg by frying it with the yolk-side up. ▶
"I like my eggs sunny-side up, with wheat toast."

▲ **Out of this world** —especially wonderful or great.
"This pizza is out of this world!"

Sitting on top of the world —feeling very happy. ▶
"Jason has been sitting on top of the world since he saw his good test scores."

Options for Reaching All Students

Beginning
Language: Guess Idioms

Ask each student to make an original illustration of one of the idioms on page 152. Then have other students guess which idiom or saying each illustration depicts.

Advanced
Writing: Use Idioms in Writing

Have students work in pairs to create a short story or dialogue that uses all four of the idioms on the page. Have them try to create an interesting story and use the idioms in as natural a way as possible. Remind students to capitalize and punctuate dialogue correctly.

Home Connection
Make a Space Idioms Book

Have students ask family members what space idioms are common in their home countries. Encourage students to share their findings with the class. Have students write and illustrate a multilingual class book of space idioms. Encourage students to find a logical way to organize their books (e.g., moon idioms followed by star idioms).

CHAPTER 8

Tell what you learned.

1. How is the Earth like other planets in the solar system? How is it different?
2. Choose a planet you would most like to visit. Write a letter to the U.S. space organization NASA and tell why you want to travel there. Give two reasons.
3. Pick what you think is the most important event listed on the Space Exploration Time Line. Tell why you picked it.
4. What is the most interesting fact you learned about the planets? What other things would you like to learn about the planets?

Assess ✓

Activity 1: Students should be able to mention two or three ways in which Earth is similar to and different from other planets.

Activity 2: Evaluate students' reasons for their choice.

Activity 3: Evaluate the choice based on the reasoning given for its selection.

Activity 4: Evaluate students' ability to restate an appropriate fact and extend their knowledge to other space-related topics.

Have students complete the Chapter Self-Assessment, Blackline Master 31. Have them choose the product of one of the activities to include in their portfolios. Add the results of any rubrics, checklists, self-assessments, or portfolio assessments, Blackline Masters 2–18 and 31.

Listening Assessment

BLACKLINE MASTER

Make sure that each student has a copy of Blackline Master 73 from the Teacher's Resource Book. Play the tape several times and have students fill in the chart.

CREAM TAPE

See Chapter 8 Resources, page T116d, for the Listening Assessment tapescript.

Options for Assessment

Strategy Assessment

Make a Time Line

Have students make time lines about events of the current school year. If necessary, help them brainstorm events to include. Evaluate their abilities to understand this type of graphic organizer.

Writing Assessment

Write a Story About Space Travel

Ask students to pretend they are astronauts who have traveled to the planet of their choice. Have them write stories about their trips. Their stories should include a description of their planet's appearance and physical features. Remind them to tell the entire story from the astronaut's point of view. Encourage them to illustrate their stories with photos or drawings.

Language Assessment

BLACKLINE MASTER

Use Blackline Master 72 in the Teacher's Resource Book.

Standardized Test Practice

ACTIVITY BOOK

Use pages 80 and 81. Answers: **1.** The earth rotated on its axis. **2.** Bar **3.** Pluto **4.** Venus

Wrap-Up

Activities

Field Trip

Help students compare the distances of the planets from the Sun and from each other. Take the class to a football field or other area that is about 100 yards long. Ask ten students to represent the Sun and the nine planets. Using one inch for each one million miles, line students up from the Sun as follows: Mercury, 3′; Venus, 5′7″; Earth, 7′9″; Mars, 11′9″; Jupiter, 40′4″; Saturn, 76′3″; Uranus, 148′8″; Neptune, 233′; Pluto, 305′. When you return to the classroom, help students write a language experience story about what they did and learned. Help beginning speakers make a contribution to the story, even if it is just providing the name of the student who represented a certain planet.

Music: The Planets

Bring a recording of Gustav Holst's The Planets to class. Explain that each movement of the piece is inspired by a different planet. Ask students to listen carefully to each movement and think about how the music evokes the planet. Then identify and play a short portion of each movement. Ask students to describe the music and how it makes them feel. Encourage them to recall what they know about the planets' Roman namesakes. Tell students that Pluto had not yet been discovered when this music was written. Ask them to describe what kind of music they would write for Pluto.

Time Line

Have students research to find out about recent space exploration events. Have them create a time line describing these events, using the time line on pages 136–137 as a model. Students can include this time line as part of the unit project display. They can also incorporate media into their time line by setting up videotapes or audio tapes that visitors can play or websites that they can explore.

Discussing the Theme

Review with students what they know about the solar system. Choose from the following activities that will demonstrate to students how much they have learned and how useful that information is:

- Have students tape-record a list of new words learned.
- Have students draw a picture of the solar system and label each planet.
- Play a game with the class. Name the planets one at a time, and encourage students to try to be the first to call out a word describing that planet. For example, for Venus students might say *hot*; for Jupiter, *big*. Continue naming the planets in random order until students run out of descriptive words.
- Have students discuss situations in which the words they have learned will be useful—for example, in science class, in looking at the night sky with a friend, in listening to news reports about currents events in space exploration.

Sharing the Project

Use the invitation form, Blackline Masters 32–33, to invite family members to school to see the model planets and solar system mural.

Help each student practice presenting information about the celestial body he or she worked on. When family members arrive, have a brief presentation about the planet models and solar system mural.

If the class has access to a kitchen, you might have students make cookies in the shapes and colors of the planets to serve as refreshments.

Signs of Success!

Duplicate a copy of this checklist for each student.

Name: ______________________________

Refer to the checklist below for a quick demonstration of how a student is progressing toward transitioning out of ESL instruction.

Objectives

Describes the solar system.

- ☐ Describes the Solar System.
- ☐ Tells why space seems black.
- ☐ Tells how ancient peoples interpreted the universe.
- ☐ Cites some literary examples inspired by the Sun and moon.
- ☐ Describes different physical characteristics of the planets.
- ☐ Relates some events in the history of space exploration.
- ☐ Names idioms that relate to space.

Language Awareness

Understands/Uses:

- ☐ prepositions of position
- ☐ words for *big*
- ☐ *little* versus *few*
- ☐ nationalities ending in *-ese* and *-an*
- ☐ synonyms
- ☐ present tense to state general facts
- ☐ comparatives
- ☐ dates; *before* and *after*
- ☐ unreal conditionals
- ☐ words that describe
- ☐ ordinal numbers
- ☐ superlatives
- ☐ idioms

Hears/Uses:

- ☐ homonyms

Learning Strategies:

- ☐ Reads a diagram.
- ☐ Uses charts to make comparisons.
- ☐ Reads a time line.

Comments

____

Planning Guide

CHAPTER 9

Settling the West

Objectives

Tell how, why, and when immigrants and other settlers moved to the West.

Describe a prairie biome and what life was like there for settlers in the late 1800s.

Recognize the problems created by increased contact between settlers and Indians.

Vocabulary Focus

Geography-related words, such as *grasslands, prairie, mountain, river, ocean.*

Place names, such as *California, Rocky Mountains, Europe.*

Transportation words, such as *wagon train, transcontinental railroad.*

Lesson	Content Focus	Language Awareness Objectives	Learning Strategies
Preview pp. 154–155 Tell what you know.			
Present pp. 156–157 Settling the West	Social Studies	**Grammar** Capitalization of Place Names	Use maps in textbooks.
Practice pp. 158–159 Getting and Settling the Land	Social Studies	**Grammar** The Suffix *-less*	
Practice pp. 160–161 How did the settlers get to the West?	Social Studies	**Grammar** Passive Voice	Scan.
Connect pp. 162–163 Biomes of the West: Grasslands and Forests	Social Studies/ Science	**Grammar** Amount Words: *Many/Few/Little*	Use previously learned information.
Connect pp. 164–171 *Sarah, Plain and Tall*	Social Studies/ Literature	**Spelling** Quotation Marks: Recognize Unattributed Dialogue **Grammar** Negatives	Use a dictionary to increase vocabulary.
Connect p. 172 "Home on the Range"	Social Studies/ Language	**Phonics** Long *o*	
Assess p. 173 Tell what you learned.			

CHAPTER 10

Industry Changed the Nation

Objectives

Describe the Industrial Revolution.

Identify some industrial leaders and inventors in the United States.

Tell about the causes and effects of the reform movement.

Describe the life of Andrew Carnegie.

Sing some songs of the Industrial Revolution.

Vocabulary Focus

Invention words, such as *patent, telephone, phonograph.*

Industrial words, such as *assembly line, factory, business, reform.*

Song words, such as *canal, lumber, whistle, brick.*

Lesson	Content Focus	Language Awareness Objectives	Learning Strategies
Preview pp. 174–175 Tell what you know.			
Present pp. 176–177 The Industrial Revolution	Social Studies	**Grammar** Expressions of Time	Read on to get meaning.
Practice pp. 178–179 The Nation's Industrial Leaders and Inventors	Social Studies	**Grammar** Appositives	Use a time line.
Practice pp. 180–181 Bringing Reform	Social Studies	**Vocabulary** Phrase *because of*	Predict content.
Connect pp. 182–183 Charting Changes	Social Studies/ Math	**Grammar** Question Formation	
Connect pp. 184–187 *Andrew Carnegie*	Social Studies/ Literature	**Grammar** Recognize Unreal Conditions	
Connect pp. 188–189 Songs of the Industrial Revolution	Social Studies/ Literature	**Vocabulary** Rhyming Words	Compare and contrast.
Connect p. 190 "Brother, Can You Spare a Dime?"	Social Studies/ Literature	**Language Function** Making Requests	
Assess p. 191 Tell what you learned.			

Resources

Chapter 9

Support Materials

PICTURE CARDS

Numbers 5, 6, 8, 9, 12, 14, 15, 17, 18, 20, 22, 24, 26, 28, 29, 30, 31, 35, 36, 39, 43, 45, 49, 50, 51, 56, 58, 59, 64, 66, 69, 71

ACTIVITY BOOK

Pages 82–91

BLUE TAPE

Side 1: *Sarah, Plain and Tall,* pages T164–T171

Side 2: "Home on the Range," page T172

DISK

Writer's Notebook

LET'S TALK CARD

96 cards to start conversations.

STORYTELLING

Storytelling Anthology: *Worlds Together*

Phonics

PHONICS

Newcomer Phonics, pages 46–49

Assessment Materials

BLACKLINE MASTER

Language Assessment, Blackline Master 80

Listening Assessment, Blackline Master 81

CREAM TAPE

Side 1: Listening Assessment, page T173

Listen carefully. You will hear a story about the settlers to the West. Write down the story. You will hear the story once. Then you will hear it again more slowly. Begin to write. Then you will hear it one more time. Check what you wrote.

Many settlers came to the West of the United States during the 1800s. They came from the East and from Europe. They wanted better lives for themselves and their families. The first settlers came in wagons. Later settlers came on railroads.

Support for Newcomers

Newcomer Book C, Survival language for absolute beginners. For overview, see pages xxviii–xxix.

Newcomer Teacher Suggestion Book, Chapter 9, pages 24–25

HomeLink Penguin Readers

The Fall of the House of Usher and Other Stories

For Extended Reading

A Frontier Fort on the Oregon Trail by Scott Steedman, Peter Bedrick Books, 1994. The triumphs and hardships of the many people who followed the Oregon Trail. **Level: Beginning**

Homesteading: Settling America's Heartland by Dorothy Hinshaw Patent, Walker & Co, 1998. Read about the families who settled America's prairies after the 1862 Homestead Act. **Level: Average**

A Multicultural Portrait of the Move West by Petra Press, Benchmark Books, 1993. How minorities and women viewed the move westward. **Level: Advanced**

Pioneers by Martin W. Sandler, HarperTrophy, 1999. This overview of the pioneer experience is brought to life by stunning photographs and prints. **Level: Average**

Ten Mile Day and the Building of the Transcontinental Railroad by Mary Ann Fraser, Henry Holt & Co., 1996. The fascinating story about the race to complete the first railroad to cross the North American continent. **Level: Beginning**

The Treeless Plains by Glen Rounds, Holiday House, 1994. The story of how the settlers came to realize the worth of the "treeless plains." **Level: Beginning**

West by Steamboat by Tim McNeese, Crestwood House, 1993. Traces the important role steamboats played in the move westward before the Civil War. **Level: Average**

Related Technology

Oregon Trail 4th Edition, MECC, 1999. An old favorite made more interesting for older students.

Resources

Chapter 10

Support Materials

PICTURE CARDS

Numbers 1, 2, 4, 8, 11, 13, 14, 15, 19, 25, 26, 27, 30, 33, 34, 36, 37, 38, 41, 42, 44, 48, 49, 50, 51, 52, 54, 55, 56, 57, 59, 60, 66, 67, 70, 72

ACTIVITY BOOK

Pages 92–101

BLUE TAPE

Side 2: "The Erie Canal," page T188; "I've Been Working on the Railroad,"page T189; "Brother, Can You Spare a Dime?," page T190

DISK

Writer's Notebok

Assessment Materials

BLACKLINE MASTER

Language Assessment, Blackline Master 82

Listening Assessment, Blackline Master 83

CREAM TAPE

Side 2: Listening Assessment, page T191

Listen carefully. Circle the inventions that you hear mentioned.

The Industrial Revolution and its inventions changed the lives of people. Several inventions of the late nineteenth century greatly affected people's lives. One was the use of electricity to run machines. This led to a variety of inventions from Edison's light bulb to the computers of today. Another major invention that changed the lives of people in the United States was the automobile. People could travel long distances more easily, and the United States became a nation in which people moved often.

Support for Newcomer

Newcomer Teacher Suggestion Book, Chapter 10, pages 26–27

For Extended Reading

Henry Ford: Young Man With Ideas by Hazel B. Aird, Aladdin Paperbacks, 1986. The life of the American automotive industrialist who pioneered in assembly-line methods of mass production. **Level: Beginning**

Industrial Revolution edited by John D. Claire, Harcourt Brace & Co., 1994. This book tells the history of the Industrial Revolution and describes the changes it brought about. **Level: Average**

Mistakes That Worked by Charlotte Folitz Jones, Doubleday, 1994. Some of today's most common products were invented—by accident! **Level: Average**

The Real McCoy: The Life of an African-American Inventor by Wendy Towle, Scholastic, 1995. The story of how this African-American inventor overcame obstacles and contributed more than 50 inventions that improved people's ways of life. **Level: Beginning**

Samuel Slater's Mill and the Industrial Revolution by Christopher Simonds, Silver Burdett Press, Inc., 1990. The story of how this Englishman established the textile industry in the United States. **Level: Average**

Related Technology

The Industrial Revolution in America, Queue Inc., 1995. This well-crafted program checks for understanding and records student progress.

Project

National Time Line

This optional project can be completed over the next two chapters. In this project, students will create a giant time line of events in U.S. history during the 1800s and early 1900s. See the Unit Wrap-Up, page T191a, for ideas on sharing the project with family members.

What You'll Need

Art Materials: colored construction paper, tracing paper, photocopy paper, paints, brushes, felt-tipped markers, scissors, glue, push pins or tacks, butcher paper

Research Materials: almanacs, encyclopedias, historical atlases, easy-to-read biographies of people from the 1800s and early 1900s, books of songs and poems from the era, magazines and books with pictures related to the Westward Movement, industrialization, and urbanization

Strategies You'll Use

- Use reference resources
- Summarize events
- Understand chronology

Beginning the Project

Cover a large horizontal section of the bulletin board with a long piece of butcher paper.

Tell students that as they study this unit, they will be creating a time line summarizing major events in U.S. history during the 1800s and early 1900s.

Begin by dividing the butcher paper into 13 equal segments, each meant to represent a decade from 1800 to 1930. Then label the top of each section with the years it covers. Start with the year 1800 at the left end of the time line; place the year 1930 at the right end. Draw a horizontal, connecting line through the middle of each decade's section. Tell students they will add their time line items both above and below this middle line with leader lines pointing to the specific year in each decade that is applicable.

Talk with students about the things that can and cannot be shown on a time line. Mention things with specific dates, such as a person's date of birth, when something was invented, and dates of earthquakes and hurricanes as being good time line items. Talk about ideas and fashion trends as being hard to put on a time line because they often do not have specific beginnings and endings.

Talk as a group about some things that students may want to add to all sections of the time line, such as the national population from the census for each decade, the admission dates of new states to the Union, and each President's term in office.

Home Involvement

Send the Letter to the Family, Blackline Masters 74–79, to families, telling them that the class will be studying the development of the United States in the 1800s and early 1900s. The letter encourages family members to share information with students about events in their home countries during those same years.

Daily Discussion

Take a few minutes each day to talk about the time line and what events from the text might be added to it and how these events might be portrayed visually. Encourage students to use:

- drawn or painted pictures of key people accompanied by captions that describe the pictures' significance
- written labels, quotes, and song lyrics representing important events
- cutout magazine pictures of inventions, events, and so on
- historical maps of relevant places, such as Gettysburg located in Pennsylvania, for the Battle of Gettysburg

Try to see that all students get to actually add at least one item to the time line and do not end up merely helping more proficient students accomplish their own goals.

Help students understand that historical events do not take place at an even pace and that this will make some parts of the time line more crowded than others.

Suggest students enrich the display and fill in "empty" spots by doing library research topics such as:

- when the Oklahoma Land Rush took place
- the dates of the Trail of Tears
- when the first movie theater opened
- key Supreme Court decisions, such as approval of the separate but equal clause
- the beginning and end of Reconstruction
- when various defeated Confederate states will allowed readmission to the Union

See page T191a for ideas about sharing the time line with families and friends when the unit is completed.

Activity Book

Chapter 9

Name

Proofread and Correct

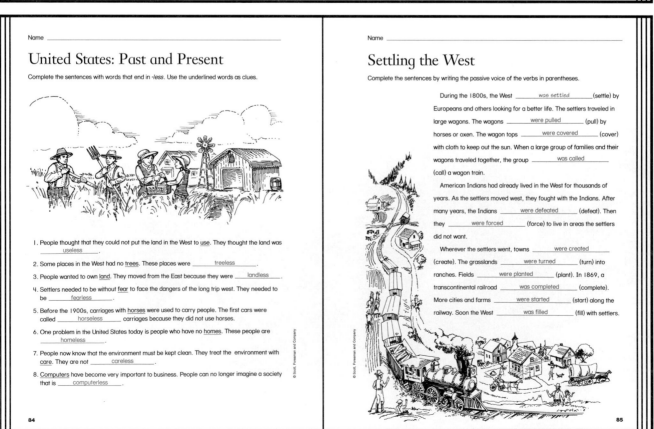

These sentences contain place names that should be capitalized. Proofread the sentences. Rewrite them to show the correct capital letters.

1. The united states changed greatly during the 1800s and early 1900s.
   The United States changed greatly during the 1800s and early 1900s.
2. Before 1800, most people lived between the atlantic ocean and the appalachian mountains.
   Before 1800, most people lived between the Atlantic Ocean
   and the Appalachian Mountains.
3. Eventually, settlers moved across the mississippi river and went as far as the pacific ocean.
   Eventually, settlers moved across the Mississippi River and
   went as far as the Pacific Ocean.
4. Many of the settlers had been born in europe.
   Many of the settlers had been born in Europe.
5. They settled in areas that later became states, such as minnesota, nebraska, and iowa.
   They settled in areas that later became states, such as Minnesota,
   Nebraska, and Iowa.

Complete the sentences.

1. I live in the city of ___Answers will vary___.
2. I live in the state of ______.
3. The nearest river is the ______.
4. The name of the country I came from is ______.

Name

Map Reading

The map below shows the years when the states west of the Mississippi River became part of the United States.

Use the map to answer the questions.

1. How many states were added to the United States in the following decades?

1840s	2	1850s	3	1860s	3
1870s	1	1880s	4	1890s	3
1900s	1	1910s	2		

2. In which year were the most states added to the United States? How many states were added?
   1889, 4 states
3. What states were added in that year?
   Washington, Montana, North Dakota, South Dakota
4. Which were the last states on the map to be added to the United States? When were they added?
   Arizona and New Mexico, 1912

Name

United States: Past and Present

Complete the sentences with words that end in *-less*. Use the underlined words as clues.

1. People thought that they could not put the land in the West to use. They thought the land was ___useless___.
2. Some places in the West had no trees. These places were ___treeless___.
3. People wanted to own land. They moved from the East because they were ___landless___.
4. Settlers needed to be without fear to face the dangers of the long trip west. They needed to be ___fearless___.
5. Before the 1900s, carriages with horses were used to carry people. The first cars were called ___horseless___ carriages because they did not use horses.
6. One problem in the United States today is people who have no homes. These people are ___homeless___.
7. People now know that the environment must be kept clean. They treat the environment with care. They are not ___careless___.
8. Computers have become very important to business. People can no longer imagine a society that is ___computerless___.

Name

Settling the West

Complete the sentences by writing the passive voice of the verbs in parentheses.

During the 1800s, the West ___was settled___ (settle) by Europeans and others looking for a better life. The settlers traveled in large wagons. The wagons ___were pulled___ (pull) by horses or oxen. The wagon tops ___were covered___ (cover) with cloth to keep out the sun. When a large group of families and their wagons traveled together, the group ___was called___ (call) a wagon train.

American Indians had already lived in the West for thousands of years. As the settlers moved west, they fought with the Indians. After many years, the Indians ___were defeated___ (defeat). Then they ___were forced___ (force) to live in areas the settlers did not want.

Wherever the settlers went, towns ___were created___ (create). The grasslands ___were turned___ (turn) into ranches. Fields ___were planted___ (plant). In 1869, a transcontinental railroad ___was completed___ (complete). More cities and farms ___were started___ (start) along the railway. Soon the West ___was filled___ (fill) with settlers.

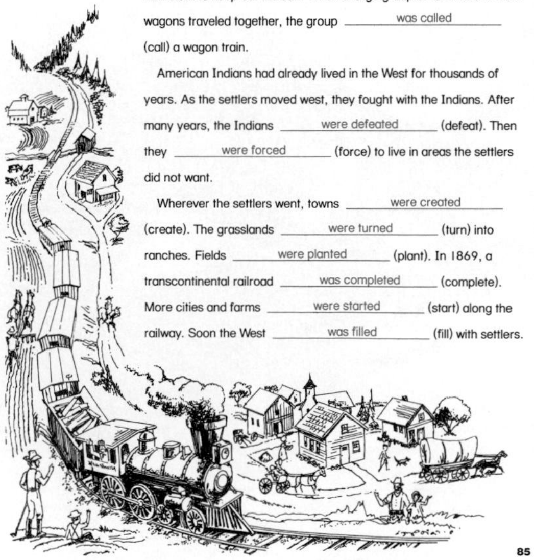

Name

Prairie or Forest?

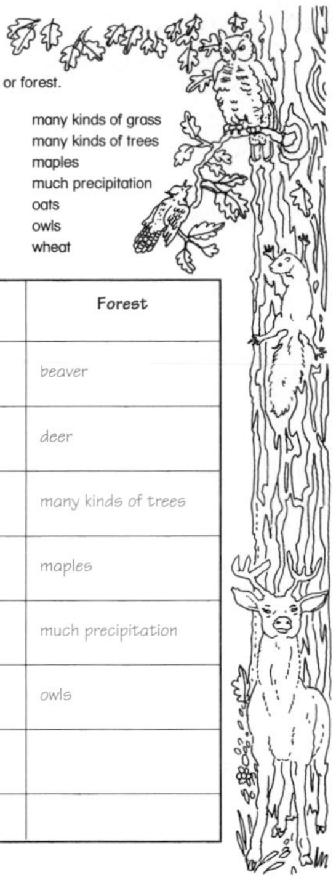

Put each item in the correct category, prairie or forest.

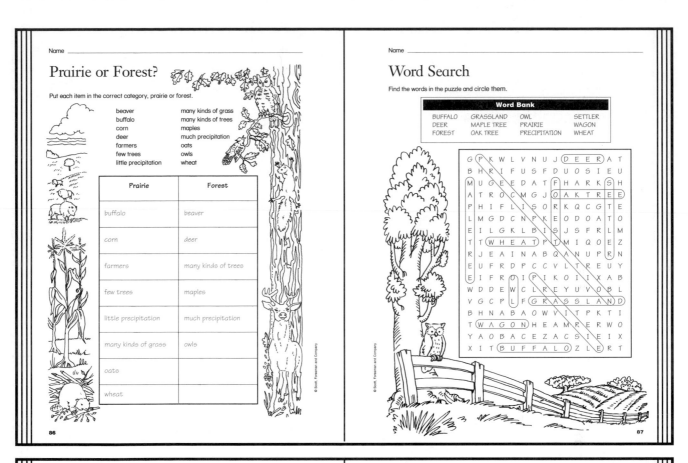

beaver	many kinds of grass
buffalo	many kinds of trees
corn	maples
deer	much precipitation
farmers	oats
few trees	owls
little precipitation	wheat

Prairie	Forest
buffalo	beaver
corn	deer
farmers	many kinds of trees
few trees	maples
little precipitation	much precipitation
many kinds of grass	owls
oats	
wheat	

Name

Word Search

Find the words in the puzzle and circle them.

Word Bank

BUFFALO	GRASSLAND	OWL	SETTLER
DEER	MAPLE TREE	PRAIRIE	WAGON
FOREST	OAK TREE	PRECIPITATION	WHEAT

G	P	K	W	L	V	N	U	J	D	E	E	R	A	T
B	H	R	I	F	U	S	F	D	U	O	S	I	E	U
M	U	G	E	E	D	A	T	F	H	A	R	K	S	H
A	T	R	O	C	M	G	J	O	A	K	T	R	E	E
P	H	I	F	L	I	S	O	R	K	Q	C	G	T	E
L	M	G	D	C	N	P	K	E	O	D	O	A	T	O
E	I	L	G	K	L	B	I	S	J	S	F	R	L	M
T	T	W	H	E	A	T	P	T	M	I	Q	O	E	Z
R	J	E	A	I	N	A	B	Q	A	N	U	P	R	N
E	U	F	R	D	P	C	C	V	L	T	R	E	U	Y
E	I	F	R	O	I	P	I	K	O	I	I	X	A	B
W	D	D	E	W	C	L	R	E	Y	U	V	O	B	L
V	G	C	P	L	F	G	R	A	S	S	L	A	N	D
B	H	N	A	B	A	O	W	V	I	T	P	K	T	I
T	W	A	G	O	N	H	E	A	M	R	E	R	W	O
Y	A	O	B	A	C	E	Z	A	C	S	I	E	I	X
X	I	T	B	U	F	F	A	L	O	Z	L	E	R	T

Name

Who am I?

Read the descriptions of the characters in the story *Sarah, Plain and Tall*. Then write the name of each character by his or her description.

Characters

Anna
Caleb
Papa
Sarah

Descriptions

1. I drove the wagon to get Sarah. Papa
2. I rocked on the porch as I waited. Anna
3. I liked my new shell. Caleb
4. I climbed up on the porch roof and tried to see the wagon better. Caleb
5. I had a pet cat named Seal. Sarah
6. I watched the sheep and the cows and the hawk as I waited. Anna
7. I thought the prairie land rolled a little like the sea. Sarah
8. I washed my face clean but not too clean. Caleb
9. I fed and watered the horses and hitched them to the wagon. Papa
10. I thought the sea stone was the smoothest and whitest stone I had ever seen. Anna

Name

Sound Search

Circle each word that contains the sound of long *o*. Remember, this sound may be spelled *o*, *oa*, or *ow*.

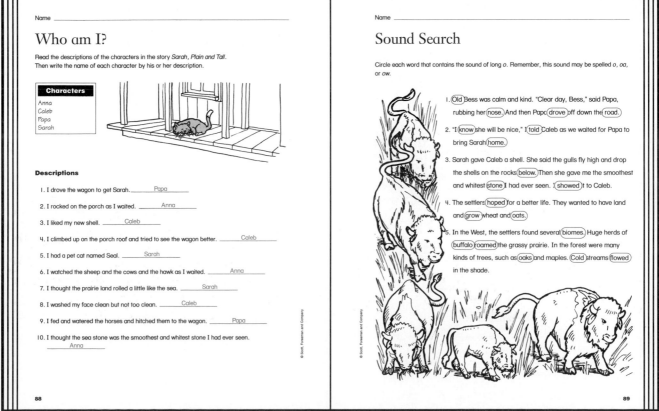

1. Old Bess was calm and kind. "Clear day, Bess," said Papa, rubbing her nose. And then Papa drove off down the road.
2. "I know she will be nice," I told Caleb as we waited for Papa to bring Sarah home.
3. Sarah gave Caleb a shell. She said the gulls fly high and drop the shells on the rocks below. Then she gave me the smoothest and whitest stone I had ever seen. I showed it to Caleb.
4. The settlers hoped for a better life. They wanted to have land and grow wheat and oats.
5. In the West, the settlers found several biomes. Huge herds of buffalo roamed the grassy prairie. In the forest were many kinds of trees, such as oaks and maples. Cold streams flowed in the shade.

Activity Book

Chapter 10

Name ______________________________

Inventions

Write the name of each invention under its picture. Use the words in the box.

Info Box

camera	light bulb	railroad
car	telephone	typewriter

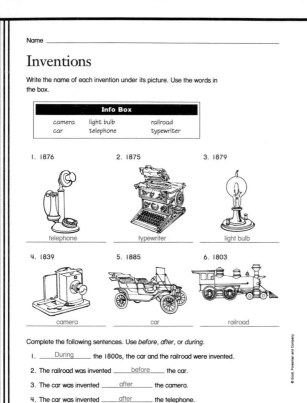

1. 1876

telephone

2. 1875

typewriter

3. 1879

light bulb

4. 1839

camera

5. 1885

car

6. 1803

railroad

Complete the following sentences. Use *before*, *after*, or *during*.

1. During the 1800s, the car and the railroad were invented.
2. The railroad was invented before the car.
3. The car was invented after the camera.
4. The car was invented after the telephone.

Name ______________________________

Inventors and Reformers

Add the phrase in parentheses to the sentence. Write the new sentence on the line.

1. Alexander Graham Bell invented the telephone. (an immigrant from Scotland)
   Alexander Graham Bell, an immigrant from Scotland, invented the telephone.
2. Henry Ford invented the assembly line. (a way to build cars quickly and cheaply)
   Henry Ford invented the assembly line, a way to build cars quickly and cheaply.
3. Thomas Edison invented the light bulb. (one of the world's most famous inventors)
   Thomas Edison, one of the world's most famous inventors, invented the light bulb.
4. The Standard Oil Company was headed by John D. Rockefeller. (a large and powerful company)
   The Standard Oil Company, a large and powerful company, was headed by John D. Rockefeller.
5. Ida Tarbell thought that John D. Rockefeller got unfair deals from others. (a writer)
   Ida Tarbell, a writer, thought that John D. Rockefeller got unfair deals from others.
6. Upton Sinclair helped to change the meat packing business. (a novelist)
   Upton Sinclair, a novelist, helped to change the meat packing business.

Name ______________________________

Because Of

Inventions

Complete the sentences with phrases that begin with *because of*. Use the information you learned in this unit.

1. Because of the phonograph, people could listen to music in their homes.
2. Because of the typewriter, people could write letters more quickly and easily.
3. Because of the ight bulb, people could have light at all times of day cheaply and easily.
4. Because of the camera, people could get pictures of themselves and important events in their lives.
5. Because of the car, people could travel from one place to another more easily.
6. Because of the telephone, people could talk to other people in different parts of the city or country.
7. Because of the assembly line, cars could be made more quickly.

People

Complete the sentences. Use *because of* and the phrases in the box.

Info Box

Sinclair's writing
Ford's assembly line

1. Because of Sinclair's writing, meat was packed more safely.
2. Because of Ford's assembly line, cars were made more cheaply.

Name ______________________________

Reading Graphs

The graph shows how many Americans were living in urban and rural areas between 1870 and 1920. Use information from the graph to answer the questions.

Urban-Rural Population, 1870-1920

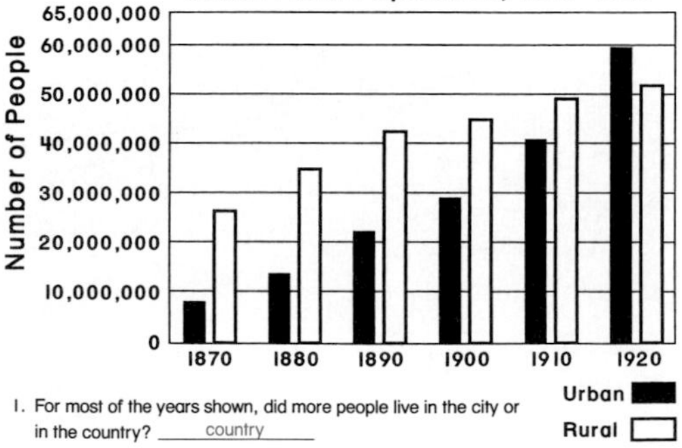

1. For most of the years shown, did more people live in the city or in the country? country
2. As you follow the graph from left to right, which group seems to be growing faster? urban
3. By which year did the urban population become greater than the rural population? 1920
4. Did either group, rural or urban, lose population between 1870 and 1920? no
5. From 1870 to 1900, did the urban population grow more or less than the rural population? Give approximate numbers.
   The urban population grew more. It grew by about 20 million people, and the rural population grew by about 18 million.

Name ______________________________

Ask the questions.

The United States grew rapidly as an industrial nation. Look at the following graph. It shows the number of cars that factories in the United States made during the 1920s. Write questions that go with the answers.

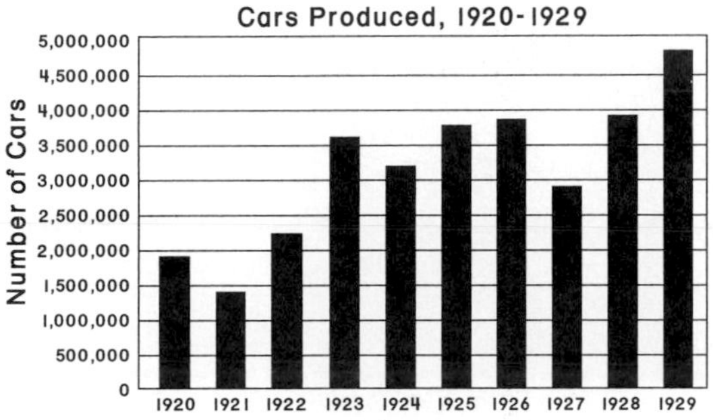

1. How many cars did factories produce in 1921?
   Factories produced almost 1,500,000 cars.
2. How many cars did factories produce in 1929?
   Factories produced almost 5,000,000 cars.
3. In what years did car production decrease?
   Car production decreased in 1921, 1924, and 1927.
4. When did factories first produce over 3,000,000 cars?
   Factories first produced over 3,000,000 cars in 1923.
5. ______________________________
   Your own answer: ______________________________

Name ______________________________

If . . .

Unscramble the words to form sentences with if.

1. a jet plane \ if I had \ I would buy \ a million dollars
   If I had a million dollars, I would buy a jet plane.
2. a lot of money \ if I were rich \ I would give away
   If I were rich, I would give away a lot of money.
3. all my favorite songs \ if I knew \ I would play \ how to play the guitar
   If I knew how to play the guitar, I would play all my favorite songs.

Complete the sentences to tell what you would do in each situation.

1. If I were twenty-one years old, ______________________________
   Accept answers that show understanding.
2. If I were in high school, ______________________________
3. If I could go anywhere in the world, ______________________________
4. If I had 10 million dollars, ______________________________
5. If I were President of the United States, ______________________________
6. If I could change two things, ______________________________

Name ______________________________

Crossword Puzzle

Use the words in the box to complete the puzzle.

Across

1. After he wrote about the meat packing industry, the government passed new laws to make food safer.
4. She was a reformer who criticized the way Rockefeller did business.
6. He was the head of a giant oil company.
7. He gave away almost $350 million during the last 18 years of his life.
8. He bought Carnegie's steel properties for half a billion dollars.

Bell Industrial Morgan Rockefeller steel
Carnegie inventors reform Sinclair Tarbell

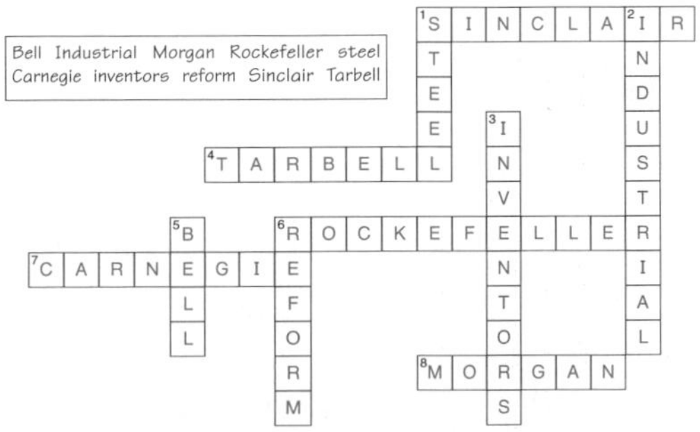

Down

1. Carnegie made much of his money in the ______ industry.
2. The ______ Revolution caused many changes in the United States.
3. Thomas Edison, Alexander Graham Bell, and Henry Ford were famous ______.
5. He was the Scottish immigrant who invented the telephone.
6. The ______ movement helped change the way big companies did business.

Name ______________________________

Can you help?

Look at the pictures. What is the person saying? Complete the requests. Begin with either *Can you?* or *Could you?*

Info Box

give me change for a dollar
tell me the time
carry this for me
show me a book about settlers in the West
give me directions
give me a piece of paper

1. 
   Can/Could you give me directions?
2. 

   Can/Could you give me change for a dollar?
3. 
   Can/Could you give me a piece of paper?
4. 

   Can/Could you show me a book about settlers in the West?
5. 
   Can/Could you tell me the time?
6. 
   Can/Could you carry this for me?

Preview

Activate Prior Knowledge

Relate Personal Experiences

Ask students to name reasons why people move to new places. Encourage students to draw on their own family's experiences with moving. Then discuss trips they have taken. Show pictures and review the vocabulary to express various means of transportation, such as *We went to Mexico by plane,. . . by ship, or . . . by car.*

Develop Language and Concepts

Present Pages 154 and 155

Have students look at the pictures. Tell students that the pictures show what the United States was like about one hundred years ago. Invite them to name or point to things in the pictures that are the same as or different from life today.

Introduce or review the Word Bank words. Then help students relate the words to the pictures.

Guide students to conclude that the United States one hundred years ago included both farms and factories. Present key words such as *industry, wagon,* and *oil well.* The car and the oil well represent the new industries and technologies that were developing at the time.

Have students answer the Talk About It questions. Encourage them to note which items are the same in their lives as well as what is different.

UNIT 5 • JOURNEYS

A Growing Nation

The United States changed greatly during the 1800s and early 1900s. Many people moved to new homes in the West. New industries began. What do these pictures show about the United States during this time?

154

Options for Reaching All Students

Beginning

Language: Transportation Words

Help students list all the ways they have traveled, such as by bus, by subway, by train, by foot. Have students draw or find pictures to illustrate each mode of transportation. Have students label each picture.

Advanced

Language: Describe a Journey

Have students work in pairs to tell each other about their journeys from where they were born to where they live now or other journeys they have made. Tell students to speak in an appropriate conversational manner and to use vocabulary their partners can understand. Encourage partners to ask questions to clarify or get more information.

Mixed Ability

Art: Make a Mural

Have students work in small groups to make murals on butcher paper that is hanging on the bulletin board. The murals should depict students' journeys to their present homes. Encourage students to add speech bubbles near individuals depicted that include one- or two-word comments on the events shown.

Word Bank

car
factory
farm
oil
wagon

Talk About It

How is life different for you now from what it was in the country where you were born?

THEME/KEY CONCEPTS

The theme of this unit is journeys. During the 1800s and early 1900s, the United States grew in size and in population as many people moved to the West. At the same time, technology and industry were beginning to change the nation from a farming, rural one to an industrial, urban one.

Chapter 9

- Thousands of people journeyed to new homes in the West, first by wagon train and later via the transcontinental railroad.
- Many of these people were Easterners or European immigrants.
- This mass migration to the West led to conflicts with the American Indians who already lived there.

Chapter 10

- In the 1800s and early 1900s, inventions changed the way people in the United States lived and worked.
- The United States produced many inventors and industrial leaders; some of these people were immigrants.
- The Industrial Revolution caused people to leave homes in farming areas and move to cities to work in factories.

Home Connection

Transportation in the Past

Have students interview older relatives or family friends to find out what kinds of transportation they used when they were younger. Have students share their findings. Then have the whole class compare and contrast transportation they use today with that used in the past by their relatives or friends. Have them list their findings in a T-Chart.

Present

Activate Prior Knowledge

Brainstorm Vocabulary

Brainstorm a list of geography-related words and U.S. place names that students know. The words can be general *(north)*, or specific (*California, Atlantic Ocean*). Write students' suggestions on chart paper. Point out that specific place names are capitalized. Add to the list as students work on this chapter.

Develop Language and Concepts

Present Pages 156 and 157

ACTIVITY BOOK

Read the text with students. Use the map to show the settlers' movements from east to west. Use Activity Book page 83. Explain that the Indians and the settlers had very different concepts of land ownership and use and that this difference led to violent conflicts. On the board, list students' responses to the question of why the settlers went west. If necessary, stimulate discussion by offering adventure and religious freedom as possible reasons. Do the Talk About It questions as a whole class.

Model a Strategy

Use Maps in Textbooks

Model using maps in social studies texts:

When I start to study a new place in social studies, I know that I need to look at a map. This helps me know where the places in the text are located. Doing this helps me better understand what I am reading.

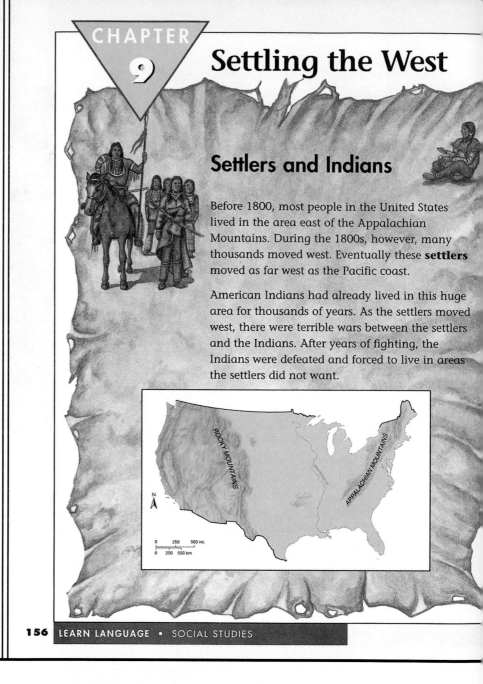

CHAPTER 9

Settling the West

Settlers and Indians

Before 1800, most people in the United States lived in the area east of the Appalachian Mountains. During the 1800s, however, many thousands moved west. Eventually these **settlers** moved as far west as the Pacific coast.

American Indians had already lived in this huge area for thousands of years. As the settlers moved west, there were terrible wars between the settlers and the Indians. After years of fighting, the Indians were defeated and forced to live in areas the settlers did not want.

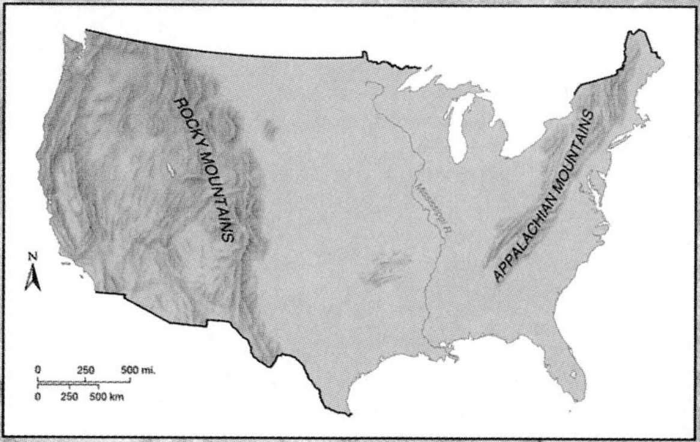

Options for Reaching All Students

Beginning

Language: Picture Sentences

PICTURE CARDS

Help students learn and chant sentences for the key word on each Picture Card that you present. Use Picture Cards 28 (family), 29 (farm), 36 (house), 45 (mountains), and 58 (river). Some sentence examples might be:

Many settlers were families.
Many settlers wanted to start farms.
Settlers had to cross mountains.

This way the students are practicing vocabulary in context. As students chant, have volunteers hold up appropriate picture cards when they hear these vocabulary words used.

Advanced

Language: Capitalization of Place Names

Ask students to make lists of place names from their home countries and to give a brief description of each place. Suggest categories, such as rivers, cities, and mountains. Review their lists with students and discuss how proper names begin with capital letters in English.

Many of the settlers had been born in Europe. Other settlers had been born in the East. However, most of these people had the same dream. They wanted a better life for their families and themselves. Most of all, the settlers wanted to own some land.

Many of the Europeans had been farmers. But their farms were too small or the soil was too poor to grow enough for their needs. Also, it was hard to buy good land. The Europeans hoped to start farms in the West. The settlers from the East wanted the same thing.

Talk About It

What reasons did your family have for wanting to come to the United States? What dreams did you have before you got here? What dreams do you have now?

Language Awareness

Grammar
Capitalization of Place Names

ACTIVITY BOOK

Write the words *United States, Appalachian Mountains,* and *Europe* on the board. Tell students that in English, place names such as these begin with an initial capital letter. When names have more than one word, then each important word begins with a capital letter. For comparison, point out that common nouns, such as *countries, states,* and *mountains* would not be capitalized because they do not refer to a specific country, state, or mountain range. Invite students to name places and write them on the board. Use Activity Book page 82.

Assess ✓

Use class discussion for assessment. Students should be able to

- describe how, when, and why Europeans and other settlers moved west
- explain the impact of the settlers' westward movement on American Indians

LOOK**AHEAD**

In the next section, students will learn how settlers obtained and settled land.

Multicultural Connection

American Indians

Divide the class into five groups. Assign each group one of the following to research and report on: the Iroquois, the Inuit, the Plains tribes, the Navaho, and the Northwest Coast tribes. Tell each group to use a variety of reference materials to find out about their assigned tribe(s) and to prepare oral and written reports for the rest of the class. Suggest that the reports include maps showing where the tribe(s) lived in general; illustrations of housing, tools, clothing, and so on; as well as text about the tribe or tribes. Remind students to check their written reports for grammar, punctuation, and spelling and to deliver their oral reports loudly and clearly.

QuickCheck

Prepositions of Time

Check students' understanding of prepositions that indicate time in phrases such as *during the 1800s, before the 1800s, in the nineteenth century.* Have them give specific examples of years that fit in each time period.

Practice

Activate Prior Knowledge

Start a K-W-L Chart

Find out what students already know about how the West was settled. Ask questions such as: *How did settlers get the land? Where did they settle?*

Use the information to make a K-W-L chart like the following on the board:

K: What We Know	Many settlers went west in the 1800s.
W: What We Want to Find Out	How did settlers get land?
L: What We Learned	

Continue to fill in the chart as the lesson progresses.

Develop Language and Concepts

Present Pages 158 and 159

Have students look at the pictures on pages 158 and 159. Ask them what they can tell about life in the West during the 1800s. Point out the sod house and how this type of house was often built where there were few trees. Discuss the map. Read the pages with students and talk about how settlers got their land. Read the advertisement on page 158. Help students identify facts and emotional arguments in it.

(Continued on page T159.)

Getting and Settling the Land

The U.S. government gave land to people who had fought in the American Revolution or the War of 1812. The government also sold land to settlers. Sometimes, rich people bought big areas of land. Then they sold pieces of it to settlers at a profit.

Many settlers just moved onto open land and started farms and ranches. Later Congress and state governments passed laws saying that these settlers owned the land they had taken.

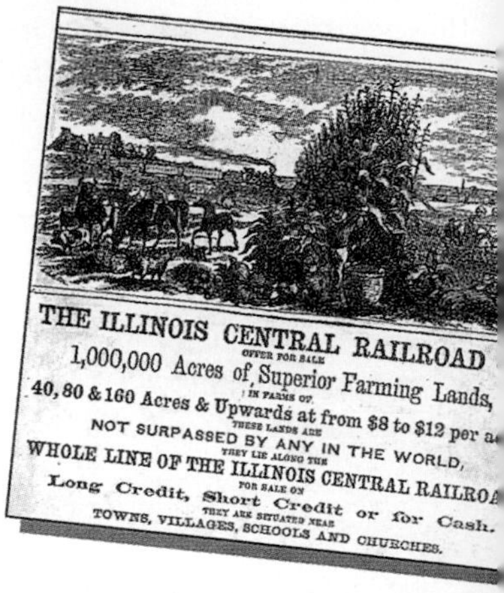
THE ILLINOIS CENTRAL RAILROAD
OFFER FOR SALE
1,000,000 Acres of Superior Farming Lands,
IN FARMS OF
40, 80 & 160 Acres & Upwards at from $8 to $12 per
THESE LANDS ARE
NOT SURPASSED BY ANY IN THE WORLD,
THEY LIE ALONG THE
WHOLE LINE OF THE ILLINOIS CENTRAL
FOR SALE ON
Long Credit, Short Credit or for Cash.
THEY ARE SITUATED NEAR
TOWNS, VILLAGES, SCHOOLS AND CHURCHES.

Options for Reaching All Students

Beginning

Language: Place Names

Have students make lists of several place names in your state, grouping them into categories, such as *towns, lakes,* and *rivers.* If students need ideas, tell them to look in atlases, encyclopedias, and other reference sources. Then have them share the lists with each other to check capitalization, spelling, and appropriateness of entry.

Advanced

Social Studies: Research a State

Divide students into small groups. Have them study atlases and other reference materials to find out all the states in the United States that are found between the Mississippi River and the Rocky Mountains. Have each group make an alphabetical list of their findings and then pick one state to study in depth.

In its study, each group should focus on geographic features, as well as important places and historical events. (Try to see that each group selects a different state.) Remind students to take careful notes. Model for them how they can use an outline to organize their information. Give examples of major headings they can use and the type of facts they can list under each heading. Have the groups report their findings to the rest of the class.

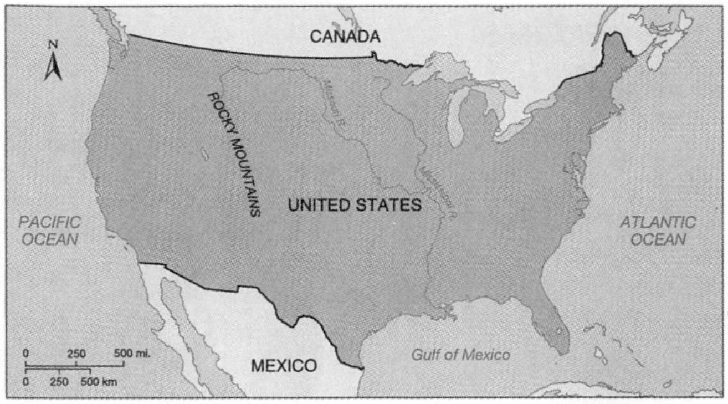

Settlers moved to almost all areas of the West. In the 1820s, people thought the area between the Missouri River and the Rocky Mountains was useless to farmers. Settlers thought they could not farm there because the land did not have forests, as the land had in their old homes. Instead, this huge flat area was **grasslands.** It looked like an ocean of waving grass and flowers. But by 1870, settlers had begun to turn this "useless" area into farms for raising wheat and corn and ranches for raising cattle and sheep.

Talk About It

Does the country where you were born have many farms and ranches? What things do people grow there?

Review the uses of land and discuss the difference between farming and ranching before having students answer the Talk About It questions.

Language Awareness

Grammar
The Suffix *-less*

ACTIVITY BOOK

Call students' attention to the word *useless* on page 159. Point out that the suffix *-less* means "without." Explain that adding the ending *-less* to *use* results in a word that means "without use." Give students other examples of words with this suffix, such as *treeless, horseless*, and *careless*. Have students do Activity Book page 84.

Assess

Use class discussion for assessment. Students should be able to

- tell how the settlers got their land and what they did with it
- explain the differences between farming and ranching

LOOK**AHEAD**

In the next section, students will learn the transportation methods that the settlers used.

Mixed Ability

Geography: Make Maps

Have students create maps of their home countries. Provide atlases in English and/or their home language, if needed. Have them show major topographical features such as mountain ranges or large rivers. Encourage students to label specific places that have special meaning to them. Invite them to present their maps and explain how these major features affect the way people live, earn money, and so on.

Peer or Cross-Age Tutoring

Language: Summarize

Have students work in pairs of mixed ability. Ask each student to tell a partner something he or she has learned about how settlers got land. Beginning learners can point to pictures and tell what they can about them. Encourage more proficient students to ask helpful questions and provide vocabulary support.

Cooperative Learning

Suffixes

List the following suffixes on the board: *-age, -ful, -hood, -ship, -ment, -ish, -like*. Have students use dictionaries to find the meaning of the suffixes and look in books to find examples of words with the suffixes in context. Have students work in small groups to prepare charts with the results for each suffix.

Practice

Activate Prior Knowledge

Relate Personal Choices

Ask volunteers to name or identify from a group of pictures the modes of transportation they use to get to school. Encourage students to discuss the reasons for their choices, such as ease of use, safety, and low cost.

Develop Language and Concepts

Present Pages 160 and 161

Have students look at the pictures on these pages and identify the modes of transportation. Read the text with students. Have students refer to the pictures and make a T-Chart to compare and contrast traveling by wagon train to traveling by rail. Use pictures or toy models to introduce the Word Bank words. Help them list the words by category: *land—bus, car, truck; sea—boat, ship; air—airplane.*

Have students do the Write About It activity.

Model a Strategy

Scan

Model how to scan:

When I start to read a new section, I scan it to see what it is about. For pages 160 and 161, I look first at the title. This tells me the section is about transportation to the West. Then I quickly look through the text and at the pictures and see that wagon trains and railroad trains are discussed.

How did the settlers get to the West?

Early settlers often went west in Conestoga wagons. These large wagons had four big wheels and were pulled by horses or oxen. The wagon tops were covered with cloth to keep out the sun and rain. A family kept all its things in the wagon.

Most of the people in a family walked. Many times large groups of families and their wagons traveled together. This was called a **wagon train.** A wagon train traveled about 12 to 20 miles (19 to 32 kilometers) a day.

Try It Out

How far could you walk in one day if you walked for ten hours? Work with a partner. Walk at a slow pace for one minute down a school hall. Measure how many feet you walked. Multiply this by 60 to figure out how many feet you could walk in an hour. Then multiply by 10 hours to see how many feet you could walk in a day. Divide by 5,280 to get the number of miles.

Options for Reaching All Students

Beginning

Math: Calculate Distance and Speed

Have students pretend that they are nineteenth century travelers taking the transcontinental railroad from New York to San Francisco, a trip that took seven days and covered a total of 2,930 miles. Ask students to calculate about how many miles the train will travel each day. (2,930 ÷ 7 = 418.6 miles)

Advanced

Math: Calculate Distance and Time

Have students work in pairs. Have them use a standard road atlas to figure out how many miles it is from St. Louis, Missouri, to Dodge City, Kansas. Then have students pretend that they are going to make that journey by wagon train at the rate of 15 miles per day. Have the pairs calculate how many days it would take to make the journey.

Mixed Ability

Social Studies: Research

Have students research two or three facts about travel west and wagon trains that are not in the text. Have them report their findings in drawings, sentences, or paragraphs. Encourage students to note the sources they consulted in case classmates want to follow up on a specific piece of information.

On May 10, 1869, a **transcontinental railroad** was completed. This made it possible to travel across the continent, from New York to California, by railroad. Now travelers could cross the continent in just ten days. Cities and farms were started along the railroad. By 1893, four more major railroad lines crossed the continent.

Word Bank

- airplane
- boat
- bus
- car
- ship
- truck

Write About It

Think of a time you moved to a new place. How did you get to the new place?

Language Awareness

Grammar
Passive Voice

ACTIVITY BOOK

Write these sentences on the board:

Settlers went west in wagons.
The wagons were pulled by oxen.

Help students understand the difference between the active and passive voices by discussing these two sentences. Tell students the passive voice is formed with the verb *to be* + the past participle. Point out the past participle for regular verbs ends in *-ed*. Have students find other examples of passive voice in the text. Use Activity Book page 85.

Assess ✓

Use class discussion for assessment. Students should be able to

- describe the process of moving west in the 1800s
- compare and contrast travel by railroad to travel by wagon train

LOOK**AHEAD**

In the next section, students will learn about the grassland and forest biomes of the West.

Cooperative Learning

Role-Play

Have students use the results of their research from the Mixed Ability activity to role-play interviews between reporters and settlers. The settlers are being interviewed about their trips west. Encourage "settlers" to use gestures, facial expressions, and other techniques to convey their feelings about the trip.

Cooperative Language Experience

Field Trip

Arrange a visit to a train station, airport, or bus depot. Brainstorm questions to ask people who work there, such as these: *How many passengers come through the facility in an average day? Where do the vehicles go? How fast do they travel?* Have the whole class write an essay with pictures about what they learned.

Writer's Workshop

My Trip

Have students write about an important trip they have taken. Have them tell how and why they traveled, what events happened on the trip, how they felt, and what they learned on the trip. Beginners can draw and caption pictures. Remind students to capitalize specific place names.

Connect

Activate Prior Knowledge

Review Vocabulary

Help students review vocabulary by asking them to brainstorm a list of plants and animals. Write the responses on the board and add to the list during the lesson.

Develop Language and Concepts

Present Pages 162 and 163

ACTIVITY BOOK

Have students study the illustrations and help them identify the animals and plants in the pictures. Use Activity Book page 87.

Read the text with students. Discuss the attributes of forest biomes and grasslands biomes. Talk about your region and ask students if it is a grasslands biome, forest biome, or some other type. Also talk about what kinds of plants and animals are found in your region or biome. Then have students answer the Write About It questions and complete Activity Book page 86.

Model a Strategy

Use Previously Learned Information

Model applying previously known facts to another topic:

I see this section talks about grasslands, which I learned about on page 159. There I learned how settlers changed their ideas about the grasslands. Now here I learn more about the grasslands. I can combine what I learned before with what I find out here to give me a fuller understanding.

Biomes of the West: Grasslands and Forests

A **biome** is a region that has a certain kind of climate and certain animals and plants. The United States has a huge grasslands biome called the **prairie.** It has many kinds of grass, but only a few trees. The prairie usually gets little precipitation. Farmers now grow wheat, oats, and corn on the prairie. Before the time of the settlers, huge herds of buffalo lived on the prairie. But by 1885, buffalo hunters had reduced the total number from 60 million to about one thousand.

Options for Reaching All Students

Beginning

Critical Thinking: Classify Foods with Grains

Display foods made from grains and model how to find ingredients listed on containers. Have students make lists of foods that contain wheat, corn, or oats. Tell students to include foods with which they are familiar, as well as ones they can discover by looking on boxes and other containers of food at home.

When their lists are complete, ask students to compare their findings with each other and create a master list on a poster for each grain. They can illustrate the poster with pictures and food labels.

Advanced

Science: Other Biomes

Divide students into small groups and assign each group another kind of biome (such as tropical rain forest, tundra, taiga, savannah, or desert) to research. Suggest that students search encyclopedias, science texts, or the Internet for information. Have groups report their findings. Presentations might include pictures and videotaped footage.

Settlers who moved beyond the prairie came to a forest biome. A forest biome gets a lot of precipitation. This makes it possible for many kinds of plants and animals to live there. A forest biome has many kinds of trees such as maples and oaks. Deer, owls, and beavers live in a forest biome.

Write About It

What kind of biomes are there in the place where you or your parents were born? (If you don't know, look in books in the library for the answer.)

Language Awareness

Grammar
Amount Words: *Many/Few/Little*

With students, review these sentences:

A prairie has <u>many</u> kinds of grass, but only a <u>few</u> trees. The prairie usually has <u>little</u> precipitation.

Help students see that the word *many* indicates a large amount while *few* and *little* indicate a small amount. Point out that *few* is used with count nouns (*few trees)*, while *little* is used with noncount nouns *(little rain)*. Present pictures of environments, such as rain forests, and have students describe them, using amount words.

Assess ✓

Use students' responses in discussion and the Write About It question for assessment. Students should be able to

- explain what a biome is
- describe grasslands and forest biomes
- talk about your region and the biomes of the countries where they were born

LOOK**AHEAD**

In the next section, students will read a story about one family's life on the prairie.

Peer or Cross-Age Tutoring

Language: Animal Names

PICTURE CARDS

Have students work in pairs to learn and practice vocabulary of animal names with the Picture Cards. Use cards 5 (bear), 6 (bird), 9 (bug), 12 (camel), 14 (cat), 15 (chicken), 20 (crocodile), 22 (deer), 24 (dog), 26 (ducks), 28 (elephant), 30 (fish), 31 (giraffe), 35 (hippopotamus), 35 (horses), 39 (kangaroo), 43 (lion), 45 (monkeys), 49 (ostrich), 50 (parrots), 51 (penguins), 64 (snail and snake), 66 (spider), and 71 (turtle). Divide the cards into several piles; give one pile to each pair of students. After a few minutes, have the pairs exchange Picture Card piles. More advanced students may want to practice dividing the cards into categories (e.g., Birds, Pets) and naming the categories.

Multicultural Connection

Environments

Have students discuss various types of environments they know about and how these environments affect the lifestyles of people who live in them. You may need to help focus some students' thoughts by asking specific questions, such as: *What kinds of clothes do people wear in your home country? Why?* Provide visual support, if needed.

Connect

Activate Prior Knowledge

Review What Has Been Learned

Review with students what they have learned in previous sections about the prairie and life there in the 1800s. List and discuss key vocabulary.

Introduce the Selection

Help students read the title, the author's name, and the introduction to the story.

Have students use a map to locate Maine and the grasslands in the Midwest (Kansas, Nebraska, South Dakota). Then have them determine in what general direction Sarah traveled. Have students study all the pictures and then try to predict what they think the story will be about. Ask students what the pictures show about this family's life on the prairie.

Read the Selection

BLUE TAPE

Read the story with students. Then read it again and present the Reader's Tips. Then have students listen to the taped version of the story on Side 1 of the Blue Tape. Ask students whether they personally prefer reading historical fiction like this selection.

Language Awareness

Spelling

Quotation Marks: Recognize Unattributed Dialogue

Have students look at the last four lines on page 166. Point out that all four of these lines use quotation marks, which tells readers that these are the exact words the book characters say. Also point out that only two of the four lines tell exactly who is speaking – Caleb. This is indicated by the phrase *he asked.* The other two lines are spoken by Anna. Readers can conclude this because Caleb and Anna have been speaking before.

Model a Strategy

Use a Dictionary to Increase Vocabulary

Model how to use a dictionary to increase vocabulary and understanding:

When I read a story, I sometimes find words I don't know, but I still understand the story. When this happens, I keep on reading, but I write down the words I don't know. When I reach a convenient stopping place, I look up the unfamiliar words in a dictionary. Then I reread the story with a better understanding. This helps me get a better grasp of the whole story's meaning and also helps me learn new words.

Help students make lists of unfamiliar words as they work through the story independently.

Options for Reaching All Students

Beginning

Critical Thinking: Make Inferences About Setting

Have students work in small groups and list words and phrases from the story that tell about life on the prairie such as "long day's trip to the train and back" and "drove off the dirt road." Have students use the details to tell about life on the farm.

Advanced

Writing: A Letter from Anna

Have students pretend that they are Anna, the story narrator. Have students write letters to Sarah while she was still in Maine, telling her what they think she would like to know about Anna and her family. Students should use their imaginations and fill in details of the story and situation as they feel is appropriate. Encourage them to write in a way that reflects Anna's voice.

Peer or Cross-Age Tutoring

Critical Thinking: Story Retelling

Have students work in pairs of mixed ability to retell the story in their own words. Remind them to include the elements of plot, character, and setting. Beginning learners can point to story pictures and make summary statements about them.

Sarah, Plain and Tall

by Patricia MacLachlan

In this story, a farmer with two children has advertised for a wife. A woman named Sarah, from the state of Maine, has answered the ad. Sarah has agreed to come for a visit to see if she and the farm family can make a life together.

Reader's Tip
Settler families needed to be large to do all the work on a farm. It was important for a parent to marry again if a mother or father died. This other adult person was needed to do work.

Language Tip
Vocabulary
Indian paintbrush is a type of plant with red and orange flowers.

Sarah came in the spring. She came through green grass fields that bloomed with Indian paintbrush, red and orange, and blue-eyed grass.

Papa got up early for the long day's trip to the train and back. He brushed his hair so slick and shiny that Caleb laughed. He wore a clean blue shirt, and a belt instead of suspenders.

He fed and watered the horses, talking to them as he hitched them up to the wagon. Old Bess, calm and kind; Jack, wild-eyed, reaching over to nip Bess on the neck.

"Clear day, Bess," said Papa, rubbing her nose. "Settle down, Jack." He leaned his head on Jack.

And then Papa drove off along the dirt road to fetch Sarah. Papa's new wife. Maybe. Maybe our new mother.

Gophers ran back and forth across the road, stopping to stand up and watch the wagon. Far off in the field a woodchuck ate and listened. Ate and listened.

Caleb and I did our chores without talking. We shoveled out the stalls and laid down new hay. We fed the sheep. We swept and straightened and carried wood and water. And then our chores were done.

Study Tip
Understand Point of View
This story is told in the first person. This means that the story teller is also in the story. This style makes the story seem very real and personal.

Language Tip
Vocabulary
A gopher is a small, furry animal. A woodchuck is a larger furry animal that sleeps in a hole in the ground all winter.

Caleb pulled on my shirt.

"Is my face clean?" he asked. "Can my face be too clean?" He looked alarmed.

"No, your face is clean but not too clean," I said.

Caleb slipped his hand into mine as we stood on the porch, watching the road. He was afraid.

"Will she be nice?" he asked. "Like Maggie?"

"Sarah will be nice," I told him.

"How far away is Maine?" he asked.

"You know how far. Far away, by the sea."

"Will Sarah bring some sea?" he asked.

"No, you cannot bring the sea."

Reader's Tip
Maggie is a neighbor woman.

The sheep ran in the field, and far off the cows moved slowly to the pond, like turtles.

"Will she like us?" asked Caleb very softly.

I watched a marsh hawk wheel down behind the barn.

He looked up at me.

"Of course she will like us." He answered his own question. "We are nice," he added, making me smile.

We waited and watched. I rocked on the porch and Caleb rolled a marble on the wood floor. Back and forth. Back and forth. The marble was blue.

We saw dust from the wagon first, rising above the road, above the heads of Jack and Old Bess. Caleb climbed up onto the porch roof and shaded his eyes.

Strategy Tip
Understand Character
Caleb keeps asking questions, and the story teller says he is afraid. Why is he afraid?

Connect

Develop Language and Concepts

Present Pages 168 Through 171

ACTIVITY BOOK Review the story with students. Encourage them to predict what they think will happen next. Ask: *Will Sarah stay with the family or will she return to Maine? Why?* Assess students' comprehension of the story by having them complete Activity Book page 88.

Encourage students to dramatize the story, acting out the scenes between Caleb and Anna and the arrival of Sarah. They can make up and/or paraphrase dialogue or pantomime actions while you or more proficient students narrate.

Language Awareness

Grammar

Negatives

Point out the last five lines on page 171, focusing on the lines *We do not have the sea* and *There is no sea here.* Tell students that these two sentences are examples of how English forms negatives:

I do not have a pet.
Lucia does not have a pet. *(third person singular)*
There are not any pets in my house. *(be verb)*

Then ask volunteers to make up some examples of their own, using personal information.

Teachable Moment

Story Elements: Character

Point out that the narrator describes Sarah as "plain and tall." Explain to students that these words offer clues not only to Sarah's physical appearance, but to her personality as well. Have students look for other clues to Sarah's character. For example, Sarah replies to Papa that the cat *will be good in the house, too.* Ask students to think about what this sentence also tells readers about her personality.

Response Activities

Personal Response

Point out to students that Caleb very much wants Sarah to like him. Ask students why they think this is so. You might also wish to point out that literature often deals with universal themes and experiences that occur in all cultures. Then ask them: *Have you ever wondered if someone liked you? How did you feel?*

Critical Response

Point out that students learn a great deal about the characters even though there are only a few pages in the story. Ask students if they think that Sarah has made a positive impression on the children and how students know.

Creative Response

Have students write a letter from Sarah to someone back in the East. Encourage them to have Sarah describe her new home and what she misses about the East.

Options for Reaching All Students

Beginning

Language: Action Commands

TPR Review those parts of the story that describe a character's actions. Then apply the actions to the class by giving commands, such as: *Water the horses. Rub her nose. Feed the sheep.* Have individual students pantomime the commands as you say them.

Advanced

Language Arts: Read the Rest of the Story

Have students read either portions or the rest of *Sarah, Plain and Tall.* Have them report back to the class about what happens in the story. Have them summarize the character development, conflicts, and resolutions.

Cooperative Learning

Make Up the Ending

Divide the class into small groups. Tell them to discuss whether they think Sarah will like the family and whether she will stay. Have them collaborate in writing an ending to the story based on their discussions. Have volunteers from each group read their endings to the rest of the class or have the groups perform their story endings as plays.

Language Tip
Vocabulary
A bonnet is a kind of hat worn by women in the 1800s.

"A bonnet!" he cried. "I see a yellow bonnet!"

The dogs came out from under the porch, ears up, their eyes on the cloud of dust bringing Sarah. The wagon passed the fenced field, and the cows and sheep looked up, too. It rounded the windmill and the barn and the windbreak of Russian olive that Mama had planted long ago. Nick began to bark, then Lottie, and the wagon clattered into the yard and stopped by the steps.

"Hush," said Papa to the dogs.

And it was quiet.

Sarah stepped down from the wagon, a cloth bag in her hand. She reached up and took off her yellow bonnet, smoothing back her brown hair into a bun. She was plain and tall.

"Did you bring some sea?" cried Caleb beside me.

"Something from the sea," said Sarah, smiling. "And me." She turned and lifted a black case from the wagon. "And Seal, too."

Carefully she opened the case, and Seal, gray with white feet, stepped out. Lottie lay down, her head on her paws, staring. Nick leaned down to sniff. Then he lay down, too.

"The cat will be good in the barn," said Papa. "For mice."

Sarah smiled. "She will be good in the house, too."

Sarah took Caleb's hand, then mine. Her hands were large and rough. She gave Caleb a shell—a moon snail, she called it—that was curled and smelled of salt.

"The gulls fly high and drop the shells on the rocks below," she told Caleb. "When the shell is broken, they eat what is inside."

"That is very smart," said Caleb.

"For you, Anna," said Sarah, "a sea stone."

And she gave me the smoothest and whitest stone I had ever seen.

"The sea washes over and over and around the stone, rolling it until it is round and perfect."

"That is very smart, too," said Caleb. He looked up at Sarah. "We do not have the sea here."

Sarah turned and looked out over the plains.

"No," she said. "There is no sea here. But the land rolls a little like the sea."

Reader's Tip
What do you think will happen? Will Sarah stay? To find out, read the rest of the book, Sarah, Plain and Tall.

Connect

Activate Prior Knowledge

Use Pictures

Have students study the picture and focus on the guitar. Ask students to tell or act out instruments they play or want to learn to play. Then ask students to speculate on why a guitar is a good instrument for people like cowboys who travel around a lot.

Develop Language and Concepts

Present Page 172

BLUE TAPE

Read the title, introduction, and text with students. Explain *range* as another word for prairie or open land. Also define *antelope*. Then play the song on Side 2 of the Blue Tape several times and encourage students to sing along. Discuss the general meaning of the song.

Language Awareness

Phonics

Long *o*

ACTIVITY BOOK

Write these words on the board:

buffalo roam
grow home

Pronounce each word and point out the various spellings that stand for the long *o* sound. Point out the pattern of vowel + consonant + *e* that signals long sounds. Have students find other words with long *o* in the chapter. Use Activity Book page 89.

Home on the Range

Many of the settlers wanted a better life. This song talks about their hopes and the beautiful countryside some believed they had found.

Oh, give me a home where the buffalo roam,
Where the deer and the antelope play;
Where seldom is heard a discouraging word,
And the skies are not cloudy all day.

Home, home on the range,
Where the deer and the antelope play;
Where seldom is heard a discouraging word,
And the skies are not cloudy all day.

Talk About It

What words in the song talk about the hope that settlers had for their lives on the prairie?

Options for Reaching All Students

Beginning

Language: The Long *o* Sound

PICTURE CARDS

Work with students as a group to practice the long *o* sound. Use Picture Cards 6 (boat), 8 (bowl), 17 (coat), 18 (comb), 56 (radio), 59 (sailboats), and 69 (telescope), as well as others. Have students list the various spellings they find for long *o*. Students can make picture collages for each spelling.

Advanced

Writing: Life in the Past

Have students work individually to write about what they think life was like for the children of settlers on the range in the late 1800s. Suggest students think about clothing, toys, friends, chores, schooling, and so on. After students write their first drafts, have them revise their work, eliminating any details that are unrelated to the main focus.

Home Connection

Musical Instruments

Have students ask their families about musical instruments that are commonly used in their home countries. If possible, have students bring in examples of these instruments or pictures of them. You might invite students and family members to play the instruments for the class.

Tell what you learned.

CHAPTER 9

1. How is travel today easier than it was for the settlers in the 1800s?
2. What do you think were the good parts of being a settler in the West during the 1800s? What were the bad parts?
3. If you could choose, would you rather live in a grassland biome or a forest biome? Why?
4. If you were a settler going west in the 1800s, what things would you bring with you? What would you leave behind?
5. What did you learn about life in the West from the story *Sarah, Plain and Tall*?

Assess

Activity 1: Evaluate comparisons based on the methods of travel discussed in this chapter.

Activity 2: Evaluate answers based on students' reasoning.

Activity 3: Evaluate answers on the basis of the validity of students' reasons for preferring one over the other.

Activity 4: Students should only list things that were available in the 1800s, and answers should reflect the necessity and suitability of various items to life on the prairie.

Activity 5: Answers should reflect the facts of the story itself.

Have students complete the Chapter Self-Assessment, Blackline Master 31. Have students choose the product of one of the activities to place in their portfolios. Add the results of any rubrics, checklists, self-assessments, or portfolio assessments, Blackline Master 2–18 and 31.

Listening Assessment

BLACKLINE MASTER

Make sure that each student has a copy of Blackline Master 81 from the Teacher's Resource Book. Play the tape and have students write the dictation.

CREAM TAPE

See Chapter 9 Resources, page T154c, for the Listening Assessment tapescript.

Options for Assessment

Vocabulary Assessment

Venn Diagram

Have students make Venn diagrams that compare settlers' lives with their own lives. Encourage students to use vocabulary that they learned in this chapter.

Writing Assessment

The American West

Have students write a brief description of what they learned about settlers in the American West of the 1800s. Remind students to use well-organized paragraphs, each with a main idea and supporting details. Pairs can exchange drafts and provide one another with constructive revision suggestions.

Language Assessment

BLACKLINE MASTER

Use Blackline Master 80 in the Teacher's Resource Book.

Standardized Test Practice

ACTIVITY BOOK

Use pages 90 and 91.
Answers: **1.** The Rocky Mountains **2.** it offered very few sources of food and fresh water **3.** Gold **4.** A prairie

Preview

Activate Prior Knowledge

Brainstorm Vocabulary

Ask students to name inventions they know about, starting with items in the classroom such as books, pencils, the pencil sharpener, computer, and so on. Have them tell whether each invention was invented long ago or recently. Discuss with students how these items affect the way they work and learn in school. Beginning learners can demonstrate how they use each item.

Develop Language and Concepts

Present Pages 174 and 175

Read the pages with students. Review the words in the Word Bank. Have students identify the pictures associated with the Word Bank terms. You may wish to show students illustrated time lines or sets of reference pictures so they can see how each item has changed over time.

Explain to students that while many people moved to the West of the United States in the 1800s and early 1900s, many other people moved to urban areas from rural ones.

Have students answer the Talk About It questions.

CHAPTER 10

Industry Changed the Nation

Word Bank

camera

car

electric light

telephone

typewriter

Tell what you know.

All these things were invented in the United States in the 1800s and early 1900s. How do they affect our lives today?

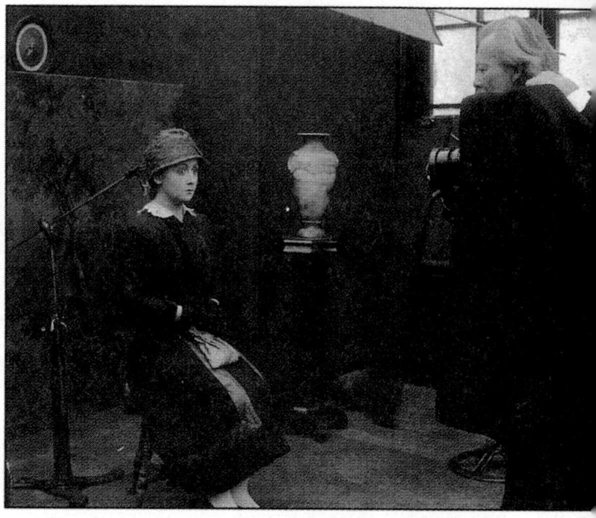

174

Options for Reaching All Students

Beginning

Language: Word Matching

PICTURE CARDS

Write the names of inventions from Picture Cards 1 (airplane), 13 (car), 30 (flashlight), 41 (lamp), and 56 (radio) on separate pieces of paper. Give pairs of students the cards and papers and have them match the words to the pictures and tell how the invention affects peoples' lives today.

Advanced

Critical Thinking: Compare and Contrast

Have each student choose a profession, such as doctor, teacher, police officer, or mail carrier. Then have students write down comparisons of these jobs today to what they think the jobs might have been like a hundred years ago.

Mixed Ability

Art: Make Collages

Have small groups make two collages with pictures cut out or photocopied from magazines and books. Label two sheets of chart paper for each group with the headings *Travel* and *Communication*. Have students paste pictures of modern inventions on the appropriate collage. For example, a cellular phone should be pasted on the *Communications* collage. Help them label each invention.

Talk About It

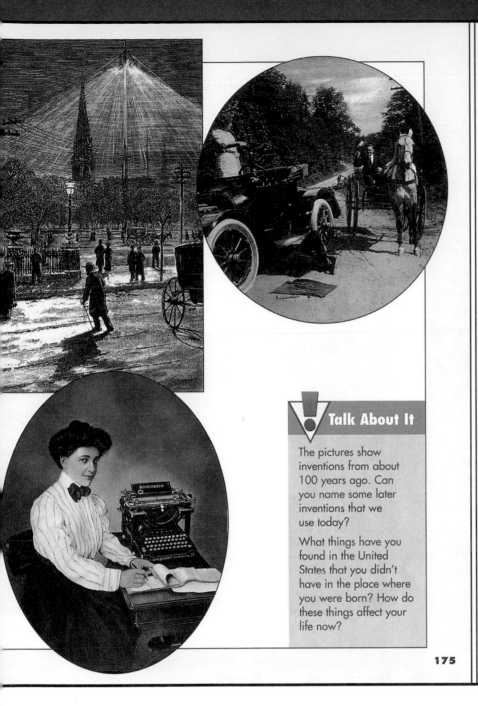

The pictures show inventions from about 100 years ago. Can you name some later inventions that we use today?

What things have you found in the United States that you didn't have in the place where you were born? How do these things affect your life now?

FYI

On page 174, the picture at the right shows an early photographic studio where people had portraits taken. Early cameras required a longer exposure time, and it was important for the subject to remain still during this process to avoid blurred images. The device attached to the woman's head would hold it still.

Cooperative Learning

Invention Guessing Game

Give students a list of inventions, including those on these pages as well as earlier and more recent ones. Add visual support as needed. Have students guess when the items were first invented. Then have them do research to determine the actual dates of inventions (children's almanacs are a good reference tool) and to confirm their guesses. Students can organize their findings chronologically and create an illustrated time line. They might also include dates and information about significant improvements to each invention.

Present

Activate Prior Knowledge

Review Previous Learning

Review with students what they know about U.S. history. Encourage them to talk about what was happening during the 1800s, such as the Civil War and the building of the transcontinental railroad.

Develop Language and Concepts

Present Pages 176 and 177

Have students study the pictures. Discuss what they show about life in the 1800s. Ask students what they think about these situations, both good and bad, and whether they think these conditions still exist, either in the United States or other countries. Then read the text with students. Explain that one meaning of *revolution* is "a sudden, big change."

Make a two-column chart on the board headed *Reasons to Live on the Prairie* and *Reasons to Live in the City*. Have students offer reasons and list them on the chart for comparison purposes.

Have students answer the Think About It questions.

Model a Strategy

Read On to Get Meaning

When I read, I don't give up when I come upon something I don't understand. Instead, I continue reading, because I may soon find

(Continued on page 177.)

The Industrial Revolution

During the 1800s, the United States changed greatly. Thousands of people left farms, ranches, and small towns to work in factories in the cities. These changes took place because of the Industrial Revolution.

Before the 1800s, there were few factories. People made things by hand at home or in small shops. Then inventors figured out how to use coal and oil to run machines. The number of factories grew quickly. Suddenly, there were more things to buy. There were faster ways to get places. There were new, easier ways of living.

Options for Reaching All Students

Beginning

Language: Opposites

Help students create a list of adjectives from the lesson: *small, fast, easy, hard, dangerous, dark,* and *young,* and write each word on a separate index card. Give students a list of the opposite terms, and ask them to match and write the opposite word on the back of the correct card. They can draw or paste pictures on the card to illustrate the two.

Advanced

Critical Thinking: Categorize

Divide students into two teams for a sentence-writing contest. Give one team a piece of paper that is labeled *Good Things About the Industrial Revolution*. Give the other team a piece of paper labeled *Bad Things About the Industrial Revolution*. Tell students to take turns writing down sentences that describe the good or bad parts of the Industrial Revolution. The "good" team, for example, might write: *There were more jobs*. The other team might write: *Working conditions were poor*. Each sentence must state a different fact. Encourage students to bring prior knowledge into their examples, if possible. The team that puts down the greatest number of appropriate, completed sentences in the allotted time wins. Remind students that sentences must begin with a capital letter and end with an appropriate punctuation mark.

These changes also caused problems. Working in early factories was hard and dangerous. Many workers were not treated well. Many people worked about twelve hours a day, six days a week. They lived in crowded, dark apartments. They often died at young ages. Children worked too. Some did dangerous jobs in coal mines and factories where adults were too large to go.

Think About It

The United States now has laws about how many hours a day people can work. It also has laws about what is the lowest amount people can be paid. Do you think these are good laws or not? Why?

information that helps me understand what came before. For example, the first paragraph mentions the Industrial Revolution. The next paragraph explains what it was. This helps me understand the first paragraph better.

Language Awareness

Grammar
Expressions of Time

ACTIVITY BOOK

List these words and phrases on the board: *during the 1800s, before the 1800s, twelve hours a day, six days a week.* Discuss how they show time relationships. Also talk about *later* and *after.* Have students make up sentences about daily activities with time-related words and phrases. Use Activity Book page 92.

Assess

Use class discussion and the Think About It questions for assessment. Students should be able to

- briefly describe what the Industrial Revolution was
- explain why they approve or disapprove of laws protecting workers

LOOK**AHEAD**

In the next section, students will learn about some U.S. industrial leaders and inventors of the 1800s and early 1900s.

Mixed Ability

Critical Thinking: Compare and Contrast

Ask small groups to brainstorm lists of items made by hand and items made in factories. Have each group discuss whether they think hand-made or factory-made goods are of better quality. Have each group make an oral report explaining its decision. You might encourage students to bring examples of hand-made and factory-made items to class.

Peer or Cross-Age Tutoring

Language: Summarize

Have students work in pairs of mixed ability. Ask them to tell each other one or more things they learned from this lesson. Tell them to restate the facts in informal, conversational language rather than formal, textbook language.

Home Connection

Working Life

Have students find out about working life from family members and adult acquaintances, including hours, machines used, safety, stresses, and other issues. Invite volunteers to share their information orally.

Encourage listeners to use responsive listening skills to clarify information.

Practice

Activate Prior Knowledge

Name Inventors

Discuss the meaning of the terms *inventor* and *invention*. Ask students to tell if they already know who invented some well-known things, such as the telephone, the lightbulb, and blue jeans.

Develop Language and Concepts

Present Pages 178 and 179

Discuss the pictures. Ask students what inventions they see and whether they know who the inventors were. Use the pictures to introduce key words such as *assembly line, telephone, phonograph,* and *microphone*.

Read the pages with students. Discuss each industrial leader, what he did, and how he contributed to the Industrial Revolution. Ask students whether these men's contributions affect life today, and if so, how. Record responses in a three-column chart, and use the chart to discuss the Talk About It questions.

Model a Strategy

Use a Time Line

Model using a time line to organize events:

Many events are described in this section. However, they are not described in the order in which they occurred. When I find a reading that is set out this way, I sometimes make a time line and place events in time order as I read about them. Then I can tell which came first and which came last.

The Nation's Industrial Leaders and Inventors

The United States was the home of many inventors and industrial leaders in the 1800s and early 1900s. John D. Rockefeller started a giant company called Standard Oil. It sold oil to use in lamps. Later, it sold gasoline to run cars.

Henry Ford figured out a system to build cars quickly and cheaply. Before this time, only rich people could afford cars. Ford's system is called the **assembly line**. In this system, workers repeated the same job all day. A worker might tighten the same part on many cars, one after another. This was possible because the parts were exactly alike.

Alexander Graham Bell was an immigrant from Scotland. He invented the telephone in 1876. By 1900, there were over 1.5 million telephones in the United States.

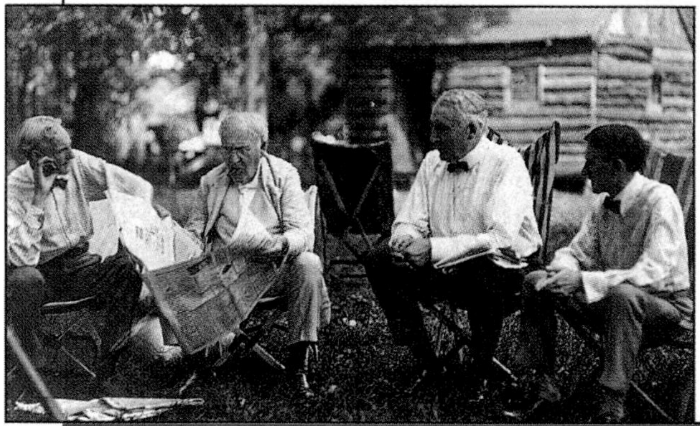

◀ Many leaders of this time were friends. This picture shows Henry Ford, Thomas Edison, U.S. President Warren G. Harding, and Harvey Firestone on vacation together in the early 1920s. Firestone's company made car tires.

Options for Reaching All Students

Beginning

Language: Learn Additional Vocabulary

Photocopy a car advertisement and distribute a copy to each student. Write the following words on the board and explain them: *bumper, wheel, hood, headlight, windshield, door, side, mirror.* Help students write these words on the corresponding parts of the car.

Advanced

Language: Research and Writing

Have each student choose one of the four men profiled here and write an expanded biography of him in their own words. Have students use encyclopedias and other reference sources. Remind them to take careful notes. Encourage students to organize their information chronologically.

Mixed Ability

Writing: Inventions

Have students list inventions that they use every day and the way in which they use these inventions. Review phrases such as *I use it to . . .* To prompt the activity, you might have a class brainstorming session. You could modify this activity for beginning learners by having them cut out pictures of inventions and helping them label each picture with its name.

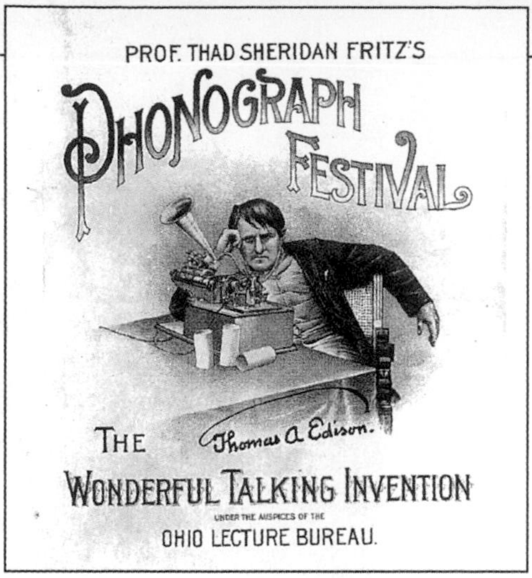

In 1877, Thomas Edison invented both the microphone and the phonograph. In 1879, he invented the light bulb. In 1891, he invented the motion picture camera. He invented so many things that people called him the Wizard of Menlo Park, the New Jersey town where he lived.

Talk About It

How do we use electricity today? How would our lives be different if we did not have electric lights?

Why do you think most of the inventors and industrial leaders at this time were men?

Language Awareness

Grammar
Appositives

ACTIVITY BOOK

Write this sentence on the board: *Tom Edison, the inventor of the phonograph, also invented the light bulb.* Explain that the underlined phrase gives more information about Edison. Point out that such phrases are a little like definitions and that they are set off by commas. Give students other examples of appositives and ask them to make up some of their own. You can write simple sentences and challenge students to insert appositives in them. For practice, use Activity Book page 93.

Assess

Use students' responses in discussion for assessment. Students should be able to

- name some U.S. industrial leaders and inventors
- tell what they invented or what system they developed

LOOK**AHEAD**

In the next section, students will read about two early reformers.

Peer or Cross-Age Tutoring
Language: Spelling Practice

Have one student write out some key words from the chapter, leaving blank spaces for the vowels. Ask a second student to add vowels in the proper places. Then have partners reverse roles. Encourage students to use their knowledge of letter-sound relationships to complete and test each word.

Cooperative Learning
Origins of Inventions

Provide students with appropriate-level resources about inventions and their origins. Have pairs of students each select one invention to research. Have the pair write a paragraph about how the invention began and illustrate it. Remind students to check their work for spelling, punctuation, and grammar. Make a bulletin board display of the papers.

QuickCheck
Write Numbers Correctly

Check students' understanding of when and where to place commas in large numbers. If necessary, remind students that years are never shown with commas, even though they are usually more than three digits.

Practice

Activate Prior Knowledge

Brainstorm Reformers

Introduce the word *reform*, using the prefix and base word to help students understand what it means. Discuss famous reformers such as Martin Luther King, Jr., and César Chávez.

Develop Language and Concepts

Present Pages 180 and 181

Read the text with students. Encourage them to relate what they read to the pictures. Discuss the purpose of political cartoons and the point of view represented in the cartoon on page 180. Ask: *Why did the artist draw the Standard Oil Company to look like an octopus?* Talk about the phrase *meat packing plant.* On the board, have volunteers create a two-column chart with the headings *Reformer* and *Accomplishment* and listing the people and accomplishments they read about here or otherwise know of. Point out that when Sinclair wrote, there were few rules governing the food industry. Brainstorm with students why food producers of the time did not follow what people now consider to be safe food production procedures.

Model a Strategy

Predict Content

Model predicting content by analyzing beginnings:

When I read an article, I look for clues in the writing to let me know what it will discuss.

(Continued on page T181.)

Bringing Reform

By the early 1900s, many people thought that some things about business and industry needed to be changed. One of these people was Ida Tarbell. She wrote about John D. Rockefeller and his company. She told how he had forced some companies out of business and how he got unfair deals from others. She said Rockefeller's giant company was too powerful.

Because of Tarbell's writings, Congress passed some laws. Rockefeller had to break up his company into several smaller ones. Some business methods Rockefeller had used were made illegal.

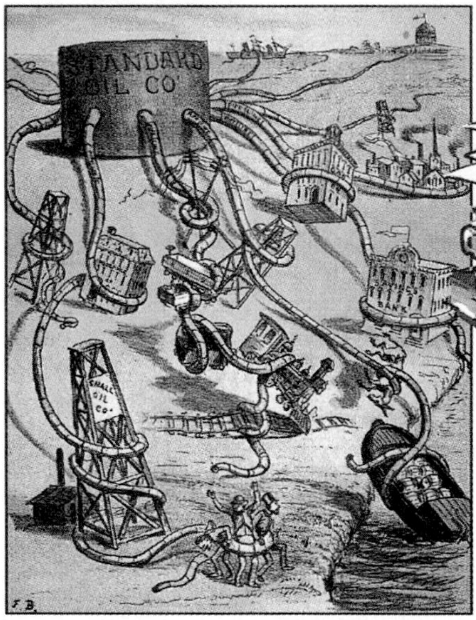

Options for Reaching All Students

Beginning

Language: Food Words

Have pairs use Picture Cards 2 (apple), 4 (bananas), 11 (butter), 14 (carrots), and so on, to practice recognizing and pronouncing food words. Have one person hold the card and the other person say the word. Have partners reverse the roles after every two or three words. Check students' pronunciation.

Advanced

Language: Read Labels

Bring in several examples of packaged foods. Have students work in small groups. Then have them read the packaging to find the following: expiration date, weight, ingredients, nutritional information. Explain that all this information is required and regulated by the government. Encourage students to write an argument in support of a new government regulation on food packaging. The new regulation can either cut back on or add to existing regulations. Remind students to use persuasive language and to give reasons that support their opinions. Model example sentences for students.

Upton Sinclair wrote about the meat packing business. He showed that food being sold to people was dangerous to eat because it was not prepared safely. Because of Sinclair's book, the government made new rules about how food could be handled. This made food safer for everybody.

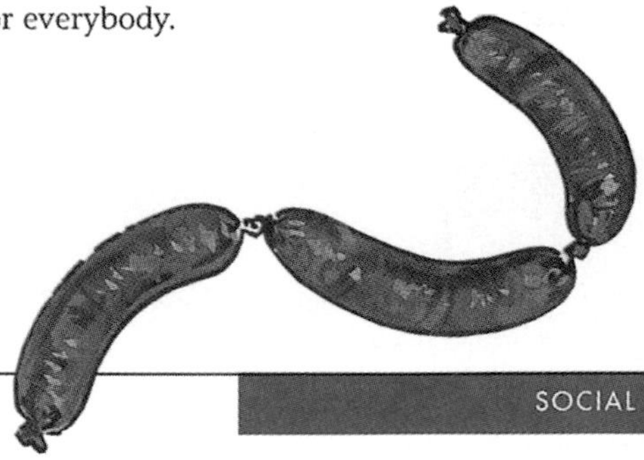

Think About It

Today the U.S. government makes safety rules about medicines, cars, and working conditions. Do you think this is a good idea? Why or why not?

What does *reform* mean?

The title of this article mentions reform, and the first sentence discusses business and industry. Based on these two points, I can predict that the article will discuss reforms in business and industry.

Language Awareness

Vocabulary
Phrase *Because of*

ACTIVITY BOOK

Have students reread the first sentence of the second paragraph on page 180. Tell them that the phrase *because of* indicates the cause of a "cause and effect" relationship. Then ask students to explain the effect of Tarbell's writing. Have them find another example of *because of* on page 181, and ask them to explain the cause-and-effect relationship indicated. Help students make up their own examples. Use Activity Book page 94.

Assess

Use students' responses in discussion for assessment. Students should be able to

- explain what reform is and give some examples

LOOK **AHEAD**

In the next section, students will use graphs to learn more about the Industrial Revolution.

Mixed Ability

Interview a Classmate

Have partners ask one another questions about what kinds of businesses are important in their home countries. If necessary, model responsive listening skills, such as summarizing, paraphrasing, and asking questions for clarification. Have students write notes about what they learned and compile them in a class "newspaper."

Cooperative Language Experience

Current Issues

Have students listen to radio and TV newscasts to learn about current social issues in the United States. Follow up by having the class make a list of issues. You might prompt the activity by presenting recordings of news reports and explaining the issues.

Cooperative Learning

Point of View

Provide students with examples of easy to understand political cartoons, opinion columns, or public service announcements. Help students identify language or picture details that reveal the artist's or writer's point of view. Discuss whether students agree with that point of view.

Connect

Activate Prior Knowledge

Discuss Patents and Inventions

Discuss with students what they may know about patents and why people patent their inventions.

Develop Language and Concepts

Present Pages 182 and 183

ACTIVITY BOOK

Read the text on page 182 with students and have them study the bar graph. Have students clarify the meaning of the bar graph by summarizing the information it contains. Trace the bars from left to right and point out the increasing pattern, or *trend*. Then ask students to suggest why they think the number of patents increased during the 1800s.

Then read the text on page 183 with students, and have them study the line graph there. Discuss whether each line on the graph shows an increasing or decreasing trend or no change. Ask them to predict how the graph would look if the decades of the 1900s were shown. You may want to point out that farmers make up less than 5 percent of the U.S. population today.

Help students answer the Write About It questions as appropriate. Have students make up additional questions based on the graph. Have students complete Activity Book page 95 for extra practice with graphs.

Charting Changes

The U.S. government gives patents to inventors. A patent says that the inventor is the only one who can make and sell the invention. In 1790, the U.S. government issued only 3 patents. In 1890, the government issued 28,304 patents. Study the graph. Why do you think the number of patents increased?

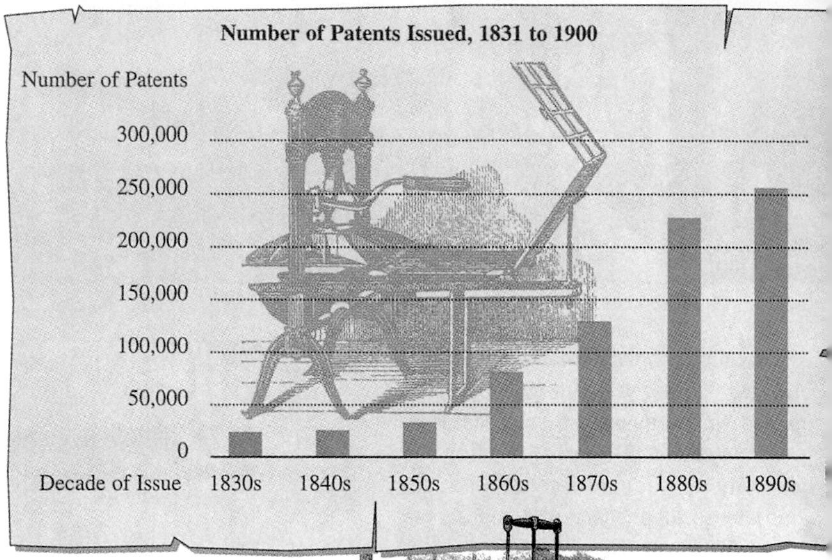

Options for Reaching All Students

Beginning

Language: Pronounce Numbers

Pronounce all the numbers listed on the graphs. Make sure students understand what each number represents. Have students repeat after you. Listen for difficulties in pronunciation and repeat as necessary. You may wish to use a place value chart or place value blocks to help students comprehend large numbers.

Advanced

Math: Make Graphs

Have small groups create simple bar and line graphs for school information, such as the school's enrollment over the last five years. Have students discuss in which situations the use of a bar graph is better than the use of a line graph. Suggest they look at and compare of variety of bar and line graphs.

Mixed Ability

Writing: Be an Inventor

Have students "create" an invention that would be useful to them. They should make a drawing of the invention and write what it is to be used for. The inventions can be fanciful ones, such as a pencil that can spell-check words.

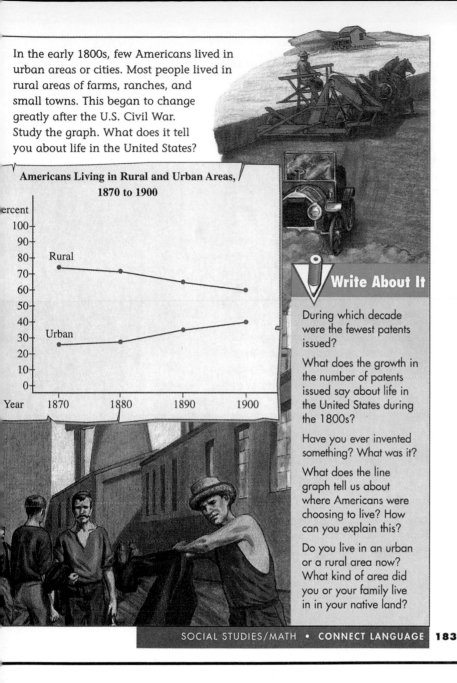

In the early 1800s, few Americans lived in urban areas or cities. Most people lived in rural areas of farms, ranches, and small towns. This began to change greatly after the U.S. Civil War. Study the graph. What does it tell you about life in the United States?

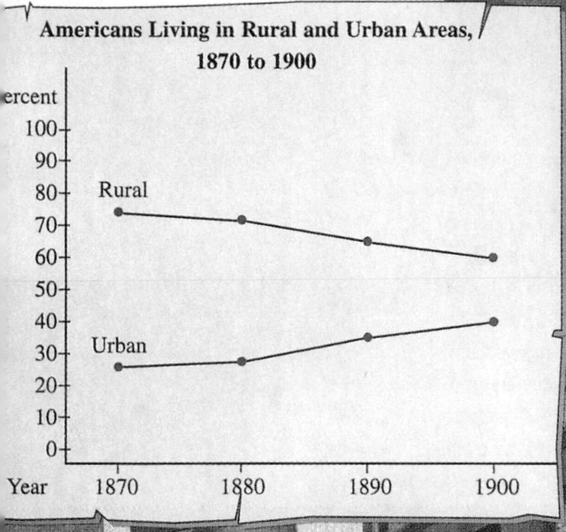

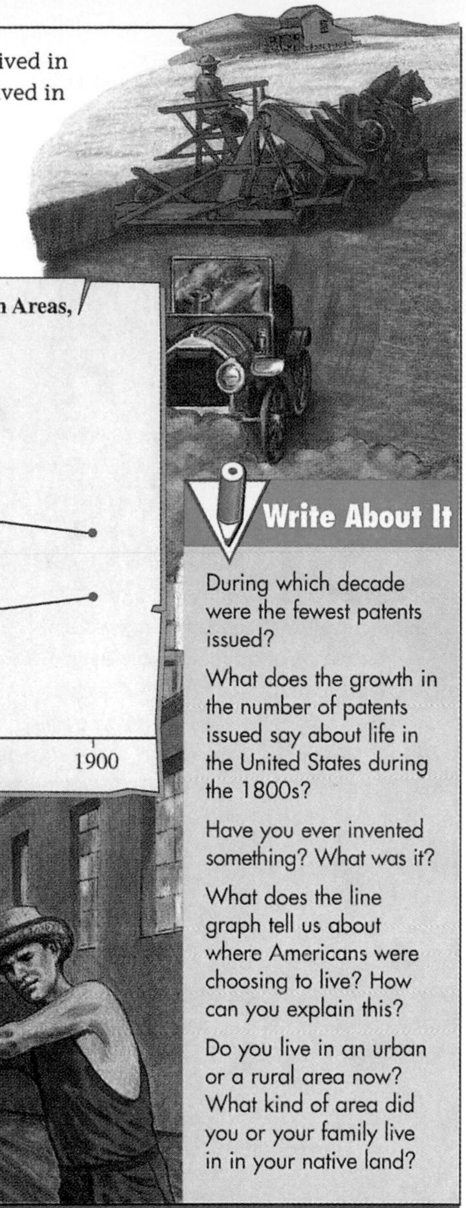

Write About It

During which decade were the fewest patents issued?

What does the growth in the number of patents issued say about life in the United States during the 1800s?

Have you ever invented something? What was it?

What does the line graph tell us about where Americans were choosing to live? How can you explain this?

Do you live in an urban or a rural area now? What kind of area did you or your family live in in your native land?

Language Awareness

Grammar
Question Formation

ACTIVITY BOOK

Point out the questions that end the paragraphs on pages 182 and 183. Talk with students about how the questions are formed. Tell students that questions ask such things as who, what, when, where, how much, and why. Point out the formation of questions with *do/did,* as well as the inversion in questions with *is/are, was/were.* Ask students to make up some questions of their own based on the information in the chapter and to complete Activity Book page 96.

Assess

Use students' responses to class discussion and the Write About It for assessment. Students should be able to

- tell when the fewest patents were issued
- tell whether more people left urban or rural areas
- state the difference between urban and rural areas

LOOK**AHEAD**

In the next section, students will read about one of America's greatest industrial leaders and philanthropists.

Cooperative Learning

100 Years Ago vs. Today

Have students use the information they learned in the chapter to compare and contrast the United States in 1890 with the United States of today. Have students work in pairs and list at least ten facts on a T-Chart. Remind students to check their spelling and the accuracy of each fact.

Multicultural Connection

Demographics

Have students discuss whether the people in their home countries live mostly in urban or mostly in rural areas or if these countries are a mixture of both. You may wish to have students research this information in almanacs or the Internet. After each student has spoken, count the total number of rural and urban countries and the number of mixed countries.

Then make a three-item bar graph on the board to show the relationship. End by asking students to speculate on why their home countries are the way they are.

You can simplify this activity by asking students whether their families came from an urban or rural area in their home country.

Connect

Activate Prior Knowledge

Relate Personal Experiences

Ask students if they have ever wondered what they would do if they suddenly received millions of dollars. Discuss people or groups students know who help others by donating money, time, or services.

Introduce the Story

ACTIVITY BOOK

Help students read the title, author's name, and the introduction. Read the article several times with them. Make a time line on the board of events in Carnegie's life that begins with his birth in 1835 and ends with his death in 1919. Break the time line into 20-year increments.

Have students do Activity Book page 98.

Language Awareness

Grammar

Unreal Conditions

ACTIVITY BOOK

Write this sentence on the board: *If I were the Queen of England, I would always wear my crown.* Tell students that this sentence describes an unreal condition since none of them will ever be Queen. Point out the first sentence in the literature selection on page 184. Give students more examples of sentences that use unreal conditions. Then have them do Activity Book page 97.

FYI

Carnegie got a job as a clerk and telegraph operator for the Pennsylvania Railroad in 1853, when he was 17 years old. During the U.S. Civil War, he helped organize the telegraph services for the Union Army. In 1865, he left the Pennsylvania Railroad to run his own companies, which later included a steel company.

Response Activities

Personal Response

Ask students to compare and contrast Carnegie's experiences as a young immigrant with their own experiences.

Critical Response

Point out that this is a factual story, but it doesn't say much about how Carnegie treated his employees. In 1892, a pay cut led to a strike, fighting, and several deaths. Ask students to tell how knowing this would or would not affect their feelings about Carnegie.

Creative Response

Point out that when Carnegie retired, he said that the second half of a rich man's life should be spent giving away money he acquired during the first half. Ask students to tell what they think a greedy rich person might say about retaining wealth.

Options for Reaching All Students

Beginning

Math: Millions and Billions

Write the words *million* and *billion* on the board. Have students look through the text on pages 184 through 187 and find all of the amounts listed in millions and billions. Then have students write these numbers as complete numerals. Check that they understand the magnitude of these numbers by reviewing place value with them.

Advanced

Social Studies: Research

Have students find Scotland on a world map or globe, and have them locate some basic facts about Scotland in an encyclopedia or almanac. Suggest students include land area, form of government, total population, major cities, and other basic facts. Have them work together to compile their information in a booklet.

Writer's Workshop

Write a Fantasy

Have students write a short personal story depicting how they would feel and where they would live if they received $1 million a month for life. Remind them to use a narrative format, including a clear beginning, middle, and end.

Andrew Carnegie

by William Jay Jacobs

Andrew Carnegie lived from 1835 to 1919. He is one of America's most famous immigrants.

If you knew that every month for the rest of your life you would receive at least $1 million, what would you do with the money?

In 1901 Andrew Carnegie sold his giant Carnegie Steel Company. Interest from his share of the sale price would bring him no less than $1 million a month, for life. What did he do with the money? He gave it all away! Indeed, during the last eighteen years of his life he gave away nearly $350 million.

The lives of rich men, said Carnegie, are divided into two parts. The first part is for getting money. The second should be for giving it away. . . .

Andrew Carnegie did not always have money to give away. In 1848, at the age of thirteen, he came to America from Scotland. He came with his father, mother, and younger brother, Thomas. His mother borrowed the money from friends to pay for their passage. In Scotland times were so hard that Andrew's father could find no work.

Young Carnegie's first job in America was in a cotton mill near Pittsburgh. . . .

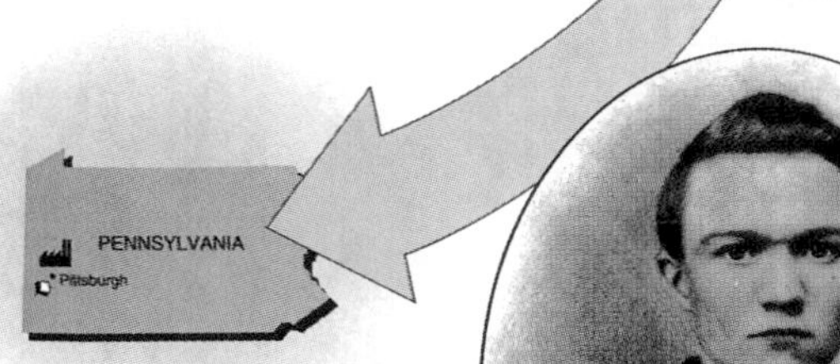

By the year 1900, he was master of the United States steel industry. He could make steel at lower cost than anyone in America or Europe. He had helped establish the United States as the largest producer of steel in the world. And it was steel that made the United States the leader among all the world's industrial nations.

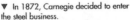

▼ In 1872, Carnegie decided to enter the steel business.

Just then—at the peak of his success—Andrew Carnegie retired. In 1901 he sold all of his properties to J. Pierpont Morgan and a group of men who had founded the United States Steel Corporation. The sale price was almost half a billion dollars. After signing the papers Carnegie turned to Morgan with a sigh of relief. "Well, Pierpont," he said, "I am now handing the burden over to you."

▲ J.P. Morgan

For nearly twenty years afterward, Carnegie did the things he most enjoyed. He read, traveled, listened to fine music, collected art, wrote books about his ideas—and gave away money.

▲ The Carnegie Hero Fund Commission makes awards for bravery.

▲ Some of Carnegie's money was used to build Carnegie Hall in New York City. It is a famous concert hall.

Connect

Activate Prior Knowledge

Use Pictures and Recall Information

Have students look at the illustrations. Ask them to recall what they learned about the Erie Canal and the transcontinental railroad in Chapters 5 and 9.

Develop Language and Concepts

Present Pages 188 and 189

BLUE TAPE

Use the pictures to introduce key words in "Erie Canal" such as *canal, barge, mule,* and *bridge.* Play the song on Side 2 of the Blue Tape for students while they follow along. Then ask students to sing along with the tape. Students can also learn this verse:

We'd better be on our way, old pal
Fifteen miles on the Erie Canal.
'Cause you bet your life I'd never part with Sal,
Fifteen miles on the Erie Canal.
Get up there, mule, here comes a lock,
We'll make Rome about six o'clock,
One more try and back we'll go,
Right back home to Buffalo.

Ask students to name facts about the canal that the song tells them. Have a volunteer write the facts on the board. Read the introduction to "I've Been Working on the Railroad" with students. Play the tape, asking students to join in the singing. See the additional verses under Mixed Ability below. Discuss what facets of the Industrial Revolution these two songs represent.

Songs of the Industrial Revolution

The Erie Canal

The Erie Canal was a major transportation route of the 1820s and 1830s. Mules walked on the shore and pulled the boats and barges on the canal.

I've got a mule. Her name is Sal,
Fifteen miles on the Erie Canal.
She's a good old worker and a good old pal,
Fifteen miles on the Erie Canal.
We've hauled some barges in our day,
Filled with lumber, coal, and hay,
And we know every inch of the way
From Albany to Buffalo.

Low bridge, everybody down!
Low bridge, for we're coming to a town!
And you'll always know your neighbor,
You'll always know your pal,
If you ever navigated on the Erie Canal.

Options for Reaching All Students

Beginning

Language: Practice Pronunciation

Read the words to both songs line by line, with students repeating each line after you. Have individual students tape-record their recitations and self-monitor their pronunciations. Point out strategies students can use if they have difficulty, such as thinking about letter-sound relationships they know.

Advanced

Language: Riddles

Have pairs make up riddles using key words from the songs. Each partner makes up a riddle for the other person to guess. Pairs can write their riddles on note cards with answers on the back. They can create a quiz game for the class to play. For example: *I use boats for transportation.* (Erie Canal)

Mixed Ability

Music: More Verses

Students can learn these additional verses to "I've Been Working on the Railroad."

Dinah, won't you blow (2 times)
Dinah, won't you blow your horn?
Dinah, won't you blow (2 times)
Dinah, won't you blow your horn?

I've Been Working on the Railroad

Thousands of people worked long hours in all kinds of weather to build the transcontinental railroad. Many of these workers were immigrants from Ireland and China.

I've been working on the railroad,
All the live-long day,
I've been working on the railroad,
Just to pass the time away.
Don't you hear the whistle blowing,
Rise up so early in the morn;
Don't you hear the captain shouting,
"Dinah, blow your horn!"

▲ Chinese immigrants did some of the most dangerous jobs, such as building the tunnels for the transcontinental railroad.

Language Awareness

Vocabulary
Rhyming Words

Write these pairs of words on the board: *Sal* and *Pal*, *down* and *town*. Point out that these are words that rhyme. Ask students to find other pairs of words in these songs that rhyme. Point out that songs and poems written in the English language frequently use rhyming sounds at the ends of lines. Have students come up with further pairs of rhyming words. Challenge more proficient students to write pairs of sentences that end in rhyming words.

Model a Strategy

Compare and Contrast

Model assessing tone to compare and contrast:

I can tell that the tone of the first song is cheerful by reading words such as "good old pal" and "you'll always know your neighbor." The second song's tune is one of complaint—the singer says he is just passing time and complains about early rising and long days.

Someone's in the kitchen with Dinah,
Someone's in the kitchen I know,
Someone's in the kitchen with Dinah,
Strumming on the old banjo, and singing
Fee-fi-fiddlee-i-o (3 times)
Strumming on the old banjo.

Cooperative Learning

Careers: Research

Have students do research on jobs that interest them. Have them decide on a standard format to report information, such as education needed, skills needed on the job, and typical tasks. Have students gather their information into a class booklet. The *Occupational Outlook Handbook* is a good source of information on jobs.

Peer or Cross-Age Tutoring

Role-Playing

Have students act out interviews between people in this unit and TV reporters. Have students work in pairs to help each other with their parts. Then have them present their interviews to other pairs. Remind students to make their conversations more lively by adding gestures and using appropriate facial expressions, and to speak loudly and clearly.

Connect

Activate Prior Knowledge
Use Pictures

Show images of the United States during the Depression from social studies texts and other sources, including documentaries. Discuss the hard economic times of the period when no jobs were available.

Develop Language and Concepts
Present Page 190

BLUE TAPE

Introduce key words such as *dime, tower, bricks, mortar, lime,* and use paraphrasing to clarify meaning. Read the title and the introduction with students. Then play the tape several times and encourage students to join in. Have students point out pairs of words that rhyme. Use the Talk About It questions for further emphasis on content.

Language Awareness

Language Function
Making Requests

ACTIVITY BOOK

Write the phrases *can you* and *could you* on the board. Tell students how these two phrases are used in English to make polite requests to obtain help or assistance from someone else. Have students make up sentences that use these two phrases. Have students do Activity Book page 99 for additional practice.

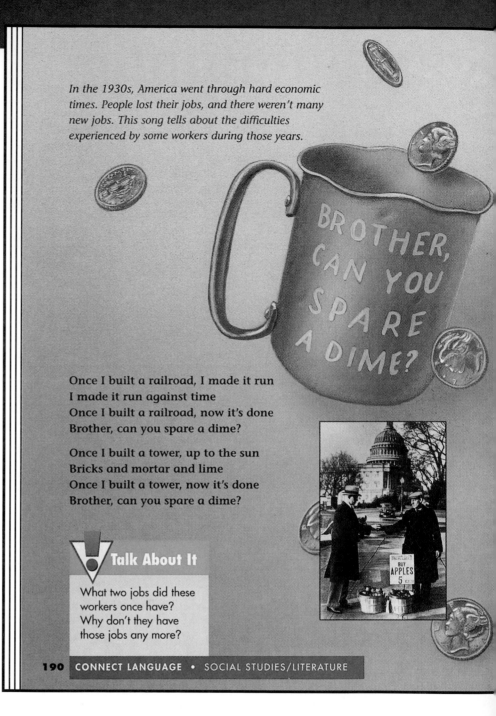

In the 1930s, America went through hard economic times. People lost their jobs, and there weren't many new jobs. This song tells about the difficulties experienced by some workers during those years.

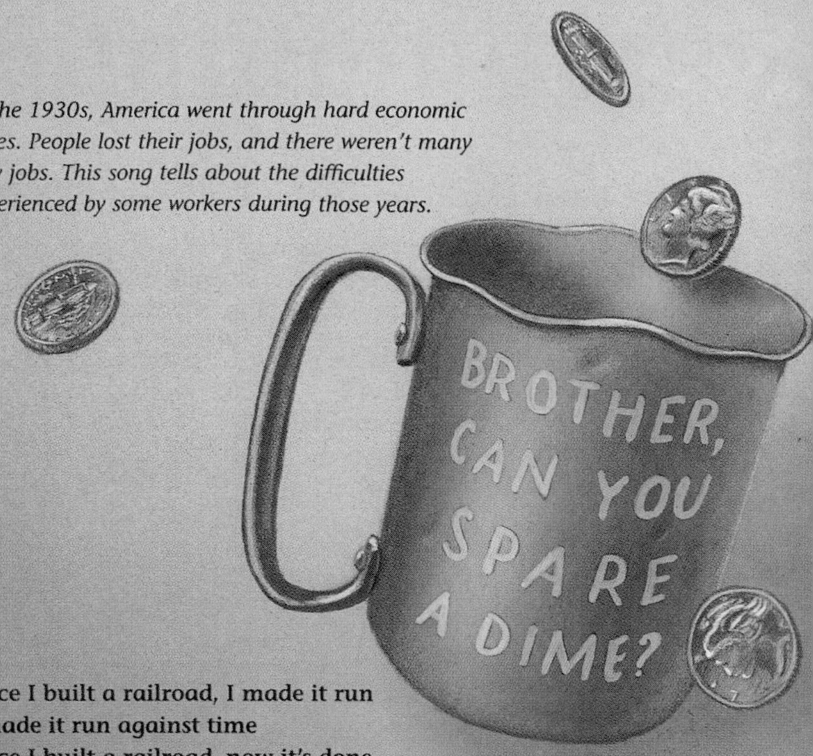
BROTHER, CAN YOU SPARE A DIME?

Once I built a railroad, I made it run
I made it run against time
Once I built a railroad, now it's done
Brother, can you spare a dime?

Once I built a tower, up to the sun
Bricks and mortar and lime
Once I built a tower, now it's done
Brother, can you spare a dime?

BUY
APPLES

Talk About It

What two jobs did these workers once have? Why don't they have those jobs any more?

190 CONNECT LANGUAGE • SOCIAL STUDIES/LITERATURE

Options for Reaching All Students

Beginning
Language: Rhyme

Discuss with students the song's rhyme scheme. Help them brainstorm a list of other words to rhyme with *run* and *time*. Have students make lists of the words and arrange them in alphabetical order.

Some students may have difficulty spontaneously thinking of rhyming words. Help them by writing ___*un* and ___*ime* on a sheet of paper. Then say or point to the letters of the alphabet. Help them fill in the blanks with letters that create meaningful rhyming words.

Advanced
Language: Collaborative Profile

Invite students to look at the picture of the tin cup and state in their own words what the question on the cup means. Ask students to tell what they think the song tells about society at that time. Discuss the modern social problem of homelessness. Have students suggest ways to help homeless people.

Tell what you learned.

CHAPTER 10

1. How did life in the United States change between 1800 and 1900? What new kinds of jobs did people have by 1900?

2. Have you ever visited a factory? What was made there? Do you think it was dangerous or safe to work there? Why?

3. Many people say that the United States is going through another revolution of information and machines such as computers. What do you think they mean by this?

4. Would you rather live in a rural or in an urban area? Why?

Assess √

Activity 1: Evaluate responses based on the comparisons that can be made from the text.

Activity 2: Check that students grasp the meanings of *safe* and *dangerous*.

Activity 3: Evaluate students' understanding of the continuing changes in all societies.

Activity 4: Check that students can state the differences between rural and urban living.

Have students complete the Chapter Self-Assessment, Blackline Master 31. Have students choose the product of one of the activities to place in their portfolios. Add the results of any rubrics, checklists, self-assessments, or portfolio assessments, Blackline Masters 2–18 and 31.

Listening Assessment

BLACKLINE MASTER

Make sure each student has a copy of page 83 from the Teacher's Resource Book. Play the tape several times and have students complete the activity.

CREAM TAPE

See Chapter 10 Resources, page T154d, for the Listening Assessment tapescript.

Options for Assessment

Vocabulary Assessment

Social Studies: Time Line

Have students work in small groups to compile lists of inventions dating from the 1800s to today. Have students place pictures, dates, and names for the inventions on a time line that they create on the bulletin board.

Writing Assessment

Write Creatively

Have students pretend that they are as rich as Andrew Carnegie and they, too, plan to give away their riches. Ask students to tell how they would spend the money and why. Have students check their work for correct usage, including subject/verb agreement, and encourage them to use a variety of sentence structures.

Language Assessment

BLACKLINE MASTER

Have students use Blackline Master 82 in the Teacher's Resource Book.

Standardized Test Practice

ACTIVITY BOOK

Use pages 100 and 101. Answers: **1.** During the 1800s, thousands of people left their farms. They came to the city. **2.** began to work **3.** Punctuation **4.** No mistake

Wrap-Up

Activities

Urban and Rural Collages

Divide students into two groups. Instruct one group to create an "Urban Collage" with pictures cut from magazines to represent the city, and the other to create a "Rural Collage" with pictures representing the country. Have students write labels, captions, or paragraphs to show what they have learned about each environment. Hang the collages in the classroom.

Prairie Life

Have the class do a creative writing exercise about life for sod busters on the prairie. Have students pretend they are sod busters and they want to write letters to family members they left behind in the East or in Europe. Suggest that students talk about how they spend their days, how they have fun, what the weather is like in summer and winter, and so on. Some students may need help in the first stage of the writing process. Help them brainstorm what the exact content of their letter will be. Then remind them to use an informal style. Make a bulletin board display of the completed letters.

Research Inventions

Have small groups of students work at the library or on a classroom computer to research items invented since 1925, such as radar, transistors, computers, and the polio vaccine. Tell students to draw a picture of each invention or its use. Suggest students label the pictures with some or all of the following information: name of invention, purpose of invention, name of inventor(s), nationality of inventor, and year invented. Arrange time for students to present their findings to the rest of the class. Students can compile their pictures in alphabetical or chronological order and bind them together to make a book.

Discussing the Theme

Review with students the main events in the development of the United States during the 1800s and early 1900s. Choose from the following activities that will demonstrate to students how much they have learned and how useful these types of information are to them:

- Have students tape-record a list of words they learned in this unit.
- Have students write down as many types of transportation as they can. Ask them to share their lists, and write the lists on the board. Prompt students to tell which forms of transportation were available to settlers before the coming of the transcontinental railroad and which have been invented since then.
- Have students identify specific interests that they have about U.S. history during the period studied. Discuss ways of locating literature that will satisfy those interests.
- Discuss with students the two conflicts presented in the unit: settlers vs. American Indians and industrialists vs. reformers. Help students create T-Charts for each of the two conflicts.
- Have students discuss situations in which the words they have learned will be useful, such as in science class, social studies class, and when traveling.

Sharing the Project

Use the invitation form, Blackline Masters 32–33, to invite family members to school to view the completed time line.

Prepare for the classroom visit by having volunteers rehearse presenting a sentence or two each about each section of the display.

Refreshments might feature foods produced in a prairie biome, such as wheat crackers, corn chips, and cheese.

Signs of Success!

Duplicate a copy of this checklist for each student.

Name: ______________________________

Refer to the checklist below for a quick determination of how a student is progressing toward transitioning out of ESL instruction.

Objectives

- ☐ Tells how, why, and when settlers moved west.
- ☐ Describes prairie and forest biomes and life in the 1800s.
- ☐ Discusses problems between settlers and American Indians.
- ☐ Describes the Industrial Revolution.
- ☐ Identifies industrial leaders and inventors.
- ☐ Tells about industrial change and reform.
- ☐ Describes the life of Andrew Carnegie.

Language Awareness

Understands/Uses:

- ☐ capitalization of place names
- ☐ the suffix *-less*
- ☐ passive voice
- ☐ *many/few/little*
- ☐ negatives
- ☐ quotation marks
- ☐ expressions of time
- ☐ appositives
- ☐ phrase *because of*
- ☐ question formation
- ☐ unreal conditions
- ☐ requests

Hears/Pronounces/Reads:

- ☐ long *o*
- ☐ rhyming words

Learning Strategies:

- ☐ Uses maps in textbooks
- ☐ Scans
- ☐ Uses previously learned information
- ☐ Uses a dictionary to increase vocabulary
- ☐ Reads on to get meaning
- ☐ Uses a time line
- ☐ Predicts content
- ☐ Compares and contrasts

Comments

____

Planning Guide

CHAPTER 11

Citizenship

Objectives

Describe the requirements for becoming a naturalized citizen and the meaning of good citizenship.

Tell about the Statue of Liberty, Ellis Island, and immigration experiences there.

Vocabulary Focus

Words relating to the meaning of citizenship, such as *equality, vote, responsibility.*

Words relating to immigration symbols, such as *statue, island, museum, gift.*

Lesson	Content Focus	Language Awareness Objectives	Learning Strategies
Preview pp. 192–193 Tell what you know.			
Present pp. 194–195 All Are Equal	Social Studies	**Grammar** *By* + Gerund Answers to *How* Questions	Use a Venn diagram.
Practice pp. 196–197 Becoming a Naturalized Citizen	Social Studies	**Language Function** Expressions of Necessity *Must* and *Have To*	Understand use of bulleted text.
Practice pp. 198–199 Being a Good Citizen	Social Studies	**Spelling** Spelling Rules for Gerunds	
Connect pp. 200–201 Facts About Immigration	Social Studies/ Math	**Grammar** Present Perfect	
Connect pp. 202–205 The Statue of Liberty and Ellis Island	Social Studies/ Reading	**Phonics** Recognize Silent Letters in Words	
Connect pp. 206–213 *Coming to America: Letters from Rifka*	Social Studies/ Literature	**Phonics** Words with Double *ss* **Grammar** Sequence of Tenses: Use of *Would*	
Connect p. 214 "America the Beautiful"	Social Studies/ Literature	**Phonics** Words That Rhyme	
Assess p. 215 Tell what you learned.			

CHAPTER 12

Government

Objectives

Describe the United States as a democracy.

Name the three branches of government.

Discuss the Constitution and some key amendments.

List some views on the meaning of the United States.

Vocabulary Focus

Forms of government, such as *democracy, dictatorship, communism, monarchy.*

Words that describe United States government, such as *Constitution, laws, amendments.*

Words that describe the three branches of government, such as *legislative, executive, judicial, Congress.*

Words about being an American, such as *promise, merits, flag, motto.*

Lesson	Content Focus	Language Awareness Objectives	Learning Strategies
Preview pp. 216–217 Tell what you know.			
Present pp. 218–219 A Government of Laws	Social Studies	**Grammar** *Or* to Signal Appositives or Explanations	
Practice pp. 220–223 The Three Branches of Government	Social Studies	**Spelling** Colons **Grammar** Two-Word Verbs with *Out*	Understand text organization. Use diagrams to get meaning.
Connect pp. 224–225 Amending the Constitution	Social Studies/ Math	**Grammar** Present Perfect with *Since*	Use a time line.
Connect pp. 226–227 The United States: Its People and Its Meaning	Social Studies/ Literature	**Language Function** Speech Fillers	
Connect p. 228 "Hang Out the Flags"	Social Studies/ Literature	**Phonics** Consonant Blends	
Assess p. 229 Tell what you learned.			

Resources

Chapter 11

Support Materials

ACTIVITY BOOK — Pages 102–111

DISK — Writer's Notebook

PURPLE TAPE — Side 1: *Coming to America: Letters from Rifka,* pages T206–T213

Side 2: "America the Beautiful," page T214

LET'S TALK CARD — 96 cards to start conversations.

STORYTELLING — Storytelling Anthology: *Worlds Together*

Phonics

PHONICS — *Newcomer Phonics,* pages 42, 64, 74

Assessment Materials

BLACKLINE MASTER — Language Assessment, Blackline Master 90

Listening Assessment, Blackline Master 91

CREAM TAPE — Side 2: Listening Assessment, page T215

Listen carefully. You will hear about some of the requirements to become a U.S. citizen. Write down what you hear. You hear the information once. Then you will hear it again more slowly. Begin to write. Then you will hear it one more time. Check what you wrote.

People who want to become citizens of the United States need to do certain things.

1. They must live in the United States for five years.
2. They must be at least eighteen years old.
3. They must be able to read, write, and speak some English.
4. They must know something about the history of the United States.

Support for Newcomers

Newcomer Book C, Survival language for absolute beginners. For overview, see pages xxviii–xxix.

Newcomer Teacher Suggestion Book, Chapter 11, pages 28–29

HomeLink Penguin Readers

The Adventures of Huckleberry Finn

For Extended Reading

Becoming a Citizen: Adopting a New Home by Fred Bratman, Raintree Steck-Vaughn Pubs., 1993. A discussion of immigration and the process of becoming a citizen. **Level: Advanced**

Ellis Island by Richard Conrad Stein, Children's Press, 1994. Read about the history, closing, and restoration of Ellis Island and about the immigrants who passed through it. **Level: Beginning**

Immigration by Kelly C. Anderson, Lucent Books, 1993. An overview of the issues concerning immigration to the United States, including adjusting to American life, illegal immigration, and refugees. **Level: Advanced**

Quilted Landscapes: Conversations With Young Immigrants by Yale Strom, Simon & Schuster, 1996. Twenty-six young people from all over the United States tell about their experiences and views as immigrants. **Level: Average**

The Statue of Liberty by Craig A. Doherty and Katherine M. Doherty, Blackbirch Marketing, 1996. The story of how the statue came to stand on an island in New York Harbor. **Level: Average**

The Vote: Making Your Voice Heard by Linda Scher, Raintree Steck-Vaughn, 1996. What does it mean to be a U.S. citizen? Learn all about free speech, interest groups, voting, taxes, jury duty, and running for office in this introductory book. **Level: Beginning**

Related Technology

Compton's Interactive Encyclopedia 1999 Deluxe, Mindscape, 1998. Allows students to study citizenship and create a database of information.

Resources

Chapter 12

Support Materials

ACTIVITY BOOK

Pages 112–121

PURPLE TAPE

Side 2: "Hang Out the Flags," page T228

DISK

Writer's Notebook

Phonics

PHONICS

Newcomer Phonics, pages 20–29

Assessment Materials

BLACKLINE MASTER

Language Assessment, Blackline Master 92

Listening Assessment, Blackline Master 93

CREAM TAPE

Side 2: Listening Assessment, page T229

Listen carefully. The student is talking about what he learned in social studies class. Circle the amendments he names. Then match those amendments with what they do.

In social studies class, we studied the changes to the United States Constitution. They are called amendments. Many amendments gave more people the right to vote. When the United States began, only white men could vote. In 1870, the Fifteenth Amendment was put into effect. It gave African American men the right to vote. The Nineteenth Amendment was put into effect in 1920. It gave many more people the right to vote. It gave women the vote. More recently, the Twentieth Amendment lowered the voting age. People can vote when they are only eighteen years old.

Support for Newcomer

Newcomer Teacher Suggestion Book, Chapter 12, pages 30–31

For Extended Reading

The Congress: America's Lawmakers by Gary M. Stern, Raintree Steck-Vaughn, 1993 An examination of the origins, function, and notable acts of our government's legislative branch. **Level: Average**

The Founding Presidents: A Sourcebook on the U.S. Presidency edited by Carter Smith, Millbrook Press, 1995. Various contemporary materials describe and illustrate the political and personal lives of the United States Presidents from George Washington to James Monroe. **Level: Advanced**

The Judiciary: Laws We Live By by Lila E. Summer and Samuel G. Woods, Raintree Steck-Vaughn, 1993. A description of the U.S. legal system and how it works for citizens. **Level: Average**

Rights and Responsibilities: Using Your Freedom by Frances Shuker-Haines, Raintree Steck-Vaughn, 1993. A look at voting in the United States. **Level: Average**

Shh! We're Writing the Constitution by Jean Fritz, Paperstar, 1998. A behind-the-scenes look at how the Constitution came to be written and ratified. **Level: Beginning**

Related Technology

Portraits of American Presidents, Ignite, 1994. Provides facts about 42 presidents, including Clinton.

Project

Citizenship Theater

This optional project can be completed over the next two chapters. In this project, students will write and act out plays and scenes relating to U.S. citizenship. See the Unit Wrap-Up, page T229a, for more ideas on sharing the project with family members.

What You'll Need

Collect materials for making costumes, scenery, and props: sheet or curtain, curtain rod, fabric, old clothing, needles and thread, string or yarn, scissors, safety pins, construction paper, cardboard, paints, crayons, magic markers, makeup, suitcases and other props, spotlights

Strategies You'll Use

- Brainstorm
- Take notes
- Understand key words

Beginning the Project

Divide the class into small groups. Explain that each group will plan and perform its own short play about United States citizenship. Assign one of the following themes to each group:

- a contemporary family's decision to move to the United States
- a United States resident's experience with the process of naturalization
- a family's immigration to the United States in the late 1800s

Tell students that if they prefer, they can develop their own themes. Remind them to brainstorm ideas and take notes for their plays as they progress through the unit.

Home Involvement

Send the Letter to the Family, Blackline Masters 84–89, to families, explaining that the class will be creating and performing short plays about United States citizenship. The letter encourages families to help students plan appropriate costumes, props, and scenery for the plays.

Daily Discussion

Take a few minutes each day to talk about the plays. Give the groups time to brainstorm ideas, write dialogue, and rehearse. Assure students that stories and dialogue can be very simple. Encourage groups to develop dialogue through repeated rehearsals and to use vocabulary from the unit. Point out to students that ideas for the plays can come from previously learned information (gathered through the students' own experiences, conversations, and observations) as well as from information contained in this unit. The plays can be based on the personal or family experiences of group members or can be purely fictional, but should include ideas presented in the unit. As the groups progress with their plays, set aside class time for the preparation of props and scenery.

Information About Plays

Discuss the basic structure of a play. Explain that most plays are built around a *conflict.* They build to a *climax* and end with a *resolution.* Make sure students understand that a conflict is not necessarily a fight or an argument. It may also entail a clash of values, opinions, actions, or personalities. Point out that the climax is the most exciting part of the play. It is the scene that all the other action builds up to. Explain that the resolution is the solution to the conflict. Have groups brainstorm specific stories for their plays, bearing in mind the key words: *conflict, climax,* and *resolution.*

Discuss the jobs involved in producing a play, as shown in the chart below. Groups should decide how the responsibilities will be divided and shared among group members.

Theater Jobs

- **Writers** prepare either a script for actors to memorize or an outline that actors can improvise from.
- **Actors** perform the roles in a play.
- The **director** helps actors develop their roles and makes technical decisions, such as how to light the play and how to switch from scene to scene.
- **Set designers** create the scenery and props for a play.
- **Costume designers** develop ideas for costumes and accessories.

Activity Book

Chapter 11

Name ______________________

Facts About Population

Every ten years the government of the United States counts the number of people who live in the country. Study the list. Answer the questions.

Population of the United States, 1790-1990

Year	People
1790	3,929,000
1800	5,308,000
1810	7,240,000
1820	9,638,000
1830	12,861,000
1840	17,063,000
1850	23,192,000
1860	31,443,000
1870	38,558,000
1880	50,189,000
1890	62,980,000
1900	76,212,000
1910	92,228,000
1920	106,022,000
1930	123,203,000
1940	132,165,000
1950	151,326,000
1960	179,323,000
1970	203,302,000
1980	226,542,000
1990	248,710,000

1. In what year did the United States have the largest population? 1990
2. In what year did the United States have the smallest population? 1790
3. By what year had the U.S. population passed 100,000,000? 1920
4. In what year was the U.S. population about 76,000,000? 1900
5. By what year had the U.S. population passed 200,000,000? 1970
6. Abraham Lincoln was elected President of the United States in 1860. About how many people lived here then? About 31,000,000
7. Ronald Reagan was elected President of the United States in 1980. About how many people lived here then? About 227,000,000

Name ______________________

The Pledge of Allegiance

Read the Pledge of Allegiance. This is a basic statement of a person's loyalty to the United States.

> I pledge Allegiance to the flag of the United States of America, and to the Republic for which it stands, one nation, under God, indivisible, with liberty and justice for all.

Find the words below from the pledge in the puzzle. Circle them.

ALLEGIANCE	JUSTICE
AMERICA	LIBERTY
FLAG	NATION
GOD	REPUBLIC

M	F	N	R	O	E	S	Q	X	I
A	L	L	E	G	I	A	N	C	E
M	A	E	P	F	D	V	H	R	N
E	G	J	U	S	T	I	C	E	A
R	C	X	B	T	G	O	D	Q	T
I	P	K	L	X	L	K	D	F	I
C	T	L	I	B	E	R	T	Y	O
A	S	V	C	H	S	O	F	P	N

Name ______________________

Becoming a Citizen

Study the list. Use the facts to write complete sentences about becoming a citizen. Use *have to* or *must* in each sentence.

Naturalized Citizens

- speak English
- live here for 5 years
- be at least 18 years old
- support the United States above all others
- know about U.S. history and government

You have to/must speak English.

You have to/must live here for five years.

You have to/must be at least 18 years old.

You have to/must support the United States above all others.

You have to/must know about U.S. history and government.

In school, you must follow certain rules. List three of them here. Use complete sentences.

Answers will vary.

Name ______________________

Duties of a Citizen

Classify the duties and rights of a citizen. Put each item in the box in the correct column. Some may go into both columns.

equality before the law	freedom of speech
obeying the laws of the nation	being on a jury
paying taxes	respecting the rights of others
voting	ability to own property

Duties of a Citizen	Rights of a Citizen
obeying the laws of the nation	equality before the law
paying taxes	voting
voting	freedom of speech
being on a jury	ability to own property
respecting the rights of others	

Find the words in the box in the puzzle. Circle them.

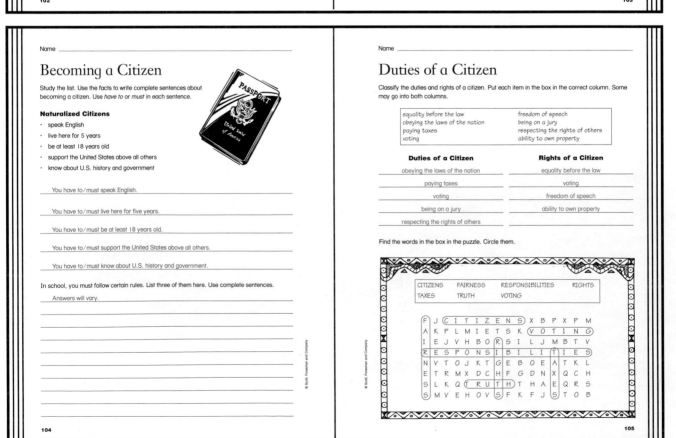

CITIZENS	FAIRNESS	RESPONSIBILITIES	RIGHTS
TAXES	TRUTH	VOTING	

F	J	C	I	T	I	Z	E	N	S	X	B	P	X	P	M
A	K	P	L	M	I	E	T	S	K	V	O	T	I	N	G
I	E	J	V	H	B	O	R	S	I	L	J	M	B	T	V
R	E	S	P	O	N	S	I	B	I	L	I	T	I	E	S
N	V	T	O	J	K	T	G	E	B	O	E	A	T	K	L
E	T	R	M	X	D	C	H	F	G	D	N	X	Q	C	H
S	L	K	Q	T	R	U	T	H	T	H	A	E	Q	R	S
S	M	V	E	H	O	V	S	F	K	F	J	S	T	O	B

Name ______________________

Being a Good Citizen

Read the sentences. Write in the correct word forms. Use words ending in *-ing*. Be sure to spell them correctly.

(Be) ___Being___ a good citizen is important. It means (respect) ___respecting___ the rights of others. It means (pay) ___paying___ taxes on time. It means (vote) ___voting___ in all elections. It means (tell) ___telling___ the truth in court, and (help) ___helping___ others when they need it. (Be) ___Being___ a good citizen means (care) ___caring___ about the future of the United States and (do) ___doing___ what you can for the good of all.

Write what being a good citizen means to you.

____

____

____

____

____

____

Name ______________________

Immigrants and Naturalized Citizens

Study the table. Fill in the blanks.

Immigrants and Naturalized Citizens, 1930 to 1980

Years	Immigrants	Naturalized Citizens
1930s	528,431	1,518,464
1940s	1,035,039	1,987,028
1950s	2,515,479	1,189,946
1960s	3,321,677	1,120,263
1970s	4,493,314	1,464,772

This table shows how many immigrants entered the United States between ___1930___ and ___1980___. The fewest immigrants came to the United States during the decade of the ___1930s___. This small number was because of the hard economic times in the United States and other places in the world during those years. Many of the 1,518,464 people who became naturalized citizens during the ___1930s___ arrived before that time. The greatest number of immigrants came to the United States in the ___1970s___. But the greatest number of people became naturalized citizens during the ___1940s___. The fewest people became naturalized citizens during the ___1960s___.

UNITED STATES OF AMERICA

Name ______________________

Words to Know

Use the clues to fill in the crossword puzzle.

Across

3. woman who wrote a poem that says, "Give me your tired, your poor"
4. place where the Statue of Liberty and Ellis Island are located
5. people of this nation sent a gift to the people of the United States
6. size of the island on which the Statue of Liberty is located
8. place where poor immigrants were admitted to the United States

Down

1. name of a famous U.S. symbol
2. people who were admitted to the U.S. through Ellis Island
7. what Ellis Island is today
9. what the Statue of Liberty holds in her outstretched hand

	1 S											2 I
	T											M
3 L	A	Z	A	R	U	S						M
	T											I
	U											G
4 N	E	W	Y	O	R	K	H	A	R	B	O	R
	O											A
	5 F	R	A	N	C	E						N
	L											T
6 T	I	N	Y				7 M					S
	B						U					
	8 E	L	9 L	I	S	I	S	L	A	N	D	
	R		A				E					
	T		M				U					
	Y		P				M					

Name ______________________

Letters from Rifka

These sentences are based on the story "Letters from Rifka." Some sentences are incorrect. Rewrite the sentences to make them correct.

1. Rifka was immigrating to the United States from Poland.
   Rifka was immigrating to the United States from Russia.
2. Rifka was crossing the Pacific Ocean.
   Rifka was crossing the Atlantic Ocean.
3. Rifka had never seen some of her brothers.
   Rifka did not remember some of her brothers.
4. Rifka was writing the letter on Ellis Island.
   Rifka was writing the letter on the boat.
5. Rifka was afraid about answering the questions at Ellis Island.
   Rifka was not worried about answering the questions at Ellis Island.
6. The trip across the ocean seemed fast to Rifka.
   The trip across the ocean seemed slow to Rifka.
7. To Rifka, the United States was a place to begin a new life.
   ____
8. Rifka saw the Statue of Liberty from the ship.
   ____

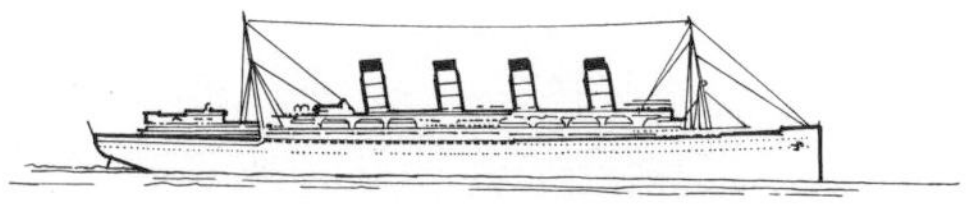

Activity Book

Chapter 12

Name ____________________

The First Amendment

Read about the First Amendment.

Amendment 1

The government cannot pass laws that make any religion the official religion of the country. The government cannot make laws that stop people from speaking and writing what they wish. It cannot make laws that stop people from holding peaceful meetings or from asking the government to correct a wrong.

Write *Yes* for the examples that would involve the First Amendment. Write *No* for the examples that would not involve the First Amendment.

Yes 1. The government passes a law that says only certain people can make speeches about health care issues.

No 2. The government passes a law that says all people must pay more taxes.

No 3. The government passes a law that changes where the border is between the states of Texas and Louisiana.

Yes 4. Some neighbors get together to talk about the amount of crime in their neighborhood.

Yes 5. People decide themselves which church they want to go to.

No 6. A young person decides to join the U.S. Army after graduating from high school.

No 7. A company decides to sell its products for less money.

Yes 8. A parent writes a letter to the editor of the newspaper in support of plans to build a new high school in town.

Name ____________________

Which Branch of Government?

Read the list. Then match the items with the three branches of government.

- makes the laws
- approves the laws
- hears court cases
- has 100 senators
- is headed by the President
- has 9 members
- meets with leaders of other countries
- decides if laws are constitutional
- has 435 representatives

Legislative

makes the laws
has 100 senators
has 435 representatives

Executive

is headed by the President
approves the laws
meets with leaders of other countries

Judicial

hears court cases
has 9 members
decides if laws are constitutional

Name ____________________

The Branches of Government

Use the clues to complete the crossword puzzle.

Across

2. where the President lives
3. name for the part of Congress with 100 members
6. how many Presidents there can be
7. name for the part of Congress with 435 members

Down

1. name for the highest court in the country
2. name of the first U.S. President
4. the number of branches of government
5. what Congress makes

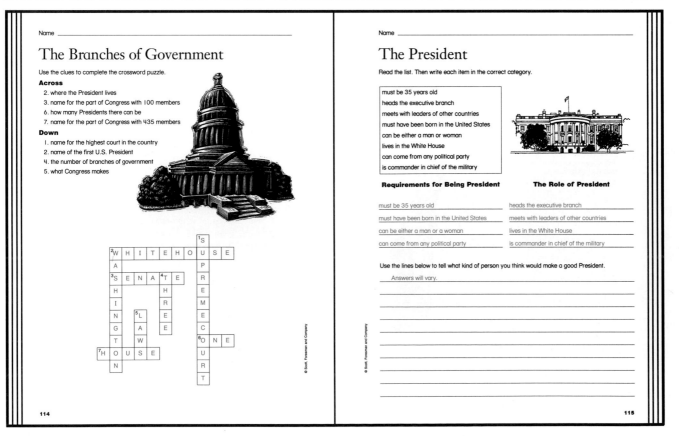

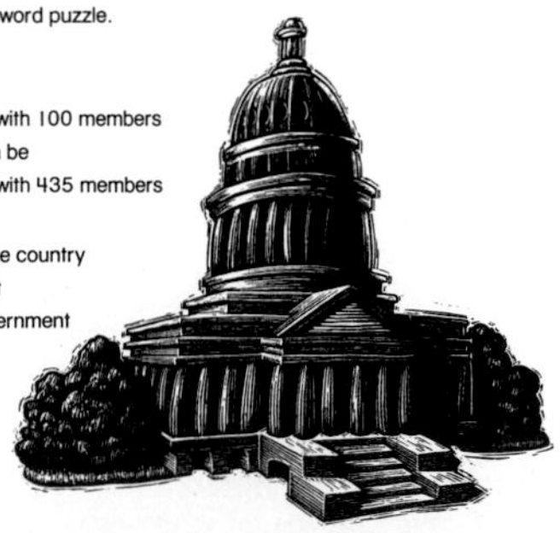

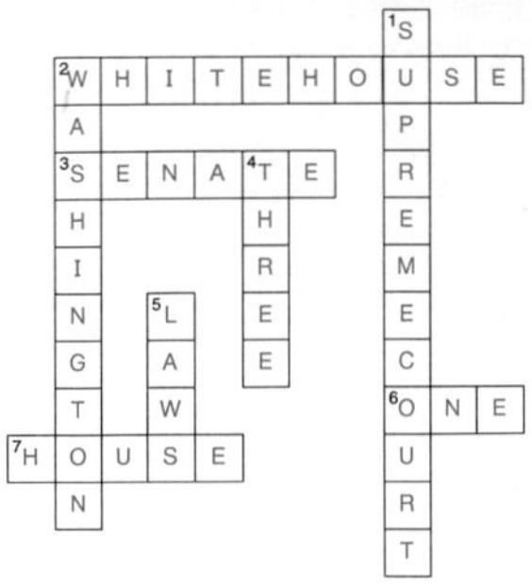

Name ____________________

The President

Read the list. Then write each item in the correct category.

- must be 35 years old
- heads the executive branch
- meets with leaders of other countries
- must have been born in the United States
- can be either a man or woman
- lives in the White House
- can come from any political party
- is commander in chief of the military

Requirements for Being President	The Role of President
must be 35 years old	heads the executive branch
must have been born in the United States	meets with leaders of other countries
can be either a man or a woman	lives in the White House
can come from any political party	is commander in chief of the military

Use the lines below to tell what kind of person you think would make a good President.

Answers will vary.

Name ________________________________

Since When?

Study the time line about the history of the United States. Write sentences that follow the example. Use *since* in your answers.

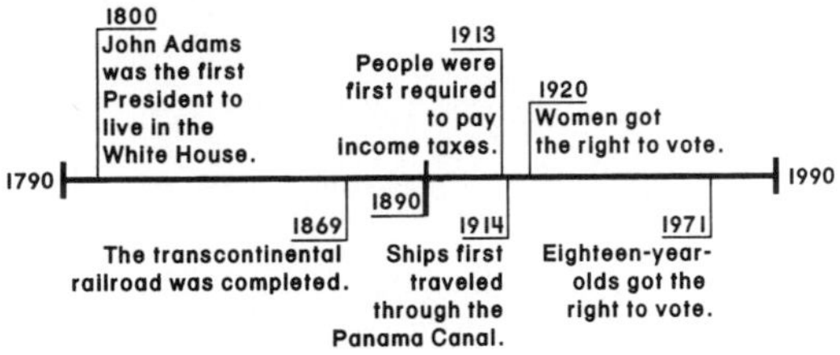

1. Presidents (live) White House

   Presidents have lived in the White House since 1800.

2. Women (vote)

   Women have voted since 1920.

3. People (travel) transcontinental railroads

   People have traveled on the transcontinental railroads since 1869.

4. Ships (travel) Panama Canal

   Ships have traveled through the Panama Canal since 1914.

5. Eighteen-year-olds (vote)

   Eighteen-year-olds have voted since 1971.

6. People (pay) income taxes

   People have paid national income taxes since 1913.

Name ________________________________

Write your own feelings.

Write your own saying or paragraph about what the United States of America means to you. Use some of the words from the Word Bank if you wish.

Word Bank	
democracy	laws
equality	opportunity
fairness	responsibilities
freedom	rights
immigrant	voting

Answers will vary.

Name ________________________________

Words to Know

Find these words in the puzzle. Circle them.

AMENDMENT
AMERICA
BILL OF RIGHTS
CONGRESS
HOUSE
LEGISLATIVE
PRESIDENT
SEPARATION OF POWERS
SENATE
SUPREME COURT
VOTE

J	P	R	O	S	F	G	D	X	T	B	U	S	L	X	V	F	C
K	R	V	X	D	A	X	B	H	S	C	D	J	G	T	P	K	D
S	E	P	A	R	A	T	I	O	N	O	F	P	O	W	E	R	S
E	S	T	M	X	M	F	L	M	D	N	K	L	T	M	O	LO	U
A	I	O	E	U	E	B	L	H	V	G	H	T	E	C	V	K	P
D	D	N	N	M	R	G	O	L	T	R	I	G	H	T	S	A	R
A	E	X	D	G	I	D	F	X	X	E	P	B	C	G	K	N	E
K	N	P	M	H	C	P	R	L	H	S	E	N	A	T	E	H	M
C	T	N	E	U	A	E	I	G	C	S	M	T	J	X	S	U	E
F	H	M	N	I	A	B	G	K	O	N	X	E	H	L	D	C	C
A	V	O	T	E	U	K	H	O	U	S	E	O	X	M	T	X	O
S	T	L	X	F	T	D	T	O	S	B	U	V	L	J	H	V	U
M	V	C	L	E	G	I	S	L	A	T	I	V	E	N	T	U	R
K	X	U	B	S	L	V	N	F	N	X	D	C	H	F	A	B	T

Name ________________________________

Consonant Blends

Complete each word in the sentences below, using *fl*, *br*, *dr*, *pr*, *st*, or *sp*.

1. The U.S. __fl__ag has 13 stripes and 50 __st__ars.
2. __Fl__ags __fl__ap when there is a __br__eeze.
3. The __St__atue of Liberty __st__ands in New York Harbor.
4. The __Pr__esident of the United __St__ates lives in the White House.
5. Congress is the legislative __br__anch of government.
6. Congress is the __br__anch of government that decides how to __sp__end the government's money.
7. __St__udents should __st__udy about the history of the United States.
8. New citizens __pr__omise to obey the laws of the land.
9. One __sp__ecial holiday is __Pr__esidents' Day. It honors Washington and Lincoln.
10. Many immigrants came to the United States to fulfill their __dr__eams.

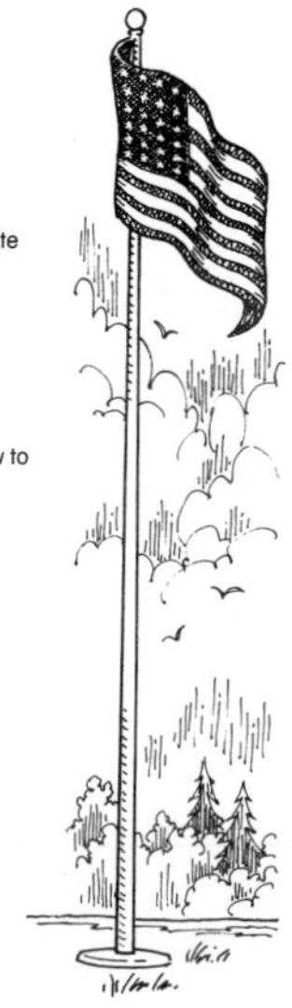

UNIT 6

Preview

Activate Prior Knowledge

Relate Personal Experiences

Ask students what they knew about the United States before they came here. Talk about why their families came. Introduce and develop the concepts of *freedom* and *opportunity.* Ask students what they already know about U.S. government.

Develop Language and Concepts

Present Pages 192 and 193

Read the questions on page 192 with students. Have them study the pictures on the page. Have them comment on the pictures, connecting them to the words in the Word Bank. Help students define each of the Word Bank terms in their own words.

Point out the image of President Woodrow Wilson giving one of his two inaugural addresses, and invite students to share what they know about the role of the U.S. president.

Also point out the suffrage marchers shown on page 193 and tell students that women in the United States did not have the vote until 1920. Then ask students to tell, if they know, who was allowed to vote in their home countries.

Introduce the concept of participation in government and freedom to participate in connection with the pictures of voting.

Point out the picture of the U.S. Capitol. Tell students that it is in Washington, D.C.

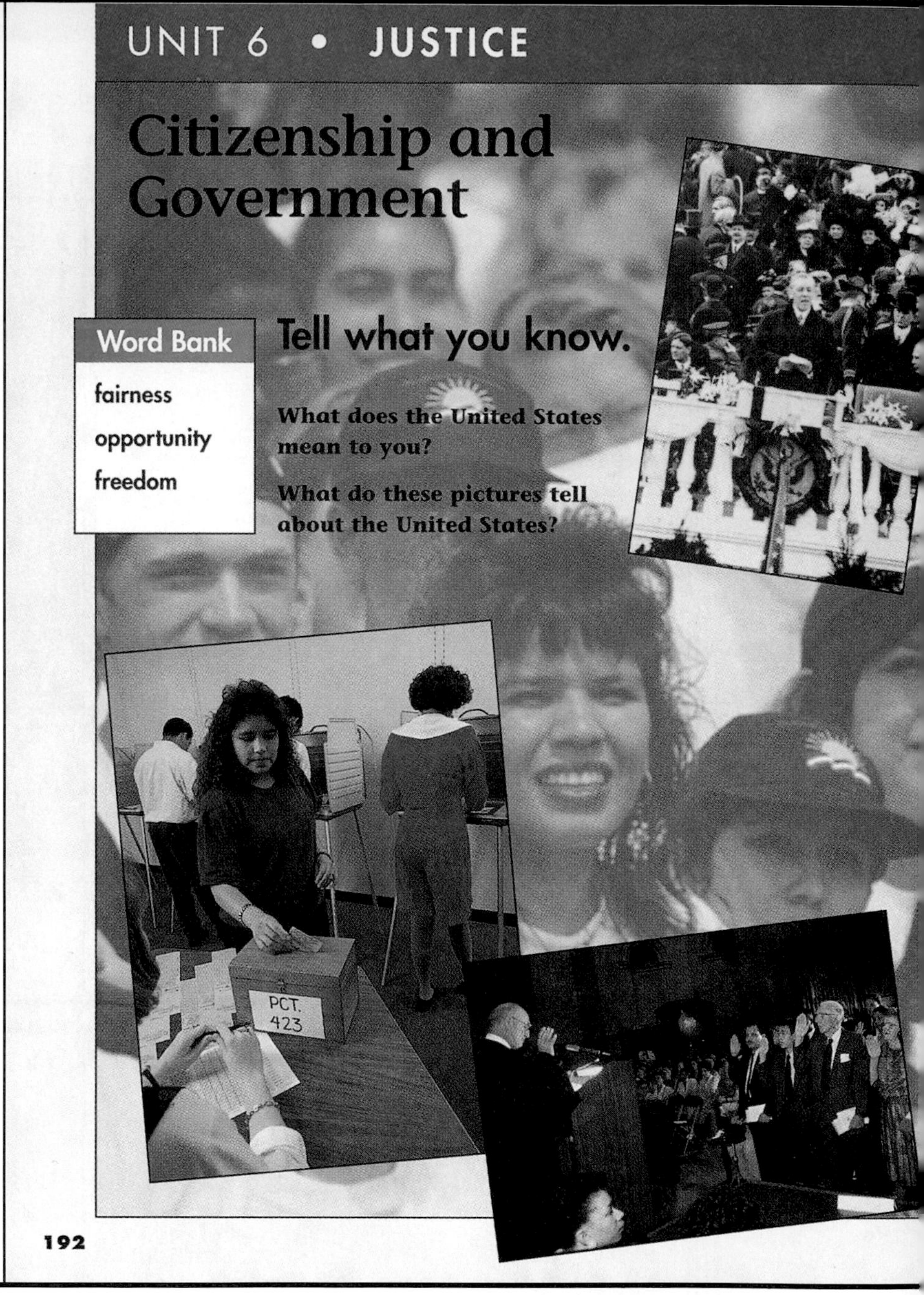

UNIT 6 • JUSTICE

Citizenship and Government

Word Bank

fairness

opportunity

freedom

Tell what you know.

What does the United States mean to you?

What do these pictures tell about the United States?

192

Options for Reaching All Students

Beginning

Social Studies: Design a Flag

Have students study the current U.S. flag. Talk with them about the 13 stripes standing for the original 13 colonies and the 50 stars standing for each of the states. Then divide students into pairs to design a new flag for the United States. Later, students should describe their creations to the rest of the class. Students should explain the reason for each color and element that they put in their designs. Remind students to speak loudly, clearly, and slowly so that their classmates can hear and understand them.

Advanced

Social Studies: Use Pictures

Have students look at these two pages and write sentences that describe the freedoms and opportunities that are depicted in the pictures. Model some sample sentences for students. Brainstorm and list useful vocabulary or phrases they might use.

Talk About It

Talk about where you were born. What did people there say about the United States? Do you think they were right or wrong? Why?

THEME/KEY CONCEPTS

The United States is a nation of immigrants and is based on the principles of freedom and democracy.

Chapter 11

- The United States is a democracy based on the principle of equality before the law for all.
- Many of the nation's myriad immigrants have become naturalized citizens.
- Many people have immigrated to the United States to create better lives for themselves and their families.

Chapter 12

- The government of the United States is a government of laws.
- The Constitution is the core of U.S. government.
- The government is divided into three branches.

FYI

Woodrow Wilson was President of the United States from 1913 to 1921. Wilson was the driving force behind the League of Nations, the forerunner of the United Nations.

Present

Activate Prior Knowledge

Recognize Similarities

Tell students that the United States celebrates every July Fourth as Independence Day and that these celebrations often include fireworks displays as shown here. Ask students to tell or draw chalkboard sketches of national celebrations that took place in their home countries.

Develop Language and Concepts

Present Pages 194 and 195

ACTIVITY BOOK Have students study the pictures and read the text. Help them understand that there are two ways for a person to become a citizen of the United States.

Point out that the promised equality is before the law, meaning that all citizens have the same rights and responsibilities. This equality does not mean that all people will be equal in everything, such as income or job status.

Tell students that the U.S. population has more than doubled since 1930. Use Activity Book page 102.

Model a Strategy

Use a Venn Diagram

Model creating a Venn diagram:

To help me understand what is the same and what is different about citizens and those who are not citizens yet, I can create

(Continued on page T195.)

CHAPTER 11

Citizenship

All Are Equal

A **citizen** is a person who is a member of a nation. A person can be a citizen by being born in a place. A person can also become a citizen by choosing to live in a place. About 250 million people live in the United States. More than 225 million of these people are citizens. Most of these people were born in the United States. They are citizens for that reason.

Options for Reaching All Students

Beginning

Social Studies: Watch a Trial

Have students watch an appropriate segment of a televised trial and identify the judge, the lawyers, the defendants, and so on as a way to build vocabulary. In a follow-up discussion, help students share their perceptions of court proceedings. Ask leading questions to prompt their responses. Stress the positive aspects of such proceedings to them, pointing out that in the United States, going to court is one way people can use to defend themselves, secure their rights, and so on. As a way of helping students relate emotionally as well as intellectually to the proceedings, ask them to acknowledge the feelings as well as the facts conveyed in the testimony.

Advanced

Social Studies: Perform a Courtroom Drama

After they watch an appropriate segment of a televised trial, have groups of students role-play a court case for the rest of the class. Players may take the roles of judge, defendant, jury, or other appropriate courtroom characters. They may reenact what they saw on TV, perhaps with a different ending, or they may want to create their own scenarios.

Many other citizens chose the United States as their home. They began life in some other country, and they came to the United States as immigrants. After living here for five years, they can become citizens.

Many immigrants become citizens because, in the United States, all people are equal before the law. This means that all people must be treated the same. This **equality** before the law is an important reason that many immigrants want to become citizens.

Write About It

Why did your family immigrate to the United States? Why did other people you know immigrate?

a Venn diagram of two intersecting circles. One circle is for citizens; the other is for non-citizens. The overlapping section of the two circles is for the rights and responsibilities that all have.

Language Awareness

Grammar

***By* + Gerund Answers to *How* Questions**

Write these phrases from page 194 on the board: *by being born; by choosing to live*. Point out that these phrases answer the question *how*. Help students draw the conclusion that an *-ing* word follows *by* in answers. Ask other questions with *how* relating to classroom situations and have students respond with *by* + gerund.

Assess ✓

Use class discussion and the Write About It questions for assessment. Students should be able to

- describe the differences between native-born citizens and naturalized ones
- tell why their own families and others immigrated to the United States

LOOK**AHEAD**

In the next section, students will learn how to become naturalized citizens.

Mixed Ability

Social Studies: U.S. Holidays

Have students discuss celebrations that are particular to the United States, such as Labor Day and Thanksgiving. Have them discuss what they know or have experienced or interview people and look in books for information. Have students make a chart with the following information: when the holiday is celebrated, why it is celebrated, and how people often spend the day.

Cooperative Language Experience

Field Trip

If possible, take students to visit a local courthouse to view a portion of a civil trial. Also arrange for a bailiff or some other court official to give a tour of the facility, highlighting the different kinds of legal work done there. You might want to prepare students for the trip by helping them create a list of questions they hope to have answered.

Multicultural Connection

Holidays

Have students find out and discuss holidays in their home countries. Have them share their findings and compare holidays. Encourage them to identify similarities and differences in what holidays are celebrated and how holidays are celebrated around the world. Students can create a bulletin board display or a booklet to present the results of their research and discussion.

Practice

Activate Prior Knowledge

Draw on Personal Experiences

Ask students if they know anyone who is a naturalized citizen of the United States. If so, ask students to tell what they know about how that person became a citizen.

Develop Language and Concepts

Present Pages 196 and 197

ACTIVITY BOOK

Read the text with students. Have them look at the pictures and describe what the people are doing. Ask them to tell what they think about the requirements for becoming a naturalized citizen. Help students see that they probably already meet some of the requirements.

Be sure students understand that one meaning of *swear* is to make a promise, or a pledge. Then have students learn the Pledge of Allegiance. Discuss the meaning of the difficult terms and of the pledge itself. Use Activity Book page 103.

Have the students work in pairs for the Try It Out. Tell them to name their new countries and to write out the rules for citizenship. Have them share their ideas for new countries with the rest of the class and tell why they chose those particular rules.

FYI Albert Einstein

Einstein is best known for his theory of relativity (1905). He spent the last two decades of his life at the Institute for Advanced Study at Princeton.

Becoming a Naturalized Citizen

Some U.S. citizens were born in other countries. These people are called **naturalized citizens.** They came to the United States and chose to become citizens here.

People who want to become U.S. citizens must do certain things and follow certain rules. People who want to become U.S. citizens must:

- live in the United States for 5 years
- be at least 18 years old
- be able to read, write, and speak some English
- know some of the history of the United States and something about the U.S. government
- be willing to support the United States above all other nations

▲ In 1940, scientist Albert Einstein became a U.S.citizen.

Try It Out

Pretend you are going to start your own country. Make up a set of rules for people who want to become citizens. Give a reason why each rule is important to the success of your new country.

Options for Reaching All Students

Beginning

Language: Numbered List

Have students write the numbers 1 to 5 on their papers and copy down the bulleted points in the text on page 196. Tell students that the numbers they used are just another way of visually portraying information. Point out the meaning of the word *some* in rules 3 and 4, noting that naturalization candidates are *not* asked to be fluent in English or be experts in U.S. history and government. Read the rules through with students and make sure they understand them. Check comprehension by asking students to paraphrase each rule.

Advanced

Drama: Start a New Country

Have students write and perform a drama about starting a new country as suggested in Try It Out. Remind students that their drama should have a central conflict, and that the characters and plot development should support this conflict (which might center on a disagreement over which rules are important for a country's success).

People who want to become U.S. citizens must fill out papers that tell about themselves. They must go to a meeting with a government officer. At this meeting, they have to answer questions in English about U.S. history and government. They must swear to support the United States. When people have done all these things, they can become naturalized citizens of the United States.

Think About It

Do you think it is too hard or too easy to become a citizen of the United States? Why?

Language Awareness

Language Function
Expressions of Necessity *Must* and *Have To*

ACTIVITY BOOK

Point out the sentences on pages 196 and 197 that use *must* and *have to*. Tell students that these words express a necessity. Make up some further examples and have students create their own. Assign Activity Book page 104.

Model a Strategy

Understand Use of Bulleted Text

Model a strategy for understanding bullets:

When I see text with bullets, or dots, I know that it is something that can best be told visually, such as a list of equal ideas. Then, when I see these five bulleted items, I know they are five things that are all equally important and go together.

Assess ✓

Use class discussion and the Think About It questions for assessment. Students should be able to

- list the major requirements for naturalization
- express opinions about the process

LOOK**AHEAD**

In the next section, students will learn what it means to be a good citizen.

Mixed Ability

Writing: School Rules and School Information

Have students make a list of school rules for others who are new to the school. Have students include other important information that would be useful for new students to have. Remind them that rules should be brief and easy to understand. Point out that many rules begin with a verb or words, such as *never* and *always*. Beginning learners might create pictures or signs that illustrate rules.

Home Connection

Assess Citizenship Possibilities

Have students who are willing, talk with family members to find out which requirements for naturalization they or family members might already meet, such as being at least 18 years old or being able to speak some English. Respect the privacy of students who feel uncomfortable discussing these issues.

Practice

Activate Prior Knowledge

Talk About Good Citizenship

Ask students what being a good citizen of the classroom means to them. They can use words or pantomime to discuss positive behaviors and attitudes. Make a list of students' suggestions on the board.

Develop Language and Concepts

Present Pages 198 and 199

ACTIVITY BOOK

Read the lesson with students. Pause after each paragraph to help them look at the illustrations and try to identify the activities in the pictures. Help students determine the main idea of the text and the relevant supporting details. Discuss the Word Bank words, giving examples of actions that show a person is *caring, fair,* and so on.

Help students describe the responsibilities of being a good citizen of a country. Review the class list made earlier in reference to being a good citizen of the classroom. Then have students make their own lists, perhaps beginning with the head *A Good Citizen Should.* Have students number each item in their lists.

Ask them to complete Activity Book page 105 and the Talk About It questions for further practice. Encourage students to use the Word Bank words and other vocabulary discussed in class to answer the second Talk About It activity.

Being a Good Citizen

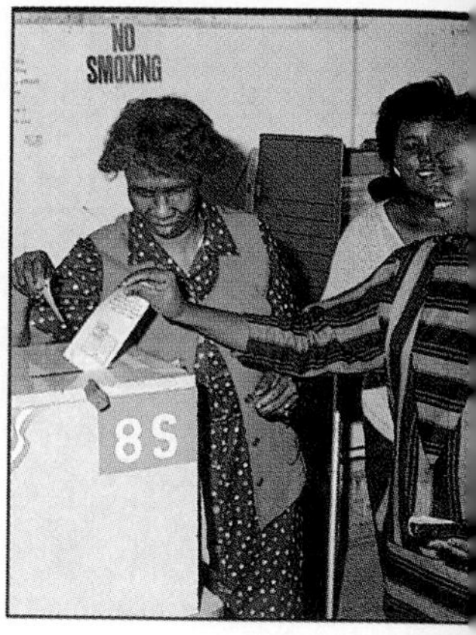

Citizens of the United States have many rights. They also have some responsibilities.

Voting is a basic responsibility of all adult citizens. The United States is a democracy. People choose their leaders by voting. Being a good citizen means voting in elections.

Another responsibility of all people in the United States, including citizens, is to obey the laws of the nation. It means paying taxes on time. It means being on a jury, and telling the truth in court.

Options for Reaching All Students

Beginning

Art: Posters

Have students study the list of responsibilities of a good citizen and then work in pairs to make posters that urge others to accept one or more of the responsibilities. Urge students to use persuasive words and appealing images. Hang the posters on the bulletin board.

Advanced

Social Studies: Write a Letter of Support

Have students write letters to various officials, such as mayors, senators, or the President, in support of some idea or legislation. Encourage students to make convincing arguments and to use formal language. Mail the letters; if any students get replies, ask them to share the replies with the rest of the class.

Mixed Ability

Social Studies: Community Project

Have students interview people in the school or neighborhood to find out about community projects they might participate in. Have students report back to class. If feasible, have students actually participate in such projects, either individually or in groups. Have students keep a journal about their experiences.

A third responsibility is to be interested in the needs of your area. It means writing to elected officials about issues you feel are important. It means helping to raise money for new library books. It means helping neighbors in need.

Being a good citizen also means believing in fairness and respecting the rights of others. Only by being fair and respecting the rights of others can people expect to be treated that way themselves.

Good citizens help each other when disaster strikes.

Word Bank

- caring
- fair
- helpful
- involved
- respectful
- responsible

Talk About It

Why do you think it is important to be a good citizen?

What words do you think describe a good citizen?

Language Awareness

Spelling
Spelling Rules for Gerunds

ACTIVITY BOOK Help students find the gerunds in the text by pointing out that *-ing* words follow the word *means;* for example, *Being a good citizen means voting in elections.* Help students create proper spellings of *-ing* words, pointing out that the final *e* is generally omitted when *-ing* is added. Write these words from the section on the board: *vote, be, obey, pay, tell, write, feel, help, raise, believe, respect, expect,* and *treat.* Ask volunteers to come to the board and write the *-ing* form of one or more. Use Activity Book page 106 for further practice.

Assess

Use students' responses to the Talk About It questions for assessment. Students should be able to

- list some aspects of good citizenship
- tell why good citizenship is important

LOOK**AHEAD**

In the next section, students will learn some statistics about U.S. immigration.

Connect

Activate Prior Knowledge

Relate Personal Experiences

Make a two-column chart on the board similar to the one on page 200 in the Student Book. Use the heading *When Our Class Came to the United States.* Then list the last ten or fifteen years in the left-hand column. Ask students to raise their hands as you call out and point to each of the years. Write the totals in the right-hand column. Leave the chart on the board for later reference.

Develop Language and Concepts

Present Pages 200 and 201

ACTIVITY BOOK

Read the text with students and help them interpret the charts. Explain that a *decade* is a period of ten years. Review place values as needed to help students read and comprehend the large numbers in the chart.

Have students study the chart on page 200 and ask them to compare and contrast the numbers of immigrants at various times. Then have students focus on the chart on page 201. Help students compare the data in the two charts. Help them discover that European immigration was heaviest before 1940 while immigration from other areas was heaviest after 1940. Have students work with partners to answer the Talk About It questions. Use Activity Book page 107 for further practice with charts.

Facts About Immigration

Some decades have been times of great immigration. Other decades have not. Study the chart and answer the questions.

Immigration to the United States, 1900 to 1990	
Decade	**Number of People**
1900s	8,795,386
1910s	5,735,811
1920s	4,107,209
1930s	528,431
1940s	1,035,039
1950s	2,515,479
1960s	3,321,677
1970s	4,493,314
1980s	7,338,062

Options for Reaching All Students

Beginning

Language: Read the Charts

Have students orally state information on the charts. Provide patterns such as:

Almost 9 million people came to the United States between 1900 and 1910.

More than 38 million people have come from Europe since 1820.

Advanced

Social Studies: Research

Have students use a variety of reference tools, including almanacs, to research the number of immigrants to the United States from specific countries, focusing on students' home countries. Have students summarize the results in chart form.

Mixed Ability

Geography: Name Continents and Countries

Use a globe or world map for naming and locating the continents. Have students tell or show on which continents they were born. Ask students to make a two-column chart listing each continent in the left-hand column and the total number of students born there in the right-hand one. Repeat the activity, using countries.

The number of immigrants from different continents has changed over time. To understand these changes, study the chart. Then answer the questions.

Where Immigrants Came From, 1820 to 1990		
Continent	1820 to 1940	1820 to 1990
Europe	32,468,776	37,045,140
Asia	1,074,926	6,098,449
The Americas	4,401,466	13,033,251
Africa	26,060	349,464

Talk About It

During which decade did the United States have the greatest immigration?

The 1930s were years of hard economic times. How does this chart show that things were not good in the United States then?

Which continent has provided the greatest number of immigrants?

Language Awareness

Grammar
Present Perfect

Have students look at the text on page 200 and talk about the meaning and structure of the present perfect. Point out that the present perfect is formed with *have* + the past participle of the verb. Explain that the past participle ends in *-ed* for regular verbs but has different forms for irregular verbs. (For example, *been* is the past participle of *be*). The present perfect refers to events that began in the past and that are still continuing. Contrast it with the past tense, using these examples:

Almost 9 million people came to the United States between 1900 and 1910.
More than 38 million people have come from Europe since 1820.

Then help students create their own sentences using the present perfect tense, using verb phrases, such as *have grown, have read,* and *have watched.*

Assess

Use students' responses to Talk About It for assessment. Students should be able to

- discuss U.S. immigration patterns

LOOK**AHEAD**

In the next section, students will study the Statue of Liberty and Ellis Island.

Cooperative Learning

Geography: Locate Where Students Were Born

Display a large world map. Have each student write his or her name on a small card. Have students pin their cards to the place where they were born and connect them to your community by attaching string to the pins. Ask: *Who came here from the farthest away? Who came the shortest distance?*

QuickCheck

Place Names

Check that students can say and spell the names of the continents in English, as well as the names of countries they and other students in the class come from. Remind them to begin each important word of a proper noun with a capital letter.

Writer's Workshop

My Impressions

Have students write about their impressions of the United States, including how it is the same and how it is different from their expectations. Have students use a T-Chart to organize their impressions before starting to write.

Connect

Activate Prior Knowledge

Talk About National Symbols

Show a U.S. flag and talk about national flags as the symbols of countries. Point out that other symbols exist for the United States and for other countries too. Ask students to tell about or draw sketches of symbols of their home countries and what those symbols mean.

Read the Selection

ACTIVITY BOOK

Have students study the pictures of the Statue of Liberty and Ellis Island. Then read the text with them. Stop frequently to assure comprehension. Have students complete Activity Book page 108 for practice with the section's vocabulary.

Ask students why they think the Statue of Liberty and Ellis Island are in New York harbor and not near an airport, which is where many immigrants arrive now.

Have students locate New York City and the continent of Europe on a world map. Then ask volunteers to trace imaginary routes the European ships might have taken in coming to New York from England, Greece, France, Norway, Ireland, Holland, and Portugal.

Have students work in pairs to answer the Think About It questions. After students have come up with their answers, have the whole class discuss them.

FYI

- **The official name of the Statue of Liberty is Liberty Enlightening the World. The mammoth copper statue was finally erected in 1886, after a lengthy campaign to raise funds to build the base. Emma Lazaus's poem was inscribed in bronze on the base of the statue in 1902.**
- **While most European immigrants came through Ellis Island, the relatively few Asian immigrants were interred in San Francisco Bay at Angel Island, where they were made to remain for six months or more. Today this treatment of Asian immigrants is widely decried as a racist tactic.**

Language Awareness

Phonics

Recognize Silent Letters in Words

Write the words *honor* and *island* on the board. Talk about the fact that some English words contain letters that are silent, or not pronounced. Pronounce the two words for students, asking them to say the words aloud after you. You may wish to have students look for other words with silent letters in the text or point out common letter pairs, such as *kn, wr,* and *mb,* in which one letter is usually silent.

Options for Reaching All Students

Beginning

Language: Items from Home

Help students make a list of things that Ellis Island immigrants probably brought with them to their new homes. Then have students illustrate and describe this list on a bulletin board display. Beside each item, have students write a reason why it would be "valuable." They might make a second list showing items their families brought to the United States.

Advanced

Language: Recite Poetry

Tell students that the text shows only the most famous part of the poem "The New Colossus" that Emma Lazarus wrote. Ask students to find the complete poem, to memorize it, and to recite it for the rest of the class. Then have students discuss how Lazarus's word choice and other poetic techniques give her poem meaning and power.

Mixed Ability

Drama: Re-create the Ellis Island Experience

Invite students to write and produce their own play about the experiences of immigrants who came through Ellis Island in the late 1800s and early 1900s. Have students play both immigrants and immigration officials. Encourage students to include the language barriers that many immigrants faced.

The Statue of Liberty and Ellis Island

For people around the world, the Statue of Liberty is a symbol of the United States. For many years, the Statue of Liberty was the first thing many immigrants saw when they reached the United States. To them, it represented what they hoped to find here: fairness, equality, opportunity, and freedom.

In 1876, the United States was 100 years old. The people of France sent a gift to the people of the United States in honor of that anniversary. The gift was a giant statue that is known as the Statue of Liberty. The statue was put up on a tiny island in New York harbor.

A poem appears on the base of the Statue of Liberty. The poem was written by Emma Lazarus. Part of the poem says:

Give me your tired, your poor,
Your huddled masses yearning to breathe free,
The wretched refuse of your teeming shore.
Send these, the homeless, tempest-tost to me,
I lift my lamp beside the golden door!

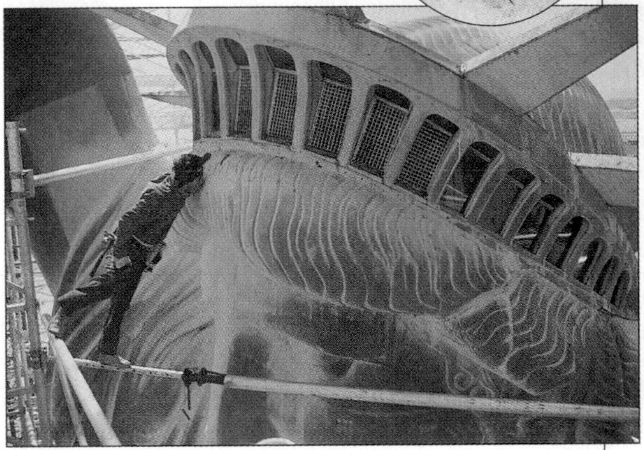

▲ The Statue of Liberty was cleaned and repaired in the 1980s.

Ellis Island is also in New York harbor, near the Statue of Liberty. Between 1892 and 1954, about 15 million immigrants entered the United States through Ellis Island. Most of them were poor people from Europe. They had sailed across the Atlantic Ocean.

Most people spent less than one day at Ellis Island. Government doctors quickly checked to see if they were sick. Only people with tuberculosis, leprosy, and a few other diseases were not allowed to enter the United States. The immigrants were interviewed for about two minutes each. If they had a little money, someplace to go, and someone to help them find work, they were free to enter.

▲ Ellis Island had a special playground for small children.

Today, Ellis Island is a museum. Visitors can tour the huge waiting room. They can see some of the things immigrants left behind and view other exhibits.

Think About It

Emma Lazarus used the words "golden door" in her poem. What do those words mean to you?

Why do you think the government wanted to be sure that immigrants had a little money and someplace to go?

Immigrants who passed through Ellis Island had crossed the Atlantic Ocean the cheapest way possible. The few rich immigrants often had better ship accommodations. They were examined on their ships. Do you think this was fair? Why or why not?

Connect

Activate Prior Knowledge

Review Information About Immigration

Have students recall what they have learned about immigration and the Statue of Liberty. Ask volunteers to tell about or act out their own travel experiences when they arrived in the United States. Develop a class word web of related words.

Introduce the Selection

Present Pages 206 Through 209

Have students read the title of the story and the name of the author. Ask them to predict what the story will be about. Read the introduction with students. Ask students to imagine what it must have felt like to be 13 years old and traveling alone for months. Have students find Russia on a world map and look at it in relation to the United States. Help students see that Rifka had to travel across Europe and the whole Atlantic Ocean to reach New York harbor.

Read the Selection

PURPLE TAPE

Read the story with students. Then read it again and discuss the Reader's Tips at the appropriate points. Play the tape of the story on Side 1 of the Purple Tape several times.

Talk about the people in the story; make a list of names on the board and ask students to tell who these characters are in the story. Talk about the themes that are introduced in the story.

Language Awareness

Phonics

Words with Double *ss*

Write these words on the board: *Russia, pass, cross,* and *homeless.* Then point out that each word uses a double *ss* as part of its spelling. Pronounce each word for students, helping them to hear the difference between *Russia* and the others. Ask students to pronounce each word after you do. Tell students that in most cases, the double *ss* is pronounced the same way as the beginning sound in *see.* The sound in *Russia* is usually spelled with the letters *sh.*

Teachable Moment

Point of View and Letters

Point out that this is a fictional, or made-up, story. The author has used two devices to make the story more immediate: it is told from the first-person point of view and it is in the form of a letter, which lets the writer express the character's feelings and opinions in a freer fashion than if the character were talking to someone.

Options for Reaching All Students

Beginning

Language: Letter Writing

Have students recall their first days in the United States. Ask them to share their memories of those times with each other and then to write letters to a relative or friend who stayed behind. Some students may prefer to make letters in the form of captioned drawings or actual photographs of their arrival.

Advanced

Language: Creative Writing

Have students pretend they are Cousin Tovah, writing to Rifka shortly after she has gotten Rifka's letter to her. Suggest students ask Rifka how things went at Ellis Island, what the family's new home is like, and so on. Point out that while the language of the letter can be informal, students should still check their spelling, capitalization, and punctuation.

Mixed Ability

Art: The United States

Cover a large area of the bulletin board with butcher paper. Divide the class into several small groups and assign each group to work on a section of the paper. Tell students to use their section to portray their feelings about coming to the United States in both words and pictures.

Coming to America: Letters from Rifka

by Karen Hesse

Introduction
This story is about a 13-year-old girl named Rifka who has traveled across the Atlantic Ocean alone to the United States in 1920. Her family had to leave her behind in Europe because she was sick. When she was well, she had to go on by herself. Now she is writing to her cousin Tovah who stayed behind in Russia. Rifka tells Tovah she soon expects to meet her older brothers who left for the United States so long ago that Rifka does not remember them.

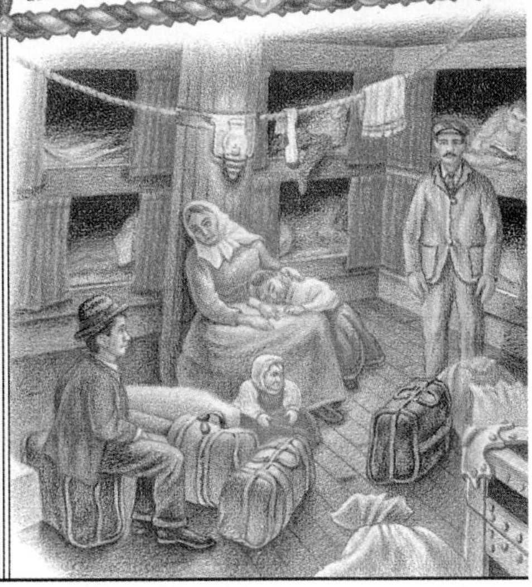

October 1, 1920
Entering New York Harbor

Dear Tovah,

Today we will arrive at Ellis Island. Today I will see Mama and smell her yeasty smell. Today I will feel the tickle of Papa's dark beard against my cheeks and see my brother Nathan's dimpled smile and Saul's wild curly hair. Today I will meet my brothers Asher and Isaac and Reuben.

Reader's Tip
Rifka says she doesn't remember some of her brothers. What does this fact say about travel and life at that time?

Language Tip
Vocabulary
Baldness means having no hair. Rifka's hair had fallen out when she was sick.

Language Tip
Vocabulary
A *tallis* is a Jewish prayer shawl. A *locket* is a piece of jewelry that has a little picture in it. A locket is usually worn on a chain around the neck.

Study Tip
Use of the First Person
An author that writes a story using *I, my, me, we,* and *us* is telling the story in the first person. This author has Rifka tell the story in the first person in a letter. How does the writing style make you feel about what has happened to Rifka? Look for the use of the first person point of view when you read other stories.

Already I am wearing my best hat, the black velvet with the shirring and the brim of light blue. I'm hoping that with the hat, Mama will not mind my baldness. I've tucked Papa's tallis into my rucksack, but Mama's gold locket hangs around my neck.

The captain said his company notified our families and they are awaiting our arrival. I must pass a screening on the island before I can go home with Mama and Papa. Papa wrote about Ellis Island in his letters.

He wrote that at Ellis Island you are neither in nor out of America. Ellis Island is a line separating my future from my past. Until I cross that line, I am still homeless, still an immigrant. Once I leave Ellis Island, though, I will truly be in America.

Language Tip
Time
Rifka is talking about several different time periods in this letter. The way to figure out what happened first, next, and last is to study the verb tenses.

Connect

Develop Language and Concepts

Present Pages 210 Through 213

ACTIVITY BOOK

Have students work in pairs of mixed ability and take turns retelling the story of Rifka's letter. Have partners ask questions to fill in the missing facts. Encourage them to act out parts of the text or use gestures to emphasize Rifka's thoughts and feelings.

Have students complete Activity Book page 109 for further comprehension practice regarding this story.

Language Awareness

Grammar

Sequence of Tenses: Use of *Would*

Direct students' attention to the sentence *I thought that we would never begin moving.* Point to the use of *would* to express an opinion after *thought.* Have students complete personal sentences using this sentence frame:

Before I came to the United States,
I thought that I would . . . .
Before I came to the United States,
I thought that it would be . . . .

Teachable Moment

The Parts of a Letter

Tell students to look over the general format of this story to recognize the parts of a letter. Assist them with identifying letter parts such as body text and salutation, or greeting. Say that the salutation *Dear* is a standard way that most letters are begun. Tell them that letters in English usually end with a short phrase such as *Sincerely yours,* or *Very truly yours,* which is called the complimentary close. In informal letters, the phrase might be *Your friend* or the like.

Response Activities

Personal Response

Ask students if they identify with the issues presented in the text. Have students compare their own experiences of immigration or those of people they know with those of Rifka's.

Critical Response

Have students analyze Rifka's character. Have them look at each paragraph and conclude what it tells them about her.

Creative Response

Have students continue the story and write about Rifka's first day in the United States.

Options for Reaching All Students

Beginning

Language: Summarize

Have students briefly summarize orally the story of Rifka: her life in Russia, her life on the ship, what she expects to find in the United States. If students have difficulty, you may wish to give them a short written summary with a few key words and names missing. Help them fill in the missing words.

Advanced

Social Studies: Research

Have students do more research on the Statue of Liberty, including information on its size and recent restoration. Have each student write a paragraph with the most interesting information he or she finds out. Have students compare paragraphs. Remind them to include a topic sentence that tells the main idea and give supporting details about the main idea.

Cooperative Language Experience

Immigrant Experience

Read aloud other stories about immigrants to the United States and show pictures from these stories if available. Discuss ways in which these stories reflect the diverse voices of people from various backgrounds. Have students write their own impressions after hearing and discussing the stories.

Papa said in his letter that they ask many questions at Ellis Island. I must take my time and answer correctly. What's to worry? I am good at answering questions. Even if they ask me a thousand questions, I will have Mama and Papa near me, my mama and papa.

Strategy Tip
Understand Character
Is Rifka worried about answering questions at Ellis Island? Why or why not? What words in her letter tell you how she feels?

Just one week ago, I did not think I would ever make it to America. We drifted on the sea for days, helpless, waiting for the ship to come and tow us. I assisted with the cleanup as best I could, doing work Pieter would have done if he were there.

Strategy Tip
Recognize Feelings
Imagine what Rifka must be feeling as she describes the trip across the ocean. Look for clues in Rifka's words.

Reader's Tip
Pieter is a young man Rifka met on the boat. He drowned in the storm that caused the ship to drift.

Then, once the tow ship arrived it took so long between the securing of the ropes and the exchanges between the two ships, I thought we would never begin moving. At last, when we did, the other ship pulled us so slowly. I could swim faster to America.

In Russia, all America meant to me was excitement, adventure. Now, coming to America means so much more. It is not simply a place you go when you run away. America is a place to begin anew.

In America, I think, life is as good as a clever girl can make it.

Very soon, Tovah, I will be in this America. I hope someday you will come, too.

Shalom, my cousin,

Rifka

P.S. As I was finishing this letter a cry went up from the deck. When I went out to see what it was, I found all the passengers gathered on one side of the ship, looking up. They were looking at Miss Liberty, Tovah, a great statue of a woman standing in the middle of the harbor. She was lifting a lamp to light the way for us.

Language Tip
Abbreviations
The initials *P.S.* stand for postscript. This abbreviation is sometimes used at the very end of a letter to indicate an idea or thought that the letter writer had after the letter was finished.

Connect

Activate Prior Knowledge
Use Prior Learning

Review with students some of the other songs about America that they have learned in this program.

Develop Language and Concepts
Present Page 214

PURPLE TAPE

Read the introduction and words to the song. Help them restate the lyrics in more simple English. Play the song several times and encourage students to sing along.

FYI

Katharine Lee Bates (1859–1929) was both a poet and an educator. She wrote "America the Beautiful" as a poem but was soon encouraged to set it to the tune of a popular song of the era. Bates had become a full professor of English literature at Wellesley College in 1891, making her one of the few women in the country to hold that rank.

Language Awareness

Phonics
Words That Rhyme

Discuss words that rhyme and write these pairs on the board: *grain/plain* and *thee/sea.* Point out that even though the words rhyme, they do not necessarily use the same spellings for the same sounds.

America the Beautiful

by Katharine Lee Bates

Katharine Lee Bates, a college professor, wrote the words to this famous song in 1893, just a year after Ellis Island had opened. Although Bates was not an immigrant, her words express the sentiments of many who are. Bates was inspired to write these words when she saw the spectacular view from Pikes Peak in Colorado during a visit there.

O beautiful for spacious skies,
For amber waves of grain,
For purple mountain majesties
Above the fruited plain.
America!
America!
God shed His grace on thee,
And crown thy good with brotherhood
From sea to shining sea.

Options for Reaching All Students

Beginning
Geography: Map Reading

Have students study a map of Colorado, such as the one usually found in an encyclopedia, that indicates major physical features. Help students locate Pikes Peak and determine its elevation. Then help students determine the elevation of your area and compare the two. You might show how to round these numbers and express them as a ratio.

Advanced
Social Studies: Biography

Have students work independently to research Zebulon Pike, for whom Pike's Peak is named. Point out that you reverse the order of names when searching for information (i.e., Pike, Zebulon). Ask students to write brief biographies of the man based on their research. Remind them to organize their facts in chronological order.

Home Connection
Patriotic Songs

Invite students and family members to bring in recordings of patriotic songs from their home countries and share them with the class. Encourage students to summarize the main idea of the lyrics.

Tell what you learned.

CHAPTER 11

1. What are some of the things a person must do to become a naturalized citizen?
2. Only about 2 percent of immigrants were turned away at Ellis Island. Still, many immigrants were fearful about the exams there. Why do you think this was so?
3. What facts that you learned about immigrants were the most interesting? Why?
4. The Statue of Liberty is a symbol of the United States. What symbols do you know of from the place where you were born?

Assess ✓

Activity 1: Evaluate answers based on the number of correct items included.

Activity 2: Responses should indicate that an entry refusal, although rare, could have grave consequences for those involved.

Activity 3: Responses should indicate an understanding of the chapter content.

Activity 4: Answers will depend on where students were born.

Have students complete the Chapter Self-Assessment, Blackline Master 31. Have them choose the product of one of the activities to include in their portfolios. Add the results of any rubrics, checklists, self-assessments, or portfolio assessments, Blackline Masters 2–18 and 31.

Listening Assessment

BLACKLINE MASTER

Make sure each student has a copy of Blackline Master 91 from the Teacher's Resource Book. Play the tape several times and have students complete the activity.

CREAM TAPE

See Chapter 11 Resources, page T192c, for the Listening Assessment tapescript.

Options for Assessment

Vocabulary Assessment

Word Lists

Have students write as many words as they can that relate to the following topic areas: Good Citizens, Becoming a Citizen, the Statue of Liberty, and Ellis Island. For beginning learners, you might supply a list of words and have them sort them by topic.

Writing Assessment

Write a Letter

Have students pretend they are newly arrived immigrants and are writing letters to relatives left behind. The letters should include a greeting and a closing and should tell that the immigrant has arrived safely. Remind students to write in the first person, using informal language and verbs that agree with the subject *I*. Partners can proofread one another's letters.

Language Assessment

BLACKLINE MASTER

Use Blackline Master 90 in the Teacher's Resource Book.

Standardized Test Practice

ACTIVITY BOOK

Use pages 110 and 111. Answers: **1.** It was the best gift the U.S. could have received. **2.** tell about the meaning of the Statue of Liberty **3.** 1900s **4.** 528,431

Preview

Activate Prior Knowledge

Brainstorm Vocabulary

Write the word *government* on the board. Ask students to suggest definitions for the word as well as words associated with the concept. Write all of the suggestions on the board.

Begin a K-W-L chart in which students list what they know about U.S. government.

K: What We Know	The President heads the government.
W: What We Want to Learn	Can the President change a law?
L: What We Learned	

Have students continue to add to the chart throughout the unit.

CHAPTER 12

Government

Tell what you know.

The United States is a democracy. Its government is of the people, by the people, and for the people. What do these pictures tell you about the United States government?

216

Options for Reaching All Students

Beginning

Social Studies: Choose a Leader

Divide students into groups of five or six and tell each group they need to choose a leader. Encourage students to explore and discuss different ways of choosing, such as voting, volunteering, and appointing.

Advanced

Social Studies: Elections

Have students contact the local election board to find out how people in your community register to vote and where some nearby polling places are. Have students use the information gained from these interviews to prepare short oral reports on local elections.

Cooperative Language Experience

Field Trip

Take a field trip to a local board of elections office and have an official show students how voting actually takes place in your community. If possible, have students see and try out a real voting booth and examine a ballot. Then have students write a class story about their experience.

Word Bank

- communism
- democracy
- dictatorship
- monarchy

Talk About It

What kind of government was there in the place where you were born?

Develop Language and Concepts

Present Pages 216 and 217

Read the text with students and talk about the terms in the Word Bank. Give a simple definition for each term and, as appropriate, examples of countries that currently use these systems of government. Then have students comment on the pictures.

Talk with students about what a democracy is. Point out that whenever people live together, they will sooner or later form some kind of government. Explain that people need to have a system to work together.

Have students read and discuss the Talk About It question. Make a list of the countries and types of government on the board as students mention them. Accept students' terminology for the types of governments. Suggest that students who don't know about the type of government where they were born might want to ask older family members for information.

FYI

The photos here show President John F. Kennedy making his inaugural address on January 20, 1961, and the U.S. Senate in the early 1980s.

Present

Activate Prior Knowledge

Review Previously Learned Facts

Ask students to think back to earlier units in the book and to list facts that they learned about U.S. history in those units. If necessary, remind students of the Civil War, the Westward movement, and the Industrial Revolution.

Develop Language and Concepts

Present Pages 218 and 219

ACTIVITY BOOK Read the text with students, pausing after each paragraph to help with pronunciation and vocabulary. Then have students study the pictures and captions. Ask students to speculate on why such great care is taken to protect the original signed Constitution, as evidenced by the picture of the National Archives on page 219.

Point out that in the United States, even the President must obey the same laws as ordinary citizens. Ask students to compare this with how things worked in their home countries.

Talk about why the Bill of Rights is so important to the smooth functioning of democracy. Be sure students realize that this lays down some of the basic rights of citizens that the government cannot take away or try to circumvent. Have students complete Activity Book page 112 and answer the Think About It question.

A Government of Laws

A **constitution** is a list of the basic laws and principles of a group. The Constitution of the United States is the world's oldest written constitution. It is the general plan for the organization and operation of the government of the United States. Because of the Constitution, the United States is governed by the rule of law. Nobody is above the law. All laws in the nation must agree with the Constitution.

▲ Men from each state approved and signed the Constitution on September 17, 1787.

218 LEARN LANGUAGE • SOCIAL STUDIES

Options for Reaching All Students

Beginning

Social Studies: Write Rules

To help students understand the difficulty of determining what should or should not be a law, divide them into groups of four or five and tell them to come up with ten rules that everybody should follow in this class. Have recorders from each group put their rules on the board. Then have the whole class compare and contrast the lists. Help students recognize the logical, ethical, and emotional appeal of various rules. Then have them point out any problems a recommended rule might cause.

Advanced

Social Studies: Research

Divide students into small groups and assign each group a specific Constitutional amendment to research. Help students summarize the main idea of their assigned amendment to make sure they understand it. Tell students they can find copies of the complete Constitution and all amendments in almanacs, encyclopedias, and civics

People can see the signed copy of the Constitution in ▲ Washington, D.C.

The Constitution describes the organization of the national government. The Constitution tells what powers the national government has. The Constitution says what powers are to be shared by the national and state governments. The Constitution also says what powers belong only to the state governments.

In 1791, the first ten **amendments,** or changes to the Constitution, were approved. These ten amendments are called the Bill of Rights. The Bill of Rights says that people have religious and political freedom. It says that people have the right to a trial in front of a jury.

Think About It

Why should citizens of the United States learn about the Constitution?

Language Awareness

Grammar
Or to Signal Appositives or Explanations

Write this sentence on the board: *The first ten amendments, or changes to the Constitution, are called the Bill of Rights.* Talk about the use of the comma and the word *or.* Explain how it helps students know that additional or explanatory information will follow. Give students some more examples. Then ask them to make up some of their own. Check that they can tell when *or* is used to signal a choice and when it is used to signal an apppositive.

Assess ✓

Use class discussion for assessment. Students should be able to

- identify the Constitution as the core document of U.S. government
- tell what the Bill of Rights is

LOOK**AHEAD**

In the next section, students will read about the three branches of government and the separation of powers among them.

texts. You may wish to provide appropriate resources at a suitable reading level. Students should try to find out when each amendment was adopted and why it was instituted; then they should make oral reports to the rest of the class on their findings. Remind students to speak slowly, loudly, and clearly so that their classmates can hear and understand them.

Mixed Ability

Social Studies: State and Local Laws

Divide students into four groups and assign each group one of the following areas of state and/or local laws to find out about in your community: speed limits, sales and income taxes, the death penalty, and funding sources for public schools. Each group should determine what the local and state laws say about their assigned topic and make a poster that describes their findings. Each group should then make an oral report to the rest of the class on their research and use their poster as a prop. Groups should keep a careful record of the source of each fact in case a classmate wants to check the validity of any information presented.

Practice

Activate Prior Knowledge

Apply Ideas to New Situations

Ask students to speculate about what might happen if one person or group had a great deal more power than all other persons or groups. You might want to give an example such as the following: one class can decide where the entire school will go on a school trip or what time lunch will be for the rest of the year. Ask students what problems they think might result from this system.

Develop Language and Concepts

Present Pages 220 and 221

Read the text with students, and provide pronunciation help with difficult terms if necessary. Help students restate information in their own words to check that they comprehend the concepts.

Make a chart on the board with the overall heading of *Legislative Branch*. Divide the chart into two sections, one headed *Senate* and one headed *House*. Then list appropriate facts about each in the proper column.

Help students come to see that the U.S. government, with its three branches, was created as a safeguard against any one group or individual gaining too much power over the others. You may want to tell students about reasons for the American Revolution, especially the seemingly unchecked power of the British king.

The Three Branches of Government

The Constitution of the United States divides the national government into three **branches,** or parts. These three branches make for a **separation of powers** so that no one person or group can get to be too powerful.

The **legislative** branch is the first branch. The legislative branch is the U.S. Congress. It makes the laws of the nation. The Congress meets every year in Washington, D.C.

Options for Reaching All Students

Beginning

Social Studies: Research Senators

Have students find out who the two senators from your state are. If possible, get pictures of these two people from their local offices and have students use these pictures as the center pieces of a bulletin board display that includes facts from the text about the Senate.

Advanced

Social Studies: Research Representatives

Have students find out which House member represents your district and contact that person's local office for a picture and information on the member's position on various issues. Have students make a bulletin board display of what they find out. Remind them to check the spelling of the Representative's name and any special political terms.

Mixed Ability

Math: Representation

Give students the population figures for several states along with the number of representatives each of those states has in the House. Then give students the population of your state and several additional states and have them calculate the number of representatives each has. Students will have to calculate proportions relating to the number of people represented by each House member.

The Congress has two parts: the House of Representatives and the Senate. The Senate has 100 members. Two members are elected from each state. Senators are elected for six-year terms.

The House of Representatives has 435 members. They are elected for two-year terms. The number of representatives from each state is determined by the state's population. Every state has at least one representative. California, the state with the largest population, gets 52 representatives.

Language Awareness

Spelling
Colons

Write this sentence on the board: *The Congress has two parts: the House of Representatives and the Senate.* Point out to students what and where the colon is and how the words that follow it explain the information that came before it. Give students some more examples of sentences using colons. Then ask them to write some examples of their own. Have volunteers put their examples on the board and explain them to the rest of the class.

Model a Strategy

Understand Text Organization

Model how to use text organization to understand and predict content:

The first paragraph in this section tells me that there are three branches of government. The second paragraph mentions the legislative branch. I can predict that the next pages will explain the other two branches. I will look for their names as I read. I will use the three branches to try to organize the facts and remember the important ones. For example, as I read the first paragraph, I will ask myself what the important things are mentioned about the legislative branch.

Cooperative Learning

U.S. History

Have students work in groups and research a topic on the American Revolution or the early history of the United States, such as the Boston Tea Party, the Constitutional Convention, George Washington, and so on. Help students find appropriate-level print or electronic sources on the topics. Have each group create a written report as well as giving an oral report on five interesting facts they learned.

Encourage students to go through all the steps of the writing process for a short research paper. Have them take notes and organize their findings into an outline. Have them check their first drafts for logical organization and correct mechanics. Have them prepare a final version.

Develop Language and Concepts

Present Pages 222 and 223

ACTIVITY BOOK

Read the text with students. Tell them that the diagram is a visual portrayal of the system of checks and balances that keeps any one part of the government from becoming too powerful. Use Activity Book page 113.

Point out the picture of George Washington. Tell students that he led the patriot army during the Revolutionary War. Ask students to speculate on why Washington is sometimes called the "Father of Our Country." Use Activity Book page 115 for further practice.

Make a three-column chart on the board, headed *The U.S. System of Government.* Then divide the chart into three equal sections, headed *Legislative, Executive,* and *Judicial.* Have students come to the board and write facts from the lesson under the appropriate headings. Use Activity Book page 114 for further practice.

Have students answer the Think About It questions.

Model a Strategy

Use Diagrams to Get Meaning

Model a strategy for using diagrams to understand information:

When I look at diagrams, I study the symbols and words carefully to help me understand the information. Diagrams help convey information in a visual form. I can use these visual clues to help me understand the concepts. For example, this

(Continued on page T223.)

The **executive** branch is the second branch. It is headed by the President of the United States. The President is elected for a four-year term. The President lives in the White House in Washington, D.C. The President approves the laws made by Congress. The President is commander in chief of the armed forces. The President deals with foreign governments. The President carries out the laws made by Congress and other duties.

▲ George Washington was the first President of the United States.

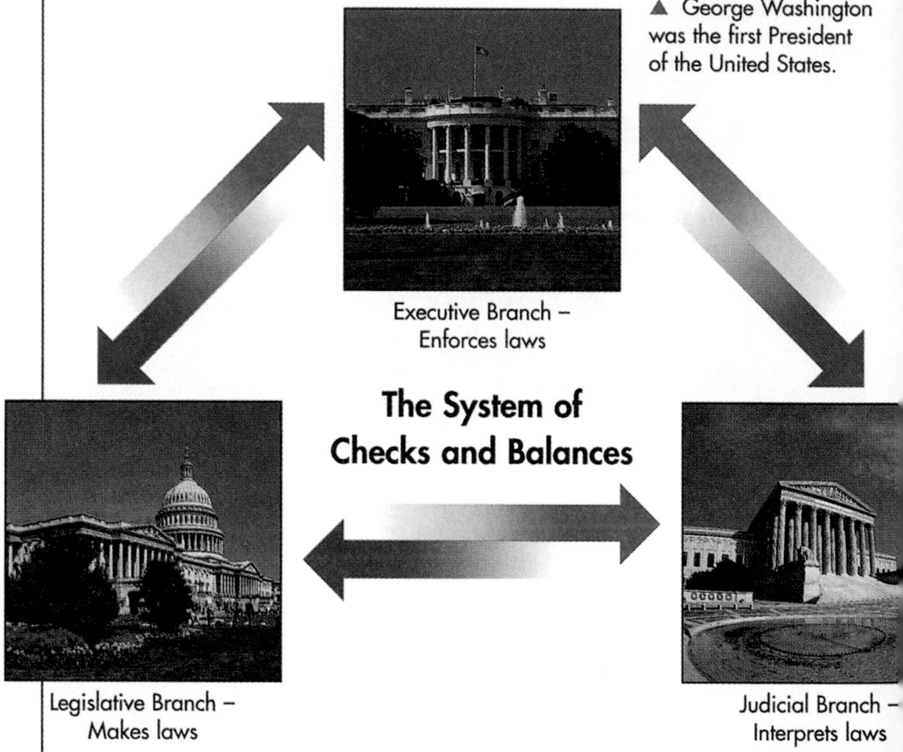

Options for Reaching All Students

Beginning

Language: The Symbolism of Words

Discuss with students the symbolism of the word *branches* as referring to the three main parts of U.S. government. Talk about how the three parts can be described as being like the branches of a tree. Have students draw "trees of government" with three branches, labeling each one.

Advanced

History: Famous Jurists

Have students pick one of these famous Supreme Court Justices to research and write a report on: John Marshall, Oliver Wendell Holmes, Louis Brandeis, Thurgood Marshall, Earl Warren, Sandra Day O'Connor, John Jay, Felix Frankfurter, Hugo Black, William O. Douglas. Remind students that each paragraph in their report should have a clear main idea and supporting details.

Mixed Ability

Social Studies: Branches of Government

Have students work together as a class to develop a visual model of the United States government. Review each of the branches and help students determine the key jobs in each branch and make a list of which offices are elected and which are appointed.

The **judicial** branch is the third branch of government. The judicial branch is the national court system of the country. The Supreme Court is the highest court. Its main job is to decide if laws or actions by government officials are allowed by the Constitution. The court has nine members. The President chooses them, and the Senate votes to approve them. The nine members are appointed for life.

Think About It

In the 1980s, California had 45 representatives. In the 1990s, California has 52 representatives. What does this tell about the population of California?

Some people say that the President is the most powerful person in the world but also has the hardest job in the world. What do you think they mean by this?

diagram uses words to name each branch of the government and tell what each branch does. The arrows are symbols that remind me that the three branches work together. No branch is more important or more powerful then the other branches.

Language Awareness

Grammar
Two-Word Verbs with *Out*

Put the phrase *carries out* on the board. Have students reread the last sentence on page 222. Help them recognize that the sentence would have a different, and nonsensical, meaning if the word *out* were eliminated. Write the words *figure out, look out,* and *find out* on the board in sentence context. Discuss the meaning of each.

Assess

Use class discussion for assessment. Students should be able to

- name the three branches of government and describe their duties
- tell how the members of each branch are chosen

LOOK **AHEAD**

In the next section, students will learn about key amendments to the Constitution.

Connect

Activate Prior Knowledge

Recall Prior Learning

Ask students to recall what they learned about the Constitution and the Bill of Rights earlier in this chapter.

Develop Language and Concepts

Present Pages 224 and 225

Read the title and the text with students. Then have them study the time line. Talk about what a time line is: a visual portrayal of when things happened in the past and in what order. Point out the year labels at the top and bottom of the line. Help students interpret the time line by asking what years the time line covers, what kinds of events are shown, how many years passed between various events, and so on.

Model a Strategy

Use a Time Line

Model a strategy for using a time line:

When I find a time line, I first check to see if there is a title that will help me. This time line's title tells me that it shows some of the amendments, or changes, to the Constitution. Then I look for the years the time line covers. This will give me a general idea of what the time line might include. Then I look at the specific items; this lets me know exactly what the time line can tell me.

Amending the Constitution

The Constitution has been in use for more than 200 years. During all that time, there have been only 27 amendments. Many of the most important amendments have been about the right to vote. These amendments have made it possible for more people to vote.

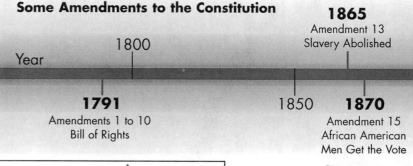

Some Amendments to the Constitution

Year

1791 Amendments 1 to 10 Bill of Rights

1800

1850

1865 Amendment 13 Slavery Abolished

1870 Amendment 15 African American Men Get the Vote

Options for Reaching All Students

Beginning

Critical Thinking: Make a Personal Time Line

Have students make time lines of the significant events in their lives. Have them make their time lines on construction paper or other fairly sturdy material. Help them begin by talking with them about the time frames their time lines should cover. Also help them use the textbook as a model for creating horizontal time lines. Point out that increments of five years might be a convenient organization. Suggest that the time lines begin with the five-year segment that includes their birth. Students may either indicate the important events in their lives with short verbal descriptions or with drawings or family photographs. Encourage them to title their time lines with descriptive phrases such as *Carmen's Life*. Hang the completed time lines on the bulletin board in a display.

Advanced

Critical Thinking: Make a Historical Time Line

Divide students into small groups and give each group a long sheet of butcher paper. Tell students that they are going to work as groups to make historical time lines of important events in the history of the United States during the 1900s. Write these events on the board and tell students to include them on their time lines:

1971
Amendment 26
Voting Age Lowered to 18

1900

1920
Amendment 19
Women Get the Vote

1950

2000

Write About It

In what century did African American men get the right to vote?

In 1971, the voting age was lowered from 21 to 18. How many years have passed since then?

Language Awareness

Grammar
Present Perfect with *Since*

ACTIVITY BOOK

Write this sentence on the board: *The Bill of Rights has been in force since 1791.* Talk about how this sentence tells when something began in the past and is still happening. Review the form of the present perfect: *has/have* + past participle. Then talk about *since* as being the word that alerts readers to when in the past something began. Give students some more examples such as *Since 1971, people over 18 have been able to vote.* Have students create their own sentences that use the present perfect tense using verb phrases such as *have grown, have read, have watched,* and *since.* Use Activity Book page 116.

Assess

Use students' responses to the class discussion and the Write About It questions for assessment. Students should be able to

- interpret the time line
- talk about some of the major amendments to the Constitution

LOOK**AHEAD**

In the next section, students will read several different views on what it means to be an American.

1914 – World War I began; 1918 – World War I ended; 1929 – the Great Depression began; 1933 – Franklin D. Roosevelt became President; 1939 – World War II began; 1945 – World War II ended; 1963 – President John F. Kennedy was assassinated; 1969 – U.S. astronauts walked on the moon; 1974 – Richard M Nixon resigned as President of the United States.

Make a display of the completed time lines on the bulletin board.

QuickCheck

Check that students know how to say dates aloud. Ask them to say important dates in their lives, such as when they were born, when they started school, when they came to the United States, and so on.

Writer's Workshop

Amendments

Have students each choose one amendment on the time line and write about its importance to the idea of democracy. Have students exchange drafts. As a class, develop an editing checklist that students can use to review each other's work.

Connect

Activate Prior Knowledge

Examine Pennies

Pass a few pennies around the class. Have students examine the pennies and find the bust of Abraham Lincoln, whom they studied in Unit 3, on one side. Tell students the building on the other side is the Lincoln Memorial in Washington, D.C. Talk about the building as a symbol of the United States.

Develop Language and Concepts

Present Pages 226 and 227

ACTIVITY BOOK Read the title of the lesson and the introduction with students. Then read the cartoon together. Ask students to summarize what the cartoonist is trying to say about people in the United States. Explain the concept of the United States as a "melting pot" of all nations and groups. Have students look at the two-page spread and its art. Point out the *E pluribus unum* quotation and the fact that it refers to "one." Ask students to infer further what this phrase means. Then read the Lyndon Johnson quotation together. Talk about what President Johnson was trying to convey. Then work together as a class to write additional phrases or sayings that students agree convey the meaning of the United States. Have students complete Activity Book page 117 as part of this exercise.

For practice with the important vocabulary in this chapter, have students do Activity Book page 118.

The United States: Its People and Its Meaning

The United States means different things to different people. Here are some examples.

Options for Reaching All Students

Beginning

Social Studies: Recognize Symbols

Give several small groups of students a dollar bill and several coins. Ask them to find all the symbols of the United States they can and make a list of these things. Students may want to look at pages in their textbooks for some ideas about which symbols to look for. Have students work together as a group to make a bulletin board collage of their own versions of these American symbols. Help students write a label for each symbol, stating its name, where it can be found, and what idea it represents.

Advanced

Critical Thinking: Interpret Quotations

Discuss the fact that literature is one of the primary means by which culture is transmitted. Then put this quotation on the board:

One flag, one land, one heart, one hand,
One nation, evermore!

Tell students that it was written by Oliver Wendell Homes, Sr., a famous

The promise of America is a simple promise. Every person shall share in the blessings of this land. And they shall share on the basis of their merits as a person. They shall not be judged by their color or by their beliefs or by their religion or by where they were born or the neighborhood in which they live.

Lyndon Johnson, 36th President of the United States

"E pluribus unum." (From many, one.)

Motto of the United States of America

Write About It

Which one of these best expresses your feelings about the United States? Write something that expresses your feelings.

Language Awareness

Language Function
Speech Fillers

Point out the use of *Well, let's see* in the cartoon. Explain that people commonly use such speech fillers to give them time to think of an answer. Introduce other fillers such as *hmmm*. Also present *really* as a noncommittal response to show that one is listening. Have pairs of students carry on conversations for several minutes and see how many speech fillers they can use.

FYI

- **The Great Seal of the United States was adopted on June 20, 1782. It is used to authenticate important documents. The eagle holds an olive branch of 13 leaves and 13 olives in one claw and 13 arrows in the other to signify a desire to live in peace but the ability to wage war when necessary.**
- **The phrase *E Pluribus Unum* appears on the face of the Great Seal of the United States and was suggested in 1776 by a committee that included Ben Franklin, John Adams, and Thomas Jefferson. Since 1873, the phrase has been legally required to appear on every U.S. coin that is minted.**

writer and physician of the 1800s, and the father of Oliver Wendell Holmes, Jr., a famous Supreme Court Justice. Analyze the American cultural beliefs embedded in this poem. Then ask students to think about this quotation's applicability to today and to write their ideas as short essays.

Cooperative Learning

Language: Cartoons

Provide students with books or copies of cartoons of various types, such as political cartoons and humorous comic strips. Have students work in groups to read and explain the cartoons. Help them analyze the cartoonist's purpose and point of view. Provide help on vocabulary and cultural meaning as needed. Have groups share their favorite cartoons as appropriate.

Multicultural Connection

Cartoons

Encourage students to describe or bring in examples of cartoons of various types from their home countries. Encourage students to translate or summarize the cartoons. Ask them to identify political and/or cultural beliefs that the cartoons represent.

Connect

Activate Prior Knowledge

Relate Personal Experience

Have students talk about when and where they have seen the U.S. flag displayed. Ask them to compare and contrast this with what they remember about flag displays in their home countries.

Develop Language and Concepts

Present Page 228

PURPLE TAPE

Read the poem with students. Use gestures and simple explanations to clarify vocabulary. Play the poem on Side 2 of the Purple Tape several times and invite students to read along. Help students identify the poem's rhyme scheme and help them appreciate the poem's vivid sensory language.

Language Awareness

Phonics

Consonant Blends

ACTIVITY BOOK

Write the following sets of words on the board: *flag, free; breeze, bright; droop, drifting.* Then underline the consonant blends in each grouping as you pronounce the words and have students repeat them after you. Have students name other words that use these consonant blends: *fl, fr, br, dr, pr, st, sp.* For practice with consonant blends, have students complete Activity Book page 119.

Hang Out the Flags

by James S. Tippett

This is Flag Day.
Hang out the flags;
Watch them rise with the breeze
And droop when it sags.
Hang out the flags.

Hang them from short poles;
Hang them from long.
See their bright colors
Shimmering strong,
Drifting along.

Flags mean our Homeland,
Country we love.
Let them sparkle in sunshine
Proudly above,
Showing our love.

Flags are for you,
And flags are for me.
Hang out the flags
For all men to see.
Let them hang free.

Talk About It

The feeling of love for one's country is called patriotism. Can new citizens to a country feel patriotism? Why do you think so?

Options for Reaching All Students

Beginning

Language: Consonant Blends

Have students look back through this unit to find other examples of words with consonant blends. Have students list these consonant blends in several columns on writing paper. Suggest that they title their columns with the following blends: *br, dr, fl, pr, st,* and *sp.* Have students practice saying the blends aloud, both in isolation and within the listed words.

Advanced

Language: Flag Day

Tell students that in the United States, Flag Day is celebrated on June 14. Have students work in pairs to find out the origin of this special day and how it is observed. Have students write about what they have learned. They may want to concentrate on one aspect, such as the first Flag Day. Remind them to capitalize all proper nouns.

Home Connection

The Meaning of the United States

Have students tell what the United States means to them. Write the responses on the board. Then have students ask one or more adults the same thing. Have students compare and contrast the two groups. You may want to categorize these beliefs into several columns on the board with headings such as *What Kids Believe, What Adults Believe, What Everybody Believes.*

CHAPTER 12

Tell what you learned.

1. The U.S. government is a system of checks and balances. What does that mean?

2. If you could add an amendment to the Constitution, what would it be?

3. Which branch of the government – legislative, executive, or judicial – would you prefer to have a job in? What job would you like to do? Why?

4. The President lives in the White House, but many people say that it is the people's home. What do you think they mean by this?

Assess ✓

Activity 1: Evaluate students' understanding of the phrase.

Activity 2: Evaluate students' ability to describe and comprehend that an amendment affects the entire country.

Activity 3: Evaluate answers for their depth of understanding of the three branches and of the types of jobs each includes.

Activity 4: Responses should indicate that the White House, like all government buildings, belongs to all the people.

Have students complete the Chapter Self-Assessment, Blackline Master 31. Have them choose the product from one of the activities to include in their portfolios. Add the results of any rubrics, checklists, self-assessments, or portfolio assessments, Blackline Masters 2–18 and 31.

Listening Assessment

BLACKLINE MASTER

Make sure each student has a copy of Blackline Master 93 from the Teacher's Resource Book. Play the tape several times and have students complete the activity.

CREAM TAPE

See Chapter 12 Resources, page T192d, for the Listening Assessment tapescript.

Options for Assessment

Vocabulary Assessment

Make Word Webs

Have students create word webs for each branch of the United States government. Ask them to write the name of the branch in the center of the web and then write as many words as they can think of for each branch. Once students have completed their initial web, you might challenge them to add as many synonyms as possible. Provide thesauruses for them to consult.

Writing Assessment

U.S. Government

Have students think about the U.S. system of government. Have them write a four-paragraph paper analyzing it. The first paragraph should state the essay's main idea. Paragraph two should state the positive features of the U.S. government. Paragraph three should state ways the system could be made even better. Paragraph four should state the conclusion.

Language Assessment

BLACKLINE MASTER

Use Blackline Master 92 in the Teacher's Resource Book.

Standardized Test Practice

ACTIVITY BOOK

Use pages 120 and 121. Answers: **1.** a constitution **2.** amendments **3.** Congress **4.** Income

Wrap-Up

Activities

Letter

Help students write a letter to a local elected official, such as a mayor, city council member, or state representative. Review the parts of a letter. Remind students to use formal English and to check their work carefully for capitalization, punctuation, and spelling (especially of the official's name). Possible content might include comments about a local issue of interest to the class, questions about the official's job and responsibilities, or an invitation to speak to the class about working in government. Have students send their letters and share any responses they receive.

Community Groups

Have students research local service organizations that help the community, such as the Kiwanis Club or the Chamber of Commerce. Help students plan a way to contribute to their community, either by working with an established group or by starting their own project to raise money for a good cause, help neighbors in need, or improve the environment. Have students write proposals, using persuasive language to tell the benefits of their plan. If feasible, have students put their plans into action.

Patriotic Songs

Teach the class patriotic songs about the United States, such as "America," "God Bless America," and "You're a Grand Old Flag." Discuss the similarities and differences between the songs. After listening to several songs, have students state and explain their personal preferences. Ask students why they think countries have patriotic songs.

Community Survey

Have the class learn about their community's diversity by surveying neighbors and local business people. Have each student ask at least two community members from what country they or their ancestors immigrated from to the United States. Have students pool their findings to create a world map with stars marking the countries of origin.

Discussing the Theme

Review with students how the requirements for citizenship and the structure of government determine the character of a nation. Choose from the following activities that will demonstrate to students how much they have learned and how useful that information is:

- Have students tape-record a list of new words learned.
- Have students diagram the basic structure of United States government, labeling each branch. Review with the class how the branches work separately and together.
- Discuss with students the differences between United States government and the governments of their home countries. Encourage each student to contribute at least one fact about the government of his or her home country.
- Remind students that Ellis Island served as the gateway to the United States between 1892 and 1954. Have them draw pictures showing their own arrival in the United States.
- Have students discuss situations in which the words they have learned will be useful, such as in social studies classes, in discussing local politics, and in working to become a naturalized citizen.

Sharing the Project

Use the invitation form, Blackline Masters 32–33, to invite family members to school to see the students' plays.

Provide class time for dress rehearsals. After the rehearsals, help students critique one another's plays. You might want to make audio or videorecordings of one or more rehearsals so students can evaluate and improve their movement, placement, gestures, volume, stress, pacing, and pronunciation.

Help students create a name for their theater groups, such as "The Ellis Island Players," and make simple programs listing the plays and the students involved in each. You might have students write brief biographies to include in the program. Photocopy the programs for distribution at the performance.

After the plays, serve typically American refreshments, such as lemonade, apple pie, or popcorn.

Signs of Success!

Duplicate a copy of this checklist for each student.

Name: ______________________________

Refer to the checklist below for a quick determination of how a student is progressing toward transitioning out of ESL instruction.

Objectives

- ☐ Can describe the process of naturalization.
- ☐ Tells about the Statue of Liberty and Ellis Island
- ☐ Describes the United States as a democracy.
- ☐ Names the three branches of government.
- ☐ Discusses the Constitution and some key amendments.
- ☐ Lists views on the meaning of being an American.

Language Awareness

Understands/Uses:

- ☐ *by* + gerund answers to *how* questions
- ☐ expressions of necessity: *must* and *have to*
- ☐ spelling rules for gerunds
- ☐ present perfect
- ☐ sequence of tenses: use of *would*
- ☐ *or* to signal appositives or explanations
- ☐ colons
- ☐ two-word verbs with *out*
- ☐ present perfect with *since*
- ☐ speech fillers

Hears/Pronounces/Reads:

- ☐ silent letters in words
- ☐ words with double *ss*
- ☐ words that rhyme
- ☐ consonant blends

Learning Strategies:

- ☐ Uses a Venn diagram
- ☐ Understands use of bulleted text
- ☐ Understands text organization
- ☐ Uses diagrams to get meaning
- ☐ Uses a time line

Comments

____

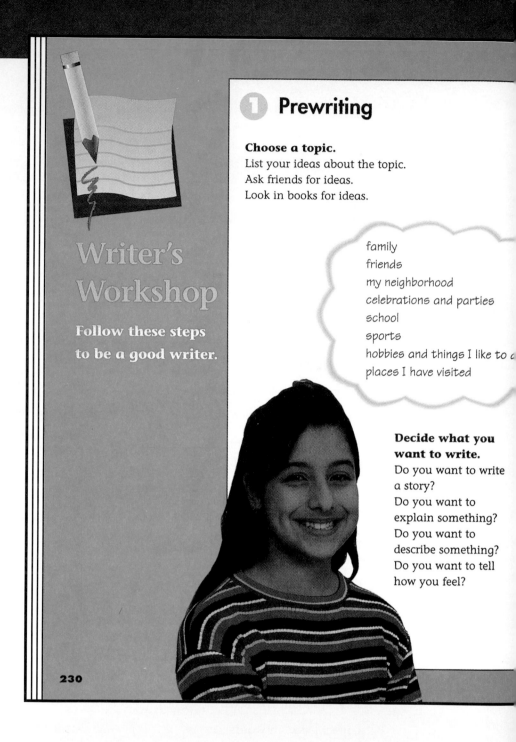

Writer's Workshop

Follow these steps to be a good writer.

1 Prewriting

Choose a topic.
List your ideas about the topic.
Ask friends for ideas.
Look in books for ideas.

- family
- friends
- my neighborhood
- celebrations and parties
- school
- sports
- hobbies and things I like to
- places I have visited

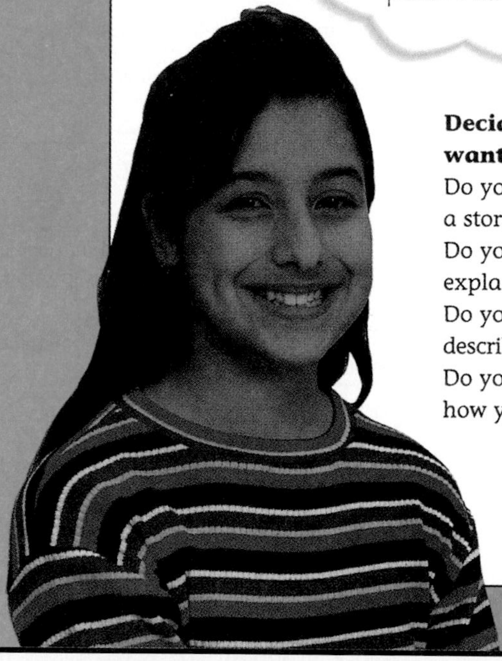

Decide what you want to write.
Do you want to write a story?
Do you want to explain something?
Do you want to describe something?
Do you want to tell how you feel?

Focus your topic.
Use a graphic organizer.
Focus on one idea.

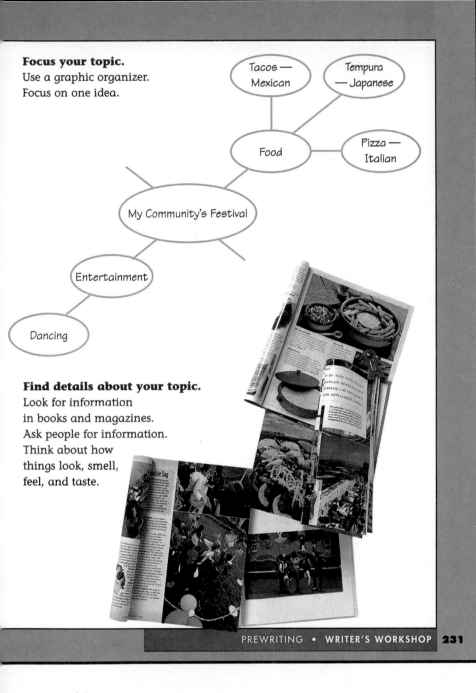

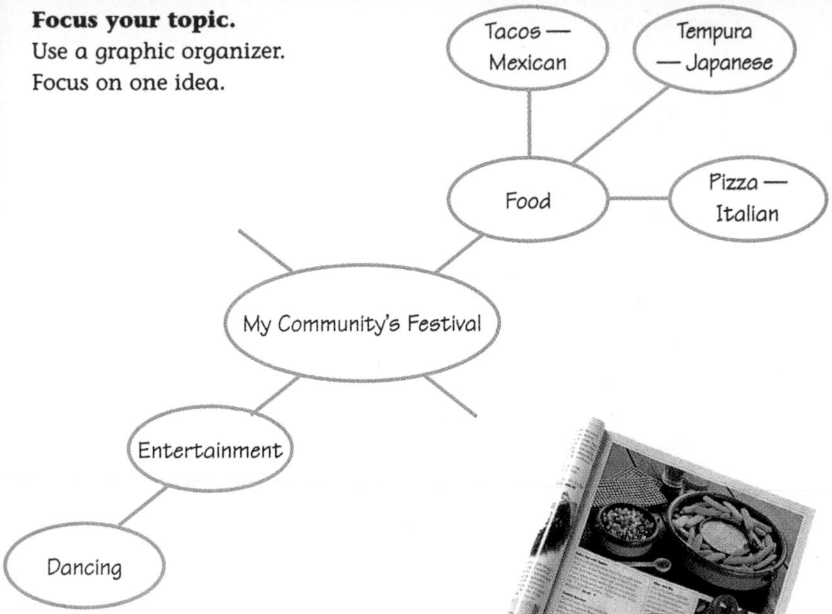

Find details about your topic.
Look for information
in books and magazines.
Ask people for information.
Think about how
things look, smell,
feel, and taste.

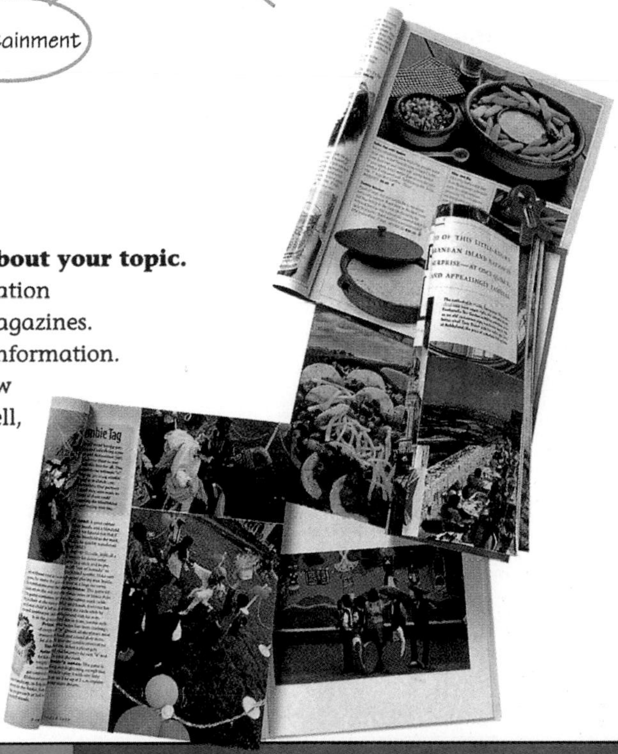

② Drafting

Get what you need.
Get paper and pencils.
Get your graphic organizer and list of ideas.
Sit in a comfortable place.

Set a goal.
How much will you write now?

Read your notes.
What do you want to say first?

Keep writing.
Write down all your ideas.
Don't worry about spelling and punctuation now.

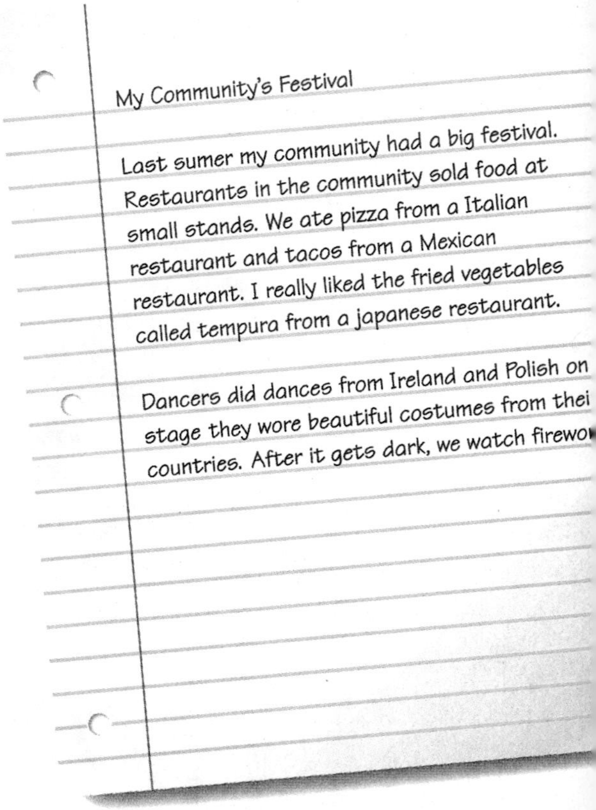
My Community's Festival
Last sumer my community had a big festival.
Restaurants in the community sold food at
small stands. We ate pizza from a Italian
restaurant and tacos from a Mexican
restaurant. I really liked the fried vegetables
called tempura from a japanese restaurant.
Dancers did dances from Ireland and Polish on
stage they wore beautiful costumes from thei
countries. After it gets dark, we watch firewo

③ Revising

Read what you wrote. Ask yourself:
Does my story have a beginning, a middle, and an end?
Is my information correct?
What parts should I keep?
What parts should I leave out?

I think I need a better ending.

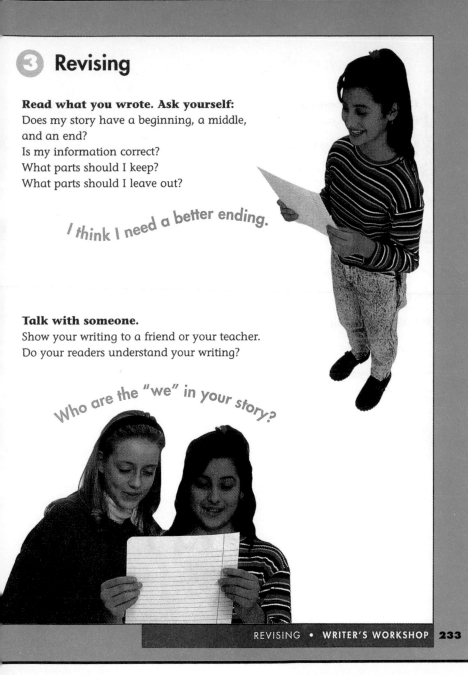

Talk with someone.
Show your writing to a friend or your teacher.
Do your readers understand your writing?

Who are the "we" in your story?

4 Proofreading

Check your spelling.
Look in a dictionary or ask for help.

Look for capital letters.

Look for correct punctuation.

Make a new copy.

≡	**Make a capital.**
/	**Make a small letter.**
∧	**Add something.**
℘	**Take out something.**
⊙	**Add a period.**
¶	**New paragraph.**

My Community's Festival

Last sum(m)er my community had a big festival. I went to the festival with friends from my school. Restaurants in the community sold food at small stands. We ate pizza from a(n) Italian restaurant and tacos from a Mexican restaurant. I really liked the fried vegetables called tempura from a japanese restaurant.

Dancers did folk dances from Ireland and ~~Polish~~ Poland on a stage⊙ they wore beautiful costumes from their countries. After it ~~gets~~ got dark, we watch(ed) fireworks. ¶ I want to go to the festival again next summer so I can taste more foods. I can't wait!

5 Presenting

Share your writing.
Read it aloud to your family or classmates.
Make a book. Lend the book to your family or classmates.

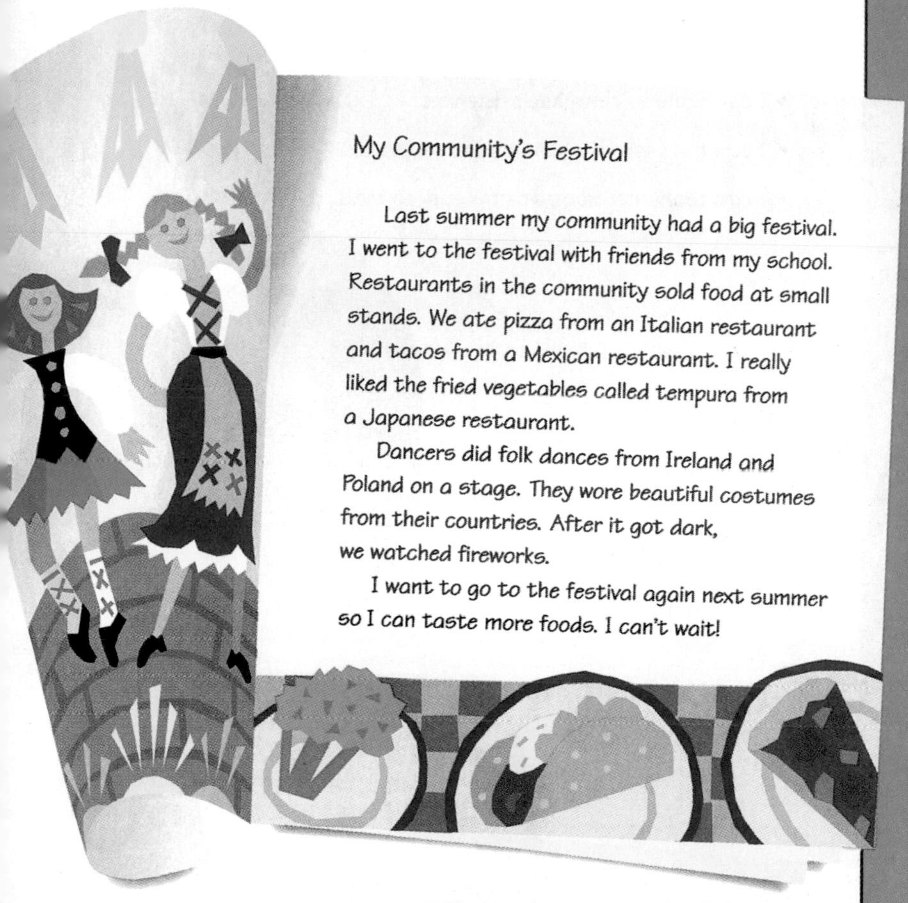

My Community's Festival

Last summer my community had a big festival. I went to the festival with friends from my school. Restaurants in the community sold food at small stands. We ate pizza from an Italian restaurant and tacos from a Mexican restaurant. I really liked the fried vegetables called tempura from a Japanese restaurant.

Dancers did folk dances from Ireland and Poland on a stage. They wore beautiful costumes from their countries. After it got dark, we watched fireworks.

I want to go to the festival again next summer so I can taste more foods. I can't wait!

What a Good Writer Can Do

- I plan before I write.
- I can write about things I know. I can write about my family, my school, and myself.
- I can write stories with a beginning, a middle, and an end.
- I can ask others to read my work.
- I can write in complete sentences.
- I can put periods at the end of sentences.
- I can make my handwriting easy to read.

Scott Foresman

ESL

Scope and Sequence

SCOPE AND SEQUENCE 1

Chapter		Objectives	Content Focus	Language Awareness Objectives	Learning Strategies
1	**Families**	Tell who is in a family; tell what families do; tell how families change.	social studies, science, reading, literature	plurals, pronouns, present tense, capital letters, initial *f*, color words	Use what you know; predict content.
2	**Growing and Changing**	Tell new things children can do as they grow; tell how children and animals grow and change.	science, math, literature	adjectives that mean "more," plurals, prepositions *in* and *on*, color words, proper nouns, offering to do something, typographic devices, initial *g, l, b*	Use picture clues; compare and contrast; use pictures to get meaning; main idea; draw conclusions.
3	**At School**	Tell how children get to school; tell what's seen at school; name rules; tell what's done at school.	social studies, math, literature	pronouns—*I* and *we,* days of the week, question words, *many,* contractions, initial *m,* initial *c* /k/, initial *d, y,* greetings	Use pictures; recognize patterns; understand a process; paraphrase/retell; use context clues.
4	**Learning**	Name some things done alone and some things done in a group; name things practiced at school; tell how children feel at school; tell what's learned in school.	social studies, health, reading, literature	giving praise, infinitives, verbs, verb *can,*pronouns, multiple meanings—*like, if*	Use picture clues; recognize cause and effect; recognize repetition.
5	**Neighbors**	Tell where people live; tell what neighbors are; tell what a community is; tell how maps help people.	social studies, math, literature	question words, initial *n,* capitalization, opposites, initial *p,* plurals, words for noises, position words, initial *s,* initial *r,* rhyming words	Generalize; use a map; brainstorming; use what you know; make inferences; draw conclusions.
6	**Animals and Their Homes**	Name places where animals live; name animals that live in trees, in ponds, and in fields; name animals that are pets; tell how to care for pets.	science, math, reading, literature	prepositional phrases, initial *t,* verbs, number and verbs, initial *w,* names for animal babies, future tense, initial *h*	Reread; use pictures; visualize word problems; make predictions based on prior knowledge.
7	**How You Can Feel Safe**	Name places where safety is important; name people who help keep others safe; name rules that help people stay safe.	health, science, literature	word families, verbs + *-er,* multiple meanings, rules, initial soft *g,* short *i,* word order, punctuation, exclamation mark	Use what you know; compare and contrast; predicting; use selective attention; recognize reality and fantasy; make predictions.

Chapter		Objectives	Content Focus	Language Awareness Objectives	Learning Strategies
8	**How You Can Feel Healthy**	Tell benefits of exercising; name ways to keep clean and healthy; name foods that assist growth and good health.	health, math, literature	adjectives—adding *-y,* pronoun—*they,* antonyms, count vs. noncount nouns, days of the week, period, short *a,* expressing gratitude	Use pictures; use a chart; finding the total
9	**Using Our Senses**	Name the senses; tell how to take care of the eyes and ears; tell how to make high and low sounds; tell what body part is used for each sense.	health, science, literature	verbs, antonyms, plural forms, giving instructions, capital letters, short *o,* multiple meanings—*went,* places in a house, past tense	Imagining; understand cause and effect; generalize; make predictions; recognize reality and fantasy; draw conclusions.
10	**How We See and Hear**	Compare how people and animals see; compare how people and animals hear; compare things seen and heard.	science, math, reading, literature	short *e,* expression *very well,* capitalization and punctuation, numerals and number words, questions and answers, short *u,* rhyming words	Activate prior knowledge; following directions.
11	**The Four Seasons**	Name the four seasons; name the months of the year; tell how the weather changes from season to season; tell what seasonal things people do; tell how people dress according to the weather in each season.	science, social studies, reading, literature	phrases, root words, consonant blend *cl,* capitalization/punctuation, adjectives, contractions	Predict content; get information; understand that numerals show sequence; compare and contrast.
12	**Trees**	Tell ways people can save and protect trees; tell ways people use trees; tell why people and animals need trees.	social studies, science, literature	long *a,* period and question mark, opposites, verbs, pronoun—*they,* adjectives—color words, superlatives, adjectives of size—*small/long/wide*	Use pictures for meaning; visualize; use planning; use pictures to get meaning; understand type conventions; understand commas and periods; use context clues.

SCOPE AND SEQUENCE 2

Chapter		Objectives	Content Focus	Language Awareness Objectives	Learning Strategies
1	**People and Places**	Name different kinds of groups; tell what different groups do; name places in a community; give reasons why people go to each place; name states in the U.S.; begin recognizing animal groups and their places.	social studies, science, literature	present tense; sentence patterns; capitalization; irregular plurals; rhyming words with long *a, e,* and *i;* informal English expression *OK;* statements showing approval; verbs	Use picture details; read maps; use pictures to get meaning; recognize fact and fantasy; summarize.
2	**Animals and Their Habitats**	Name animals and some of their attributes; understand what animals get from their habitats; tell about groups animals belong to; tell about pets and their habitats.	science, math, reading, literature	subject/verb agreement, short *a,* explaining choices, comparatives, similes, rhyme	Use pictures for meaning; understand patterns; understand main idea; count how many; remember details.
3	**How People Work**	Name community workers; tell how workers help us; name work-places; understand what people's needs are; tell the difference between needs and wants; tell what animals' needs are.	social studies, science, reading, literature	verbs, related words, words *needs* and *wants,* contractions, rhyme	Use pictures for meaning; use title to predict; note repeated words; find a way to classify; use what you know.
4	**What Animals Do**	Tell ways animals work to meet their needs; tell how animals protect themselves; tell how protective coloration works.	science, math, literature	subject/verb agreement; blends *sm, sk,* and *spr;* giving directions; punctuation; contractions; verbs; describing; rhyme	Recognize main idea; recognize sentence patterns; follow directions; understand specialized language; use prior knowledge; use pictures to get meaning; summarize.
5	**How We Have Fun**	Name toys and games; name ways to play alone and to play with friends; tell how to get exercise while playing; name ways that exercise is good for you; tell which parts of the body are used with different exercises.	health, math, literature	final consonant *s /z/,* long *i,* number and present progressive tense, irregular past tense, future tense, pronouns, contractions, addressing family members and friends	Visualize; use imagery; recognize cause and effect; use pictures for meaning.
6	**How Things Move**	Tell which things can be pushed or pulled; understand force; tell what magnets do; understand pushing and pulling activities that are fun.	science, social studies, reading, literature	consonant blend *tr,* adjectives, prepositions, present progressive, future tense, imperatives	Use picture clues; ask questions to get information; use word structure; use context clues.

Chapter		Objectives	Content Focus	Language Awareness Objectives	Learning Strategies
7	Plants We Eat	Name the parts of plants; tell what each part of a plant does; name plants we eat; tell which parts of plants we eat; name grains and foods made from grains.	science, social studies, literature	consonant blends *st* and *str, a few* and *a lot (of),* count vs. noncount nouns, passive expressions, sentence patterns, nouns and verbs, long *o* spelled *ow* and *oa*	Use pictures for meaning; understand that numerals show sequence; find a way to classify; locate patterns; explain a process; summarize.
8	Where We Buy Food	Tell where fruits and vegetables are grown; tell where foods are purchased; tell which foods can be purchased at which places; name kinds of restaurants.	social studies, math, reading, literature	phrases, capitalization, making requests, numerals and number words, possessives, long *a*/short *a,* pronouns	Preview text; monitor meaning; plan to read orally; use pictures and text to predict; use context clues.
9	Day and Night	Name things in the sky; tell what causes night and day; tell about the sun; tell about the moon; tell why a calendar is important.	science, social studies, literature	homophones, compound words, expressing time, irregular past tense, comparatives, similes, describing, pattern and rhyme	Use a diagram; generalize; predict content; make comparisons; use context; use prior knowledge.
10	Long Ago and Today	Tell about the first people in North America; tell about early Spanish settlers of North America; tell about the Pilgrims; name U.S. holidays.	social studies, math, literature	telling why, time expressions, ordinal numbers, questions and answers, present tense, onomatopoeia	Understand chronology; use a calendar; summarize.
11	Where We Find Water	Name sources of water; tell how some bodies of water differ; find bodies of water on a map; tell what happens when there is too much or too little water; tell how water can be saved.	social studies, science, literature	adjectives, capitalization, expressions of amount—*little, a lot (of),* long *a,* short *u,* possessives, informal expressions, short and long *i*	Use context clues; use a map; visualize; preview a story; recognize cause and effect; paraphrase/retell.
12	Water and the Weather	Tell how rain makes people feel; tell about clouds; tell where rain comes from; tell about water vapor; tell about the water cycle.	science, math, reading, literature	related words, forming questions, prepositional phrases —*from the, to the,* comparatives, punctuation, rhyming words, compound words	Check inferences; self-assess; preview directions; solve problems.

SCOPE AND SEQUENCE 3

Chapter		Objectives	Content Focus	Language Awareness Objectives	Learning Strategies
1	**Life on a Farm**	Tell what farmers do; identify products that come from a farm; tell how wheat is grown; read a thermometer.	social studies, science, literature	singular and plural nouns, subject-verb agreement—*is/are,* simple present tense, recognize commands, /p/ and /b/	Use time expressions; follow directions; recognize patterns in English.
2	**Life in the City**	Tell about a community; name services and goods in a city; solve math story problems; name parts of a city; name state capitals; name the five food groups.	social studies, math, health, literature	sentence structure, consonant sounds /g/ and /k/, capitalization of proper nouns, numbers as words, slang/informal English, extending an invitation, present progressive tense, the *s* sound	Reread; use a map; recognize opinions; type conventions; draw conclusions.
3	**How You Use Light**	Name lights used in the past and today; read a time line of lights; tell uses of lights in a community; explain how people use their eyes to see.	social studies, science, reading, literature	words in a series, time words, *when* and *where,* the sound of long *i,* contractions, rhyme	Recognize time and sequence; use a time line; visualize; use a diagram.
4	**What Light Can Do**	Tell what light can and cannot move through; identify what makes light bend and bounce back; use a prism to see rainbow colors; put on a shadow play.	science, social studies, literature	*some, all,* or *none;* prepositions of location *on, in, under;* commands; nouns as adjectives; communicating with sounds; expressing the same idea with different expressions; plurals of words ending in *-y;* alliteration	Explain a process; use pictures for meaning; paraphrase; recognize main idea.
5	**How You Make Sound**	Tell how sound is made; demonstrate vibrations; tell how sounds are different; name musical instruments from around the world.	science, social studies, literature	the *v* sound, *can* and *can't,* adjectives, the pronoun *it,* past tense, long *a* and short *a,* rhyme, onomatopoeia	Record information; recognize sentence patterns; use type conventions; understand specialized vocabulary.
6	**How You Use Sound**	Tell how people hear sound; name parts of the ear; tell how ears help animals survive; find out how well people hear; name inventions in communication.	science, social studies, reading, literature	the sound of *ear,* singular/plural agreement—*has/have, you* as understood subject in commands, *can* + verb + complement, *so . . . that,* long *o* and short *o*	Read a diagram; set a purpose for reading; recognize main idea; distinguish between fact and opinion.
7	**Plants, Animals, and Climate**	Describe the climate of deserts and forests; tell how a cactus can live in the desert; tell how animals live in a forest; tell how veterinarians help animals.	science, social studies, literature	*some* or *other;* adjectives; long *e;* pronouns *he, she, they; many, most, some,* and *all; they* and *them; once, twice;* words for the senses	Compare and contrast; use a Venn diagram; use picture captions; reread sentences.

Chapter		Objectives	Content Focus	Language Awareness Objectives	Learning Strategies
8	**Weather and People**	Tell how weather affects the way people live; tell how people dress for the weather; identify climates in various parts of the world; tell how to stay healthy in hot weather; tell how to stay healthy in cold weather.	social studies, health, literature	antonyms; infinitives of purpose; consonant blends *sl, pl, cl;* commands; similes; simple past tense—questions and answers; quantity expressions	Recognize cause-effect relationships; recognize main idea; use a map key; use pictures for meaning, use patterns to aid in reading.
9	**What Shelters Are Made Of**	Name materials used to build homes; tell how people found building materials long ago; tell how homes changed over time; name steps in building a beaver lodge.	social studies, science, literature	beginning and ending consonant sounds *st* and *ch, house* or *home,* past tense verbs ending in *t,* sequence words, short *i* and long *i,* identify a sentence, end punctuation, parenthetical expressions	Recognize a pattern; read a time line; use numbers.
10	**How Shelters Are Built**	Name tools and materials and tell how they are used; tell how bricks and glass are made; name simple machines; name shapes in houses.	science, math, reading, literature	forms of *build, /ks/,* subject-verb agreement—*is* and *are,* show possibility—*can be,* phrases that tell *where* or *when*	Reread to understand; understand a process; use pictures for meaning, use time words.
11	**Changing the Earth**	Tell how people affect the environment; tell about a local habitat; tell how children can save a rain forest; name endangered or extinct animals; write a letter to an environmental group.	science, social studies, reading, literature	special singular and plural nouns, consonant blends—*str* and *thr,* context and picture clues, *when* clauses, making requests, possessive adjectives	Set a purpose for reading; use pictures to follow directions; use context clues; take notes.
12	**Pollution**	Name causes of water pollution; name ways to prevent water pollution; tell how to find out how clean the air is; tell how recycling works; name things that can be recycled; tell what people can do to prevent pollution.	science, social studies, literature	gerunds, sounds /h/ and /j/, conjunctions—*and,* verbs with *up, was going to,* prepositions—*under, above;* adverbs of degree—*very, too*	Paraphrase; draw conclusions; recognize language patterns; recognize supporting details; use prior knowledge to predict; use type conventions.

Chapter		Objectives	Content Focus	Language Awareness Objectives	Learning Strategies
1	**The American West Today**	Name the states and landforms in the West; name crops farmers grow in the West; describe ranching, fishing, and mining in the West.	social studies, science, reading, literature	singular and plural nouns; verbs; /m/ and /n/; simple present tense; place an order; antonyms	Use a map key; recognize a pattern; read money amounts.
2	**Settling the West**	Explain why people went west; describe the trip west; tell what settlers took with them; talk about the Oregon Trail; talk about the dangers and benefits of prairie fires.	social studies, science, literature	*want* + infinitive; household items; /w/; habitual *would;* quotation marks; recount past activities; exclamations; metaphors	Set a purpose for reading; visualize; use pictures for meaning; recognize a personal title.
3	**You Are a Living Thing!**	Explain that all living things are made of cells; describe how cells grow; tell why living things need energy; demonstrate that yeast is a living thing; tell how people communicate.	science, social studies, reading, literature	/k/ and /s/ spelled *c;* simple present vs. present progressive tense; questions with *what* and *how;* onomatopoeia; describe activities with other people; using *cannot*	Use pictures for meaning; classify to understand; use chronology to understand.
4	**Living in Your Ecosystem**	Define an ecosystem; explain how an ecosystem works; make an ecosystem; use bat facts to solve math problems.	science, math, literature	compare—*as* + adjective + *as;* conjunctions—*when* and *as;* diphthong /oi/; *how many* and *how much;* prepositions of location; noun phrases with *who;* express obligation	Use labels to understand; prepare for an activity; use pictures for word meaning; visualize a relationship.
5	**The First Americans**	Name some American Indian shelters and the resources used to build them; identify the parts of a buffalo and how they were used; describe American Indian crafts; tell what an archaeologist does; name some materials that are good insulators.	social studies, science, literature	pronoun *they;* sentence patterns with *use . . . for;* present perfect tense; sequence words *first, second, third, last;* deductions with *must be;* /j/; fraction words, words with *ing*	Classify information; use numerals for sequence; predict content; use context clues; visualize story details.
6	**The Aztec Indians**	Name some crops that Aztec farmers grew; describe Aztec arts and crafts; name foods that come from the Aztecs; explain how the Aztec calendar worked.	social studies, math, literature	past tense verbs; consonant blend *st;* expressing preference; *before* and *after;* adverbs; *I am . . .*	Use context clues; set a purpose for reading; paraphrase.

Chapter		Objectives	Content Focus	Language Awareness Objectives	Learning Strategies
7	**You Are What You Eat!**	Explain that people need food for energy; describe a balanced diet; describe a food pyramid; tell where foods grow.	health, social studies, literature	compare past abilities to present abilities with *can/couldn't;* expressing people's needs; *yes/no* questions with *did;* adverbs *well* and *poorly;* /ü/ and /yü/; /fr/	Use graphics for information.
8	**Let's Eat!**	Use a diagram to explain digestion; tell what saliva does; explain why people feel hungry; describe how people learned about vitamins.	science, social studies, literature	words for parts of the body; *when* clauses; *yes/no* questions with *do/does;* /v/ and /b/; express obligation; prepositional phrases; define foreign words; *I like* + noun vs. *I like* + infinitive	Understand specialized vocabulary; use phonetic spellings; use pictures for meaning; read to find information.
9	**Life in the Rain Forest**	Tell where rain forests grow; name types of species that live in a rain forest; describe a food chain in a rain forest; tell the history of rubber.	science, social studies, literature	prepositions *above, below, along, through;* give examples with *such as;* pronoun referents; /l/ and /r/; comparisons; frequency expressions; present and past tenses	Identify main idea; use pictures for meaning; use a map key; use punctuation to read.
10	**Using Our Forests**	Tell why people need trees; explain why people need rain forests; find rain forest products; describe a rain forest scientist; tell how people are trying to save the rain forests.	social studies, science, reading, literature	consonant blends *gr* and *tr;* past tense of irregular verbs; possibility—*might;* present progressive tense; use *please*	Use graphics to compare; use prior knowledge.
11	**Regions of Our Country**	Identify directions on a map; name regions of the U.S.; read a map; make a map; recognize state symbols.	social studies, science, literature	form plurals; capitalization of proper nouns; /sh/; expressions of amount—*some, most, each, a lot of;* polite requests; rhyme scheme	Use sources of information; recognize patterns.
12	**State Histories**	Tell events in the history of California; read a time line; read a population bar graph; read a population line graph.	social studies, math, literature	ordinal numbers; irregular past-tense verbs; prefix—*re;* comparatives and superlatives; digraph *th;* express wants; /kw/ sound represented by *qu;* contractions	Read time lines; use prior knowledge; read a line graph; use pictures for meaning; understand author's point of view.

SCOPE AND SEQUENCE 5

Chapter		Objectives	Content Focus	Language Awareness Objectives	Learning Strategies
1	**The Science of Sound**	Tell what sound is; tell how people hear; make and use an ear trumpet; read a decibel graph.	science, math, literature	the *v* sound, singular and plural nouns, action words as directions, comparatives, rhyming sounds, the long *o* sound	Recognize cause and effect; use a graph; use pictures to predict.
2	**Uses of Sound**	Make sounds of different pitch; tell how musical instruments make sound; make a musical instrument; name events people celebrate with music.	science, social studies, literature	superlatives; passive voice expressions; count vs. non-count nouns; the sound /ng/ in the final position; time expressions; suffixes *-er, -ist;* idioms	Use a graph; use classification; work cooperatively; use pictures for meaning; use intonation.
3	**The Earth Is Not Flat!**	Tell why the Indies were important; identify Columbus and describe his voyage; tell about the meeting of Columbus and the Taino people; explain how a compass works.	social studies, science, literature	use language for buying, selling, and trading; past-tense verbs; word origins; digraphs in the final position, *-sh, -th;* verb tenses; asking questions; expressions of frequency	Use pictures for meaning; visualize; make inferences; make a model to understand meaning.
4	**The Aztecs and the Spaniards**	Describe the Aztec city of Tenochtitlán; explain how Cortés conquered the Aztecs; name the parts of a horse; make an Aztec sun god mask.	social studies, science, reading, literature	prepositions *in, on;* saying dates; /ėr/ spelled *er, ir, ear, or;* making general statements; verbs in directions; rhythm and rhyme	Identify main idea; use patterns; understand a process.
5	**Precious Water**	Explain differences between fresh water and salt water; tell why living things need water; name ways people use water; do an experiment with salty water.	social studies, science, literature	capitalization of proper nouns; infinitives; use of *as;* the pronoun *it;* /y/ in *Yaya* vs. /j/ in *magical;* the sound of /v/; clauses with *that*	Find a topic sentence; read on to get meaning; recognize supporting details; record observations; summarize.
6	**The Forms of Water**	Name the forms of water; explain the water cycle; do a water cycle experiment; describe water sources in the Sahara Desert.	science, social studies, literature	sounds for *s,* the *-tion* ending, long vowel sounds, simple present tense for presenting facts; asking questions	Use pictures for meaning; use context to get meaning; follow directions; use imagery to understand poetry.
7	**Coming to America**	Name countries from which settlers came; tell why settlers came to America; tell about a journey to America; describe a beaver.	social studies, science, reading	time expressions; short *a,* long *a;* past progressive tense; describing; transportation words; *there is, there are*	Visualize story details; formulate opinions; summarize.

Chapter		Objectives	Content Focus	Language Awareness Objectives	Learning Strategies
8	**Life in the Colonies**	Tell something about Jamestown; become familiar with the names of the thirteen colonies; tell something about the New England, Middle, and Southern Colonies; read a graph on tobacco exports.	social studies, math, literature	infinitives; names of languages; past tense of irregular verbs; comparisons— *more, less*; verbs joined by *and;* comparisons—*as* + adjective + *as;* short *i* and long *i*	Recognize cause and effect; use a Venn Diagram; read a bar graph; make predictions; use context clues; paraphrasing.
9	**What Do You Read?**	Tell why people read; name materials people read; identify the parts of a front page; identify the sections of a newspaper; use word clues to solve story problems.	language arts, math, literature	infinitives; letter-sound correspondence—*f, ph, th;* report information; clauses with *that;* use of *do;* make exclamations	Use pictures to answer questions; read story problems; decode unfamiliar words.
10	**What Makes a Good Story?**	Define setting, characters, and plot; read a plot diagram; write a plot diagram; tell about storytelling around the world.	language arts, social studies, literature	subject/verb agreement—*is, are;* present tense verbs; question marks; the sound /s/ spelled *c;* idioms; consonant digraph—*sh;* contractions; expressing approval and disapproval; rhyming words	Recall the plot; make a plot diagram; skim and scan; use pictures for meaning; set a purpose for reading; ask questions to understand word meanings.
11	**Problems with England**	Tell that America's thirteen colonies belonged to England; explain why some colonists were angry with England; describe what happened at the Boston Tea Party; write and solve a sales tax problem.	social studies, math, literature	*only/many,* idioms, irregular past tense, the short *e* sound, sound words, indefinite pronouns and adverbs, the present perfect tense, long and short *i*	Draw conclusions; take notes; recognize point of view; follow directions.
12	**The War for Independence**	Identify Thomas Jefferson as the writer of the Declaration of Independence; identify George Washington and describe conditions at Valley Forge; tell what happened at the Battle of Yorktown; use capital letters; name important beliefs in the Declaration of Independence.	social studies, language arts, literature	pronouns—*they, he, it;* describe conditions; sounds *or* and *ar;* capitalization of proper nouns; adjective/pronoun—*these*	Summarize; use a time line; generalize; read on to get meaning.

Chapter		Objectives	Content Focus	Language Awareness Objectives	Learning Strategies
1	**Digging Up Fossils**	Describe dinosaurs; tell how scientists learn about dinosaurs; tell when dinosaurs lived; compare old and new ideas about dinosaurs.	science, art, literature	plurals; the idiom *turn into; before* and *after;* consonant *p;* consonant blends *pl* and *pr;* past tense of *be;* antonyms; conjunctions *or* and *and;* synonyms	Use headings; recognize patterns in English; read a chart; use action words in directions; remember details keep track of details.
2	**Digging Up Ancient Objects**	Name ancient Egyptian artifacts; tell how archaeologists learn about the past; tell about ancient Egyptian burial; tell about King Tut's tomb; tell about hieroglyphics.	social studies, language, reading, literature	letters *f* and *ph;* past tense; expressions *years old/years ago;* large numbers; quantity words *all/most/many/several;* rhyme	Use diagrams for meaning; keep track of chronology.
3	**Types of Fitness**	Name various types of physical fitness; describe steps one must take to be fit; identify body parts; understand and use commands in exercises; make a fitness plan; talk about games played around the world.	health, social studies, literature	*when* clauses; numbers expressed as words; gerunds; present tense; initial consonants *b* and *f;* contractions	Rehearse steps; read a chart; use reference resources; use techniques to memorize.
4	**Olympic Challenges**	Describe the history of the Olympic Games; explain how the modern games differ from the ancient Olympics; name various Olympic events; identify skills Olympic athletes need; explain the nature of Greek myths.	social studies, math, literature	irregular past tense; expression *such as*; ordinal numbers; superlatives; subject pronouns; conditional sentences; regular past tense; basic punctuation rules	Use a map; use a graphic organizer; categorize information; predict before and during reading.
5	**Life Underwater**	Name the areas of the ocean; name the things found in the ocean; compare the areas of the ocean; tell why things float; name the oceans of the world.	science, social studies, literature	comparatives with *-er;* adjectives —position and agreement; articles *a* and *an*; expressions *surrounds/ is surrounded by;* greetings/farewells; antonyms; irregular past tense verbs; long *e*, vowel digraphs *ea/ee*	Identify main topics; follow order in an experiment; use dialogue to evaluate characters; use pictures for meaning.
6	**Taking Care of the Ocean**	Tell how people use the ocean; tell how people pollute the ocean; name some solutions to pollution; tell how students can help the environment; tell about aquaculture.	social studies, science, reading, literature	questions with *how*/answers with *by* + *-ing; stop/start* + *-ing;* expressions *less* and *more;* consonant digraph *sh; wh-* questions in the past tense; consonant *s*	Use a graphic organizer; find information in a newspaper article.

Chapter		Objectives	Content Focus	Language Awareness Objectives	Learning Strategies
7	**The Roman Empire**	Tell how the ancient Romans built their empire; describe the ancient Romans as builders; discuss the nature of Roman law; identify Latin words in English; discuss contributions of the ancient Romans.	social studies, language, reading, art	regular and irregular past tense; the verb *be* + adjective; hard and soft *c;* prefixes; amounts and container words; plurals	Read a map key; find the topic sentence; use prior knowledge; follow a recipe.
8	**Volcanoes in History**	Describe the eruption of Mount Vesuvius; discuss what archaeologists learned from Pompeii; tell what a volcano is; retell an ancient Roman myth.	social studies, science, literature	verbs and infinitives; passive verbs; consonant blends and digraphs with *s;* capitalization of proper nouns; discourse connectors; prepositional phrases of direction; regular and irregular past tense; letter *v*	Make personal connections; summarize to remember information; use a graphic organizer; visualize a story.
9	**What Makes Things Move?**	Explain why objects move; identify everyday activities that use motion; explain the effects of friction and gravity; experiment with friction and gravity.	science, math, literature	present tense; shape words; comparisons with *-er;* superlatives with *-est;* quotation marks for dialogue; action words; rhyming words with different spellings	Predict, monitor one's work; use context clues to find meaning.
10	**Physics of Roller Coasters**	Explain how a roller coaster works; experiment with the forces that make a roller coaster run; learn about synonyms and the use of a thesaurus.	science, math, reading, literature	words that show a sequence; expressions with *up;* conditional sentences; math words for averaging; express excitement; synonyms and antonyms; slang	Visualize; read a chart; understand words with multiple meanings; use word groups to remember new words.
11	**Handling Stress**	Describe some of the physical effects of stress; identify situations that cause stress; name ways to deal with stress; discuss school and differences among schools attended.	health, language arts, literature, reading	*may; have to;* end punctuation; giving advice; greetings and introductions; infinitives; telling "why"; stating rules; comparisons *good/better/best*	Paraphrase/retell; solve a problem; state main idea; identify with characters; compare and contrast.
12	**Getting Information**	Describe sources of information; tell how to use an encyclopedia as a reference tool; describe information found in magazines and newspapers; use graphic organizers to connect information.	study skills, language, reading, literature	appositives; quotation marks; questions and answers; colon; *wh-* questions; cognates	Understand chronology; understand magazine articles; evaluate an article; use graphic organizers; read on to get meaning.

Chapter		Objectives	Content Focus	Language Awareness Objectives	Learning Strategies
1	**Immigration Then and Now**	Give reasons why people immigrate; tell about the first settlers in North America; name the early English and Spanish settlements in the United States; tell where later immigrants to the United States came from.	social studies, math, literature	infinitive answers to *why* questions; past tense; expression *such as*; verbs *increase/decrease*; dialogue; action verbs; expressions *there was/there were*; short *a*	Make a time line; read large numbers; visualize the story.
2	**Gifts from Many Lands**	Tell how immigrants have brought their culture to the US; tell how people borrow customs and language from other groups; describe how different ethnic groups celebrate; identify place names from other cultures.	social studies, language arts, reading, literature	information questions; *when* clauses; words for nationalities ending in *-ese* and *-an;* capitalization; imperatives; vowel digraphs *oo* and *ou*	Use cognates; use paragraphs to follow meaning.
3	**How the Eyes Work**	Identify parts of the eye and how they work together; explain how pictures are formed and transmitted to the brain; compare human eyes to those of bees; learn idioms about eyes and seeing.	science, language arts, reading, literature	position words; present tense: third person singular; hard and soft *c;* gerunds; negative present tense; greetings and farewells	Learn science vocabulary; use a diagram to get meaning; compare and contrast.
4	**Looking at Colors**	Name different kinds of radiant energy; describe how light is comprised of different colors with different wavelengths; explain where rainbows come from; tell how artists use color to affect the viewer's mood.	science, art, literature	the conjunction *but;* present perfect; position of adjectives; *all/most/many/some/several/few;* past tense; *sh, sl,* and *sp;* words that describe sequence; *like* used for comparison	Scan text to predict content; read a scientific process; use diagrams to visualize instructions; identify values; understand italics.
5	**Life in the Middle Ages**	Name classes of people during the Middle Ages; describe life in a castle; explain how a boy became a knight; tell about the legend of King Arthur.	social studies, health, literature, art	negative past tense; pronouns; gerunds; frequency adverbs; antonyms; sentence structure; future expressions; possessive forms	Recognize patterns in text; use reader's tips; make inferences; analyze a legend.
6	**Trade in the Middle Ages**	Describe how people traveled; tell how towns grew; identify products Europeans imported and exported; tell about the journeys of Marco Polo; explain how the Black Death spread through Europe.	social studies, health, literature	names of occupations ending in *-er;* verbs + infinitives; past perfect verb tense; irregular past tense verbs ending in *-aught* and *-ought;* giving reasons with *because* and *so that;* idioms	Track cause and effect; use maps; revise predictions and self-correct; understand the use of italics.

Chapter		Objectives	Content Focus	Language Awareness Objectives	Learning Strategies
7	**Reading Stories**	Tell about types of reading materials; identify story elements; tell about story genres; tell how scientists test ideas.	language arts, science, literature	question words; irregular plurals: changing *-y* to *-ies*; *may/might; yes/no* questions; use of italics for emphasis; interjections; long *e:* vowel digraphs *ie/ea;* contractions	Use an idea web; identify genre; use pictures to get meaning; identify story elements; identify a fantasy.
8	**Writing Stories**	Tell about languages and alphabets; tell about the parts of a dictionary; name types of writing; tell about different kinds of writers; write about yourself.	language arts, careers, reading, literature	capitalization of place names, languages, nationalities, and book titles; words with multiple meanings; common punctuation; verbs that express necessity; words that describe people; long *o:* vowel digraphs *ow, oa*	Look up words in a dictionary; prepare to write.
9	**Mysteries in History**	Tell about the Inca civilization in South America; describe the end of the Inca civilization; tell about the historical site of Machu Picchu; describe various features of the Andes Mountains.	social studies, science, literature	position of adjectives; passive voice; cause and effect with *so* and *since;* comparatives and superlatives with *-er* and *-est;* real conditionals; expressing opinions; present and past tenses; express likes and dislikes	Keep track of main idea; use maps; use new information; take notes on main ideas.
10	**How Science Solves Mysteries**	Describe the process scientists use to solve mysteries; explain hypotheses scientists have about whales' songs; tell about the mystery of the Loch Ness Monster.	science, math, reading, literature	*why* questions; digraphs *ch* and *tch*; cause and effect; math vocabulary; connecting words *however* and *but;* sensory words	Paraphrase; read math problems; follow arguments.
11	**Desert Life**	Describe conditions found in the desert; name deserts of the world; tell how plants, animals, and people survive in the desert; name animals that live in the desert.	science, social studies, literature	adjectives ending in *-y;* present tense; ordinal numbers, prepositions of time; *because* clauses; negatives; intensifiers; long *a*	Identify main idea and supporting details; use information to understand characters' feelings; visualize.
12	**Water in the Desert**	Describe how plants and animals adapt to lack of water and to sudden rainfalls; explain how cities, towns, and farms get water; identify ways to conserve water; describe other solutions to the water shortage problem.	science, math, reading, literature	present tense: third-person singular and negative; appositives; transitions; forming questions about amounts; *start/stop* + gerund; vowel digraphs *aw, a* and *al*	Read diagrams; guess word meanings; use context clues.

SCOPE AND SEQUENCE 8

Chapter		Objectives	Content Focus	Language Awareness Objectives	Learning Strategies
1	**Growing Up**	Name physical characteristics family members share; describe the growth of boys and girls between ages 9 and 15; tell how heredity influences growth; name foods from the different food groups.	health, math, reading, literature	comparatives; present tense *has/have* and *is/are;* plural forms; possessive adjectives; superlatives; opposites	Understand key words; use a chart; understand directions.
2	**Life Cycles of Plants**	Name the parts of a plant; name the four main parts of a flower; describe the life cycle of a plant; tell how plants and animals are interdependent; identify parts of plants that people can eat.	science, math, literature, reading	words that describe; initial consonant *p;* consonant blends *pl* and *pr;* count and noncount nouns; position words; capitalization of place names; expressing intention with *going to* or *will;* past tense; punctuation	Use pictures for meaning; follow a sequence; make inferences; recognize cause and effect; visualize story details.
3	**Changing Weather**	Name kinds of weather; tell what makes weather change; tell how we know that air has weight; tell what causes storms; use weather idioms and sayings.	science, language arts, literature	conjunctions *and* and *or;* imperatives; present tense; adjectives that end in *-y; he/she/they;* past tense; *ou* and *ow*	Follow directions; track cause and effect; infer word meaning; understand story elements; read on to get meaning.
4	**Predicting the Weather**	Name the ways we get information about weather; tell about meteorologists; tell about the tools meteorologists use; tell who uses weather forecasts; read a weather map.	science, math, reading, literature	future with *will;* the expression *use (it) to;* clauses with *so* to express purpose; *there is/there are;* future with *going to;* the letter *l;* long *a*	Use a graphic organizer; understand specialized vocabulary; recognize text organization; use a map key.
5	**The United States Before the Civil War**	Describe the prewar economies of the North and the South; tell about slavery and the abolitionist movement; talk about Harriet Tubman and the Underground Railroad.	social studies, math, reading, literature	words that contrast; passive voice; italics for titles; expressions for comparison; past tense; contractions	Recognize main ideas and supporting details; use encyclopedias; understand textbook explanations.
6	**War Between North and South**	Tell how people were affected by the war; describe the results of the war; name the leaders and some famous people of the war; tell how the songs of the era describe the times; tell how literature describes the war.	social studies, music, literature	use commas in numbers; stating opinions; occupation words ending in *-er* and *-ist;* future tense with *will* and *going to;* action words; words that paint pictures; position words; prefix *un-*	Understand chronology in biographies; understand characters' feelings; summarize events.

Chapter		Objectives	Content Focus	Language Awareness Objectives	Learning Strategies
7	**The Sun**	Describe the solar system; explain why space appears to be black; tell how ancient peoples interpreted the universe; cite some literary examples that were inspired by the Sun and moon.	science, social studies, literature	prepositions of position; words for big; *little* vs. *few;* nationalities ending in *-ese* and *-an;* homonyms; synonyms	Read a diagram.
8	**The Planets**	Describe different physical characteristics of the planets; describe some major events in the history of space exploration; name idioms that relate to space.	science, math, literature, language arts	present tense to state general facts; comparatives; dates—*before* and *after;* unreal conditions; words that describe; ordinal numbers; superlatives; idioms	Use charts to make comparisons; read a time line.
9	**Settling the West**	Tell how, why, and when immigrants and and other settlers moved to the West; describe prairie and forest biomes in the late 1800s; recognize problems caused by increased contact between settlers and Indians.	social studies, science, literature, language	capitalization of place names; the suffix *-less;* passive voice; amount words *many/few/little;* quotation marks with unattributed dialogue; negatives; long *o*	Use maps in textbooks; scan; use previously learned information; use a dictionary to increase vocabulary.
10	**Industry Changed the Nation**	Describe the Industrial Revolution; identify some U.S. industrial leaders and inventors; tell about the causes and effects of the reform movement; describe the life of Andrew Carnegie; sing songs of the Industrial Revolution.	social studies, math, literature	expressions of time; appositives; phrase *because of;* question formation; unreal conditions; rhyming words; making requests	Read on to get meaning; use a time line; predict content; compare and contrast.
11	**Citizenship**	Describe the requirements for becoming a naturalized citizen and the meaning of good citizenship; tell about the Statue of Liberty, Ellis Island, and immigration experiences there.	social studies, math, reading, literature	*by* + gerund answers to *how* questions; expressions with *must* and *have to;* spelling rules for gerunds; present perfect tense; silent letters in words; words with double *ss;* use of *would;* words that rhyme	Use a Venn diagram; understand the use of bulleted text.
12	**Government**	Describe the U.S. as a democracy; name the three branches of government; discuss the Constitution and some key amendments; list some views on the meaning of the U.S.	social studies, math, literature	*or* to signal appositives or explanations; colons; two-word verbs with *out;* present perfect with *since*; speech fillers; consonant blends	Understand text organization; use diagrams to get meaning; use a time line.

NOTES